THE JEW OF LINZ

AD MAIOREM DEI GLORIAM, in total sympathy with the spirit of enquiry which informs the vast stream of European and American civilization and which ultimately ferrets out all chicanery.

THE JEW OF LINZ

WITTGENSTEIN, HITLER AND THEIR SECRET BATTLE FOR THE MIND

KIMBERLEY CORNISH

Century · London

This edition published by Century Books Limited 1998

1 3 5 7 9 10 8 6 4 2

Copyright © 1998 Kimberley Cornish

Century
Random House UK Ltd, 20 Vauxhall Bridge Road, London SW1V 2SA

Arrow Books Ltd
Random House UK Ltd, 20 Vauxhall Bridge Road, London SW1V 2SA

Random House Australia (Pty) Limited
20 Alfred Street, Milsons Point, Sydney,
New South Wales 2061, Australia

Random House New Zealand Limited
18 Poland Road, Glenfield,
Auckland 10, New Zealand

Random House South Africa (Pty) Limited
Endulini, 5a Jubilee Road,
Parktown 2193, South Africa

Random House UK Limited Reg No 954009

A CIP catalogue record for this book
is available from the British Library

Papers used by Random House UK Limited are natural, recyclable products
made from wood grown in sustainable forests. The manufacturing processes
conform to the environmental regulations of the country of origin.

ISBN 0 7126 7935 9

Printed and bound in the United Kingdom by
Mackays of Chatham plc, Chatham, Kent

Contents

Acknowledgements

I would like to acknowledge the help of Sinead Williams and Margaret Wanklyn of the Latrobe University Library Research Service LASER (now sadly defunct) whose cheerful following up of obscure references greatly eased my research tasks, and, above all others, of my wife, Cecilia Joyner, without whose patience and support through very difficult times this work would not have seen publication.

Introduction

Once I knew a brave and intelligent man – a Jew – one of the numberless
bits of human flotsam cast out of Europe by Adolf Hitler. With his own
eyes and dressed in the blue and white uniform of a Jewish youth organization, he had seen the Führer drive past him in cavalcade into his native
Czechoslovakia. He had escaped from Czechoslovakia and fought
honourably in the British Army while his family was consumed in the
Holocaust. On returning to his native land, full of hope, he saw Stalin's
writing on the wall and had to run yet again.

Along with many Holocaust survivors, he found sanctuary in Australia.
His experiences, as he later related, had turned him into an intensely political creature and the study of politics became his obsession. His experiences
had immunized him against totalitarianism on both sides of politics. In
Australia, he reacted to the prevailing intellectual political ambience.
Having escaped Czechoslovakia, he found the universities to be suffering
from a profound unconcern with the dangers of the totalitarian Left. The
Nazis had been crushed with the Soviet Union as ally and there was a
legacy of trust that endured in the universities longer than elsewhere. He
felt that Australian academics generally were blindly sympathetic to the
policies of the Soviet Union and the person of Joseph Stalin. He thought
this sympathy to be neither entirely innocent nor harmless, so he began to
write in defence of liberty and thereby became controversial.

He was invited to teach at the University of Sydney by David
Armstrong, but, in a nationally notorious and shameful scandal, a politically
organized faculty strike forced him out to take up another appointment at
the University of Melbourne. Here he shepherded a generation of students
through the arcana of political argument. He was a wit and as fabulous a
raconteur as Australia has ever seen. He was a great force for good. His name
was Frank Knopfelmacher and he deserves to be remembered.

I was never his student but I benefited greatly from his conversation.
Among the very many things he said that gave me cause to ponder was an
off-hand remark he made to me about the origins of Nazism. He said that

he had always suspected there was a Jewish hand in it and that this hand might have belonged to Otto Weininger – the Viennese doctor and admirer of Wagner who took his own life because he was Jewish.[1] Dr Knopfelmacher's idea was that Nazism was a sort of expropriation by gentiles of the Jewish 'self-hatred' that one finds in Weininger and in other turn-of-the-century Viennese such as the journalist Karl Kraus. He was pessimistic, however, about the truth behind the matter ever emerging.

Dr Knopfelmacher is now dead and my own work shows, as we shall see, that he was wrong in his suspicion of Weininger, though Weininger did have a cameo role to play in forming the mysterious mind that really mattered. And he was also wrong in his suspicion that Jewish self-hatred was connected with the origins of Nazism. But he was quite correct that there was a Jewish hand in it, or at least a hand that was three quarters Jewish. It belonged to a brilliant man who claimed to be a Jew (though the Orthodox will challenge this) and who achieved posthumous world-wide fame in another area. In fact he claimed to be one of 'the greatest of Jewish thinkers'. His role in the origins of Nazism was not active, but passive; indeed, he was perhaps the very first victim of Hitler's bullying. Hitler hated him with an all-consuming fire. After a late start, he dedicated himself to fighting Hitler. He was desperate and resorted to evil means that seriously damaged Great Britain, the nation Dr Knopfelmacher admired above all others. To paraphrase the prophet Isaiah,[2] this man made a covenant with death (in the form of Stalin) and with Sheol he had an agreement. Between Hitler and Stalin the forces of evil were a house divided and he used the one against the other. His role has been a closely guarded secret for sixty years and this secrecy has distorted our knowledge of one of the main causal factors of the twentieth century, the origins of Hitler's anti-Semitism. It has also distorted our knowledge of the nature of Nazism.

That Nazism contains something wicked is obvious, but that it might require vigorous and difficult intellectual effort to comprehend is not at all obvious. The metaphysics of Nazism lie deep, however, and Political Science departments which dismiss it as unworthy of study are not studying Nazism, but something else – a straw man of their own creation. Nazi metaphysics cannot be understood without profound philosophical reflection. It is, in fact, a Hitlerian perversion of a doctrine discovered – or rediscovered – by the genius of this Jew. This Jew was a great philosopher – indeed, one of the very greatest – but his doctrine too has been, as he wrote, 'variously misunderstood, more or less mangled or watered down' and 'in the darkness of this time' unlikely 'to bring light into one brain'. Because of this, the true causes of much of our own bloody century lie shrouded in mist. To dispel the fog, to understand the genius of Hitler and this Jew, we must make some philosophical investigations. We shall find that the forces that shaped Dr Knopfelmacher's life – Nazism, the Holocaust, the Stalinist triumph in Eastern Europe and even the political orientation of Australian universities – were all influenced by this Jew whose unknown hand Dr Knopfelmacher sensed. In fact, unknown to Dr Knopfelmacher, his own political activities in Australia were being reported to prominent Australian Communists by this Jew's chief Australian disciple, who was named publicly by a Royal Commission in Victoria into the Communist Party.[3]

Political Science departments tend to dismiss Nazism as a political doctrine. The Holocaust ensures that it is treated as institutionalized racism or mass insanity and the student is left amazed that such lunacy could ever have come within a whisker of running the world. Plato or Marx might be studied for political ideas, but not Hitler – but then he was under-estimated all his life. Hitler is even now mistakenly thought to lack intellectual depth.

What I shall be suggesting in this book is that one of the central doctrines of Nazism was not an invention of Hitler's but the perversion of a philosophical idea that has very deep and ancient roots. This idea is also central to much of Wittgenstein's work and in Part II I try to show that it was through him that Hitler first encountered it. It is not an easy idea to grasp and Part III is devoted to unravelling it and to demonstrating that Wittgenstein did base an important part of his thought on it. This part also investigates the historical background to the idea and some of the critiques that have been made of it.

There is also another strand to our investigation, which is pursued in Part I. This is concerned not with Wittgenstein's influence on Hitler but rather the reverse. My contention is that hatred of Hitler and his doctrines drove Wittgenstein into a secret life that until now has never been revealed or even suspected.

What holds these strands together is that they deal with the mutual influence of two extraordinary – and extraordinarily different – men. What the reader is about to consider is pioneer detective work, and on the face of it, utterly implausible.[4] To show its plausibility, we must make some preparatory historical investigations, and to begin with we must turn our attention to a certain Jew of the Austrian city of Linz.

Part I

ONE

The Jew of Linz

Who was the first Jew Hitler refers to in *Mein Kampf*, the mysterious young Jewish boy of Linz who first inclined him along the path of anti-Semitism? Did he survive the Holocaust? There is not much to go on in Hitler's book, merely a sentence or two revealing that this boy attended the same school as Hitler. Nonetheless, it is possible to make a fair bet as to who he was and this 'fair bet' is astonishing. Indeed, while European Jewry was turned to ashes, this Jew not only survived the Holocaust but played a significant role in bringing Hitler down. His role in history and the Nazi defeat has been a major secret of the Cold War.

There is a good deal of information available about pre-Great War Austria and its prominent (and not so prominent) families. Let me sketch the background of one such prominent *fin de siècle* Viennese family, the Wittgensteins, and their famous son, Ludwig. (In referring to Ludwig, I shall follow the universal practice of other writers and call him simply 'Wittgenstein', except where this would lead to confusion. The other family members I shall refer to by including their first names.) The more general Viennese milieu in which the Wittgensteins moved has been studied intensively and a number of books and biographies are available.[1]

Wittgenstein is celebrated today as a seminal twentieth-century thinker, a logician and philosopher of the very first rank. Much of his work was produced in England, primarily at Cambridge. He was born into a fabulously rich Viennese family of Jewish descent on 26 April 1889. Details of the family background are obscure, but his paternal great-grandfather appears to have been one Moses Meier, who took the name of his employer (an aristocrat named Wittgenstein) after a Napoleonic decree of 1808 required Jews to adopt a surname.[2] His son, Hermann Christian Wittgenstein, adopted Christianity and acquired a reputation as somewhat of an anti-Semite, forbidding his daughters to marry Jews. Hermann's son, Karl – Wittgenstein's father – ran away to America and spent time in New York. Following his return to Austria, he became managing director of a steel rolling mill. Ray Monk's standard biography

7

of Wittgenstein outlines the meteoric career that then ensued:

> In the ten years that followed he showed himself to be perhaps the most astute industrialist in the Austro–Hungarian empire. The fortunes of his company – and, of course, his own personal fortune – increased manifold, so that by the last decade of the nineteenth century he had become one of the wealthiest men in the empire, and the leading figure in its iron and steel industry. As such, he became, for critics of the excesses of capitalism, one of the archetypes of the aggressively acquisitive industrialist. Through him the Wittgensteins became the Austrian equivalent of the Krupps, the Carnegies, or the Rothschilds.[3]

Karl organized a cartel between his own steel works at Kladno and the Rothschild steel works at Wittkowitz that controlled the iron and steel output of Central Europe. Centred on Bohemia in the Czech lands, the Wittgenstein cartel produced over sixty per cent of the Empire's iron and steel and controlled its railroad and tyre industries.[4]

Karl's wife, Leopoldine (née Kalmus), though brought up as a Catholic, was also of Jewish descent. Their son Ludwig shared the nominal Catholicity of the household, but the family's Jewish origins were very well known in Vienna and throughout Austria. Ludwig and his brother Paul, for example, wanted to join a gymnastic club but failed to meet the criterion of Aryan origin.[5] I shall also mention here (and document later) that Karl Wittgenstein, on a number of occasions, felt forced to deny in papers with an empire-wide circulation that his business practices were dubious. In short, the Wittgenstein family were fabulously rich, of Jewish descent and subject to allegations that their wealth was acquired unethically.

Three of Karl Wittgenstein's sons were homosexual. In 1904, Ludwig's brother Rudolf was driven to suicide over it. Monk writes on Rudolf's death that in a farewell letter

> he said it was because he had 'doubts about his perverted disposition'. Some time before his death he had approached 'The Scientific-Humanitarian Committee' (which campaigned for the emancipation of homosexuals) for help, but, says the yearbook of the organization, 'our influence did not reach far enough to turn him away from the fate of self-destruction'.[6]

Bartley mentions that brother Hans, who killed himself in 1902, was also homosexual.[7] It is now clear from published material that Wittgenstein was similarly oriented. This issue was once controversial, but Monk's book has established the matter beyond doubt, quoting Wittgenstein's own words from his diary concerning his dealings with his male lover Francis Skinner, in Norway. Wittgenstein recorded that with Skinner he was 'sensual, susceptible, indecent' and that he 'Lay with him two or three times. Always at first with the feeling that there was nothing wrong in it, then with shame.[8] I raise the matter here only because of its possible relevance for what is to come later.

Wittgenstein was not athletic or sporting, suffered from a high-pitched voice and, at this early stage of his life, a stammer.[9] McGuinness records a further relevant fact for our purposes, that he

> was delicate and sensitive in temperament, and almost certainly in health also. By the age of fourteen it is known that he had to be excused gymnastics at school and his history even before the hardships of the First World War is one of minor operations and surgical appliances (he had apparently a double rupture).[10]

The family wealth allowed Karl to have his sons Paul and Ludwig educated at home, and McGuinness refers to the tutors and governesses of Ludwig's first fourteen years.[11] The atmosphere at home was one of rarefied high culture, particularly in music, Brahms, for example, being a frequent visitor to the family musical salon.[12] But in the second semester of the academic year 1903/4,[13] for reasons that are unknown, the father decided to send Ludwig away from this cosseted, highly cultured environment to a state school. The fateful one chosen was far away from Vienna, the *Realschule* in Linz. McGuinness describes it as a school for dayboys and states that Wittgenstein lived at the home of a master at the Gymnasium. Not surprisingly (one might think, inevitably), given the change of environment, Wittgenstein did not do well at school. Monk accounts for this in the following very important passage:

> His poor results may in part be due to his unhappiness at school. It was the first time in his life he had lived away from the privileged environment of his family home, and he did not find it easy to find friends among his predominantly working-class fellow pupils. On first setting eyes on them he was shocked by their uncouth behaviour. 'Mist!' ('Muck!') was his initial impression. To them he seemed (as one of them later told his sister Hermine) like a being from another world. He insisted on using the polite form 'Sie' to address them, which served only to alienate him further. They ridiculed him by chanting an alliterative jingle that made play of his unhappiness and of the distance between him and the rest of the school: 'Wittgenstein wandelt wehmutig widriger Winde wegen Wienwarts' ('Wittgenstein wends his woeful windy way towards Vienna'). In his efforts to make friends, he felt, he later said, 'betrayed and sold' by his schoolmates.[14]

It is clear from this, and many other references in the biographies, that his time at the *Realschule* was desperately unhappy. The school, however, is not something that can be simply dismissed as an unhappy but ultimately unimportant interlude in his life. On the contrary, it is of enormous significance because there was another student attending there who was to become even more famous than Wittgenstein. This other student was none other than the man whose actions were to shape the twentieth century: Adolf Hitler. McGuinness writes on this:

> The *K.u.k Realschule* in Linz has its small place in history, since Adolf Hitler attended it from 1900 to 1904. Hitler was a few days older than Ludwig, but during the year in which they overlapped he was in the IIIrd class while Ludwig was in the Vth. It seems that he was a year behind and Ludwig a year ahead of the average. The school counted as a stronghold of German nationalism and Hitler in *Mein Kampf* mentions one history master who traced all that was glorious back to the Teutonic tribes. There were a handful of Jews, rather isolated, but, by the rough standards of the schoolboys, not persecuted. One former pupil explained that if a Jew were called *Saujud!* in a quarrel, this would only be in the formulaic manner in which a Bavarian would refer to a *Saupreuss*.[15]

McGuinness, unfortunately, tells us neither the name of the former pupil nor to whom the explanation was given. His account can be compared with a passage in Jetzinger's book, *Hitler's Youth*, reporting a conversation that Jetzinger had in 1938 with one Herr Keplinger, who knew Hitler at the Realschule.

> Once Adolf shouted at another boy, '*Du Saujud!*' ('You filthy Jew!') The boy concerned was staggered; he knew nothing of his Jewish ancestry at the time and only discovered it years later . . .[16]

McGuinness, in his biography of Wittgenstein, has informed us, on the authority of a 'former pupil', that '*Saujud!*' was used at the school, but that it had no more significance than analogous epithets directed at Prussian Germans. Jetzinger informs us that it was used, not just by any student at the school, but specifically by Adolf Hitler! And Hitler used it not against a Jew, but against a boy of Jewish descent. For any reader with a nose for historical connections, I imagine the nose has already twitched. We ask ourselves the question, 'Who might this unfortunate student have been?' and unavoidably there comes a startling suspicion. But is what this suspicion suggests really so much as possible? Let us investigate . . .

Hitler was born on 20 April 1889, just six days before Wittgenstein.

Monk records that the year Hitler and Wittgenstein overlapped at the school was the school year 1904-5[17]. Alan Bullock's standard biography of Hitler says that he started attending the Linz Realschule in September 1900.[18] Monk states also that 'There is no evidence that they had anything to do with one another.' Perhaps not. But a photograph of Hitler aged fourteen at the school also shows the fourteen-year-old Wittgenstein standing less than an arm's length away from him, one row down and to the left.[19] This photograph has been blown up and enhanced by the Identification Division of the Victoria Police Department using specially developed proprietary software. The image of the individual I am claiming to be Wittgenstein has been 'aged' ten years and compared with photographs of the adult Wittgenstein. The police personnel involved in the operation used standard police photographic identification procedures and state that the identification is 'highly probable', the highest degree of certainty the Department offers.[20] The matter of the photograph has not been raised elsewhere, but is clearly of great significance for our hypothesis.

Detail from a school photograph, Linz Realschule. Hitler is at the top right position; Wittgenstein is on row below, three from the right © AKG London.

The last sentence of the quote from McGuinness also deserves further consideration: 'One former pupil explained that if a Jew were called *Saujud!* in a quarrel, this would only be in the formulaic manner in which a Bavarian would refer to a *Saupreuss.*'

Now why a Bavarian? Weren't the students Austrian? Not all of them so described themselves. We know for certain that one of Wittgenstein's fellow students described himself as Bavarian. Thus Hitler, in *Mein Kampf*, describes his parents as 'Bavarian by blood'.[21] And he also notes that 'The German of my youth was the dialect of Lower Bavaria.'[22] On the '*Saupreuss*' reference, we might also note the following snippet in Bradley Smith's book, describing the views of Hitler's father, Alois Hitler:

> What Alois could not tolerate, as a devoted subject and servant of the crown, was the suggestion that the Habsburg realm be destroyed and that the Austrian Germans become dependent on the Prussians, whom he thoroughly disliked.[23]

'*Saujud*', of course, is an expression we can easily imagine to have issued forth from Hitler. But if the young Adolf shared his father's feelings about the Prussians, then '*Saupreuss*' might have been part of his vocabulary as well. Let us now turn to consider what Hitler said in describing his own development.

He was at pains to deny that he came from an anti-Semitic household, writing of the growth of his anti-Semitism that

> Today it is difficult, if not impossible, for me to say when the word 'Jew' first gave me ground for special thoughts. At home I do not remember having heard the word during my father's life-time. I believe that the old gentleman would have regarded any special emphasis on this term as cultural backwardness. In the course of his life he had arrived at more or less cosmopolitan views which, despite his pronounced national sentiments, not only remained intact, but also affected me to some extent.[24]

Hitler goes on to say that at school there was nothing to change this inherited picture, but he adds a very interesting qualification. This paragraph contains Hitler's very first reference to a Jew having a negative effect upon him:

> At the Realschule, to be sure, I did meet one Jewish boy who was treated by all of us with caution, but only because various experiences had led us to doubt his discretion and we did not particularly trust him . . .[25]

This paragraph – a mere forty words in English translation – is the focus of our investigation. Our speculation, as is obvious by now, is that this 'one Jewish boy' Hitler refers to, the very first link in the chain of hatred that led to Auschwitz, was none other than Ludwig Wittgenstein. I am suggesting, then, that Ludwig Wittgenstein is referred to in *Mein Kampf*.

How likely is it that Hitler's unknown Jew was really Wittgenstein? McGuinness notes that there was only a 'handful' of Jews at the school. This is supported by Hitler's own observation that 'There were few Jews in Linz.'[26] Had we known there was only one student of Jewish descent at the school, the case would be settled and there could be no doubt at all that Hitler's Jew was Wittgenstein. The case is not settled yet, of course, but there are some further factors to consider in assessing the probabilities that we shall come to in a moment.

Quite apart from their strikingly unusual personalities, a little research shows that the two youths shared common interests to a quite unusual degree. Both displayed a youthful enthusiasm for Schopenhauer and for music. Wittgenstein, in fact, was, at this stage, somewhat of a Wagner devotee, having learnt *Die Meistersinger* by heart.[27] Before he was twenty, he had heard it thirty times.[28] *Die Meistersinger* was also Hitler's favourite opera.[29] John Toland records:

> Hanfstaengl found that Hitler knew Die Meistersinger 'absolutely by heart and could whistle every note of it in a curious penetrating vibrato, but completely in tune'.[30]

Hitler later astounded a group of German musicologists by demonstrating that he knew the libretto of *Lohengrin* by heart. This is rather more than one would expect, even from schoolboys keen on Wagner. One would not, in fact, expect such detailed knowledge even from music graduates. Where did Hitler's knowledge of Wagner come from? Hanfstaengl suggests it might date back to Hitler's days in Linz:

> Over the course of time I taught him to appreciate the Italian operas, but in the end it always had to be Wagner, *Meistersinger, Tristan and Isolde* and *Lohengrin*. I must have played them hundreds of times and he never grew tired of them. He had a genuine knowledge and appreciation of Wagner's music, and this he had picked up somewhere, probably in his Vienna days, long before I knew him. The seed may even have been sown in Linz, where at the beginning of the century there was a pupil of Liszt called Göllerich, who was the local orchestra conductor and a Wagner enthusiast, but wherever it was, it had become part of Hitler's being. I came to see that there was a direct parallel between the construction of the *Meistersinger* prelude and that of his speeches. The whole interweaving of *leitmotifs*, of embellishments, of counter-point and musical

contrasts and argument, were exactly mirrored in the pattern of his speeches, which were symphonic in construction and ended in a great climax, like the blare of Wagner's trombones.[31]

Göllerich? Or someone else? (We shall bring out the important connection between Liszt, Wagner and the Wittgenstein family in the next chapter.)

The two schoolboys also shared an interest in architecture and a fascination with the power of language. Hitler's criticisms in the paragraph quoted are framed in the third person – 'various experiences had led us to doubt his discretion' – but sound almost personal, as though the boy might have been indiscreet about something affecting Hitler and his cronies. About this, of course, we know absolutely nothing, but my own experience of adolescents at schools who share a passion for common intellectual interests is that they tend to drift together. And each was possessed of a personality so dominating as to count as remarkable within twentieth-century history.

Hitler's talent for whistling *Die Meistersinger* 'in a curious, penetrating vibrato' was mirrored in Wittgenstein's virtuoso skill at whistling. Monk writes of the recollection of one of Wittgenstein's later acquaintances as follows:

> He recalls Wittgenstein's ability to whistle whole movements of symphonies, his showpiece being Brahms's St Anthony Variations, and that when other people whistled something wrong, Wittgenstein would stop them and firmly tell them how it should go – something that didn't endear him to his fellow-workers in the dispensary.[32]

Here is Theodore Redpath's account of this trait of Wittgenstein's:

> A more amusing musical episode, trivial but significant, occurred one day when he was talking with me about Bizet. He evidently liked Bizet, and he told me that Bizet had appealed to Nietzsche as 'Southern music', in contrast with the 'Northern music' of Wagner. I had recently been playing to myself through a piano score of *L'Arlésienne* and had enjoyed the work keenly. I told him how much I had liked it, and he said he liked it too. I asked him if he remembered the opening theme of the Overture and started to hum it. He said I had not got it quite right, and he tried to whistle it correctly, as he thought. He was very proficient at whistling and sometimes whistled splendidly to piano accompaniment. This time, though, he didn't get the melody right, and I had the face to say so and tried to whistle it correctly myself. My whistling was not as technically skilful as his, but this time I am pretty sure that it was at least accurate. He was annoyed and burst out: 'We *are* a couple of asses!' I fear I continued to

believe that I was not one of them, but I let the matter drop. He didn't respond kindly to correction, and he was also at times over-confident and even rash in expressing opinions.[33]

How might the two Wagner-admiring whistlers of the *Realschule* have interacted? Compare the reports of Wittgenstein's habitual correction of others with Waite's report of a particular sensitivity of Hitler's:

One evening during the war, Hitler was whistling a classical air. When a secretary had the temerity to suggest that he had made a mistake in the melody, the Führer was furious. He showed his vulnerability – and his lack of humour – by shouting angrily, 'I don't have it wrong. It is the composer who made a mistake in this passage.'[34]

There is also the fact that the Wittgenstein family shared anti-Semitic views to some degree. That they did is undeniable and has been remarked upon before.[35] McGuinness[36] quotes a report of Wittgenstein's father saying 'In matters of honour one does not consult a Jew.' Consider also this passage of Wittgenstein's from the previously noted section (pp 314–15) in Monk's biography, comparing the Jews to a 'tumour':

Within the history of the peoples of Europe the history of the Jews is not treated as their intervention in European affairs would actually merit, because within this history they are experienced as a sort of disease, and anomaly, and no one wants to put a disease on the same level as normal life [and no one wants to speak of a disease as if it had the same rights as healthy bodily processes (even painful ones)]. We may say: people can only regard this tumour as a natural part of their body if their whole feeling for the body changes (if the whole national feeling for the body changes). Otherwise the best they can do is *put up with it.*

You can expect an individual man to display this sort of tolerance, or else to disregard such things; but you cannot expect it of a nation, because it is precisely not disregarding such things that makes it a nation. I.e. there is a contradiction in expecting someone both to retain his former aesthetic feeling for the body and also to make the tumour welcome.[37]

Other of Wittgenstein's passages from this period state that Jews are incapable of original thought and that they are naturally secretive.[38] The family was quite certainly anti-Semitic, for, as we have already seen, 'Hermann Wittgenstein, indeed, acquired something of a reputation as an anti-Semite, and firmly forbade his offspring to marry Jews.'[39] McGuinness tells us that Gustav Freytag's book *Soll und Haben*, was read rather later in the Wittgenstein family than elsewhere, but not that this book is one of the greater anti-Semitic works of the nineteenth century.[40] Monk also quotes a dream report made by Wittgenstein, in which Wittgenstein records, 'I think: must there be a Jew behind every indecency?'[41]

It is surely remarkable to find such sentiments (dating to 1931) coming from the hand of an Austrian of Jewish descent who thought of himself as Jewish. And it is equally remarkable that thinking in racial terms is traceable in Wittgenstein's thought to well before National Socialism appeared on the political scene; for as early as 1914, he had written:

> . . . I feel the terrible sadness of our – the German race's – situation. The English – the best race in the world – cannot lose. We, however, can lose, and will lose, if not this year then the next. The thought that our race will be defeated depresses me tremendously, because I am German through and through.[42]

Clearly, Wittgenstein saw himself as German and explained the outcome of historical struggles (just as did the fifteen-year-old Hitler) in racial terms. Now let us return to Linz and Hitler.

The *Encyclopedia Judaica* article on Linz gives the Jewish population of the town in 1880 as 533.[43] Assuming an equal division of the sexes, and allowing a little for population growth, one broadly estimates roughly 300 male Jews in the city in 1904. We do not have to estimate the number of Jews at the *Realschule* from these figures, because the figures are already on record. Werner Maser reports that there were fifteen Jews in the school Hitler attended:

> of the school's 329 pupils fifteen were Jewish . . . At the beginning of 1902 Hitler's class, 1B, consisted of twenty-eight Catholics, six Jews and five Protestants.[44]

The other snippet of information that Hitler provides (besides the fact that this boy was Jewish and outside the circle of 'us') was the ground for his exclusion; specifically, that his discretion was doubted.

It so happens that the doubts Hitler expressed about the boy's 'discretion' tie in rather well with another characteristic of Wittgenstein that is clearly recorded in the biographies, his almost fanatical attitude to what he regarded as 'honesty'. Wittgenstein is said to have valued honesty above all other qualities in personal relationships, but I have used the word 'fanatical' because of the strange manner in which this came out in him. He saw the process of being honest as demanding that he make confessions to others; later on, at Cambridge, insisting on confessing personal and inti-

mate details of his life to embarrassed colleagues, such as the philosopher
G.E. Moore.[45]

This characteristic is a common symptom in a certain type of neurotic.
Such people tend to be lonely individuals and the act of confession can be
used as a means of establishing a sort of intimacy or bond – a rapport – with
the person to whom they are confessing. The dialogue runs: 'Look, I'm
being honest with you. I'm telling you what a rotten, contemptible person
I am! Can't you see I must really like/respect you to tell you this dreadful
secret?' If the person being confessed to does not want to play the role, the
intimacies revealed can make the whole experience highly unpleasant. Here
is another record in Monk's biography of how others experienced
Wittgenstein's confessions:

> For both Rowland Hutt and Fania Pascal, listening to the confession was an
> uncomfortable experience. In Hutt's case, the discomfort was simply embar-
> rassment at having to sit in a Lyons cafe while opposite him sat Wittgenstein
> reciting his sins in a loud and clear voice. Fania Pascal, on the other hand, was
> exasperated by the whole thing. Wittgenstein had phoned at an inconvenient
> moment to ask whether he could come and see her. When she asked if it was
> urgent she was told firmly that it was, and could not wait. 'If ever a thing could
> wait,' she thought, facing him across the table, 'it is a confession of this kind and
> made in this manner.' The stiff and remote way in which he delivered his
> confession made it impossible for her to react with sympathy.[46]

After reading this, one realises that if someone were to say of
Wittgenstein that his discretion was to be doubted, then that person would
be guilty not of some unjustified slander but of understatement.[47] One
should have no difficulty at all in seeing that people who feel bound to make
'confessions' to others in this manner, particularly to adolescent boys,
might be in for major rejection, perhaps even contempt.

Now this 'confessional characteristic' is traceable not just to
Wittgenstein's later life, but as far back as his time in Linz. We know from
his own words that he felt forced to make these 'confessions' to others at
the *Realschule*. There are, for example, the following barely comprehen-
sible notes Wittgenstein made about his inner life during the period (circa
1904), which seem tied up with some sort of sexual experience.[48] (Monk
tells us that 'P' stands for 'Pepi' and 'G' for Wittgenstein's sister
Margarete.)

> Realschule class first impression. 'A shower'. Relation to the Jews. Relation to
> Pepi. Love and pride. Knocking hat off. Break with P. Suffering in class.
> Halfway reconciliation and further break with P. Seeming innocence I learn the

facts of life. Religiosity, G's influence on me, talk about confession with my colleagues. Reconciliation with P and tenderness.

That is, Wittgenstein wrote of a 'talk about confession with my colleagues' as something that occurred while he was at the *Realschule*.[49] If the identity between Wittgenstein and the 'one Jewish boy' of *Mein Kampf* is correct, then something like this would explain Hitler's complaints about the boy's lack of discretion. What a refined and cultured Viennese might see as a brave act of soul-baring, less precious country lads might see somewhat differently, particularly if his confessions to others adversely affected them, as might well be possible. If those confessions had the further neurotic element that is evident in the Lyons restaurant incident then they might take a very dim view of it indeed.[50]

Wittgenstein, then, must be considered a prime candidate to be this very Jew whom Hitler mentions as first forming his own anti-Semitism. He fits perfectly. It is clear that Wittgenstein was very much on the outside and did not enjoy fellowship with the other pupils; at least to this extent they distrusted him, just as Hitler said happened with the 'one Jewish boy'. And McGuinness has stated of the handful of Jews that 'they were not persecuted', presumably meaning 'not persecuted for being Jewish'. Yet Wittgenstein clearly did suffer from persecution.

We may wonder how much the persecution involved in Wittgenstein's case (the '*Saujud*' reference apart) was not so much anti-Semitic as of a particular person.[51] One can see why adolescent boys would have found him obnoxious: his background and personality worked against him and isolated him. He had family connections to the Jewish Rothschild dynasty through his father's control of the very heights of Central Europe's economy in the iron and steel cartel he created. His family was fabulously rich. Wittgenstein, then, as somewhat of an objectionable prig in the eyes of the other boys (whom he regarded as muck, and addressed as '*Sie*'), would have been the most noteworthy subject for jibes at the school for just these reasons, regardless of whether other Jews suffered the same treatment (which apparently they did not). And small, unathletic, stuttering, homosexual adolescents notoriously are treated badly by their fellows.

The circumstantial evidence that Wittgenstein is indeed referred to in *Mein Kampf*, that he is a reasonable candidate to identify as 'the Jew of Linz', is therefore strong. We also must consider that we are dealing here with two of the twentieth century's most spectacularly unusual personalities confined together in a school, with, as it were, three hundred also-rans. Wittgenstein's personal and family traits would have made him so perfect a specimen for picking on in the eyes of the other boys that it is unlikely that he would have had a rival. In addition, he did not commence with an age-group cohort in 1900, as did Hitler, but started the school as an outsider between semesters, after the other boys had already had four years to form their own friendships and groups. Surely, the probability of having two such perfectly victimizable individuals at a school has to be unlikely.

Years later during the First World War, while in service on a captured Russian boat in Poland, Wittgenstein was jeered at by the crew and wrote:

> There is an enormously difficult time ahead of me, for I am sold and betrayed now just as I was long ago at school in Linz.[52]

The event referred to here, whatever it might have been, could be identical with the 'lack of discretion' episode Hitler refers to in *Mein Kampf*. Whatever it was, it clearly mattered to Wittgenstein, sticking in his mind ten years later. It sounds as though Wittgenstein confided something sensitive and important to someone, who then blabbed.[53] When Wittgenstein was twenty-three, he confided to David Pinsent that he had suffered desperate loneliness – accompanied by thoughts of suicide – for nine years. This serves to locate the origin of his feelings of loneliness to the critical year at the *Realschule*.

In the second volume of *Mein Kampf* there is even a passage about betrayal and discretion (that quality notably lacking in the Jew of Linz) though here it sounds as if Hitler were the one betrayed:

> How often, during the War, did we hear the complaint that our people were so little able to be *silent*! How hard this made it to withhold even important secrets from the knowledge of our enemies! But ask yourself this question: What, before the War did German education do to teach the individual silence? Even in school, sad to say, wasn't the little *informer* sometimes preferred to his more silent schoolmates? Was not and is not informing regarded as praiseworthy 'frankness', discretion as reprehensible obstinacy? Was any effort whatever made to represent discretion as a manly and precious virtue? No, for in the eyes of our present school system, these are trifles . . . And this is the place to say that a teacher, for instance, must on principle not try to obtain knowledge of silly children's tricks by cultivating loathsome tattle-tales . . . A boy who snitches on his comrades practises *treason* and thus betrays a mentality which, harshly expressed and enlarged, is the exact equivalent of treason to one's country. Such a boy can by no means be regarded as a '*good, decent*' child; no, he is a boy of undesirable character. The teacher may find it convenient to make use of such vices for enhancing his authority, but in this way he sows in the youthful heart the germ of a mentality the later effect of which may be catastrophic. More than once, a little informer has grown up to be a big scoundrel! This is one example among many.[54]

'The little informer' – Wittgenstein was both little and a confessor of sins to others. And Hitler was asked to leave the school at the end of the year. Could there be a connection here? Some commentators have attributed the origins of Hitler's anti-Semitism to his time in Vienna, after he had left the *Realschule*. They attribute its growth to his reading anti-Semitic pamphlets. One need not doubt that Hitler read anti-Semitic pamphlets in the capital, but it seems to me a lunatic hypothesis that these alone could have been the source of such all-consuming hatred. There is in any case evidence that his anti-Semitism began earlier. The '*Saujud!*' reference has already been considered. And Maser writes:

> Kubizek maintains that when they first met in 1904 – at a time, that is, when Hitler was attending the school – his friend's attitude was already 'distinctly anti-Semitic'.[55]

There is also an account, in Waite's study of Hitler's psychology, of the time after his father's death in 1903 when the Hitler family enjoyed some financial independence:

> Glorying in a life of leisure as critic and patron of the arts in the provincial capital, he joined the local museum and library and rarely missed a performance of the Linz opera. He dressed immaculately, in white shirts, flowing cravats with stickpins, a broad-brimmed black hat set at a confident angle, and well-cut tweed suits which were the envy of the young men of the town. In winter, he donned a silk-lined black overcoat. For the opera, he affected black kid gloves, an ivory-handled walking stick, and a top hat.[56]

How many of the *Realschule* boys besides Hitler attended the opera regularly? The school contained at least one other opera attender and that one from a family to whom all the expensive frippery required for opera attendance was mere pin money. The conductor Bruno Walter visited that boy's home. Gustav Mahler, the conductor at the Vienna Opera House, also visited that boy's home. Brahms gave private performances at that boy's home. And the man acknowledged by music historians as the greatest violinist of the nineteenth century – Wittgenstein's cousin, Joseph Joachim – grew up in the same house as his father.[57] Later we shall see that this cousin was hated above all other Jews by Hitler's idol, Richard Wagner.

Hitler was interested in art, but that other boy came from a home in Vienna graced with paintings by von Alt and Klimt and sculptures by Rodin and Mestrovic.[58] Jones states of Hitler's own paintings that

> Few drawings exist from these early years, but those that do remain show a

somewhat unskilled hand at work on paintings, primarily architectural in nature, and in the style of Rudolph von Alt, an Austrian master.[59]

Whatever one might think of Hitler's artistic tastes, he knew his art. And if Jones is correct that Hitler's art was modelled on von Alt's, then he would have made it his business to find out everything about him, just as he did with Wagner, who was his musical exemplar. That von Alt originals were held in the home of a school-fellow is therefore no small matter. We shall see later that Karl Wittgenstein was in any case a patron of very great importance in the Austrian art world.

Hitler's doodles © Bayerische Staatsbibliothek

Hitler is recorded by Martin Bormann in Hitler's *Table Talk* as saying that 'Jewry had raised Brahms to the pinnacle. He was lionised in the salons.'[60] Which salons was Hitler referring to? If we can locate them, then we might know whom he considered to constitute Jewry. In Vienna, the chief such salon, so far as Brahms was concerned, was the Palais Wittgenstein, where some of his compositions had their first public performance.

Of that pregnant school year 1904, we have also the following report of Hitler in Linz:

> ... the city certainly impressed upon Hitler a sense of class distinction. He made 'no friends and pals' at the *Realschule*. Nor was the situation any better at the home of ugly old Frau Sekira, where for a time he boarded with five other schoolmates his age during the school week. He remained stiff, aloof, a stranger. One of the former boarders recalls: 'None of the five other boys made friends with him. Whereas we schoolmates naturally called one another du, he addressed us as Sie . . .'[61]

Curious this, for we recall reports of someone else at the school with this very mannerism. It is remarkable to find it commented upon in records of two different *Realschule* students of the school year 1904/5. The other person, in fact, had a personality so extraordinary and compelling that his expressions and mannerisms were still detectable in philosophy lecturers at Cambridge a decade after he died. Should we simply dismiss it as coincidence and conclude that in 1904 some of the boys (the two most interesting ones from the historian's point of view) just happened to have been particularly polite to the others? Hitler's affectation in this regard appears not to have been permanent, for Jetzinger records his 1938 talk with Keplinger:

'Did you ever meet Hitler again in later life?'
'Yes, in the summer of 1927. I was in Munich on business and rang him up. He sent a car round at once and I found him waiting for me in front of the Brown House, in shorts and a shirt, because of the heat.'
'How did you greet him?'
'I said, "Servus, Hitler."'
'Did he answer with "Thou", or "You"?'
'"Thou", of course! I wouldn't have taken "You" from a class-mate!'[62]

Wittgenstein's sister, Hermine, reports of this '*Sie*' locution in her brother that

One of his school-fellows told me much later that Ludwig had appeared to all of them as if blown in from an alien world. He had a completely different life-style from theirs, addressing his school-fellows, for example, with the formal pronoun '*Sie*'; which created a barrier, apart from the fact that his interests and the books he read were totally different from theirs. Presumably he was somewhat older than the boys of his class, and in any case, disproportionately more mature and more serious. But above all he was uncommonly sensitive, and I can imagine that to him his school-fellows in turn seemed to stem from another world, from a terrible one![63]

The occurrence of this '*Sie*' locution then, in both Wittgenstein on the one hand and Hitler on the other, has separately been seen as remarkable by various relatives, school-fellows and historians. None of them, however, has commented on the striking fact that this remarkable mannerism occurred in *both* of that year's most historically important school-fellows. Hitler's continued use of '*Sie*' was commented upon by Albert Speer:

When Eckart died in 1923 there remained four men with whom Hitler used the *Du* of close friendship: Hermann Esser, Christian Weber, Julius Streicher, and Ernst Roehm. In Esser's case he found a pretext after 1933 to reintroduce the formal *Sie*; Weber he avoided; Streicher he treated impersonally; and Roehm he had killed.[64]

In *Mein Kampf*, Hitler complains of the 'infamous deception' of Jews trying to appear 'Germanic' and states of the Jew that 'of Germanism he possesses nothing but the art of stammering its language'.[65] He had previously mentioned the Jews of Linz in this regard (on the same page as he mentions the 'one Jewish boy'), saying:

> In the course of the centuries their outward appearance had become Europeanised and had taken on a human look; in fact I even took them for Germans.

Certainly, Wittgenstein scores here both on the count of stammering and of trying to appear Germanic and not Jewish. Most readers of *Mein Kampf* would take the reference to 'stammering' here as an unjustified abuse of Jews in general. I wonder, however, if he might not have had the individual young Wittgenstein in mind.

The whole section of 'Nation and Race' in *Mein Kampf* traces the process by which 'The Jew' has infected the Aryan race. It rails against 'the German princes' and states:

> it is thanks to the German princes that the German nation was unable to redeem itself for good from the Jewish menace.[66]

'The Jew' marries into the nobility:

> The Jew almost never marries a Christian woman; it is the Christian who marries a Jewess. The bastards, however, take after the Jewish side. Especially a part of the high nobility degenerates completely.[67]

Now Wittgenstein bore an aristocratic name and the Wittgensteins from whom old Moses Meier drew the name were a princely family with a castle, in Bad Laasphe, in the German county of Wittgenstein.[68] Hermann Christian Wittgenstein, Ludwig's grandfather, had indeed married a Jewess. Monk reports of Wittgenstein at Cambridge:

> An impression Wittgenstein quite often made, and which no doubt appealed to his vanity, was of being aristocratic. F. R. Leavis, for example, once overheard him remark: 'In my father's house there were seven grand pianos,' and immediately wondered whether he was related to the Princess Wittgenstein who figures in the annals of music. It was, in fact, widely believed in Cambridge that he was of the princely German family, the Sayn–Wittgensteins.[69]

If he gave this impression at Cambridge, one imagines he might also have given it at the *Realschule* to Hitler.[70] And this possibility should lead us to enquire into this 'Princess Wittgenstein who figures in the annals of music'. Who was she?

This 'Princess Wittgenstein' whom Leavis mentions was the mistress of Franz Liszt, whose illegitimate daughter by another mistress, Cosima, married none other than the anti-Semitic composer, Richard Wagner. That is, a 'Wittgenstein' had an adulterous affair with the father-in-law of the man whom Hitler admired most for his Teutonic blood purity, etc.[71] Cosima – the future Frau Wagner – hated Princess Wittgenstein, who, as we shall see, was responsible for taking the young Cosima away from her mother.

The singer Dietrich Fischer-Dieskau writes of Cosima's marriage to Wagner following her abandonment of Hans von Bulow:

> At the time of the ceremony, Cosima was assailed by conflicting emotions. There was no word from her father, nor from her mother Countess Marie d'Agoult . . . and there was no word from old Frau von Bulow, who felt resentful and scornful towards the 'fallen woman'. But what troubled Cosima most was the hatred of Princess Sayn-Wittgenstein, her father's mistress and lifetime companion, a cold, nasty woman who grew more and more sanctimonious with age, apparently forgetting that she herself had once abandoned family, money, and honour for Liszt.[72]

This writer also notes that

> The Jew-baiting Chamberlain doubtless encouraged Cosima's 'idee-fixe': her ever latent anti-Semitism, which some biographers have ventured to tie in with the Jewish ancestry of her step-mother Princess Wittgenstein, whom she despised all her life.[73]

This reference to a Jewish background of the Sayn-Wittgensteins is obviously noteworthy. Houston Stewart Chamberlain, like Wagner a seminal anti-Semite, was Wagner's son-in-law and met Hitler in the 1920s. Hitler praised him in *Mein Kampf* and attended his funeral. There is a report dating from 1923 of the reading material in Hitler's bookcase, which included Chamberlain's biography of Wagner.[74] If he read it, then Hitler knew of the Sayn–Wittgenstein connection to Wagner, whether or not he knew of it from his school-days. Hitler, of course, attended the Wagner music festivals at Bayreuth and made a point of meeting Winifred Wagner and the aging Cosima Wagner.

Bartley[75] points out that Wittgenstein's obituary in *The Times* stated that Wittgenstein *was* a Sayn-Wittgenstein and that 'some members of the

Sayn-Wittgenstein family have on occasion indicated that they are related to Ludwig Wittgenstein's family'. If there really is a Sayn-Wittgenstein family connection through to the anti-Jewish hates of Wagner and Chamberlain, then this would be of the very first importance. As it happens, however, there is an even more direct and important link between Wagner's hates and the Wittgensteins, whose details are the subject of a later chapter.

There is a further point to note about the 'Nation and Race' section of *Mein Kampf.* Describing the process of Jewish infiltration, Hitler writes of the 'court Jew':

> With his deftness, or rather unscrupulousness, in all money matters he is able to squeeze, yes, to grind, more and more money out of the plundered subjects, who in shorter and shorter intervals go the way of all flesh. Thus every court has its 'court Jew' – as the monsters are called who torment the 'beloved people' to despair and prepare eternal pleasures for the princes. Who then can be surprised that these ornaments of the human race ended up by being ornamented, or rather decorated, in the literal sense, and rose to the hereditary nobility, helping not only to make this institution ridiculous, but even to poison it? Now, it goes without saying, he can really make use of his position for his own advancement. Finally he needs only to have himself baptised to possess himself of all the possibilities and rights of the natives of the country. Not seldom he concludes this deal to the joy of the churches over the son they have won and of Israel over the successful swindle.[76]

This passage, with its references to 'court Jews' and to Jews converting to Christianity, raises the question of whom Hitler thought he was alluding to. What historical fact did he have in mind? One thinks, perhaps, of the Rothschild family or of the court Jew subject of the Nazi propaganda film *Jew Süss.* The Rothschilds had been court Jews, but then they never wavered in their Jewish affiliation, so whoever he had in mind, Hitler was not referring to them.

Professor Anscombe, one of Wittgenstein's literary executors, mentioned to me a conversation she once had with Wittgenstein, in which she had asked him about the origin of the name 'Wittgenstein'. He replied that his ancestors had been court Jews. And unlike the Rothschilds, the Wittgenstein family had indeed converted to Christianity.

Further, Hitler's allegations of Jewish stock market manipulation, etc. all fit the activities of Ludwig's father, Karl Wittgenstein. Karl Wittgenstein's newspaper articles over the period 1888-1905 have been collected and published by J. C. Nyiri.[77] Wittgenstein's articles on tariffs and the nationalities question (and defending cartels) are punctuated by two public declarations in 1900 that he had not been engaged in dubious stock market manipulations. The first declaration was published in the *Arbeiterzeitung* (the organ of the Socialist Party) on 20 June 1900 and the second on 24 June 1900. Karl Wittgenstein's first declaration notes that

> Certain newspapers have reported for a long time and continue to report about certain operations that connect me with the stock exchange.[78]

Karl Wittgenstein goes on to deny the allegations, but the important point here is that it is evident the allegations were continuing and widespread and public (indeed, empire-wide) and that therefore some notoriety attached to his name. McGuinness's own description of Karl Wittgenstein's business affairs runs as follows:

> Wittgenstein detached himself from his industrial affairs only gradually and not without controversy. Towards the end of 1898 his colleagues attempted to distribute some of the reserves of the Prague company which, in part, had been only recently accumulated. This seemed to be a transparent stock exchange manoeuvre and was severely criticised in the official newspaper. It is even said that the heir-apparent, the Archduke Franz Ferdinand, intervened. In the event the distribution was delayed for a year and the Credit-Anstalt directors left the Prague company's board while Wittgenstein himself left that of the Credit-Anstalt. It can hardly have been an accident that the value of the shares (which had fallen by 27 fl on the day Wittgenstein left the steel board) was driven up in this manner just when he was divesting himself of his interests: a year later Karl Kraus was able to point out[79] that on the one hand the dividend had in fact fallen from 60 to 50 florins and the shares by 100 fl and on the other Wittgenstein had declared that he had nothing more to do with the company.[80]

Karl Wittgenstein's writings appeared also in papers other than the *Arbeiterzeitung*. Here is a list of some of his other articles, as given in Nyiri's book but rearranged into chronological order. (The list is by no means exhaustive.)

- Impressions of Travels in America, *Neue Freie Presse*, August 1888
- Fairy Tale of the Currencies, *Neues Wiener Tagblatt*, 1892
- The Confiscation of the Scythes in Judenburg, Kindberg and Murzzuschlag, *Neue Freie Presse*, 1892
- The Confiscation of the Scythes in Judenburg, Kindberg and Murzzuschlag, *Neue Freie Presse*, 1892 (a second letter defending himself against an article claiming the Wittgenstein works were operating against the spirit of the law. The earlier letter of Wittgenstein complained

against the authorities confiscating the three Wittgenstein scythe-works products and sealing his warehouse. These letters together cover ten pages in Nyiri's reprint.)

- Cartels in Austria, *Neue Freie Presse*, 1894
- On a World Trip, *Neue Freie Presse*, 1898
- The Causes of the Development of Industry in America, *Zeitschrift des Osterr. Ingenieur und Architekten Vereines*, 1898
- A Declaration by Herr Wittgenstein, *Arbeiterzeitung*, 1900
- A Second Declaration by Herr Wittgenstein, *Arbeiterzeitung*, 1900
- Moderne Handelspolitik, *Neues Wiener Tagblatt*, 1901
- The Politics of Illusion, *Prager Tagblatt*, 1902
- Hungarian Grain and Austrian Scythes, *Neues Wiener Tagblatt*, 1902
- Blind America, *Industrie*, circa 1902
- Letter to the Editor of *Industrie*, 1902
- Free Trade and Protection, *Zeitschrift des Osterr. Ingenieur und Architekten Vereines*, 1903
- New Year Reflections, *Bohemia*, 1905
- The Industrial Depression of Imperial Germany and the Economic Situation in Austria (no publication or date given)

Karl Wittgenstein, then, was not an industrialist *simpliciter*, but one who took an active role in the popular intellectual life of the empire by writing in quality newspapers over a period of many years.

As it happens, following the Anschluss, the *Neue Freie Presse* and the *Neues Wiener Tagblatt* were closed down on Hitler's direct instructions, whereas other Jewish-owned newspapers in Germany and Austria were allowed to continue publication after being purged of Jews.[81] That Hitler read the *Neue Freie Presse*, at least in his Vienna days, is clear from *Mein Kampf*, where, on the page opposite the reference to the young Jewish boy of Linz, he writes, 'I zealously read the so-called world press (*Neue Freie Presse, Wiener Tagblatt* etc.)', and continues, after pages of anti-Semitic diatribe, with

> And now I began to examine my beloved 'world press' from this point of view. And the deeper I probed, the more the object of my former admiration shrivelled. The style became more and more unbearable; I could not help rejecting the content as inwardly shallow and banal; the objectivity of exposition now seemed to me more akin to lies than honest truth; and the writers were – Jews.[82]

Indeed they were: one of them was Karl Wittgenstein, who attacked government policy on taxes, tariffs and protection of farmers in these very newspapers.[83] Again I remind the reader that Hitler's father, Alois, was a customs official. In 1901, Karl had written, 'Wir alle waren in unserer Jugend Freihandler und sind es zum Teile noch' – 'We were all proponents of free trade in our youth, and still are, in part, today.'[84] How might a person whose career was based upon the collection of customs duties view newspaper articles denouncing government policy, especially when they were written by an industrialist with strong Jewish connections and of dubious public reputation? Surely, if he were a 'well-informed person' – as he was described in his obituary – he would react with a somewhat jaundiced eye. Indeed (given the family propensity we know of in his son) perhaps even extreme rage, since abolition of tariffs would do away with his livelihood and call into question the *raison d'être* of his life. He seems in any case to have had decided views about people of influence in Vienna, for Hitler records:

> I have much to thank my father for. He was a customs official. He knew Austrians and Bavarians, Germans and Slavs, Italians and French. For him Austria was always just a part of the great German Fatherland. Even as a child I heard my father say that Vienna was ruled by a clique, a mongrel crew which had collected in the capital. Later I was able to check this for myself.[85]

McGuinness mentions also that Karl's activities had *racial* consequences within the empire:

> . . . the struggle of its nationalities was indeed, as Wittgenstein said, a struggle for bread, but the growth of industry accentuated the contrast between the races and the more successful he was in expanding his enterprises and in employing Czechs for wages that Germans would not accept, the more he contributed (as Karl Kraus pointed out)[86] to Slavicizing the industrial regions of the Czech lands and to sharpening the racial conflict.[87]

Karl Wittgenstein's business affairs were particularly evident in the crucial year 1904:

> The major metallurgical concerns had close connections with the banks, but Wittgenstein's *Prager Eisenindustrie-Gesellschaft* was apparently in a position to act as an independent agent. In 1904 the *Bohmische Montangesellschaft* was formally merged with the Wittgenstein company; the newly merged company had a share capital of 24.5 million crowns. This was one of the most profitable enterprises in the Czech lands, and indeed, in the entire dual monarchy. By 1912 the firm had a share capital of 36 million crowns, and its net profit

amounted to almost 16 million crowns.[88]

One should expect that news of such major changes in the empire's industrial base of 1904 would not be unknown to well-informed newspaper readers in Linz. Remembering that the son of the great industrialist responsible attended the local school, I suggest that it might be profitable to read some of *Mein Kampf*'s anti-Semitic fulminations, which *sound* general, as directed not at Jews in general but rather against Jews seen under the aspect of Haus Wittgenstein.

The fact that Karl Kraus turned his pen against Karl Wittgenstein is also significant. Kraus was not just some minor journalist, but a twentieth-century Austrian literary phenomenon in his own right. Wistrich[89] quotes Kraus's observation in *Die Fackel*[90] about anti-Semitism concerning Moritz Benedikt, editor of the *Neue Freie Presse*, and the Wittkowitz steel works, which were managed by Karl Wittgenstein's relative and mentor, Paul Kupelwieser, and were part of the Wittgenstein cartel:

> Some obscure Jews have been beaten up, a few teachers have not been promoted – but Rothschild's profits from municipal business grow. And since Herr Benedikt has for the last twenty years successfully persuaded the Viennese Jews that they have no real interest other than the balance-sheet of Wittkowitz [the Rothschild–owned iron works] it is therefore no surprise that the readers of the Neue Freie Presse feel very comfortable under Lueger's regime.[91]

Wistrich also notes that Kraus's writings were spared the bonfires of the 1933 Nazi book-burning 'because he had exposed the international conspiracy of world Jewish finance'.[92] Well, he certainly wrote about Karl Wittgenstein.

The relative positions of the Rothschild works at Wittkowitz and Wittgenstein's Prager Eisenindustrie-Gesellschaft in the earlier period up to 1890 is clear from the following:

> Of the major iron and steel producers, the Witkowitz works remained the most powerful. Throughout the period under discussion the works remained the private possession of the great Rothschild and Gutmann brothers private banking houses. The Prager Eisenindustrie-Gesellschaft . . . stood second to the Witkowitz enterprises in iron and steel production, and was the most dynamic of the firms in moving toward greater concentration within the industry.[93]

Rothschild and Wittgenstein – here is 'Jew monopoly capital' with a vengeance; the iron and steel cartel, the controlling power at the very core of the empire's economy. The importance of this cannot be overemphasized. Previous accounts of Hitler's anti-Semitism have assumed he had no acquaintance with any Jew of substance and that his opinions were formed from reading anti-Semitic pamphlets during his time in Vienna. It is now reasonably clear that Hitler – at a very impressionable age – had a school-fellow link to the family of the single most significant Jewish-controlled industrial sector of the empire. And that family was such that Hitler could not fail to be aware of it. The elder Wittgenstein runs the empire's iron and steel industry, has a reputation for sharp practice, and pontificates about trade matters in papers with an empire-wide distribution. His stuttering, homosexual son thinks his schoolmates to be muck. This homosexual son has one homosexual brother who kills himself in the very enrolment year 1904 and another homosexual brother who had killed himself two years previously. Surely young Ludwig must have been the very talk of Linz!

In a speech given in Munich on 28 July 1922 Hitler complained of the Jews:

> ... these apostles who talk their tongues out of their heads, but who spend the night in the Hotel Excelsior, travel in express trains, and spend their leave for their health in Nice – these people do not exert their energies for love of the people. No, the people is not to profit, it shall merely be brought into dependence on these men. The backbone of its independence, its own economic life, is to be destroyed, that it may the more surely relapse into the golden fetters of the perpetual interest slavery of the Jewish race. And this process will end when suddenly out of the masses someone arises who seizes the leadership, finds other comrades and fans into flames the passions which have been held in check and looses them against the deceivers. That is the lurking danger, and the Jew can meet it in one way only – by destroying the hostile national intelligentsia.[94]

I point out, in connection with Hitler's complaint about the Jews holidaying in Nice, that McGuinness refers to 'the double-eagles casually thrown onto the table at Monte Carlo on the way from the restaurant' by Karl Wittgenstein.[95] Without doubt, some other European Jews holidayed on the Riviera, but those to whom Hitler referred as 'The Jews' so holidayed and Karl Wittgenstein so holidayed. If each of the points of coincidence we have marshalled carries only a spider's strand of evidentiary weight, collectively they are beginning to support a very substantial load.

Hitler's main interest at the time, of course, as an aspiring artist, might well have been art, rather than industry or politics. But here again, Karl Wittgenstein was as influential as any man in Europe.

'No Jews at the Hotel Excelsior!' © *Ribbentrop Collection*

The history of the 'Secession' movement is chronicled in any reasonable account of twentieth-century art.[96] The Secession was a breakaway art movement formed in 1897 whose most prominent member was Gustav Klimt, the painter of a famous portrait of Ludwig Wittgenstein's sister. The movement was anti-classicist and rebelled against the restrictions the Academy placed on their exhibiting in the Vienna Kunstlerhaus. In 1902 the Secessionists organized an exhibition honouring Beethoven, a statue of whom by Max Klinger was the centrepiece.[97]

The fate of this centrepiece statue of Beethoven can be gleaned from a passage in McGuinness's book describing Karl Wittgenstein's Alleegasse house and its furnishings:

This became, though the family of course never called it so, the Palais Wittgenstein, the centre of their lives, with its Dienstmann sitting on his stool outside, the business-rooms on the ground floor, the card-tray where the children were careful to put the tame Princess's card on top, the imposing stair-case, the large music room, and the numerous proteges and tutors and servants. But in it, as well as the equestrian portrait of himself by Kramer and later the fashionable portrait by Laszlo, which any successful businessman might have, he assembled a collection of pictures painted between 1870 and 1910 of much more modern inspiration – Segantini, Rudolf von Alt, and Klimt among them. These were set off by sculptures by Rodin and Mestrovic, and a famous one of Beethoven by Max Klinger.[98]

The Secessionists' centrepiece sculpture by Klinger, then, ended up in Karl Wittgenstein's hands.[99] But his connection to the Secession movement was more intimate than simply being a purchaser of Secessionist art works, for Karl Wittgenstein financed the Secession building, which still stands. Jones outlines the background to the Secession movement:

> The principal aim of the group was to exhibit, something the more conservative Kunstlerhaus had in the past prevented. Exhibit they did, and with a vengeance, in 1898. Their first exhibition was held in rooms rented on the Park Ring virtually out from under the rival Kunstlerhaus group who had been about to rent them. The show was a smashing success financially. There were paintings by members of the group including Klimt and Moll, plus paintings by foreigners such as Whistler that were completely new to the Viennese. . . . The Viennese loved it. More than 57,000 visitors saw this first show, and some 218 of the works displayed were sold. But when the profits earned from the show were put to use to build a permanent exhibition hall on the Friedrichstrasse across the Karlplatz from the Kunstlerhaus and behind the Academy, the Viennese were no longer so sure in their opinion of these self-styled rebels. The austere lines of this cube-shaped building designed by Olbrich earned the place such nicknames as 'the Mahdi's Tomb' and 'the gilded cabbage', which referred to the cupola adorning the building. . . . Bahr describes the scene during the construction of the Secession building: 'You can see a crowd of people standing around a new building. On their way to work . . . they stare, they interrogate each other, they discuss this thing. They think it strange, they have never seen anything of the kind, they don't like it, it repels them. Filled with serious reflections, they pass on their way, and then turn round yet again, cast another look backwards, don't want to depart, hesitate to hurry off about their business. And this goes on the whole day!'[100]

The Secession building, therefore, was something of an architectural scandal. Now Monk informs us of Karl Wittgenstein's financing of it, and of his artistic interests in general:

> After his retirement from industry Karl Wittgenstein became known also as a great patron of the visual arts. Aided by his eldest daughter Hermine – herself a gifted painter – he assembled a noteworthy collection of valuable paintings and sculptures, including works by Klimt, Moser and Rodin. Klimt called him his 'Minister of Fine Art', in gratitude for his financing of both the Secession Building (at which the works of Klimt, Schiele and Kokoschka were exhibited), and Klimt's own mural, *Philosophie*, which had been rejected by the University

of Vienna. . . . The Wittgensteins were thus at the centre of Viennese cultural life.[101]

Compare the Wittgensteins' grand patronage of art with the struggling efforts of a certain impoverished would-be artist from Linz, who hawked his drawings to tourists in Vienna so that he could live in a men's home! Wouldn't he at least have gone inside the Secession building, just off the Ring, to look at the odd exhibition during his Vienna years? Toland comments on Hitler's habits, '. . . he haunted the Ringstrasse, inspecting it and adjoining areas by the hour . . .'[102] Would he not have known about the background to the scandalous Secession building – as he did of so much Viennese architecture – and of Klimt's 1905 portrait of Wittgenstein's sister? (When the Nazis came to power, some of the Secession artists, particularly Schiele and Kokoschka, suffered state campaigns against their work.)[103] And earlier, in Linz, would not Hitler, as an art student, have known about the most dynamic art movement of the day and its great patron? It is demonstrable that, in Vienna, Hitler personally approached a founder of the Secession movement, Alfred Roller, of whom Vergo writes:

> Together with Moser, Olbrich and Hoffmann, he was one of the founding members of the Secession.[104]

Schwarzwaller, in his book *The Unknown Hitler*, states that when Hitler left Linz for Vienna he was able to get access to Roller, an internationally famous painter of stage scenery, via an introduction 'from a friend in Linz'.[105] Schwarzwaller writes:

> Roller was the co-founder of the Vienna Secession Art Movement, as well as being an instructor at the School of Applied Arts. Gustav Mahler had picked him as the stage designer for the Imperial Opera, and he created the scenery for Mahler's productions of all of Wagner's operas and, later, the premieres of Richard Strauss' operas.
>
> Roller gladly received Hitler and gave him some friendly advice but was unable to take him on as a private student due to time constraints. He recommended the budding young artist to Panholzer, a seasoned educator, sculptor and drawing teacher. Panholzer accepted Hitler as his pupil. Later, when he was Führer, Hitler loved to brag that he'd been a pupil of Professor Alfred Roller, which wasn't the truth, although during his first year in Vienna, he attended every opera performance for which Roller had designed the scenery. Hitler's blind reverence for Roller went so far that in 1935 he suggested the now 74-year-old man be called to Bayreuth to become a stage designer. Roller died that same year.[106]

Roller had been the editor of the Secession's own journal, *Ver Sacrum*, one of the outstanding periodicals of its day.[107] *Ver Sacrum*, however, had ceased publication in 1903 over the issue of commercialization of art.[108] Now the Secession movement in the crucial year 1904-5 had split into two opposing groups: the Klimt-gruppe – the followers of Klimt – and the Nur-Maler – the pure painters. Vergo's account of the split runs:

> The origins of this jealousy may be traced back to the debacle over the 1904 World's Fair at St Louis, at which the Secession had, somewhat belatedly, been invited to exhibit by the Austrian Ministry of Education. A special booklet published by the Secession in connection with this invitation indicates that the committee, faced with the choice of arranging an exhibition purely of paintings or creating some more 'monumental' kind of display, had decided in favour of a whole room designed by Hoffmann, where it was decided to show pictures by Klimt, among them *Philosophy* and *Jurisprudence*, and precious little else. . . . The debate which this decision provoked, above all in the press, became so heated that the Secession was finally prevented from exhibiting in St Louis at all; but it is not difficult to recognize, in the attacks directed against Klimt and his party, the particular animus evoked by the continuing collaboration between Klimt and Hoffmann, and the indignation at the neglect of the other painters within the association. From this point onwards, the Secession polarized itself into two opposing groups: the *Klimt-gruppe*, which included the architect Otto Wagner, the designers Hoffman and Moser, and the painter Carl Moll; and the *Nur-Maler* (pure painters) with Engelhart at their head.[109]

In 1905 the Secession split and in 1906 the Österreichischer Kunstlerbund (Austrian Artists' Union) was founded. Roller, the Imperial Opera stage designer and director of the School of Applied Art, as a rival of Hoffmann, was in the anti-Klimt (and thus anti-Wittgenstein) group.[110] It is therefore understandable that Hitler approached him. Hermann Bahr – 'the man from Linz', who was a card-carrying member of the Secession – had published a book in 1903, *Gegen Klimt* ('Against Klimt'), in which he labelled Klimt an 'outlaw'. Hitler in later life often expressed solidarity with successful Linz artists against the Viennese. In his *Table Talk*, for example, he rallies to the musician Bruckner, from Linz, against Brahms, from Vienna. Here too, Hitler's sympathies were with Bahr and against Klimt – and the Wittgensteins.

So, clearly, Hitler *did* know about the Secession movement, at least when he moved to Vienna. And Werner Maser's study of Hitler even has a passage describing his artistic efforts just after the Great War that locates Hitler's acquaintance with the Secession to as early as 1898, when he would have been about ten years old:

At about this time he asked the well-known and highly esteemed artist Max Zaeper to give an opinion of his recent work. Zaeper was so impressed by the quality of Hitler's watercolours and drawings that he sought a second opinion from Professor Ferdinand Staeger, a colleague of Czech extraction. Staeger's romantic-mystical pictures painted in a naturalistic style had first come to Hitler's attention at the Vienna Secession's exhibition held in 1898 at No 12 Friedrichstrasse in protest against the conservatism of the artistic 'establishment'.[111]

The Secession had grown from strength to strength. Knowledge of the exhibitions it organized and their content was essential for any Austrian art student. Its sixteenth exhibition, in 1903, included works by Manet, Monet Renoir, Degas, Pissaro, Sisley, Cezanne, van Gogh, Toulouse-Lautrec, Vuillard, Bonnar, Denis, Redon, Renoir, Gauguin, Vermeer, Tintoretto, Velasquez, El Greco, Goya, Delacroix, Daumier, Whistler and the Japanese Hokusai and Utamaro.[112] What a list! One would expect that the young Hitler, who aspired to be an artist, would have known about this great exhibition in the Secession building, even before he decided to approach Roller. (The eighteenth exhibition of the Secession, on the other hand, also in 1903, was devoted entirely to Klimt, with Wittgenstein support.) Could Hitler not have known that the son of the great Secession patron, Karl Wittgenstein, was identically the 'Saujud' homosexual, stuttering, truss-wearing Ludwig Wittgenstein from Vienna, the new boy at his own school, the same age yet two years ahead of him, whom the schoolboys persecuted? Or should we rather believe that Wittgenstein would have been discreet about his background? Well, writing of Wittgenstein's period as a primary school teacher at Trattenbach after the First World War, Bartley notes that

> he went out of his way to ensure that the villagers would know who he was, or at least that they would know of his family's wealth and influence, of his own education and aristocratic background, and of his academic achievement in England.[113]

Bartley supports this claim with eye-witness testimony:

> Shortly after his first arrival in Trattenbach, Wittgenstein was visited by Hansel (who came to see him – as did his friends Drobil, a sculptor, and Nahr, the Wittgenstein family photographer – approximately every second month throughout his sojourn in the villages). While taking lunch together in the inn, Wittgenstein and Hansel talked about life in Vienna in voices that the villagers present, listening intently, easily overheard. One of Wittgenstein's remarks to

Hansel which is still remembered is this: 'Ich hatt einst einen Diener, der hieß Konstantin' ('I once had a servant named Konstantin'). Later during Hansel's visit, Wittgenstein and he cornered poor George Berger in the school office, and Wittgenstein demanded to know what the villagers had to say about him. Berger reports that he replied reluctantly, fearing Wittgenstein's temper: 'The people take you to be a rich baron.' Wittgenstein was satisfied with this answer, but remarked to Berger that although he had indeed been rich, he had given all his money away to his siblings 'in order to do a good deed'.[114]

Perhaps he saw going out of his way to proclaim his background in this manner as just being honest. But if such behaviour was part of his character as a grown man at Trattenbach, how much more likely is that as a schoolboy he was similarly indiscreet, as was the 'one Jewish boy' about whom Hitler complained?

That there were only fifteen Jews in the whole school needs emphasis. How could any other student have stood out more from the rest than a homosexual, truss-wearing, stuttering, Austrian equivalent of a Carnegie, Krupp or Rothschild? Wittgenstein stood out 'as if blown in from an alien world' as his sister described his relations to his school-fellows. On our hypothesis, of course, this Jew was not one of the fifteen registered Jews at the school, but then this might explain why researchers appear to have drawn a blank trying to locate the unknown Jew who provoked Hitler's anti-Semitism as someone at the school; for if our hypothesis is correct, this Jew was hidden in the Catholic registrations.

Pauley's book contains an interesting passage on Vienna's 'hidden Jews', which is worth noting. He writes:

Although the census of 1923 revealed that there were just over 201,000 registered Jews in Vienna and another 19,000 in the federal states, no one knew how many people there were of Jewish origins in Austria (or for that matter in Germany). As noted earlier, the Nazis themselves discovered after the Anschluss that there were only 34,500 Viennese who met the Nuremberg definition of a full-blooded Jew who had not already been counted as such in the most recent Austrian census. (The Nuremberg Laws, it will be recalled, defined a full-blooded Jew as someone with at least three Jewish grandparents or someone who practised Judaism and had two Jewish grandparents.)[115]

The Nuremberg Laws, which defined who was a Jew in the eyes of the Nazis, might have been drawn up with Wittgenstein in mind – he had three Jewish grandparents. And if Pauley's figures (that there were about a sixth as many 'hidden Jews' as officially registered as Jews in the Viennese population) applied proportionately also to the *Realschule* student population of fifteen Jews, then there would have been about two or three students 'of Jewish descent' (but not officially Jewish) at the school.

Wittgenstein's 'submarine' status as a hidden Jew would have been shared by only one or two others. In fact we must expect there to have been fewer submarine Jews in the provincial towns because the possibility of submarine status is a function of anonymity; and while the anonymity allowed by big cities has become a by-word, in smaller towns, everyone tends to know everyone else's business and family background. The possibilities of anonymity, therefore, are reduced. As an illustration, consider the corresponding figures for Jews in Hungary in 1941:

HUNGARIAN JEWS, 1941

	Budapest	The Country	Total
Official Jews	184,453	540,554	725,007
'Nuremberg' Jews	62,350	37,650	100,000
Total	246,803	578,204	825,007

(Source: © 1994 courtesy of the Jewish Holocaust Museum and Research Centre, Elsternwick, Australia.)

In Budapest, 62,350 out of 246,803, or about a quarter of those counted as Jews, were not officially Jewish in the eyes of the Jewish community. In the country, however, the proportion was only 37,650 out of 578,204, or about a fifteenth.

If a roughly similar phenomenon applied to the distribution of Jews in Austria, then the 'Vienna' estimate of Pauley's figures (that there were about a sixth more hidden Jews than there were of those who were Jewish in the eyes of the Jewish community) should also be adjusted downwards for the country; from one sixth to one fifteenth.[116] We ought then to expect that alongside the fifteen acknowledged Jews at the school there would be one submarine Jew. We do know the identity of one such – Ludwig Wittgenstein – and it is most unlikely that there would have been more than a tiny number of others. We have the guarantee of Keplinger's testimony that of this very tiny group one was picked as a Jew by Adolf Hitler.

Did Hitler refer to Wittgenstein later? There is an interesting reference in Hitler's first speech on Austrian soil, which he gave back in Linz, on 12 March 1938:

I thank you for your words of greeting. Above all I thank all of you assembled here who have borne witness that it is not the will and the wish of some few only to found this great Reich of the German people. Would that on this evening some of our international seekers after truth whom we know so well could not only see the facts but later admit them to be facts. When years ago I went forth from this town, I bore within me precisely the same profession of faith which to-day fills my heart. Judge of the depth of my emotion when after so many years I have been able to bring that profession of faith to its fulfilment.[117]

We should remember that when Hitler made this speech, he had achieved the great goal he stated as his aim in the opening chapters of *Mein Kampf* – because one blood demands one Reich, Austria should be united with Germany. It was his moment of triumph. He was hailed as a greater German than Bismarck. And yet he referred back to the days of his youth and stated his regret that certain people were not there to witness his triumph. What are we to make of Hitler's reference to 'our international seekers after truth whom we know so well'? Knowing his hates, one might suppose that he was referring to Jews. But it is obviously a most peculiar description to apply to Jews generally. Why call Jews 'international seekers after truth'? One can mentally scan the normal anti-Semitic arsenal of epithets ('blood-suckers', 'rootless cosmopolitans', 'Christ-killers', etc.) to be struck by how out of place it sounds. It sounds like the sort of description one might apply to philosophers rather than to Jews. Perhaps it is not so peculiar, however, if the reference was aimed at another *Realschule* graduate who really was now a philosopher – at Cambridge. There would be no problem at all in describing an Austrian philosopher in Cambridge as an 'international seeker after truth'. And if his former fellow-student Ludwig Wittgenstein really were the veiled referent of this description in Hitler's speech, then the added rider describing him as someone 'whom we know so well', would seem to indicate some so far unsuspected intimacy of contact in the days of Hitler's youth in Linz. Hitler, when asked in the late twenties why he was anti-Semitic, always replied that it was something 'personal'.

That Hitler till the end of his days had an obsession with making Linz a greater centre of art than Vienna is well known. Art treasures looted from all over Europe were to be sent to Linz for the Adolf Hitler museum. His plans for the Hitler museum were discussed with the astonished director of the Linz museum as early as 12 March 1938 in the Weinziger Hotel in Linz. That is, on the very same day that he wished that the 'international seekers after truth' – whom he knew so well, but who were unfortunately somewhere else – might witness his triumph, he set up plans to make Linz the art capital of Europe.

Historians have seen Hitler's plans for the glorification of Linz as something separate from his hatred of Jews; as a sort of 'help the home town' pork-barrelling that one might find equally in successful politicians of democratic countries. But if the thesis of this chapter is correct, that is to misread the psychology of Hitler, who was doing it to rub the noses of the Viennese Wittgensteins into the dirt. It was all of a piece with his hatred of Jews, recognizably part of the same pathology. And it was life-long. The plans for Linz and the Hitler museum were his consolation in the Berlin bunker as the sound of the Russian guns drew steadily closer. This was an unfulfilled part of his life. As for the Jews . . . well, he had shown them. And as for the Wittgenstein steel complex in Kladno, he'd set up the Hermann Goering steelworks in Linz, which now owned the Wittgenstein cartel's Wittkowitz plant. Jews couldn't laugh at him now – and never would again! Indeed not. He had achieved his goal of ridding Germany of Jews, the 'Final Solution'.

If I am right, Wittgenstein's complex, prickly personality (whose characteristics were striking and which is remarked upon in all the memoirs) was a contributory cause of the events that climaxed in the extermination of European Jewry. Hitler, I suggest, with *his* complex, prickly personality, was repelled by Wittgenstein and came to attribute what he saw as Wittgenstein's particular personality defects to Jews in general. Tied in with this transfer of hatred to Jews was the unparalleled wealth and power of the Wittgenstein family in Austrian industrial and cultural life in contrast to Hitler's background as an essentially small-town yokel from Braunau. Of course Hitler recounts his later experience of other Jews as well, in an attempt to justify his anti-Semitism, but the Jewish boy at the Linz *Realschule* is the very first and the only one referred to as an individual Jew whom he had met, rather than as a type. Something happened between Hitler and Wittgenstein at the *Realschule*. We face, I think, the astounding possibility that the course of the twentieth century was radically influenced by a quarrel between two schoolboys.

TWO

The Spies of Trinity

That Wittgenstein attended school with Adolf Hitler is remarkable. There is a further fact about Wittgenstein revealed in the biographies that is every bit as remarkable but that no commentator appears to have found worth anything more than the mere noting. This is that Wittgenstein was offered the chair in Philosophy at Kazan University in the Soviet Union in 1935.[1]

What is remarkable about this offer is that academics in Soviet universities at the time were being systematically tortured and murdered for the slightest deviation from the Party line. The merest whisper in criticism of Marxism or the Great Leader was a certain ticket to a drawn-out death by starvation in a forced labour camp. Why then would the Soviet government think Wittgenstein's work to be of such compelling importance that he should be rewarded with the chair in Philosophy at the university that Lenin himself had attended?

To anyone at all familiar with the literature on the nature of the Soviet state in the thirties, it is clear that there is no possibility at all that such an offer could have been made to a non-Marxist foreign philosopher. The fact that it was, shows that things are neither quite as they seem nor as every Wittgenstein biographer and commentator has taken for granted. The offer raises the question whether Wittgenstein rendered some signal service to the Communist cause.

Can we glean, at this remove, any indication of what such a signal service might have been? Let us first see what we know of the development of Wittgenstein's political views.

The Austrian state that survived the Great War was a fragment of its former self. Vienna, which had been the ancient seat of emperors, the pride and vibrant hub of a vast and prosperous multi-racial empire, was now a drain on the remnant state that owned it as capital. The city faced bitter poverty and many of its greatest families had been ruined. The Wittgenstein family, on the other hand, emerged from the Great War amongst the very richest in Europe. The wise and far-seeing Karl, as Bartley outlines, had invested his fortune in America before the war started:

Before his death on 20 January 1913, Karl Wittgenstein, founder of the Austrian iron and steel industry, had transferred virtually all his liquid capital into American stocks and bonds, principally in the United States Steel Corporation. And thus the fortune, which was giving Ludwig alone an annual income of 300,000 Kronen (gold crowns in 1914), prior to the start of the war, had been vastly augmented by the prosperity of the nation whose forces had helped bring about his own country's defeat.[2]

One must imaginatively put oneself in the position of a starving citizen of post-war Vienna. Surely if news of the Wittgenstein family's war-time business dealings had emerged in the violent political turmoil of post-war Austria, it could not but have caused immense resentment? Even during hostilities, the family had withdrawn support from its nation's war effort and attended to multiplying its own assets. Thus:

> As for the money that had been left in Austria during the war, for the most part Karl Wittgenstein's brother Ludwig, who had managed it, invested it in government bonds. But prior to the end of the war and the great inflation, he had sold most of the bonds to buy real estate, one of the few things in Austria whose value was augmented by inflation.[3]

Prudent, yes, but hardly patriotic.[4] And the reader must now place himself in Wittgenstein's position at the cessation of hostilities. His older brother Karl had killed himself, the third of his brothers to take this course. His sole surviving brother Paul – a pianist of genius – had lost an arm and been imprisoned by the Russians in Siberia. The society was politically riven and Austrian children were not merely hungry but literally dying of starvation, at least partially from the effect of the blockade, which continued past 1918. In the autumn of 1919, Wittgenstein wrote a letter to Bertrand Russell saying that the city was starving.[5] He obviously felt for the sufferers. Indeed, he must have felt that the world was in ruins, for certainly his world was in ruins, destroyed by British allies and the British blockade. Yet, in the very midst of this colossal ruin, he stood to inherit one of Europe's more considerable fortunes; one, moreover, which had been multiplied many times from investments with the enemies of his own country.

What would one expect to be the likely effect of this upon the political views of the young Wittgenstein? Wittgenstein's renunciation of his inheritance lends some support to thinking that his move was indeed towards the left.

Another common view of Wittgenstein is the complete opposite of this: that, to the extent that he had political inclinations at all, he was conservative – a supporter of the status quo. In Fania Pascal's memoir, for example, we read:

> At a time when intellectual Cambridge was turning Left he was still an old-time conservative of the late Austro-Hungarian Empire.[6]

Some of Wittgenstein's recorded pronouncements would seem to support what Mrs Pascal says. On the other hand, there is a considerable body of evidence indicating that the reality was the exact opposite of this view. Indeed, later we shall see that her testimony, for political reasons, might have been designed deliberately to mislead.

Wittgenstein taught in primary schools from 1920 to 1926, in a number of locations in Austria, the last of which was Otterthal. During this period, in September 1922, he wrote to his friend Paul Engelmann that 'The idea of a possible flight to Russia which we talked about keeps on haunting me.'[7] Let us note that this was written well after the Russian revolution and the imposition of a bloody dictatorship. Six weeks after he left Otterthal, on 3 June, Wittgenstein's mother died and, soon after, Wittgenstein entered a monastery in retreat. He camped there for three months in a toolshed of the garden. Here is Bartley's description of Wittgenstein's time in this monastery:

> The remainder of that summer he spent in retreat in a monastery of the Barmherzige Brüder in Hütteldorf, a suburb of Vienna. Although Wittgenstein worked as a gardener, as he had done once before, he entertained seriously the idea of becoming a monk. The monastery no longer exists, and its buildings now serve as a home for destitute mothers and their children; yet some of the old retainers still remain, and a few remember Wittgenstein as 'a very good and highly industrious gardener – and a left-winger'.[8]

Wittgenstein's opinions in 1926, then, were so pronounced that the characteristic for which he was remembered, apart from the excellence of his gardening, was not his philosophy but his politics – he was a 'left-winger'. Three years later, Wittgenstein – who seems to have wanted to flee to the Soviet Union – was to return to Trinity College, Cambridge. The reasons for his return are to this day quite opaque, for commentators unanimously agree that he detested academic life and academics. Malcolm writes on this that

> He had an abhorrence of academic life in general and of the life of a professional philosopher in particular. He believed that a normal human being could not be a university teacher and also an honest and serious person. . . . Wittgenstein

could not stand the society of academic colleagues.[9]

Clearly, despite this, he forced himself to adopt the life. In 1929, Wittgenstein was to return to Cambridge from a Vienna where in the previous year or two, striking workers had been shot in the streets.[10] If he were a left-winger in 1926, we must expect that he would have been radicalized by the events of 1927 and their aftermath into being a rather more committed left-winger. For twelve years, until imposition of the even worse discipline of Adolf Hitler, Vienna was the playground of warring political gangs. The experiences that produced English left-wingers in the thirties, bad as they might have been, were in no way comparable with the experiences of those unfortunate enough to have suffered life in Vienna.[11] The Austrian philosopher Paul Feyerabend, for example, matter-of-factly recalled from the days of his youth 'the dead bodies and the blood-spattered streets I saw in Vienna during the civil war of 1934'.[12]

Now Wittgenstein had a number of particularly interesting contemporaries at Trinity College, among them the future spies Guy Burgess, Kim Philby and Anthony Blunt. (Donald Maclean attended nearby Trinity Hall.) All of them came to Communism in close proximity to Wittgenstein's return to Cambridge. Philby started at Trinity in October 1929, Burgess in October 1930 and Maclean, at Trinity Hall, in 1931.[13] Blunt was elected to a Trinity fellowship in 1932.[14] All the Trinity spies were therefore close contemporaries of Wittgenstein's. It is noteworthy that they all shared his homosexuality.[15] Philby also shared Wittgenstein's stammer, which was still evident at this time, as we know from some lines in Julian Bell's poem about Wittgenstein:

> . . . who, on any issue, ever saw
> Ludwig refrain from laying down the law?
> In every company he shouts us down,
> And stops our sentence stuttering his own;[16]

Of course the mere fact of their attending Trinity College at the same time proves nothing about whether Wittgenstein knew them, but know them he did. Anthony Blunt, for example, the 'fourth man' of the Cambridge spy ring, attended a special supper meeting of the Apostles called by John Maynard Keynes to welcome Wittgenstein's return to philosophy at Cambridge. ('Apostle' is the term used to describe any member of the Cambridge Conversazione Society, which was founded by twelve members in 1820. Renowned for secrecy, its members have included an entirely disproportionate number of prominent British intellectuals.) There were a number of other Communists present: Alister Watson (who Blunt later claimed was the man who taught him Marxism and who Peter Wright reports was still meeting his KGB controllers in the 1960s)[17] was there, as were George Thomson and Julian Bell among others.[18] At this meeting, certainly with Communist support, Wittgenstein was elected as an honorary member of the Apostles.[19] He had already been a member before the Great War, but was excommunicated in 1912. At this meeting his excommunication was revoked.

The presence of Julian Bell (Virginia Woolf's nephew) with Anthony Blunt is not surprising, since both were Apostles, but the connection between these two was closer than simple common membership of the Apostles might indicate. John Costello quotes from a letter of Julian Bell to his mother, Vanessa Bell, concerning the nature of his relationship to Anthony Blunt. The relationship lasted for six months until about September 1929:

> Julian Bell's letter to his mother, dated March 14, 1929, announces that his 'great news is about Anthony'. Couched in the matter-of-fact terms that might be expected of the eldest son of Virginia Woolf's sister, he informed Vanessa: 'I feel certain you won't be upset or shocked at my telling you that we sleep together – to use the Cambridge euphemism.'[20]

Andrew Boyle records that Bell also had some involvement with Guy Burgess, at least in 1933:

> Burgess, not to be outdone by the impassioned Marxist fervour of a freshman called John Cornford . . . threw himself into organizing occasional demonstrations, such as the anti-war march to the War Memorial on Armistice Day 1933. The marchers endured taunts, jeers and a shower of rotten eggs and bruised tomatoes hurled by rowing men and 'hearties' from Jesus College and elsewhere, while policemen looked on stolidly. No truncheons were drawn, no bones broken. And Burgess, seated beside Julian Bell, his fellow Apostle, in the latter's veteran sports car, scattered the phalanx of counter-demonstrators like the navigator of a tank by guiding the vehicle's nose straight at them.[21]

We shall see later that Julian Bell intended writing a PhD thesis on Wittgenstein, so Wittgenstein certainly had a great effect upon his thinking. There is a little further information about the Blunt/Bell/Wittgenstein relationship in Costello's book, for, speaking of Wittgenstein, he writes:

> At the reunion dinner of the Apostles in Wittgenstein's honour, he appears to

have offended Bell's fiercely socialist morality. Blunt sprang to his friend's defence. A fierce verbal dispute erupted. Keynes sent a sharp 'My dear Blunt' note to Anthony on March 19 [1929] taking him to task for being 'upset by what you think happened when Wittgenstein returned to the Society'. Keynes curtly told Blunt, 'The facts are not at all as you suppose.' Both he and Julian were to be summoned to lunch 'early next term to talk about it'.

Despite Keynes's talking to, neither Bell nor Blunt reconciled themselves to Wittgenstein. According to John Hilton, Blunt made Cambridge's adopted philosophical genius 'one of his not rare, "betes noires"'. The assignment of Wittgenstein to a suite on Blunt's staircase in Bishop's Hostel further increased the young man's discomfort.

Never one to abandon a vendetta, Blunt encouraged Bell to write four pages of barbed couplets for The Venture,[22] attacking Wittgenstein's self-righteousness.[23]

Interesting this, and a highly condensed mine of information. Wittgenstein and Anthony Blunt, both homosexuals and Apostles, lived in the same hostel on rooms of the same staircase.[24] Blunt's homosexual lover had been offended by what he thought was an assault on socialist morality by Wittgenstein, but both he and Blunt were reassured of Wittgenstein's political correctness by John Maynard Keynes! And Bell wrote a poem taking off Wittgenstein's views on aesthetics.[25]

Bell later moved in with Lettice Ramsey, the widow of Frank Ramsey,[26] whom Wittgenstein referred to in the preface to the *Philosophical Investigations* as an influence upon him second only to Piero Sraffa, whom we shall consider later. Like Bell, Lettice Ramsey's politics were also ultra'leftist. She was the photographer of the famous shot of the six Marxist Apostles who took over the society.[27] Another Ramsey sister, Margaret, was a Communist Party member and married George Paul, a left-wing student of Wittgenstein's who later took up an academic post teaching philosophy at Melbourne University, another fact to which we shall return. Suffice to mention here that George Paul, Margaret Ramsey, Allen Jackson and Douglas Gasking – all Wittgenstein's Cambridge disciples – were under surveillance in Australia by ASIO, the Australian Security Intelligence Organization, the antipodean equivalent of MI5.[28] Transcripts of Jackson's telephone conversations with high-ranking Australian Communists were made by ASIO virtually from its inception in 1950 and now are available from the Australian Archives in Canberra.

Now the reader must bear in mind that whatever Anthony Blunt's faults, he still ranks as one of the great aesthetes of the twentieth century. He was Keeper of the Queen's Pictures and a theoretician of the first rank in art theory. In his Cambridge days, we know that on the same staircase as he, lived a homosexual Austrian philosopher with pretensions to knowledge about the ultimate nature of aesthetics; to wit, that aesthetics lies in the realm of 'the inexpressible' and that nothing whatever can meaningfully be said about it. The fourth line of the extract from Bell's poem, below, records Wittgenstein's great fault in Bell's eyes:

> Unceasing argues, harsh, irate and loud,
> Sure that he's right, and of his rightness proud.
> Such faults are common, shared by all in part,
> But Wittgenstein pontificates on Art.[29]

Julian Bell's brother Quentin Bell, writing some sixty years later, recalls of Anthony Blunt, 'I knew that Anthony was practically the only person in Cambridge who took an interest in painting,'[30] but this is obviously not quite right: there was another; a philosopher. This philosopher, who pontificated on Art, had a father who financed the enormously influential Secession movement in Vienna and who ensured that his children knew the prominent musicians, artists and art works of the time. This philosopher, to say the least, was not reticent in conveying his opinions to others. Indeed, Bell adds in his poem that Wittgenstein

> . . . numerous statements makes
> Forever his own vow of silence breaks:
> Ethics, aesthetics, talks of day and night . . .

Blunt's first academic interest, before switching to Modern Languages, had been mathematics, the subject whose foundations were the subject of Wittgenstein's lectures. Like Blunt, Wittgenstein had a particular interest in architecture, having even designed and built a great house in Vienna in the style of Adolf Loos.[31] He had visited Vienna in the 1928 Easter vacation.[32] (Goronwy Rees reports Burgess making a trip to Vienna also,[33] as did Philby a little later.)

Blunt's fellow academic aesthete and architect/philosopher had attended school with Adolf Hitler, against whose movement (and on whose person) the Comintern was gathering intelligence frantically from all over the world. This philosopher's family had extensive contacts with socialists in Vienna and was strongly left wing himself; indeed, as we shall see, a Stalinist.

Now Penrose and Freeman, in their study of Anthony Blunt, have a passage that is quite incredible. They write:

The main forces responsible for recruiting young men at Cambridge into the party were James Klugmann and John Cornford, aided by their lieutenant, Sam

Fisher. Fisher said that Klugmann was 'the archrecruiter, who roped them in by the score at Trinity'. At one time, Fisher said, there were fifty Communist Party members in that one college, although that was followed by mass resignations when there was 'a dispute over poetry' – the details of which have long been forgotten.[34]

Reflecting upon this passage, we ask ourselves why the cadre should be split by a dispute over poetry. We are considering here devotees of Bolshevism! The passage is quite striking on the face of it and it seems most peculiar that an aesthetic dispute might lead to 'mass resignations' within a Communist Party. We know, however, of one particular dispute by Communists (indeed by Comintern agents) over poetry at Cambridge at the time. This dispute even found expression in a *cause celèbre* poem; in Julian Bell's poem criticizing Wittgenstein's philosophy of aesthetics. Bell had even written to the *New Statesman* in December 1933:

> in the Cambridge that I first knew, in 1929 and 1930, the central subject of ordinary intelligent conversation was poetry. . . . By the end of 1933 we have arrived at a situation in which almost the only subject of discussion is contemporary politics, and in which a very large majority of the more intelligent undergraduates are Communists, or almost Communists.[35]

The writer of this piece was a self-described Marxist who was to give his life for that cause and whose transition from poet to politically activist Communist took place precisely in the period he describes in the letter to the *New Statesman*. Was this, then, the content of Fisher's reference to the long-forgotten dispute over poetry? As a post-graduate Bell intended writing a PhD thesis on Wittgenstein:

> . . . he had considered submitting to the English Board (for the PhD) a topic on Wittgenstein. But George Rylands had dissuaded him, pointing out that to offer such a topic to the English faculty would be much the same as sending Swinburne's 'Dolores' to Queen Victoria as a birthday ode. So that was abandoned, and he eventually gave up the whole idea. . . .[36]

If it were indeed Bell's poem on Wittgenstein that led to the mass resignations, then Wittgenstein must have carried considerable pull with Communist students. We know from Bartley's report that he was a 'left-winger', but there is in any case additional evidence of the strength of his left-wing opinions and left-wing associations in Monk's report of the Communist George Thomson's views:

George Thomson, for example, who knew Wittgenstein well during the 1930s, speaks of Wittgenstein's 'growing political awareness' during those years, and says that, although he did not discuss politics very often with Wittgenstein, he did so 'enough to show that he kept himself informed about current events. He was alive to the evils of unemployment and fascism and the growing danger of war.' Thomson adds, in relation to Wittgenstein's attitude to Marxism: 'He was opposed to it in theory, but supported it in practice.' This chimes in with a remark Wittgenstein once made to Rowland Hutt (a close friend of Skinner's who came to know Wittgenstein in 1934): 'I am a communist, at heart.' It should be remembered, too, that many of Wittgenstein's friends of this period, and particularly the friends on whom he relied for information about the Soviet Union, were Marxists. In addition to George Thomson, there were Piero Sraffa, whose opinion Wittgenstein valued above all others on questions of politics, Nicholas Bachtin and Maurice Dobb. There is no doubt that during the political upheavals of the mid-1930s Wittgenstein's sympathies were with the working class and the unemployed, and that his allegiance, broadly speaking, was with the left.[37]

Now the long-standing public image of Wittgenstein is of a twentieth-century secular saint, a troubled, non-political genius, akin to Wordsworth's Newton, 'voyaging through strange seas of thought alone'. This image completely obscures the historical reality: his sympathies were not, as Monk misleadingly writes, 'broadly speaking' with the left. As we shall see, so far as political support for the Soviet Union was concerned, the man was a hard-core Stalinist.

Now if, behind Hitler's blanket castigation of Jews in *Mein Kampf*, lies some so far unexplained encounter with the House of Wittgenstein, then we must scrutinize very carefully the outline of Jewish development Hitler presented therein. In this outline, Hitler has the 'Court Jew' first converting to Christianity, then controlling the economy through the stock exchange, degrading art via commercial control of it and, finally, working for the success of Bolshevism. Since each step in this process up to the last does indeed match known facts about the Wittgenstein family history,[38] it is inescapable that we should compare the last step Hitler describes – working for Bolshevism – with what is known of the life of Ludwig Wittgenstein.[39]

Let us note immediately that Wittgenstein's philosophy is not Marxist.[40] On the other hand, we have seen that the source he acknowledged in 1945 as the chief stimulus for his ideas was Piero Sraffa:

Even more than to this – always certain and forcible – criticism I am indebted to that which a teacher of this university, Mr P. Sraffa, for many years unceasingly practised on my thoughts. I am indebted to this stimulus for the most consequential ideas of this book.[41]

Sraffa, an economist, *was* a Marxist.[42] In fact he appears to have been a particularly zealous one, for Costello writes of the testimony of Michael Straight, who later confessed his Soviet recruitment to the FBI:

> According to Straight, other moles included the Italian Marxist economist Piero Sraffa, whom Keynes had brought over to Cambridge and who was in danger of deportation if his party affiliation was revealed.[43]

Sraffa, then – the chief influence upon Wittgenstein – was, on Straight's testimony, a Communist and a 'mole'. (Sraffa was also a close friend of Antonio Gramsci, the Italian Communist theoretician.)[44]

In 1978 (as a politically wet-behind-the-ears naif) I visited one of Wittgenstein's former pupils of the 1930s, the retired Professor of Philosophy at Monash University, A. C. Jackson (himself a leading Australian left-wing academic) at Queenscliff in Victoria and asked him some questions about his recollections of Wittgenstein. He assured me that Wittgenstein's politics were ultra-left-wing and that he had strong sympathy for Stalin and the Soviet Union. Jackson is in any case on record in print elsewhere as saying that Wittgenstein was 'a bit of a Stalinist',[45] though his testimony to me was rather more emphatic than this suggests. (Jackson's own ASIO records in the Australian Archives, which I read eighteen years later, include a transcript of an intercepted conversation passing on his assessment of the political activities of Dr Frank Knopfelmacher and David Armstrong to the well-known Australian Communist leader Judah Waten.) This is supported by Rush Rhees' account of a conversation he had with Wittgenstein towards the end of the 1939–45 war:

> Again and again Wittgenstein would say 'the important thing is that the people have work'. He would have said this in 1935 as well, although there were not the problems of 'reconstruction' then. He thought the new regime in Russia did provide work for the mass of the people. If you spoke of regimentation of Russian workers, of workers not being free to leave or change their jobs, or perhaps of labour camps, Wittgenstein was not impressed. It would be terrible if the mass of the people there – or in any society – had no regular work. He also thought it would be terrible if the society were ridden by 'class distinctions', although he said less about this. 'On the other hand, tyranny. . . ?' – with a questioning gesture, shrugging his shoulders – 'doesn't make me feel indignant.'[46]

By 1945, when this conversation took place, cumulative deaths in Soviet labour camps and from collectivization of agriculture were many, many times the total of the Holocaust. In the Ukraine alone, well over five million people had been deliberately starved to death in the terror famine – the now infamous 'harvest of sorrow' – as a matter of intentional government policy. What Wittgenstein found highly offensive, however, was not Soviet tyranny, but the thought that the Soviet state was not a classless society:

> The suggestion that 'rule by bureaucracy' was bringing class distinctions in Russia, however, did arouse his indignation: 'If anything could destroy my sympathy with the Russian empire, it would be the growth of class distinctions.'

He clearly was committed to a rather rosy view of what the Russian revolution had wrought. Monk notes:

> ... even after the show trials of 1936, the worsening of relations between Russia and the West and the Nazi-Soviet Pact of 1939, Wittgenstein continued to express his sympathy with the Soviet regime – so much so that he was taken by some of his students to be a 'Stalinist'.[47]

Indeed he was. Monk quickly reassures the reader that 'This label is, of course, nonsense.' But on this critically important matter we should, I am proposing, give some credence to Wittgenstein's contemporaries. Jackson – the source of Monk's description of Wittgenstein as 'a bit of a Stalinist' – when I spoke to him, had no doubt at all as to Wittgenstein's political inclinations: Wittgenstein supported the foreign policy of the Soviet Union, its internal policies of repression and the leadership of Joseph Stalin. Theodore Redpath even offers the frightening reminiscence that Wittgenstein 'had sternly though salutarily declared that to be a good politician one needed to have a good purge'.[48] Wittgenstein chastised Norman Malcolm for doubting his belief that the British government engaged in political assassination, became 'extremely angry' and 'kept the incident in mind for several years'.[49] Douglas Gasking, a former Wittgenstein student and Communist Party member at Cambridge, said to me, in response to my enquiry about Wittgenstein's politics, that he was 'of the left'. What a Cambridge Communist Party veteran like Gasking might consider to count as 'of the left', of course, is likely to be considerably more to the left than an uninformed reader would gather from reading Monk's 'broadly speaking' qualification.

The 'Stalinist' label was applied to Wittgenstein by left-wing and Communist students in a notably left-wing university whose alumni were to form the most successful spy ring known to history. The difference between being 'merely left wing' and 'Stalinist' at Cambridge was quite clear. Politics at Cambridge was a very serious business. Everyone was left wing; not everyone was Stalinist. The 'Stalinist' label, then, is something whose implications need to be pondered very carefully, for Wittgenstein's Cambridge disciples were to colonize philosophy departments across the English-speaking world.

George Paul, for example, who married Frank Ramsey's Communist sister, Margaret, greatly advanced the Communist cause in Australian universities, from 1939 to 1945, before leaving for a position at University College, Oxford. Douglas Gasking and Allen Jackson, his successors at Melbourne and both students of Wittgenstein's, were also left-wingers. Gasking, who rose to the Chair, described himself as 'an old Bolshevik Wittgensteinian' and had been a Communist Party member at Cambridge.[50] Selwyn Grave, the Australian philosopher/historian, in his mild, under-stated fashion, writes of Jackson, 'His sympathies were markedly leftist and he came under public notice for them.'[51] Indeed. He was publicly named by the Victorian Royal Commission investigating the Communist Party.

Wittgensteinian influence at the University of Melbourne had a role to play in producing Australia's own spy, Ian Milner, who defected to Czechoslovakia rather than face questioning. The Milner case is peripheral to our theme, however, and I do not propose to follow it up here.[52]

Wittgenstein's friends alone are a guarantee that he came to the attention of Western counter-intelligence agencies in the investigations at Cambridge that followed the defections of Burgess, Philby and Maclean.[53] In fact Costello reveals that the British counter-intelligence agencies intercepted letters written well before this from 'Frostlake Cottage, Malting Lane, Cambridge', and displays a photograph of one dated 10 February 1929 in the final (un-numbered) pages of his book. Special Branch, then, had the dwelling which Wittgenstein shared with Dobb in 1929 under close surveillance.

Wittgenstein certainly held to his political allegiance very late. In 1939, after Stalin had already liquidated tens of millions of innocents, Wittgenstein told Drury:

> People have accused Stalin of having betrayed the Russian Revolution. But they have no idea of the problems that Stalin had to deal with; and the dangers he saw threatening Russia.[54]

Theodore Redpath recalls a film he discussed with Wittgenstein:

... it may be worth my mentioning a particular case in which Wittgenstein quite definitely and intentionally communicated to me his attitude on a fundamental matter. I used to go quite often to what was then called the Cosmopolitan Cinema ('the Cosmo', for short), which later became the Arts Cinema, and was ably managed by Norman Higgins. Well-chosen films, both British and foreign, were shown there. One evening I saw an English film in which Ralph Richardson took the part of a landowner, who seemed to me a thoroughly decent sort of chap, but who was morally condemned by the film, apparently simply for being a landowner. This struck me as grossly unfair, and not long afterwards I happened to tell Wittgenstein what I thought. His reply struck me, as so much of what he said used to do. He said that simply being a landowner could have been quite bad enough. I was not wholly convinced by that, but I was interested to find him saying something so clear-cut, despite the fact that he did not, so far as I knew, have any political affiliations at the time.[55]

That so many of Wittgenstein's companions, students, etc. were Marxists, given the atmosphere of the times, is hardly surprising. The problem is not that they were Marxists, but rather that, of a Trinity population of fifty or so Communist undergraduates, at least one of his students – Watson – turned out to be a spy while others of his students established the Communist Party in Cambridge, served as its secretaries, converted some of the famous group of three Cambridge spies and gave their lives for the Party in Spain. It was his students – Bell, Cornforth, Haden-Guest and Cornford – who formed the nucleus of the whole Trinity College Communist explosion. It might be, of course, that these four came to their Communism independently of each other. On the other hand, if at the core of the explosion there was a single initiating hand striking matches, then we must look very carefully at whichever academic was of most influence upon these particular four.

John Le Carre, in his introduction to the book by Page, Leitch and Knightley, *Philby, The Spy Who Betrayed a Generation*, offers a passage that most students of the Cambridge recruitment think has turned out to have been about Anthony Blunt. Blunt, however, appears not to have been politically active in the initial Communist ferment, and this fact alone should incline us to consider other possibilities:

This book is massively incomplete, as the authors are the first to admit. We should never forget the gaps. In this most Marxian of novels, where thesis and antithesis are endemic to protagonist, institution and reader alike, it is arguable that even the principal character is still missing. In the lives of Burgess, Maclean and Philby we discern his hand, his influence, his shadow: never once do we see his face or consciously hear his name. He is the Soviet recruiter. For these men were recruited. By whom? Between the ages of nineteen and twenty-one, it seems, these children of Cambridge were recognized, courted and consciously seduced into a lifetime of deceit. By whom? As they grew to manhood, and the youthful dream of an adventurous crusade gave way to the tedium and fears of criminal betrayal, who sustained them in their faith? . . .

When a boy of twenty gives himself body and mind to a country he has never visited, to an ideology he has not deeply studied, to a regime which even abroad, during those long and awful purges, was a peril to serve; when he remains actively faithful to that decision for over thirty years, cheating, betraying and occasionally killing, surely we must speculate on the nature of his master; no novitiate can last indefinitely without a confessing father. He understood us better than we understood ourselves: was he our countryman? He recruited only gentlemen: was he himself a gentleman? He recruited only from Cambridge: was he a Cambridge man? All three recruits would travel far on the reputations of their families alone: was he too a man of social influence?[56]

Given his recruits, the presumption must be not just that the recruiter was a Cambridge man, but that he was a (probably homosexual) Trinity College man with connections to the Apostles. This presumption is not too difficult a matter to research from material in the public record. There is not an enormous number of names to be sieved – a mere few thousand – and the exercise is worth the effort. (One imagines the security agencies went through exactly the same procedure in the 1950s, but if so, the results do not appear to have percolated through to the public domain.) It is well known that, like Blunt and Burgess, Wittgenstein was an Apostle, but it is not generally realized how few names are on the suspect list at Trinity College from this cause alone. Besides Blunt and Burgess, then, let us see how many other individuals qualify as homosexual, Trinity College Apostles.

The *Cambridge Review* Extra Numbers for the period 1929-35 provide a complete list of all Trinity College academic staff and students together with their addresses. It is a matter of a few mouse-clicks to scan the data for each year with a desk-top scanner, merge the lists for each year and then sort the names alphabetically by their addresses. If the Soviet recruiter was teaching or studying at Trinity College during the period, his name must appear on the list of 2,659 distinct names and addresses that results. It is a fascinating exercise to peruse the clusters of names that emerge when the names above are sorted by their addresses. It shows, for example, who else lived with Philby or the others over the period and who were their near neighbours. Some few of the people involved are still alive, however, and it is not our business to raise possibly unjustified suspicions outside our main theme. Accordingly, and on the advice of my editor concerning space restrictions, I shall simply report on the use I have made of the list.

The next step in our investigation is to determine which of the names on the Trinity College list were also Apostles. We are not doing this because the recruiter had to have been an Apostle; we are doing it to get a handle on the numbers and names of Blunt and Burgess' Apostle associates. It is not that a few rotten apples necessarily spoil all the apples in a barrel, but in investigating how rot spreads, it is good policy for an apple epidemiologist to know which, of all the apples in England, were in the same barrel as the rotten ones he is studying.

Perhaps due to the traditional secrecy of the society, there appears to be no exhaustive list of Trinity College Apostles, but it is possible to construct one from publicly available material that gives the names of all Apostles without their colleges of origin. That is, by comparing names on the Trinity College list of those individuals attending during the period 1929-35 with the names of Cambridge Apostles from all colleges who were elected sometime in the period (say 1880-1935) we will derive the complete list of Trinity College Apostles who might have had a hand in the recruitment of the Cambridge spies.

To do this we must first complete a few subsidiary tasks. There appears to be no publicly available list of all Cambridge Apostles over the period we require, but it can be compiled by merging the lists of Cambridge Apostles from various periods that are publicly available and selecting for the timespan we are investigating. The crucial lists are available in Richard Deacon's book *The Cambridge Apostles* and Costello's book *Mask of Treachery*.[57] So far as I have been able to ascertain from publicly available material, the list that emerges is complete.[58]

CAMBRIDGE APOSTLES FROM ALL COLLEGES
ELECTED 1880-1935
(including year of election)

Ainsworth, A.	1899	Clough, A.	1883
Beck, T.	1881	Cohen, A. B.	1930
Bekassy, F. I.	1912	Collio, H. O. J.	1934
Bell, J. H.	1928	Crusoe, F. J. A.	1929
Bliss, F.	1912	Cust, H. J. C.	1883
Blunt, A.	1927	Davies, H. S.	193?
Braithwaite, R. B.	1921	Dickinson, G. L.	1885
Brooke, R.	1908	Dodgson, W.	1890
Burgess, G. de M.	1932	Doggart, J. H.	1919
Cane, A. B.	1886	Duff, J. D.	1884
Champernowne, A.	1929	Forster, E. M.	1901
Champernowne, D. G.	1934	Fry, R.	1887

Furness, J. M.	1891	Robertson, D. H.	1926
Goodhart, H. C.	1880	Rolleston, L. C.	1919
Green, W. D.	1892	Rothschild, V.	1932
Greenwood, L. H.	1902	Russell, B. A. W.	1892
Hardy, G. H.	1898	Rylands, G. H. W.	1922
Harmer, F. E.	1925	Sanger, C. P.	1892
Hawtrey, R.	1900	Sheppard, J. T.	1902
Hobhouse, A. L.	1905	Shove, G.	1909
Hodgkin, A.	1935	Smith, A. H.	1882
Keynes, J. M.	1903	Smith, H. B.	1885
Lintott, H. J. B.	1929	Smyth, A. E. A. W.	1897
Llewellyn Davies, C.	1889	Spicer, R. H. S.	1920
Llewellyn Davies, T.	1889	Sprott, W. J. H.	1920
Llewelyn-Davies, R.	1932	Strachey, G. L.	1902
Lucas, D. W.	1925	Strachey, J. B.	1906
Lucas, F. L.	1914	Sydney-Turner, S. A.	1902
Luce, G. H.	1912	Sykes Davies, H.	1932
Macarthy, D.	1896	Tatham, H. F. W.	1885
Macnaghten, M.	1891	Taylor, C. F.	1910
Marsh, E. H.	1894	Thompson, G. D.	1923
Marshall, M. O.	1914	Trevelyan, G. M.	1895
Mayor, R. J. G.	1889	Trevelyan, R. C.	1893
Mclean, N.	1888	Turner, H. H.	1880
Mctaggart, J. M. E.	1886	Walter, W. G.	1933
Meredith, H. O.	1900	Watkins, A. R. D.	1925
Moore, G. E.	1894	Watson, A. G. D.	1927
Norton, H. J. T.	1906	Wedd, N.	1888
Noyce, C. W. F.	1934	Wedgwood, R. L.	1893
Penrose, A. P. D.	1919	Whitehead, A. N.	1884
Penrose, L. S.	1920	Wilson, H. F.	1881
Proctor, P. D.	1927	Wittgenstein, L.	1912
Raleigh, W. A.	1882	Woolf, L.	1902
Ramsey, F. R.	1921	Wyse, W.	1880
Rawdon-Smith, A. F.	1937		

By comparing names on this list with those on the list of those attending Trinity College we can work out who were Apostles at Trinity College during the period when the spies were recruited. Here, then, is the final list: the precipitate of Cambridge Apostles elected between 1880 and 1935 who were also attending Trinity College for some or all of the period 1929-1935. If the Soviet recruiter were a Trinity College Apostle, he was one of the names on the following list. I include the date that each was elected as an Apostle and a brief comment on how well each fits the characteristics of the individual for whom we are searching. When I give the description 'sexuality unknown' in some of the following, I am simply indicating that I have not come across material allowing a definite judgment.

55

Name	Year Elected	Comment
Blunt, Anthony	1928	Spy. According to Michael Straight, recruited after Guy Burgess and therefore not the recruiter. Homosexual.
Burgess, Guy	1932	Spy. Not believed to be the recruiter by any writer with a background in intelligence. Homosexual.
Cohen, Andrew	1930	Left Cambridge in 1932. This seems an unlikely move for a recruiter of spies, though Phoebe Pool reported to Anita Brookner that Cohen needed warning that he was under an MI5 investigation.[59] Sexuality unknown.
Duff, James	1884	46 years since his election to the Apostles. Too old.
Hardy, Godfrey Harold	1898	Mathematician and pro-Communist president of the pro-Bolshevik National Union of Scientific Workers 1924-6. A suspect. Homosexual.
Hodgkin, Alan	1935	Sir Alan was elected too late and in any case had the political views of a Quaker. Probably heterosexual.
Llewelyn-Davies, Richard	1932	Lord Llewelyn-Davies' move into town-planning seems an unlikely career path for a recruiter of spies, though Sir Isaiah Berlin publicly announced he was a Communist. (Costello, p 651.) Heterosexual.
Lucas, Frank Lawrence	1914	Trinity, then King's. Conservative, patriot, gassed in the Great War, worked at Bletchley Park. Unlikely to have been a traitor. Sexuality unknown.
Moore, George Edward	1894	An academic of purest ray serene. Simple minded from a practical point of view and an unlikely traitor. Probably heterosexual.
Robertson, Dennis	1926	Thought Philby's politics suspect and refused to be his referee for the Civil Service Examination.[60] Sought treatment from Freud in Vienna for his homosexuality.
Rothschild, Victor	1932	Under heavy suspicion. Heterosexual.
Trevelyan, George M.	1895	Historian and helper of Guy Burgess. Probably heterosexual.
Wittgenstein, Ludwig	1912	Took up arms against British allies in the Great War. A Stalinist who intended settling in the Soviet Union and the only non-Briton on the list. His brother maimed and his country destroyed by Britain and her allies. Believed the British Government to practise murder via its security agencies. Homosexual.

On the dates, the only possible Trinity College Apostles elected between the wars who might have recruited the Cambridge spies are Dennis Robertson, Andrew Cohen, Alan Hodgkin, Richard Llewelyn-Davies and Victor Rothschild. They all seem too close in age to the recruits, however, for it is unlikely that the mentor role of a recruiter could be filled by a contemporary of the recruits; it would probably require an older man. With the possible exception of Lord Rothschild (to whom we will return later), these others pursued careers singularly bereft of obvious opportunities for espionage. We should therefore include in our investigation the names of Apostles recruited before the Great War. One must exercise a degree of caution, of course, but of the Apostles elected to the society before the Great War, it seems that the only possible candidates are the mathematician G. H. Hardy, the historian George Trevelyan and the philosopher Ludwig Wittgenstein. Hardy and Trevelyan, whatever their flirtations with socialism and Guy Burgess, appear to have been patriotic Englishmen.[61] Certainly no one could describe either of them as 'Stalinist'.[62] Wittgenstein, however, *was* so described by his own students. In addition, he had fought against the Allied cause in the Great War, lost one brother and had his sole remaining brother maimed. He had no cause to love England.

To see Wittgenstein's name emerge in a precipitate of so few possibilities from an original list of over two and a half thousand Trinity College students and staff must make one sit up and start. It is clear that he must be a suspect, and perhaps even a prime suspect, as the man Le Carre wrote about – the mysterious Cambridge 'talent spotter', the Comintern recruitment agent who set up the Cambridge spy ring. But is it really likely that he was? Is it possible that this persecuted homosexual boy from Hitler's school saw Communism as the only hope of resisting the Nazis and therefore threw in his lot with Stalin and the Comintern?

The global strategic importance of Wittgenstein's Cambridge connections is worth bearing in mind. Lytton Strachey's brother, Oliver, for example, was head of a Bletchley Park cryptanalysis group. The role of his fellow homosexual Alan Turing (who attended his lectures) at Bletchley on the Enigma decrypts is too well known to document. And the Cavendish physicists form a Who's-Who of the British and American atomic weapons programme. His friends not only could, but did, win global wars.

The Russians chose some peculiar types as agents. Guy Burgess was successful precisely because he was too outrageous to be considered seriously as a spy. Wittgenstein also had an extraordinary personality. His leftist persuasion and homosexuality are aspects that one imagines the Russians might have worked on had they targeted Cambridge for penetration, as of course they did. His frequent trips to the continent and his country hikes, etc. would have made him ideal for unsuspicious contacts with Russian controllers. Fania Pascal writes:

He was the most elusive of men, shrouding his comings and goings in mystery.

Once, maybe twice, he called with a rucksack on his back, as if he had just arrived by train, perhaps from abroad, yet you would not ask him where he came from.[63]

The ability of this elusive man to mould the lives of his own students and acquaintances was so marked as to have become a byword. His lover, Francis Skinner, was persuaded by Wittgenstein to forgo a promising mathematical career in order to become a worker at the Cambridge Scientific Instrument Company, thereby imbibing the purer spirit of the proletariat.[64] Fania Pascal raises the question 'Was Wittgenstein good or bad for Skinner?'[65] and recalls a conversation she had with Skinner's sister:

In a restrained way she told me of the consternation in her family when her brother, a brilliant mathematician and a scholar of Trinity College, decided to give it all up. 'Why?' she asked, '*why?*'

She continues her assessment of Wittgenstein:

His moral and practical influence on those around him strikes one as at least as significant as his work. Was it his fault that he left an imprint on the character and manner of speech of some, so that a decade after his death Roy and I recognized it in a new acquaintance, a non-philosopher?
. . . It is a staggering thought that Wittgenstein almost certainly never asked himself: Are there other people close to Francis whose attitude should be taken into account? He would treat Francis as a responsible adult able to take his own decisions, without recognizing the immense force of his own personality and how inescapably it came into play.

That Wittgenstein was so pure of heart as to be ignorant of the power of his personality to influence people seems to this cynical writer extremely unlikely. The late Cornell Philosophy Professor Norman Malcolm was another student who recorded of his student days that

Wittgenstein wished to persuade me to give up my plan to become a teacher of philosophy. He wondered whether I could not do some manual job instead, such as working on a ranch or farm.

We again see here exaltation of the virtue of manual labour. Giving advice to his students not to adopt academic life was in fact usual for Wittgenstein, for Malcolm writes: 'Wittgenstein several times renewed the attempt to persuade me to give up philosophy as a profession. He commonly did this with other students of his.'[66] Now unlike Malcolm, others of

Wittgenstein's philosophy students – the most active Cambridge Communists – *did* act in accord with the advice he gave Malcolm. Seale and McConville, in their study of Kim Philby, write:

> This hunger for physical action, for translating words into deeds that might change society, drove some of the early Cambridge comrades to 'good works' in England. For example, David Haden Guest went to work with the Young Communist League in the slums of Battersea – where the once unwashed but highminded ideologue was born anew, spruce, clean and happy. Maurice Cornforth, the Cambridge cell's chief-of-staff, threw up philosophy to become an agricultural organizer in East Anglia. A year or two later, John Cornford broke with his bourgeois background to serve the Party among the Birmingham working-class, while Donald Maclean, in spite of his first-class degree in modern languages, dreamed only of teaching English to workers in the Soviet Union, until his Russian friends persuaded him that he would be of more use in the Foreign Office. Kim's path to self-fulfilment lay in Central Europe.[67]

The first three mentioned in this extract – Haden-Guest, Cornforth and Cornford – went to these non-academic careers virtually directly from Wittgenstein's philosophy classes. Of course the students mentioned might have arrived at their decision to seek non-academic careers quite independently of each other, or perhaps simply in accord with the ethos of Marxism. But it is surely noteworthy that one of the academics who taught them is known to have urged precisely this course of action upon his students.

Let me now stress a little further the compelling power Wittgenstein exerted upon those he met. The following extract describing a student entering the inner sanctum reads, at least to this reader, as a veneration so extreme as to approach idolatry, yet it was penned by a respected British academic philosopher. (We should recall Le Carre's curiosity about the personality of Philby's mysterious recruiter and its effect upon his novice recruits.)

> At the age of 40 he looked like a youth of 20, with a godlike beauty, always an important feature at Cambridge, . . . awesome in its unearthly purity. . . .
>
> The God received him . . . in an ascetic room, beautiful in its almost total emptiness, where a wooden bowl of fruit on a table made the one note of colour. . . . The God was all he had been described as being: he looked like Apollo who had bounded into life out of his own statue, or perhaps like the Norse God Baldur, blue-eyed and fair-haired, with a beauty that had nothing sensual about it, but simply breathed the four Greek cardinal virtues, to which was added a very exquisite kindness and graciousness that bathed one like remote, slightly

wintry sunshine. . . . what Wittgenstein himself was thinking was of little importance, only much superior to the confusions and half-lights in which most philosophers of his acquaintances lived, despite their very great excellence as men. . . . There was . . . an extraordinary atmosphere that surrounded him, something philosophically saintly that was also very distant and impersonal: he was the philosophe Soleil. One had walked in his sunlight but one had not at all been singled out by the Sun. . . . the tea one drank with him tasted like nectar.[68]

In Australia, half a century later, I read this and blink. It sounds like nothing so much as westernized guru-worship. How could a sober British academic have penned a purportedly serious sketch of Wittgenstein as Baldur the beautiful? But it is not unrepresentative of other accounts of Wittgenstein in the thirties.[69] Fania Pascal remarks that

> Once he started talking he could hold you in thrall; I don't think he was aware of this gift. The man who was later to make the famous statement: 'Philosophy is a battle against the bewitchment of our intelligence by means of language' (P 109) had no inkling how he himself cast a spell whenever he said anything.[70]

Richard Deacon quotes a member of the Apostles, who, even while being unsympathetic to Wittgenstein, said:

> To listen to Wittgenstein too often was like being dragged back into the Middle Ages. One almost felt that he had been God's representative on earth and that it was Wittgenstein who had been on the Cross, not Jesus Christ.[71]

Remarkable as they sound, these reports really are accurate descriptions of Wittgenstein's effect upon Cambridge. (There are many, many similar accounts.) Let readers now ask themselves, 'What might Stalinist Wittgenstein's compelling persuasive powers have been had they been turned to achieving political ends from such impressionable material?

There is a recollection in the Rhees volume, by Rush Rhees himself, describing Wittgenstein's reaction when Rhees discussed becoming a Trotskyist Communist:

> In 1945 I was walking with Wittgenstein and I said I had been thinking I ought to become a member of the Revolutionary Communist (Trotskyist) Party.
> 'Ought to? Why do you think you ought to?'
> 'I find more and more that I am in agreement with the chief points in their analysis and criticism of present society and with their objectives.'
> 'You could agree with that as you have been agreeing up to now – without becoming a member of the party.'

'I'm inclined to tell myself *hic Rhodus, hic salta*.'

Wittgenstein stopped walking at once and grew more serious – as he did if you mentioned a problem that he'd thought about: 'Now let's talk about this.' We sat down on a park bench. He got up almost at once, because he wanted to illustrate what he said by walking in different directions.

His main point was: When you are a member of the party you have to be prepared to act and speak as the party has decided. You will be trying to convince other people. In arguing and answering their questions you cannot turn back on the party line if you now see something shaky in it and say, 'Well I can see that isn't quite right; perhaps the matter [whatever it is] goes more like *this*. . . .' If you are in the habit of trying one way, then turning back on your tracks like this and trying another, you will be no use as a party member. Perhaps the party line will change. But meanwhile what you say must be what the party has agreed to say. You keep along that road.[72]

Wittgenstein then contrasted this with what a philosopher has to do, which demands being constantly ready to change direction in working through a problem. But he concluded:

Some people speak of philosophy as a way of living. Working as a member of a communist party is also a way of living.

Wittgenstein's words here were hardly words of discouragement, except for those few with the particular calling to do philosophy. To the contrary, they must prick up the ears of any reader familiar with Wittgenstein's philosophical works, for in Wittgenstein's works the idea of a 'form of life' or a 'way of living' is of absolutely central importance. It is a technical term, referring to that which has to be accepted: 'What has to be accepted, the given, is – so one could say – forms of life.'[73] If working as a member of a Communist Party is 'a way of living', then as 'the given', it cannot be criticized – it has to be accepted.

In 1932 Wittgenstein had visited the town of Jarrow, with Drury. Jarrow had virtually complete unemployment due to the shipyard having closed and, as Drury records, 'had a terrible air of dejection'.[74] The town was something of a *cause célèbre* to the left, a Left Book Club publication on Jarrow by Ellen Wilkinson even carrying the title *The Town that was Murdered*. Drury remembers Wittgenstein approvingly quoting the views of his Communist economist friend Sraffa: 'Sraffa is right: the only thing possible in a situation like this is to get all these people running in one direction.'

If Wittgenstein really believed that working as a member of a Communist Party was a way of living, that the unemployed had to be mobilized according to a Communist economist's prescriptions, that a Party member had a duty to obey the Party line despite his own feelings – and if he passed these beliefs on to some of his impressionable, worshipful students – then this, I think, is indeed how it came about that the Cambridge spy ring was recruited. Let us now turn to investigate the political effects discernible in many of those friends and students who benefited from his instruction.

It is well known that Wittgenstein intended abandoning England to settle in Stalin's Russia.[75] He referred to the possibility of a flight to Russia in his correspondence with Engelmann in the early twenties. He had kept this dream alive, for at Trinity College he learnt Russian towards this end and essayed a preparatory visit in 1935 to scout out the possibilities. (Guy Burgess had visited the USSR in the previous year[76] and Donald Maclean told his mother in 1933 that he would be off to the Soviet Union to work as a teacher when he had finished with Cambridge.)[77] Monk writes on Wittgenstein's trip:

> Throughout the summer of 1935 he made preparations for his impending visit to Russia. He met regularly with those of his friends, many of them members of the Communist Party, who had been to Russia or who might be able to inform him about conditions there . . . Among these friends were Maurice Dobb, Nicholas Bachtin, Piero Sraffa and George Thomson . . .
>
> . . . The summer of 1935 was the time when Marxism became, for the undergraduates at Cambridge, the most important intellectual force in the university . . . It was then that Anthony Blunt and Michael Straight made their celebrated journey to Russia, which led to the formation of the so-called 'Cambridge Spy Ring', and that the Cambridge Communist Cell, founded a few years earlier by Maurice Dobb, David Hayden-Guest[78] and John Cornford, expanded to include most of the intellectual elite at Cambridge, including many of the younger members of the Apostles.[79]

Monk continues on Wittgenstein:

> . . . he was perceived as a sympathetic figure by the students who formed the core of the Cambridge Communist Party, many of whom (Hayden-Guest, Cornford, Maurice Cornforth etc.) attended his lectures.[80]

As the first of these associates, let us consider the Cambridge Marxist, Maurice Dobb. Wittgenstein returned to Cambridge on 18 January 1929 and stayed in an attic room of John Maynard Keynes, the economist. Skidelsky, Keynes's biographer, writes:

Complaining that he 'was not born to live permanently with a clergyman', Keynes gave Wittgenstein notice to quit on 2 February; Wittgenstein moved in with Frank Ramsey and his wife, then with Maurice Dobb. . . .[81]

Dobb, then, did not merely attend Wittgenstein's lectures; at one stage they shared a dwelling.

Now Costello, who examined Special Branch files on the visit of Bukharin to Cambridge, writes that

Special Branch reports on the revolutionary leader's visit indicate how by 1921 the MI5 Registry contained some bulky files on Cambridge scientists who were potential targets of, and sympathizers with, the Soviet Union. The records that have come to light show that elaborate measures were in place to monitor the activities of Needham and his cohorts, especially Maurice Dobb, who had been identified as a longtime member of the Communist faction of the Union of Scientific Workers. Dobb was already the university's leading spokesman for the new vision of the classless, scientifically run society that was to hypnotize the third wave of Cambridge undergraduate recruits to Marxism in the years to come.[82]

In fact as early as 1925 no less a personage than King George V had written to the Chancellor of Cambridge demanding to know why such a well-known Marxist as Dobb was permitted to indoctrinate undergraduates.[83] Kim Philby, in his interview with Phillip Knightley, claimed that it was Dobb who directed him to a Communist group in Paris after his return from Vienna. Costello is dismissive of Philby's claim and believes that the mysterious NKVD recruitment agent at Cambridge could not have been so notorious and open a Marxist as Dobb.[84] A certain left-wing friend of Dobb's, however, with whom he had shared lodgings, had strong connections to Socialists in Vienna.

Another of Wittgenstein's associates was Nicholas Bachtin. Bachtin was described by Fania Pascal as 'an exile from the Russian Revolution but by the outbreak of the Second World War a fiery communist'. She writes of him as

another intimate friend of Wittgenstein's, Dr Nicholas Bachtin, earlier a lecturer in classics in Southampton, then in Birmingham where he was finally Reader in Linguistics. He died a year before Wittgenstein. When just before the war we too moved to Birmingham, where my husband was appointed to the chair of German, it was when Wittgenstein was visiting the Bachtins (often accompanied by Skinner) that we saw him or both of them. 'Wittgenstein loved Bachtin,' Constance, Bachtin's widow, told me. . . .[85]

This Birmingham connection has a particular interest that comes out in an obituary of the physicist Rudolf Peierls who died on 19 September 1995, aged eighty-eight. Peierls escaped from Germany with his Russian wife, Eugenia Kanegiesser, in 1933:

> ... his wider fame rests on his part in the creation of the first atomic weapons. Together with Otto Frisch, he showed with mathematical precision that a few pounds of pure uranium could make an explosion that would devastate a city.
>
> In 1940 Mr Peierls was working with Frisch, another refugee at the University of Birmingham. They wrote a memorandum to the British government spelling out how a 'super-bomb' could be made from only a handful of a rare but easily fissionable material.
>
> In detail, they showed that the critical mass of uranium-235 needed for an explosive chain reaction was far less than previously thought and that the destructive effect of an 11-pound (5-kilogram) bomb would be the same as that of several thousand tons of dynamite. . . . In a summary of great prescience, they predicted that nuclear bombs would become weapons of mass destruction; that exploding them in the atmosphere would cause damaging radioactive fallout; that the only apparent defence would be the deterrent effect of mutual possession; and, for those who needed reminding, that German scientists were themselves already at work on a nuclear bomb.
>
> Seldom in history has a piece of paper had such consequences. To pursue their results, the British government set up the oddly named 'MAUD Committee' . . . the MAUD report convinced the many doubters among America's top military men. President Roosevelt instructed Vannevar Bush, his scientific advisor on military questions, to race ahead with what soon became, under American leadership, the vast Manhatten project.[86]

The Communist Bachtin and the Pascals, all with demonstrably close personal connections to Wittgenstein, moved to take up academic positions at Birmingham when the theory of nuclear explosions was mooted.[87] Further, Wittgenstein visited them in Birmingham 'often accompanied by Skinner'.[88]

The reader will think of Wittgenstein as a philosopher, rather than as a physicist, but he had designed and worked upon a jet reaction propellor as a Manchester engineering student. And the Cambridge mathematician J. E. Littlewood, in a personal communication to Brian McGuinness, wrote that Wittgenstein first went to Manchester to study under Rutherford.[89] (He had originally hoped to study physics under Boltzmann in Vienna, but was prevented by Boltzmann's suicide.) Lord Rutherford, of course, was *the* great twentieth-century experimental physicist and Boltzmann too, with natural constants named after him, was hardly inconsequential as a theorist. McGuinness writes:

Littlewood in the late 1960s thought that Wittgenstein came to Manchester to learn what was behind engineering and that for this purpose he intended to sit at the feet of Rutherford. The general motive is probably correctly ascribed, and it was indeed the case that a year before Rutherford had arrived at Manchester. Curiously enough in the very year that Wittgenstein came to Manchester there was a large loan of radium made to the University from the Austrian Academy of Sciences to enable Rutherford to carry further his work on radioactivity. There may well have been some direct or indirect link – his father's patronage, perhaps – between this loan and Wittgenstein's coming. . . .[90]

If what McGuinness suggests here is correct, then Wittgenstein's connection with atomic research and Lord Rutherford dated not simply to the great days of the Cavendish at Cambridge, but back to the first fumbling steps at Manchester before the Great War. He certainly had connections to Cambridge, to Birmingham and to British nuclear research. Another of his Cambridge Communist friends, the King's Apostle George Derwent Thomson, had also moved to Birmingham in 1937 to be Professor of Greek.[91] Costello continues:

. . . he was the organizer for the Communist party for many years. Significantly, Birmingham, a center for industrial and scientific research, emerges from later MI5 reports as being second only to Cambridge as a haven for academic communism. Thompson's proselytizing before and during World War II helped ensure that Britain's premier 'red-brick' university became a refuge for emigre physicist Klaus Fuchs as well as Alan Nunn May, both of whom were to supply atomic secrets to the Soviet Union.

Let us return to Wittgenstein's students who, at least in the early thirties, seem also to have been particularly ardent Communists. Consider first David Haden-Guest. Haden-Guest was one of the Cambridge Communists shot fighting in Spain for the Republic in 1938. His life was commemorated by a book, edited by his mother, Carmel Haden-Guest, and published in 1939.[92] The contributors include a number of well-known British Communists and the prominent analytical philosopher Max Black. Black points out that

The undergraduate reading mathematics at Cambridge in his first year has usually little knowledge and less interest in a subject so recondite as mathematical philosophy. That David should have been so attracted by it is in keeping with the intellectual precocity which was one of his most striking characteristics.

Letters written from Cambridge in his first year of residence show that he found time to attend lectures on philosophy in addition to his regular classes for the mathematical tripos.[93]

He went out of his way, then, to attend lectures in mathematical philosophy. These were Wittgenstein's lectures. But what did he think of Wittgenstein? His opinion comes out in a letter from which Black also quotes:

I am attending a course of lectures and 'Conversation classes' in philosophy given by the great Wittgenstein.[94] Professor Moore goes to his lectures, which is very amusing because Moore was the teacher of Bertrand Russell, and Russell the teacher of Wittgenstein. The conversation class is in the nature of a debate. I never felt so pleased with myself as when I chipped in for the first time and he said 'Precisely, you are quite right.' Of course he doesn't always say this.[95]

Another contributor to the Haden-Guest memorial volume, the Communist Maurice Cornforth, described the effect of Wittgenstein upon the 1929 intake:

I first met David when he came to Cambridge in the autumn of 1929. I had arrived at the same time, and it wasn't long before we met. . . .

In the same year, 1929, the Viennese philosopher, Ludwig Wittgenstein, also turned up in Cambridge.

Wittgenstein immediately caused an upheaval in the circles of students (and lecturers) who were studying philosophy. He proceeded to tear all our preconceived ideas to pieces. . . .

A circle of young students very quickly formed around him, and both David and I belonged to that circle. We used to sit at Wittgenstein's feet, drinking in his new ideas, and at the same time we argued furiously, both with him, and with one another. This went on for a whole year.[96]

It was following these furious arguments that Haden-Guest went from Cambridge to Gottingen to further his study in mathematical philosophy and returned to Cambridge a convinced Communist. Importantly, judging from the record, his conversion was a result of philosophical conviction. Cornforth's account of his return states:

He marched into Hall with a hammer and sickle emblem displayed in his coat.

I well remember too how David came into a meeting of the Cambridge Moral Science Club (which is the name of the students' philosophical society there) with a copy of Lenin's *Materialism and Empirio-Criticism*. He was bubbling over with excitement about it, and kept reading passages aloud, especially those parts which deal with a class basis of philosophy. Some of the students were rather shocked, others thought he had gone crazy, but he took no notice, and kept reading out the passages just the same. I remember this because it made a big impression on me personally. I went straight home and read the book, and thereupon decided to join the Communist Party. To this extent it was David's influence that made me join the Party. I was thinking about doing so, but his directness and enthusiasm made me quite decided.

David and I both joined at the same time, just after the final examinations of 1931.[97]

Cornforth too, trained in philosophy by Wittgenstein, converted to Communism on reading Lenin's philosophical work. That is, it was as philosophers, fresh from Wittgenstein's instruction – and perhaps during his philosophical instruction – that they were converted. And the historical climax of Guest's post-Wittgensteinian, Communist involvement was the gaining of a particularly noteworthy convert, one of rather more interest than Cornforth, for Costello's account of the conversion of Guy Burgess to Communism squarely involves Wittgenstein's student, David Haden-Guest:

. . . Burgess got to know David Haden-Guest, the son of a Labour MP and fellow Trinity undergraduate, who became his guide to dialectical materialism. Haden-Guest was a socialist when he abandoned his study of philosophy under Wittgenstein early in 1932. . . . Burgess was sufficiently impressed by such personal dedication to spend much of his second year reconciling his own historical theories to the dialectical materialism in Haden-Guest's copy of Lenin's *The State and Revolution*.[98]

In short, one of Wittgenstein's many Communist philosophy students inspired Guy Burgess to Communism. (Like Wittgenstein, Blunt and Bell, Burgess was a fellow homosexual Trinity College Apostle, having been elected in November 1932.)[99] Burgess, then, was recruited: he did not, in the first instance, recruit.

Peter Wright also reports Anthony Blunt as saying that Alister Watson 'schooled him in Marxism'.[100] So, on Blunt's testimony, just as one of Wittgenstein's students (Haden-Guest) taught Guy Burgess his Marxism, so another (the Apostle and spy Alister Watson) taught Marxism to Anthony Blunt.[101] (Theodore Redpath states that Watson and George Paul were Wittgenstein's students as early as 1934.)[102] Here too, Blunt was recruited – he was not the recruiter.

Now Haden-Guest was no mere dilettante Communist: he founded the Communist cell in Cambridge University.[103] This is how Cornforth described the formation of the cell:

It so turned out that there were about four or five other students in Cambridge who were also at that time coming to the same decision. We had never met them before, but they also joined the Party, and we decided to form a Group in Cambridge. We had two senior members of the University who had been in the Party for some time to guide us and keep us in order.[104] And so the Communist Party was started in Cambridge.[105]

Cornforth, unfortunately, does not name the 'four or five other students' who were foundation members, but says that

. . . we succeeded in forming a Town Branch of the Communist Party in Cambridge. This inevitably led to a division of activities, for the membership grew in the University too, and it became necessary to form a University section which met separately. I became secretary for the town and David became secretary for the University.[106]

After Cambridge and Party work in London, Haden-Guest moved to Moscow, where he taught Mathematics and Physics in the Anglo-American School. Herman Levy, a visiting English Marxist mathematics professor from the Imperial College of Science, records Haden-Guest discussing Wittgenstein's mathematical philosophy with him in Moscow. From Moscow, Haden-Guest moved to the University of Southampton and finally to the Ebro front in the Spanish Civil War, where he was shot.[107]

Another of Wittgenstein's students, as we have seen, was John Cornford. Cornford, like David Haden-Guest, was one of the legendary Cambridge Communists of the thirties. He was the son of the Trinity College philosopher F. M. Cornford. Wittgenstein, then, taught the son and knew the father. John Cornford succeeded Haden-Guest as Party secretary when Charles Madge could not take the position, and like Haden-Guest, he too died in Spain for the Party. Fania Pascal records Wittgenstein's visit to the Cornford home, in 1940, after John Cornford's death. His reaction seems most unusual.

In the early spring of 1940, before Hitler's offensive in the West, I was staying in Cambridge with my sister, who was herself at that time a visitor at the house of Frances Cornford in Madingley Road. Wittgenstein rang me there and arranged to call. I walked out along the Madingley Road towards the Observatory to meet him. . . .

He got ready to go. I said: 'Come in and have a cup of tea. Meet my sister.' He looked scared: 'I mustn't. No. I can't.' I was furious, yet I still saw him down the long drive. What an enslaver the man was! Was he reluctant because of some fear of meeting a new person? Unwilling to walk into Professor Cornford's house? Or just disinclined to comply, accustomed to act entirely according to his own wishes?[108]

We know that Wittgenstein encouraged his crippled lover, the polio victim Francis Skinner, to volunteer for Spain. He therefore viewed participation favourably, even by those most dear to him. If Wittgenstein's encouragement of such participation had a role to play in his student John Cornford also volunteering for Spain, his reluctance to confront Cornford's father – a fellow philosopher at the same college – following his son's death is readily explicable.[109] Looking scared and saying 'I mustn't. No. I can't' is a far stronger reaction than simply declining to go in.

Another Wittgenstein student was Alister Watson, whom Peter Wright refers to extensively in his book, *Spycatcher*.[110] Wright, as an MI5 investigator, was studying Cambridge graduates of the thirties with noted left-wing views and writes:

> One name stood out beyond all the others: Alister Watson. . . . He was . . . a fervent Marxist at Cambridge in the 1930s, an Apostle, and a close friend of both Blunt and Burgess.[111]

Wright reveals that Watson

> became head of the Submarine Detection Research Section at ARL.[112] It was one of the most secret and important jobs in the entire NATO defense establishment.

Wright queried Anthony Blunt about Watson, and Blunt – who had been granted immunity from prosecution if he cooperated with the investigators – named Watson as his instructor in Marxism.[113] Watson was interrogated and admitted regularly meeting three top KGB controllers: Yuri Modin, who ran Kim Philby, Sergei Kondrashev, who ran George Blake, and Nikolai Karpekov, who ran John Vassall.[114] As a result of this, says Wright, 'At MI5's insistence, Watson was removed from secret access overnight.' Wright wrote further that

> No one who listened to the interrogation or studied the transcripts was in any doubt that Watson had been a spy, probably since 1938. Given his access to anti-submarine-detection research, he was, in my opinion, probably the most damaging of all the Cambridge spies.[115]

In 1929, Wittgenstein's endless discussions with fellow Apostle Watson had prompted John Maynard Keynes to write in a letter: 'Ludwig is beginning, I think, to persecute poor Alister a little.'[116] Wittgenstein, then, found Watson to be a student of sufficient interest to justify a large investment of his time. Watson's relationship with Wittgenstein was long-standing, his name featuring in reports of those attending Wittgenstein's lectures in the 1930s. (He also introduced Alan Turing to Wittgenstein.) If Wright is correct about the dates, Watson became a spy while a student of Wittgenstein's, for Theodore Redpath records his belief about who attended Wittgenstein's lectures in the Lent and Easter terms of 1938:

. . . I believe the group included Francis Skinner, George Paul, Rush Rhees, Yorick Smythies, Francis Kitto, *Alister Watson*, Casimir Lewy and Douglas Gasking.[117]

Like Wittgenstein, Blunt and Burgess, Alister Watson was also an Apostle.

As the last two members of this subversives rogues gallery, let us consider Roy and Fania Pascal. Fania Pascal (née Feiga Polianovska) was the woman who taught Russian to both Wittgenstein and his lover, Francis Skinner. She wrote an account of her experience of Wittgenstein and Skinner in the now defunct literary magazine *Encounter*.[118] Here is Costello's sketch of her husband, Roy Pascal, and his connection to the spy Anthony Blunt:

Pascal was second only to his mentor, Maurice Dobb, in promoting the communist cause at Cambridge. . . . Pascal had also been a friend and influence on Blunt since 1929, when they were both graduates in the Modern Languages Faculty and carrying out part-time teaching to supplement their research grants. Blunt took French supervision and Pascal held classes in German.[119]

Costello continues on the same page with some further information on Roy Pascal, describing his politics after he returned to Cambridge around 1930:

. . . Pascal was a fervent Communist. His vigorously expressed politics alarmed some of the Pembroke dons, who argued that he was an unsuitable candidate for a fellowship. But he was elected despite their objections to join Dobb as a senior member of the college. By now he was also a lodger at Dobb's small house in Chesterton Lane.

Known as 'Red House', it was the epicenter of Comintern activity at Cambridge. Here Dobb worked as a tireless propagandist of the Communist cause. He was a founding member and Cambridge organizer of the Society for Cultural Relations and the League Against Imperialism but he maintained links with the Marxist scientists at the Cavendish Laboratory. 'The 'Red House', as we now know, had been under frequent surveillance by MI5 since the mid-twenties.

Monk, writing of Wittgenstein's abode over the summer of 1929, informs us that

> Wittgenstein spent the early part of the summer vacation in Cambridge, living as a lodger with Maurice Dobb and his wife at Frostlake Cottage, Malting House Lane.[120]

What was Wittgenstein's acquaintance with Dobb that he should stay with him? And how did it come about that he knew Dobb well enough to board with him on first returning to Cambridge? Who knows? But it is clear that both Wittgenstein and his Communist friend Roy Pascal had been lodgers with the Communist Maurice Dobb, albeit in different houses. Costello's account of Fania Pascal, Roy Pascal's wife, is even more suggestive:

> Pascal's pivotal role in the Cambridge Communist network owed as much to his marriage to Feiga 'Fanya' Polianovska as it did to his association with Dobb. This darkly attractive Russian Jew had met Pascal at Berlin University, where she was taking a doctoral course in philosophy. 'Fanya' was a dedicated Marxist whose revolutionary ardor was born of her experience of pogroms. Her 'darkened childhood' in the Ukraine had been 'branded by the anti-semitism of Tsarist Russia'. That the Russians granted her an exit visa to study in Berlin raises the presumption that her postgraduate work was not confined to philosophy.[121]

Costello interviewed Professor Harry Ferns (an academic friend of Roy Pascal) and reports Ferns saying:

> . . . Fanya was the iron in her husband's political soul. She also had all the right qualifications for a full-fledged Comintern agent, as evidenced by her activities at Cambridge. Fanya became an activist with the Cambridge branch of the Anglo–Soviet Society, and was soon elected to the committee of an organisation that was one of the principal links between the university and the Comintern in Moscow.[122]

Fania Pascal's article contains a striking claim, which, on the basis of the rest of what she writes, seems totally unjustified. She writes of Wittgenstein: 'Much of his life will remain forever unknown to his closest friends.'[123] This seems a strong statement from someone who is explicit that she was *not* one of his closest friends. It sounds as though she knew something about him that his closest friends did not. Yet she apologizes in her paper for making it seem 'as though it describes a friendship with the man, a thing I have no claim to'.[124] She adds, 'It must be understood that a lunch at our house or a tea with him in Trinity College were rare, isolated events.' Despite this, she claimed to know that there were significant things in his life that even those who were his friends – his closest friends – did not know about. How could she possibly have spoken so authoritatively? If, of course, Fania Pascal really were a Comintern agent, as Costello and Ferns thought, then the quote invites an altogether more sinister interpretation and, one must suppose, might well be true.

Mrs Pascal also records something very curious that Wittgenstein communicated to her before leaving for Norway in 1936:

> Before leaving for Norway he made a tour of Brittany with (as he told me) a newly acquired friend who knew the area well and was an excellent driver. 'My friend is a cripple,' he added, 'lame in one leg.' I remember this detail of a second lame friend, for it struck me as odd.[125]

Wittgenstein's first lame friend would of course have been his lover Francis Skinner but Mrs Pascal was sufficiently struck by his having a second one to record the fact for posterity, and it is indeed odd. Most readers probably would not try to fit an individual to the description. After all, how many cripples were there in England? But if one lets one's mind drift speculatively over possible candidates among known cripples with connections to Cambridge, France and Communism, an interesting candidate emerges.[126] He connects to Cambridge in a rather closer relation than mere random association for, like Wittgenstein, he was a pre-Great War Cambridge graduate. He was crippled because of a 1924 train injury between Paris and Le Havre. He is known to have had strong connections to Russian Intelligence. Like Wittgenstein, he was both homosexual and strongly influenced by the Viennese Jewish writer Otto Weininger. From a millionaire family, this man became known as 'Stalin's apologist' and was largely responsible for the horror of the Ukrainian famine being kept from Western readers through his reassuring reports in the *New York Times*. He had lived in both Paris and Moscow, where he held court in the bar of the Hotel Metropol, where Wittgenstein was to stay.

The individual I have in mind is the journalist, Walter Duranty.[127] Duranty later reported the Spanish Civil War and, as Seale and McConville report in their book on Philby, a connection between Duranty and Philby in Spain is demonstrable in the town of St Jean de Luz:

> Many British residents of Spain had fled to St Jean from the shellings, air raids and imprisonments of the Civil War, and to make themselves feel more at home

had founded the Baloney Club amid the rustic walnut and red plush of the Bar Basque. Several of the war correspondents were roped in as associate members – Alan Moorehead, Walter Duranty, the red-haired, knickerbockered Virginia Cowles, and of course Kim.

Behind the careful make-belief, what must Kim really have felt? His life was a lie. It must sometimes have been a painful one. John Cornford was killed in Spain a couple of months before Kim got there, and David Haden-Guest before he left.[128]

We shall return to Duranty and Wittgenstein's treatment of magic – Duranty's obsession – later in the book.

However this speculation about Wittgenstein's crippled travelling companion might turn out, it is clear that the circles in which Wittgenstein moved in Cambridge – his close friends and students – demonstrably included Comintern agents, probable Comintern agents and spies. And he learnt Russian from Fania Pascal, a probable Comintern agent, in order to settle ultimately in the Soviet Union and become a Soviet citizen. Wittgenstein's efforts to visit were facilitated by the economist John Maynard Keynes who introduced him to Ivan Maisky, the Russian Ambassador in London. Keynes wrote to Maisky:

> May I venture to introduce to you Dr Ludwig Wittgenstein . . . who is a distinguished philosopher [and] a very old and intimate friend of mine. . . . I should be extremely grateful for anything you could do for him. . . .
> He . . . has strong sympathies with the way of life which he believes the new regime in Russia stands for.[129]

One imagines that Keynes would have known. Whether due to Keynes's eminence or for other reasons, Wittgenstein was granted a visa and left for Leningrad on 7 September 1935, arriving five days later.[130]

Monk then remarks that he impressed the Professor of Mathematical Logic at Moscow University with his interest in dialectical materialism and that he was offered the Chair of Philosophy at Kazan University. Monk points out that Kazan had been Tolstoy's university. But this altogether misses a more recent luminary alumnus of Kazan of considerably greater importance than Tolstoy. Kazan had been Lenin's university.

Is this not striking? It would be rather like the Archbishop of Canterbury appointing a Muslim as Bishop of London. Is it credible that such an offer to a visiting non-Marxist Austro/English academic could have been made without approval from the very highest Soviet level? And why was it made? Are we to believe it was offered from disinterested Soviet intellectual respect for Wittgenstein's brand of linguistic analysis? Why would a

Communist government support a non-Marxist philosopher teaching philosophy from the chair of Lenin's university?

Also significant is a sentence in a letter of Wittgenstein's to Gilbert Pattisson: 'I am staying in the rooms Napoleon had in 1812.' The rooms sound as though he were enjoying five-star treatment courtesy of the Soviet state. Wittgenstein, an admirer of Napoleon, was notoriously frugal with his own needs and Monk points out that he was sufficiently concerned about his future to have organized the promise of a loan from Keynes prior to his departure for Russia. (Wittgenstein's five-year fellowship at Trinity ended after the academic year 1935-6, so his financial future was precarious).[131] In any case, the reference to Napoleon allows us to identify his residence in Moscow as the Hotel Metropol, a block or so from Red Square. It was in the bar of this hotel that the crippled Walter Duranty held court as the doyen of Western journalists in Moscow.[132]

The significance of this trip to Moscow has been raised before. *The Times* of London, for example, wrote:

Did Anthony Blunt's Cambridge converts to Soviet-style communism include . . . Ludwig Wittgenstein? The question is prompted by the coincidence of the sale at Sotheby's yesterday of a postcard sent by Wittgenstein from Moscow on September 18, 1935 to the Cambridge philosopher G.E. Moore. . . .[133]

Penrose and Freeman confidently dismiss the suggestion as 'a mistake', without any argument whatsoever, much as Monk dismissed the 'Stalinist' label. The date, however, is highly significant, since it suffices to establish that Wittgenstein and his fellow Apostle, the spy Anthony Blunt – whom we know he knew and whose Communist boyfriend had written a poem and hoped to complete a PhD about him – were both in Moscow from Trinity College, Cambridge, at the same time. Thus Anthony Blunt, Wilfred Blunt, Charles Fletcher-Cooke, John Madge, Christopher Mayhew, Derek Nenk, Brian Simon, Michael Straight and Michael Young sailed for Leningrad, 10 August 1935.[134]

Blunt sailed for Leningrad in early August 1935 and Wittgenstein was in Moscow in mid-September 1935. The Blunt group, of course, contained at least two spies (Blunt and Straight) and also would have been in Moscow in mid-September.

The hypothesis we are considering is not quite that of the London *Times*; that Wittgenstein was recruited by Blunt. Our hypothesis is that Wittgenstein himself was the man, the mysterious man, who fascinated John Le Carre – the long-sought Cambridge recruitment agent; the Trinity College homosexual Apostle who recruited Blunt and the other Cambridge spies. All the investigations chasing the recruiter have looked at Communist dons such as Maurice Dobb and Roy Pascal – or sympathizers such as Andrew Gow. Yet fifty years of the most intensive detective work based upon this hypothesis have yielded precisely nothing. There is no consensus as to who he was. That he must have been a remarkable individual goes without saying. That he must have had remarkable influence upon his students also goes without saying. But that he might have been one of the most brilliant minds of the twentieth century has not been suspected. Wittgenstein, though a staunch defender of Stalin, was not, so far as we know, a Party member; archetypally, he was a philosopher and a moulder of people's lives. There is no doubt at all that his students were moved by and responded to the extraordinary power of his overwhelmingly dominant and charismatic personality.

Would Wittgenstein's aggressively intelligent personality, formed in a household with an overwhelmingly dominant father, with its stutter, its love of German music and of Russian literature, have had a particular resonance for any of the Cambridge spies? We have already considered Anthony Blunt and aesthetic debate. Consider now Kim Philby, with *his* stutter and dominant father, the Arabist St John Philby:

> He was still only seventeen when he arrived at Cambridge to read history in 1929. With nothing showy or aggressive in his nature, and sustained by a quiet self-respect that he owed to St John, he spent a rather reserved and solitary first year, bringing no close friends from school and seeming to make none. Very likely his stutter was a barrier to easy sociability. . . . Joining no club, playing no sport, lacking a wide variety of acquaintance, Kim spent his hours of lonely leisure obsessively listening to the music of Beethoven, often with tears in his eyes. With characteristic orderliness he learned to refer to each work by its opus number. His room on Jesus Lane (where the rents were stiff) was dominated by a photograph of the then famous French concert pianist, Alfred Cortot. He tried to play the French horn but made little progress. Ibsen, Turgenev and Dostoevski filled his bookshelves, for in literature as in music Kim was fastidiously restrictive, maintaining there were only two or three authors worth reading. He read them repeatedly and knew them very well. One of his first acquaintances at Cambridge, Anthony McLean, recalls lending him Tolstoy's *Resurrection* in the Maude translation (and never getting it back) in exchange for Turgenev's *A Nest of Gentlefolk* in the Constance Garnett translation.[135]

What was Wittgenstein's opinion of Philby's favourite authors? He had learnt Norwegian in order to read Ibsen in the original. Of Tolstoy, he is on record as having stated that the work of Tolstoy had saved his life in the Great War. He thought the great Russian novelists, particularly

Dostoevski, among the two or three authors worth reading and was intent, through his Russian lessons, on being able to read Tolstoy and Dostoevski in the original Russian.[136] Wittgenstein – who had considered a career as an orchestral conductor – had an encyclopedic knowledge of music, knew Beethoven's works by their opus numbers and also played a wind instrument.[137] Like Blunt, Philby was learning German and might be expected to have sought out for German-speaking practice the only Trinity College staff member at the time who was a native German speaker.[138] And what of the poster Philby had upon his wall, of the French pianist, Alfred Cortot?

Cortot was a master pianist; indeed, the ranking French concert pianist of his day. He had studied in Vienna and knew the musical luminaries of Europe, including the French composer Maurice Ravel, with whom he had a close relationship. In fact he was sufficiently impressed by one piece of Ravel's, the Concerto for the Left Hand, to suggest an alternative version of it for two hands, which he actually produced. But why would Ravel and Cortot have ventured to work upon a piano concerto for only one hand in the first place?

Ravel was commissioned to do it circa 1930 by a rich Viennese who tragically had lost his right arm in the Great War, thereby cutting short a brilliant career as a concert pianist. He had been captured by the Russians and interned in Siberia, to be released to his grateful family in the pre-revolutionary turmoil. The name of this tragic character was Paul Wittgenstein and he was Ludwig's brother. The Paris premiere of the Concerto for the Left Hand took place on 17 January 1933 with Paul Wittgenstein as soloist. (Sergei Prokoviev also wrote a one-handed concerto for Paul Wittgenstein – his Fourth Piano Concerto – in 1931, indicating rather close relations to an Austrian millionaire for a Soviet composer; he would surely not have produced it for such a person on his own initiative.)[139] What between Dostoevski, Tolstoy, Ibsen, Beethoven, Prokoviev, wind instruments, Alfred Cortot's emendations of the piano concerto Paul Wittgenstein commissioned and Philby's fund-raising on behalf of the Austrian Communists, there is no doubt that Wittgenstein and Philby would have had much to stutter about together in German.

Perhaps they had a good deal more to discuss about Tolstoy and Russia, too, for surprisingly, Ludwig Wittgenstein was not the first of that name to achieve renown in European history.[140] During the Napoleonic campaign it was Lieutenant-General Ludwig Adolf Graf von Sayn-Wittgenstein who stopped Napoleon's advance on St Petersburg, earning from Napoleon the judgement that he was 'the most able of all Russian generals'. Later he was made Field Marshal and a Prince of Russia and was appointed to the Council of State. He achieved literary fame in *War and Peace* where

Tolstoy referred to him as 'the brilliant hero of St Petersburg'.[141]

Since the Meier-Wittgensteins claimed a (perhaps illegitimate) descent from the Sayn-Wittgensteins they had as impressive a family connection with Russia as it is possible to imagine. It ought surely to have alerted *somebody* investigating the Burgess/Maclean/Philby defection that the Russian hero's Cambridge namesake might be worth a little further study. It would be rather as if the KGB were to totally ignore somebody whose name was Dwight D. Eisenhower, of capitalistic sympathies, teaching students at the University of Moscow, whose students spied for the West and defected to the United States.

Wouldn't the Cambridge Ludwig Wittgenstein, a devotee of Tolstoy, have known that his namesake was mentioned in *War and Peace*? Redpath writes of Wittgenstein's view of *War and Peace*, 'Toushine, a minor character in *War and Peace*, seemed to him especially admirable, serving selflessly and effectively as a Captain without any ostentation, a symbol of the best in the Russian resistance to Napoleon.'[142] It is fairly clear, I think, that Wittgenstein was holding back from Redpath a good deal of what he must have known about the background to *War and Peace*. But perhaps he didn't hold back from Philby. The military action of the first part of *War and Peace*, leading up to Austerlitz, is in any case set in Austria, where Tolstoy records Kutuzov's burning of the Danube bridges at Braunau – Hitler's birthplace – and at Linz – where Hitler and Wittgenstein attended school. For both Hitler and Wittgenstein, *War and Peace* must have been not dry literature, but living history.

What is actually *known* about Philby's controller? The literature on this crucial matter is curiously uncertain. The man reputed to have been his first controller in Vienna was named Theodore Maly. His alleged second controller was named Arnold Deutsch.

The evidence that Maly and Deutsch were Philby's controllers, however, apparently derives from Philby himself and is therefore suspect. Nigel West writes of MI5's investigation of possible agents in place in the 1930s:

> When MI5 belatedly attempted to tackle this conundrum in the early 1960s, when the danger of moles had manifested itself dramatically through the defection of Guy Burgess and Donald Maclean in 1951, it had relied upon two main sources of information. The first was a confession written by Kim Philby in 1963 in which he asserted that he had been recruited into the NKVD by Maly, who had subsequently been replaced in 1936 by a Soviet illegal known to him only as OTTO. In return for the offer of a formal immunity from prosecution, and confronted by the weight of denunciations from defectors, Philby had admitted his guilt in an interview conducted in Beirut. He claimed that when he

had been stationed in Washington DC in 1949, he had taken the opportunity to study the FBI's files on Soviet illegals and had identified OTTO from an FBI photograph as an Austrian academic, Arnold Deutsch. While this sequence of events seemed entirely plausible, a check with the FBI revealed that the Bureau had only acquired Deutsch's picture after Philby had been sacked from SIS. Had Philby lied, or had he sought to protect some other illegal? The most likely explanation is that Philby knew his principal contact in London during 1934 and 1935 was still, in January 1963, at liberty in the West and, therefore, vulnerable.[143]

If our hypothesis about Wittgenstein is correct, the 'illegal' Philby was trying to protect was not 'at liberty in the West'; he had been dead for some twelve years, but the need to protect his identity was pressing because once it was realized who he was, it would be much easier to trace his other Cambridge converts. It seems to me that it is this – the identity of the spy ring recruiter – that is the key to the mystery of the Cambridge spy ring. Keeping investigators off the scent was clearly important, for Blunt and Philby both went to great lengths to disguise the details of their recruitment. Costello writes:

> Until Blunt's confession became publicly known, there were two prime candidates for controller of the Cambridge agents: Samuel Cahan, Moscow Center's resident in London, who was operating under diplomatic cover as first secretary of the embassy; and the longtime Tass representative in Britain, Semyon Rostovsky, who wrote under the name Ernst Henri.
>
> The case against either Cahan or Rostovsky as the Cambridge recruiter was their 'legal' status as Soviet citizens with diplomatic positions. In the decade after the Arcos debacle, Moscow generally avoided using such people to run spy rings. Any exposure of their role in the chain of command would have jeopardized not only their official status but also Moscow's hard-won restoration of Anglo–Soviet diplomatic relations. Moscow Center would also have reasoned – correctly, as we now know – that Soviet officials in London were subject to intense scrutiny by British counterintelligence. And Soviet intelligence would not have risked exposing one of its most important underground operations to such close surveillance.
>
> 'We were recruited individually and we operated individually,' Philby has declared. But all the evidence points to his recruitment and control of the Cambridge agents by the same highly sophisticated illegal. Blunt admitted as much when he told MI5 that his recruitment by Burgess was orchestrated by a middle-class Eastern European whom he knew only as 'Otto'. Blunt described him as being 'short with no neck and swept back straight hair'. But despite being shown volume after volume from the extensive MI5 Registry of photographs of Soviet agents and suspects, Blunt never matched a face and name to this indi-

vidual he vaguely recalled as being Czech.

'For some reason, we were never able to identify "Otto",' Peter Wright of MI5 wrote, disclosing that two other members of the Cambridge ring, Philby and Cairncross, had told MI5 about their contacts with the mysterious 'Otto' also without knowing or revealing his real name. During his 'confession' to MI5 officer Nicholas Elliott in Beirut shortly before his defection in 1963, Philby said that 'Otto' was a Comintern agent he had met in Vienna.

Wright concedes he was never able to identify 'Otto'. Nor did anyone else in MI5 discover why Blunt and the other surviving members of the Cambridge network were so determined to preserve the identity of the mysterious Eastern European. . . .[144]

It seems a reasonably fair bet that both Philby and Blunt were lying and that Maly and Deutsch were invoked purely as decoys. They would not, however, have chosen Maly and Deutsch as decoys all by themselves. Some thought must have gone into who was chosen to be a decoy; not just anybody would be suitable. That is, there would have been some serious research by the responsible Soviet intelligence agency to find suitable false candidates. Whichever individuals it settled upon as decoys would have had precisely the features that Western investigators following the few clues available would find decisive. And ideally, they would still have served as decoys as further facts about the true recruiter unavoidably came to light. What particular features did Maly and Deutsch share that might do the job of misleading Western investigators? Here are some obvious suggestions if our own hypothesis about Wittgenstein is correct.

1   The recruiter had a famous concert-pianist brother. Theodore Maly had a famous concert-pianist brother.[145]
2   The recruiter was not Russian, but from the Austro–Hungarian empire and with Jewish connections. Both Maly and Deutsch were Austro–Hungarian and Deutsch was an Austrian Jew.
3   The recruiter had served in the Austrian army. Maly had served in the Austrian army.
4   The recruiter had a background in philosophy and was associated with the Vienna Circle. Deutsch had a Viennese philosophical background and had studied under Moritz Schlick, completing a PhD in 1928.[146] (He would almost certainly have known Wittgenstein, given Wittgenstein's Vienna Circle discussions.)
5   The recruiter was interested in religion and mysticism. Maly was a renegade priest.

Any whisper of a background vaguely like this in connection with Philby's recruiter could then be attributed to the hapless Maly or Deutsch. Stalin had Maly, and perhaps Deutsch, murdered, just to be safe.[147] They could not have been better chosen had the Russian intelligence agency responsible had national resources available to call upon, multi-billion-rouble budgets, and a choice of any or all of hundreds of thousands of trained staff to do the necessary research work to find such a wonderful fit. But then, of course, that is exactly what it did have.

There is a further aspect of the Cambridge spy affair that might also be worth noting. It has always been a puzzle why Guy Burgess defected. Maclean was doomed by the Venona decrypts and it was only a matter of time before his arrest. Burgess, on the other hand, while leading an erratic life, was not a suspect and in no danger of arrest. Politically, his slate was clean.[148] Burgess and Maclean defected on Friday 25 May 1951. Organization for the defection would presumably have taken a few weeks. Wittgenstein had breathed his last on 28 April 1951, less than a month before. Interestingly, one of Burgess' deeds, a week after he arrived back in England, was to revisit Cambridge, on 19 May, presumably to tidy up some loose ends.[149] Perhaps he also said his last farewell at the St Giles' grave-site, for might he not have felt released from his spying obligation by the death of his mentor and decided he had earned his passage to the worker's paradise? The prophet had been denied his refuge in Russia, but his disciples were indeed now free to enter the promised land.

Suppose the case of the previous chapters is true; that Hitler's hatred of Jews was given an early and vital impetus by an unknown encounter with Ludwig Wittgenstein at school around 1904. Then Wittgenstein knew Hitler. If true, this hypothesis is not some mere historical oddity, but a fact with enormous implications, for how would we expect Wittgenstein to have reacted? Would he have viewed the growth of Nazi power with equanimity? Or would he not rather have been moved to oppose it actively? But if he was so moved, what could he, as a mere philosopher, have done? Where should we look to investigate his possible course of action?

It is clear that he could not do much as an Austrian primary school teacher, stuck in villages where, as Bartley reveals, he was regarded by the devoutly Catholic villagers as simply a little queer from the big city. But then, to a certain class of intellectual, he was powerfully charismatic. Wittgenstein's charisma might not move primary students, and it might not move Germans, but it most certainly – demonstrably – could move Englishmen. And if it could move the right *sort* of Englishmen, then perhaps this divine Baldur could play an active role in history after all.

Now, of the Trinity College dons, how many others were able to inspire their students to regard them as a god? How many were fully aware of the origins of Hitler's Jew-hate and the sort of man Hitler was? How many counted as Jewish under the Nuremberg Laws? How many had worked just across the border from Bavaria, as Nazism in Munich grew from strength to strength? How many had seen armed Nazi insurrection against the government of their country, as had Wittgenstein, or striking workers shot in the streets? How many had seen, even before 1933, doomed and broken Jewish refugees hopelessly fleeing across the mountain passes into Austria?

What must have been the temptation to think, 'Yes, I can help. I'll select people, who, in my judgement, can further the cause of the only inter-national organization that stands for armed opposition to Hitler; I will back the Comintern!'[150] Perhaps, when the task seemed too daunting, or the nervous strain too much, he dreamt of, yearned for, prayed for, sanctuary and peace in Russia. Certainly he visited it to scout out the terrain for future settlement. How many of the other Cambridge dons actively welcomed the chance to live in Russia under Stalin's regime and learned the language to that end?

Monk quotes a recollection of George Sacks, who knew Wittgenstein in Russia in 1935:

> ... we [he and his wife] heard that Wittgenstein wanted to work on a collective farm, but the Russians told him his own work was a useful contribution and he ought to go back to Cambridge.[151]

Why would the Russians have thought his work 'was a useful contribu-tion'? Is it really at all likely that they were referring here to his philosoph-ical work? What earthly interest would doctrinaire Marxists take in Wittgenstein's contributions to non-Marxist philosophy at Cambridge? This report alone is evidence that Wittgenstein's activities were in some way helping the revolutionary cause. And if Wittgenstein's Cambridge activities resulted in whole departments of MI5 coming under Russian control, it is clear why they would have preferred him in Cambridge to working on a collective farm.

In 1994 the Australian journalist Roland Perry published a sort of jour-nalistic *exposé*, 'The Fifth Man'. In this, he claimed that the 'fifth man' of the Cambridge spy ring – and by far the most damaging – was not John Cairncross, but Victor Rothschild, the third Lord Rothschild, an Apostle and fellow of Trinity College. The late Lady Rothschild, in response to an enquiry from me, replied that she never knew Wittgenstein and that so far as she was aware, neither did her late husband.[152] Since Lady Rothschild's death, however, Tom Bower, the biographer of Sir Dick White, has made the accusation that she was a former lover of Anthony Blunt. If the accusation is correct, her testimony must be viewed with an otherwise unnecessary squint. In any case, Peter Wright notes that when war broke out, Tess Mayor, as she then was, joined MI5 and 'had rooms No 5 Bentinck Street along with Blunt and Burgess'.[153] Wright quotes her as saying, 'Anthony used to come back tight to Bentinck Street, sometimes so tight that I had to help him into bed. . . . I would have known if he was a spy. . . .' The Bentinck Street building was owned by her future husband, Victor Rothschild, who was also in MI5.

The reader might recall the Rothschild name appearing earlier in our own investigation in connection with the Wittkowitz steel works. The Austrian Rothschilds were cartel partners of Karl Wittgenstein's Prager Eisenindustrie Gesellschaft and their Wittkowitz works were managed by Paul Kupelwieser, a close Wittgenstein relative. After the Great War, the works fell within the borders of the new state of Czechoslovakia, but remained under Rothschild control. What happened to ownership of the plant when Hitler took control of Czechoslovakia is the subject of a very entertaining and interesting historical anecdote because it points to active involvement in the fortunes of the Austrian Rothschilds by the English branch of the Rothschild family.

The Nazis found they could not simply expropriate Wittkowitz, because it was no longer under Austrian Rothschild ownership; it had been sold, before the Nazis could get their hands on it, to Alliance Insurance in London. Accordingly, compensation was paid to the new owners. Hitler found out later, after the money had changed hands, that Alliance Insurance was a vehicle of the English Rothschilds and hit the proverbial roof. It follows, therefore, that there were substantial business contacts between the Austrian Rothschilds and English Rothschilds in the 1930s. The Wittkowitz steelworks ended up owned by the Hermann Göring Steelworks in (where else?) Linz.[154] One thinks involuntarily of Hitler's schooldays.

The Austrian Rothschilds, of course, had had very close dealings with the Wittgenstein family through the great Austrian cartel. The English Rothschilds had had very close dealings with the Austrian Rothschilds through the Wittkowitz transfer. And the most prominent English Rothschild – Victor, scion of the family which employed Guy Burgess – and the most brilliant son of Karl Wittgenstein were now academics at Cambridge together; indeed, fellows of the same college! Both were on the same side of the political spectrum and, with their strong Jewish connections, united in opposition to Hitler. A great steelworks to which each of their families had strong historical links was transferred from the Austrian

Rothschilds to English Rothschild ownership in order to fool Adolf Hitler. And the Rothschilds' London residence was next door to the Soviet Embassy in London.[155]

In 1995, the former Australian senator, John Wheeldon, published the text of an interview with Trotsky's former bodyguard, Albert Glotzer.[156] Glotzer describes visiting Berlin in December 1931 and visiting the Liebknecht Haus, the headquarters of the Communist Party. He continues:

> From there I went to England, where I joined up with Max Schachtman. We had one large meeting with people who were disaffected with the CP. We didn't organise a group there, but we set the basis for it, and it was organised after we left.
>
> We had one mission there for Trotsky. Trotsky told me before I left that he would like me to go to see an English baron, who happened to be Jewish, who was involved with Russian trade and the movie industry. Trotsky thought he was a sympathiser of his. For some reason or other he had written to Trotsky. Schachtman and I went up to see him, but we got a cold reception. We said that Trotsky wanted to know whether he could help with getting *Whither England?* republished.
>
> He didn't respond, and when we came out we said, 'Why the hell did Trotsky want us to go and see him? This guy is so Stalinist. He's involved in the Russian trade, and he isn't going to do anything to hurt his relations with the Russians.' So I wrote to the Old Man, 'This guy isn't going to do anything for you. He's a Stalinist.'
>
> Then I went back to the States.

'An English baron, who happened to be Jewish'? There aren't many Jews in the English aristocracy and precious few barons. This information alone should enable us to identify the family whose head Glotzer referred to as a 'Stalinist'. The only possible candidate family is the Rothschilds. And the father of Victor Rothschild had killed himself in 1923. The title went to Victor's uncle, Lionel – presumably Glotzer's 'Stalinist' – but Victor succeeded to it in 1937. Victor had the singular distinction of being an Apostle, a friend of both Anthony Blunt and Guy Burgess (whom his Austrian mother employed) and a fellow of Trinity College, Cambridge. He denied ever having met Kim Philby at Cambridge, but their addresses in Jesus Lane in the early thirties, Philby at 8 Jesus Lane and Rothschild at 25 Jesus Lane, must strain the credibility of this denial somewhat. Cornforth, incidentally, lived at 62 Jesus Lane and Haden-Guest at 37 Jesus Lane. (The other, earlier, address given for Haden-Guest was A8 Bishop's Hostel, remarkably close to Blunt at A2 and C1 where Wittgenstein had stayed.)

The defector Anatoli Golitsin, who, as Peter Wright reports, was given access to the most secret files in MI5, named Victor and Tess Rothschild as Soviet agents in the spring of 1968.[157] Wright, as a very close friend of Lord Rothschild and his wife, was disinclined to accept the truth of Golitsin's allegation and attributed it to 'KGB anti-Semitism'. He commented sadly that 'With Golitsin unable to advance the penetration issue any further, MI5 were trapped in the middle of a maze.'[158] Perhaps they were. For if Lord Rothschild really were a Soviet agent, the long-sought-for leak in MI5 would have been neither Roger Hollis nor Graham Mitchell, but Peter Wright, via his discussions with Lord Rothschild about security matters. In any case, Lord Rothschild, despite repeated requests, was rather pointedly not cleared by Margaret Thatcher in her speech to the House of Commons – perhaps she was bearing in mind the sad legacy of Harold Macmillan's assurance (as Foreign Secretary) to the House of Commons in 1955, that Kim Philby was not the 'Third Man'.

Victor Rothschild was also one of three people present at one of the more significant meetings of the twentieth century. It took place in June 1940 in his three-storey apartment in London, at 5 Bentinck Street. The other two attending were Anthony Blunt and Guy Liddell, head of MI5's counter espionage division. Rothschild had recommended Blunt (who had taught him French at Cambridge) for appointment to the Security Service. The English writer Nigel West mentions 'a distinguished paediatrician' who wishes to remain anonymous, but who had been a Party member at Cambridge, recalling that Rothschild, too, had been a Party member.[159] At this meeting, Liddell accepted Rothschild's earlier recommendation and took Blunt into the service in MI5's D Division. This, in essence, is the account of the late Lord Rothschild, forty-six years after the meeting took place.[160] Liddell had also seconded the proposal that Guy Burgess join MI5.[161]

West, in another work, offers the following in brief background on the allegations concerning Guy Liddell:

> The first person to be accused of misconduct in relation to Blunt, based on allegations made by Goronwy Rees shortly before his death on 12 December 1979, was the late Guy Liddell. On 20 January 1980 Andrew Boyle wrote about Rees in the *Observer* and quoted him as having said that Burgess' 'main source must have been Guy Liddell with whom he and Anthony Blunt remained, of course, on very close terms. I was strongly convinced, though I had no direct proof, that Liddell was another of Burgess' predatory conquests. I know that dead men cannot answer back, but there was to my mind something sinister about Liddell's protectiveness in regard to both Blunt and Burgess.'[162]

This suspicion is reinforced by a reported observation of Maurice Oldfield, the former chief of MI6, about the investigation of the Fluency Committee into possible penetration of MI5, that 'If I had been in charge of the investigation . . . I would have put Guy Liddell at the top of the list.'[163] Liddell was also accused in an article in *The Times* of 31 December 1979 by David Mure, a retired intelligence officer. Mure wrote that 'he had 'come across a chain of circumstances which in my opinion, make it certain that Liddell was a Russian agent'.[164] The accusation stirred up a hornet's nest and Sir Dick White made an almost unprecedented public statement in his defence. (John Costello's own assessment of Liddell is that either he was an agent or else monumentally incompetent.)

Now every individual in the world bears a characteristic locus of connections. The business of the detective historian is to investigate these loci, to bring out the interesting, the unusual and the significant. What is particularly interesting about the three individuals at the Bentinck Street meeting is that their loci all met, in various ways, in the Wittgenstein family and not just through Trinity College. The Blunt connection has been established already. And the Rothschild connection, through both Trinity College and the Wittgenstein/Rothschild cartel in Central Europe, is evident.[165] But what of the Liddell connection?

The Liddell family includes Alice Liddell, for whom the logician Lewis Carroll wrote *Alice in Wonderland*. (Wittgenstein was a devotee of this work.) But they have also been blessed by a very strong musical tradition. West writes of Liddell's private life:

> His home, 42 Cheyne Walk, was the scene of frequent, extremely popular musical soirees where he played the cello with great skill. At one time he was rated as the best amateur cellist in the country.[166]

Where did Guy Liddell acquire such consummate skill? Was it simply natural talent or was he trained by someone who knew what he was doing musically? There is one very interesting possibility.

Liddell's mother was a talented violinist, who founded an all-female string quartet.[167] Her talents were such, in fact, that she sought to perfect them by learning from masters. She sought, as is natural, to learn from the very best violinist in the world and was fortunate to be able to realize her ambition. The very best violinist in the world, as it turns out, though of continental Jewish origins, was a frequent visitor to England and had been awarded an honorary doctorate from Trinity College, Cambridge. He was able to train Mrs Liddell and perhaps her son in his unusual bowing technique. We have come across his name before.

Mrs Liddell is named in Moser's 1901 biography of Joseph Joachim as Mrs Liddell (née Shinner), one of Joachim's faithful English disciples.[168] She is named again on p 328 as Mrs Shinner-Liddell, who during a celebratory music festival organized in Joachim's honour, affectionately employed a trick to persuade the ageing master to play Beethoven. There is no doubt they knew each other well, before the Great War. And Joachim, of course, was an adopted Wittgenstein.

Does such a connection matter? We are looking not at proof in some mathematical sense, nor are we even operating with evidence suitable for a court of law. We are simply looking at connections whose significance is connected with their very improbability. Is it not exceedingly improbable that the Wittgenstein name should connect to so many of the players in the drama we have been investigating and in so many different ways? If I am correct in my suspicions of Wittgenstein's role at Cambridge, then he was the master spy recruiter of the twentieth century. It is surely noteworthy that the mother of a deputy Director-General of a British secret agency had intimate dealings with this man's cousin. If I am correct, the Cambridge spy ring was not something that emerged *ex nihilo* in the 1930s. Indeed its roots at Trinity College go back to before the Russian Revolution and the Great War.

Do any of the facts we have unearthed establish Wittgenstein's role as recruiter? No, but they do suffice, I think, to establish him as the most likely suspect. And just to have a suspect is in itself a very great advance. Does the reader still doubt? The cure for such a doubt is simply to take up a piece of paper and complete the sentence 'Wittgenstein was offered the Chair in Philosophy at Lenin's university in 1935 because . . .'

If I am right, then, like Philby, Burgess, Maclean and Blunt, Wittgenstein too escaped the hangman. Hitler, however, blew his brains out, and Wittgenstein's role in the Soviet intelligence effort might well have been pivotal, for Wittgenstein's disciples transferred the crown jewels of British intelligence to Stalin. If so, then those Hitler *called* 'the Jews' really did contribute in an important way to his defeat, through the Enigma decrypts; though the true Jews – the real, Covenant-keeping Jews – had been murdered in their millions, going to their dreadful deaths in complete ignorance of how it all happened. But the *Saujud* of Hitler's beginning, the mysterious young 'Jew' of the Linz *Realschule*, was the very same Jew who helped bring about Hitler's end. The hidden hand of Hitler's nightmares, that of 'the Jew', really did exist and, indeed, contributed to his undoing. But 'the Jew' involved can only be referred to as such in inverted commas, for he was not a Jew, but a Catholic. And *his* 'final solution of the problems', his greatest achievement, was not the *Tractatus*, nor even the *Philosophical*

Investigations, but Hitler's finger closing on the trigger in the Berlin bunker.

It is time now to begin unravelling the second strand of our investigation, which concerns Wittgenstein's philosophy. It will turn out to be more closely connected both to the nature of history – in fact to Hitler's great discovery of 'the meaning of history' at the *Realschule* – and to the mass murders of the twentieth century than anyone has yet suspected. To understand the connection we must first take what seems to be a side-step into the history of music, specifically the music of Richard Wagner.

Part II

THREE

Wagner and Judaism in Music

The historical importance of the photograph in Chapter 1 in confirming what was already known about Hitler and Wittgenstein attending school together in 1904 is obvious. It is now clear that it is very likely that they did indeed know each other and that the onus of proof must shift to the doubters. Previous investigators have turned up no other evidence that they might have known each other, other than that they attended the same school. In the photograph, however, proximity would seem indicative of acquaintance.

The photograph, then, sustains confidence that the hypothesis is correct and that a number of historical theses that have been taken as given for half a century or more can be investigated afresh. One of these concerns the precise nature of the causal links between Richard Wagner's seminal piece of anti-Semitic propaganda *Judaism in Music* and Hitler's own anti-Semitism. One might think that the anti-Semitic nature of the tract and its momentous historical significance in reviving German anti-Semitism is sufficient all by itself to account for Hitler's interest. There are, however, some background links between Wagner's paper and the Wittgenstein name that have not been pointed out and that now take on quite remarkable importance for Holocaust research. Let us approach these links with a preliminary sketch of the background to Wagner's paper.

It appeared under the pseudonym K. Freigedank in 1850 and is the first major literary manifestation of modern German anti-Semitism.[1] Wagner sketched out a process of spiritual decay in art, the cause of which he attributed to infiltration by Jews, whose nature he saw as intrinsically unheroic and as antithetical to whatever it is that art is striving to express. What art Jews had produced was theirs, he thought, only by expropriation of the creative works of others. In music in particular, Jews suffered from the fact that the European languages they spoke were only acquired and not mother-tongues. Jews therefore were cut off from the historical community that alone is the root of creativity. Jews had their own folk sources, but these were from a withered root.

Such was the general tenor of the tract, in no way different from more recent tracts in German from the 1930s that were its lineal descendants. It originally appeared in September 1850 in the *Neue Zeitschrift fur Musik* in Leipzig. Though its authorship was known to the cognoscenti, 'K. Freigedank' was unknown to the general public and the name was not, as yet, associated with Richard Wagner, the great composer. That was to come later, and when it did, the reissued tract bearing Wagner's name came with a very interesting Afterword whose length was about equal to that of the original article. We shall consider the Afterword in a moment. For now, let us return to the Wagner/Wittgenstein links that I promised to elucidate. We have already seen in the last chapter that Wagner's wife's father, the virtuoso pianist Franz Liszt, had Princess Wittgenstein as a mistress.

I earlier quoted Dietrich Fischer-Dieskau's words on the hatred between Cosima Wagner and her father Liszt's mistress, Princess Sayn-Wittgenstein,[2] and the possible link between Cosima's anti-Semitism and the Princess's Jewish ancestry.[3] It is not generally recognized that Cosima Wagner was herself part Jewish. Her grandmother – the mother of the Countess Marie d'Agoult, Cosima's mother – was the daughter of a rich Jewish banker, Simon Moritz Bethmann of Frankfurt.[4] Whether or not this might connect her with her own anti-Semitism in general and her particular hatred of Princess Wittgenstein is a moot point. She was certainly a supporter of her husband's fateful anti-Semitism.

Wagner's book, *My Life*, contains many derogatory references to Princess Wittgenstein. As one example, writing on the close of Liszt's Dante Symphony, Wagner recalls:

> I was all the more startled to hear this lovely conception suddenly interrupted by a pompous plagal cadence which, I was told, was supposed to represent Domenico. 'No, no!' I exclaimed loudly. 'Not that! Out with it! No majestic Lord God! Let's stick with the fine soft shimmer.' 'You are right,' Liszt replied, 'I thought so too; the Princess convinced me otherwise, but it shall be as you recommend.' That was all well and good. But I was all the more dismayed to learn later not only that this close for the *Dante* Symphony had been retained, but also that the delicate ending I had liked so much in the *Faust* Symphony had been altered by the introduction of choruses in a manner calculated to produce a more ostentatious effect. This expressed everything I felt about Liszt and his lady friend, the Princess Karoline von Wittgenstein![5]

Moser's standard biography of Joseph Joachim quotes Princess Wittgenstein's description of Wagner's paper on *Judaism in Music*, which shows that Wagner's feelings were reciprocated.

Some years later, it was discovered that this article which had aroused so much excitement was, as the Furstin Wittgenstein says, 'une de ces grosses bêtises de Wagner'.[6]

Now Princess Wittgenstein was rather more than just a brief fling of Liszt's, and her impact upon Wagner's future wife Cosima was rather more than that of being simply an unwelcome intruder between Liszt and Cosima's mother. Princess Wittgenstein was the cause of Cosima being taken away from her mother as a seven-year-old girl and placed in the hands of a governess of truly horrible strictness. The following passages from the standard biography of Wagner really speak for themselves. (Cosima's mother, the Countess d'Agoult, was a moderately famous nineteenth-century writer who produced novels under the pseudonym Daniel Stern.)

Between the Cosima whom the older people of our generation knew, however, and the Cosima of 1864, many years had gone by. She was born on the Christmas Day of 1837; she died in her ninety-third year, on the 1st April, 1930, having survived Wagner a full forty-seven years. What kind of woman was the Cosima of twenty-six-and-a-half whose life became so inseparably interwoven with his in 1864?

She was no more than seven, her elder sister Blandine no more than nine, and her brother Daniel only five, when, about 1844, the ways of her father and mother began to diverge for good. Liszt resumed his vagrant virtuoso career through Europe; the Countess d'Agoult settled with the children in Paris. There they remained for the most part, in the care of Liszt's mother; Liszt did not wish them to see too much of their own mother, nor, fighting as she was just then to regain her social position in Paris, was it possible for her to impose, as constituent parts of her own household, three illegitimate children, each of them the product of an extra-marital association with a mere piano virtuoso, upon her aristocratic family and on the high French social world of that day. For years at a time the children never saw their father, who was little more than a grandiose, fantastic figure of legend to them. As time went on, and Liszt's hatred of Marie d'Agoult increased, he used his authority more and more to sequestrate and estrange the children from their mother, who, under French law, had no legal rights in them. This hatred of his was fanned by the woman with whom he had cast in his lot in 1847, the Princess Carolyne von Sayn-Wittgenstein, who detested Marie for three excellent feminine and Carolynian reasons – she was beautiful, she was intelligent, and Liszt had once adored her. Liszt's worship of his worshipping Princess combined with his resentment at Marie's unkind exposure of his human weaknesses in her novel *Nélida* (1846) to turn him completely against his former love; and the hand of the Princess is plainly evident in his unfriendly dealings with Marie in the matter of the children. . . .

In October, 1850, Carolyne brought it about that they were removed from Madame Liszt's house and placed completely in the charge of her own former governess, Madame Patersi, who was brought from Russia to Paris for that purpose. They seem to have had no child companions, no games, and few pleasures appropriate to their age. From Madame Patersi and her sister Madame de Saint-Mars, two acidulous old ladies of over seventy, they received an education of the strictest possible kind, being allowed into contact with nothing but what was held to be most admirable in literature, in music, in the theatre, and in the museums. They worked hard at their piano-playing, as became the children of Liszt; they learned English and German in addition to French. . . .

Those childhood years in Paris determined Cosima's character in its essentials for the rest of her life. In spite of all the efforts of Liszt and Carolyne, the children, as they grew older, saw their mother fairly frequently, and the more they saw her the more irresistibly they were attracted by her. Probably because they had little or no physical outlet of the customary kind for their youthful energy they bent their minds as few children could have done, or would have had need to do, to the understanding of the strange situation in which they found themselves between their mother – with her beauty and her charm, her cultivated intelligence, her delightful library, and her circle of acquaintances which included all that was most distinguished in the literary, artistic and political worlds of the Paris of that day – the dried-up, thin-lipped old dragon of a Madame Patersi, without a particle of tenderness in her composition – 'Merely water!' she would say when their eyes filled with tears and 'Just like their mother!' when one of them did something of which she disapproved – their father, a severe, remote figure, who had no understanding of children, and least of all of his own, and who wrote them letters that often did little more than modulate between sternness and downright harshness – and, in the background, the gushing but venomous Carolyne, with her blue-stocking habit of mind and her over-blown literary style, doing all she could to bring them to regard herself as their true 'mother'. They saw not only their own letters to their father and the Princess censored by their governess but their mother's letters to them 'tapped' by her and the contents passed on to Weimar.[7]

The reader should note that biographers differ greatly in their treatment of Princess Wittgenstein, largely as they respond to Richard Wagner. The 'Wagnerians' present her as a vindictive, cigar-smoking blue-stocking, whose later religious activities in Rome were pure hypocrisy. The biography of Liszt by Sacheverell Sitwell presents her in an altogether more favourable light, where the last-minute refusal of the Church to marry her to Liszt takes on the form of tragedy.[8] Either way, Newman probably accurately reflects the views of Cosima Wagner. He documents each of the assertions in these passages with references to correspondence, etc., and the picture that emerges is clear. Liszt takes up an adulterous affair with Princess Wittgenstein, who then acts to remove the future Mrs Wagner from contact with her own mother. Princess Wittgenstein tries to take over as a substitute mother and imposes a truly dreadful, disciplinarian upbringing on Cosima at the hands of aging foreigners, who evidently couldn't care less about the little girl in their charge. Indeed, the biography of Cosima Wagner by du Moulin-Eckart quotes from a letter of Liszt's mother of 1855 saying of the two governesses appointed by Princess Wittgenstein, 'Now these two ladies have taken a dislike to Cosima (*en grippe genommen*) because she has the misfortune to be like her mother.'[9] Of course Cosima hated Princess Wittgenstein! And despite the Princess's Catholicity, of course Cosima hated her Jewish background. We see here, I think, the first major historical link in a chain of causes leading to the Holocaust. At no stage in this process were Jews involved. The individuals in the drama were one and all Roman Catholics who could be described only as from families of Jewish apostates.

Another possible link is that Ludwig Wittgenstein may have been a direct relation of the Sayn-Wittgensteins. Bartley notes that his obituary in *The Times* stated that he was a Sayn-Wittgenstein and that 'some members of the Sayn-Wittgenstein family have on occasion indicated that they are related to Ludwig Wittgenstein's family'.[10] If this is so, then Ludwig was related to Liszt's mistress, Princess Wittgenstein, whom Wagner despised and Cosima hated. Monk, it is true, presents a different genealogy for Ludwig, but whatever the truth of the exact genetic relations, the matter is clearly of very great historical interest all by itself, for the Wagners hated someone bearing the Wittgenstein name.

In fact there is a quite astonishing and even closer connection to Wagner's anti-Jewish hates and the Wittgensteins traceable through an altogether different route. And survey of this route shows that someone closely connected to the Wittgenstein family was a direct target of Wagner's paper.

One of the luminaries of nineteenth-century German music was a Hungarian Jew named Joseph Joachim, a child prodigy of the violin. He is almost universally acknowledged as the greatest violinist of the nineteenth century. Moser's biography of Joachim relates how young Joseph's fortunes were assisted by a musical relative, a certain Fraulein Figdor, who, for our purposes, will turn out to have been rather important:

> Fanny Figdor of Vienna, a relation of whom the Joachim family were very fond, paid them a visit in the summer of 1839. She was Frau Joachim's niece, very musical, and, although only an amateur, a skilled and finished pianoforte player. Fraulein Figdor was delighted with her little cousin, who, in spite of his

tender years, could already play the violin so charmingly, and she joined Serwacynski in persuading the parents to have Pepi trained as a *virtuoso*. This meant that they would have to part with their darling, for although the musical atmosphere of Pesth was not unfavourable, Fanny Figdor wisely urged the removal of Pepi to Vienna, where there were finer teachers, and the opportunity for general culture greater, and where an altogether different musical atmosphere prevailed than in then secluded Pesth. The knowledge that in Vienna Pepi would be well cared for in his grandfather's house, made it easier for the parents to part with their promising child; and the relations there were generous enough to undertake the cost of his education and living.

So three travellers, Herr Joachim, Fanny Figdor, and little Pepi, set out cheerfully, with the mother's blessings, for the old imperial city on the Danube, which, for the next five years, was to be a second home to the little violinist.[11]

Moser recounts some amusing but inconsequential incidents concerning Joachim's life in the Figdor home and of his training under Joseph Bohm and then outlines the next stage in his education, which, once again, involved the redoubtable Fanny Figdor:

As, five years earlier, Fraulein Figdor's visit to Pesth had been the immediate occasion of the child's removal to Vienna, so now this artistic lady exerted her whole influence to have the boy sent to Leipzig for further development in his art. Fraulein Figdor in the meanwhile had married the merchant Wittgenstein, and lived with her husband in Leipzig. Thence she wrote to her relations in Vienna, letters full of admiration for the artistic activity of the town which, by the efforts of Mendelssohn and Schumann, had been raised to be a model for all the musical towns of Germany for coming decades. Frau Wittgenstein said, with the assurance of second-sight, that Leipzig was the only place where the splendid talents of her young cousin could attain to artistic maturity; and the sequel has proved how very right she was.[12]

Who was this musical 'Fraulein Figdor' who married 'the merchant Wittgenstein'? Could she have been related to Ludwig Wittgenstein's family? Indeed she was. She was Ludwig Wittgenstein's grandmother.[13] A German biography of Wittgenstein relates:

In 1839, the grandfather Herman Christian (1803-78) married Franziska Figdor, who came from one of the most prominent old Jewish families.[14]

Felix Mendelssohn and Robert Schumann had been working to raise the Conservatoire in Leipzig to a position of the first order and Frau Franziska Figdor/Wittgenstein was determined that Joachim should attend that institution.[15] He came to live with the Wittgensteins in Leipzig in the spring of 1843, but Mendelssohn, after hearing him play, declared, to the Wittgensteins' delighted surprise, that he needed no further training at all. He stayed with the Wittgensteins and his local reputation grew apace:

Joachim had now become a local celebrity, but, fortunately for him, his relations in Leipzig had not forgotten their intention to give him a thoroughly good education. The Wittgensteins, in their reasonable and kindly way, took care that the boy should not grow conceited, rather did they strive to develop his character side by side with his great talents. Like other boys of his age, he had to submit to home discipline, going to bed early and getting up betimes. The only exception to this was made in his connection with Mendelssohn. Wherever the latter performed, whether publicly or privately, the boy was permitted to be present, and it is one of the most touching instances of Mendelssohn's kindness that on most of these occasions he himself accompanied the boy home.[16]

These passages suffice to establish that Mendelssohn knew the Wittgensteins and visited the family home. Moser's biography of Joachim even contains a copy of a letter written by Mendelssohn from London to Hermann and Fanny Wittgenstein in Leipzig, informing them of the unparalleled success Joachim had experienced on his London tour under Mendelssohn's baton.[17] And the Wittgenstein family had strong connections to other prominent musicians, the daughters being taught by Clara Schumann.[18]

Hermann Wittgenstein (1802–1878), whom Fanny Figdor had married, was a prosperous wool-merchant in Leipzig, Wagner's home town. The marriage had taken place in Dresden, another Wagner haunt. The number of Jewish families in Dresden and Leipzig at the time was restricted by legislation to about one hundred,[19] so, given that the Wittgensteins were friends of Mendelssohn, Brahms and the Schumanns, it is not impossible – indeed likely – that they had some contact in the small musical community with Wagner as well. In fact if we allow that Joseph Joachim, Fanny Figdor's cousin, whom Monk says Hermann Wittgenstein adopted at the age of twelve, was also a Wittgenstein, then we can be quite certain there was contact, for as we shall see, Wagner hated Joachim above all other German musicians.

Their early relationship appears to have been excellent. Hans von Bulow, in a letter to his mother dated 12 October 1853, wrote:

On Thursday we six young people (Joachim, Cornelius, Pruckner, &c.) travelled with Liszt, the Princess Wittgenstein, Princess Marie, and her cousin Eugen W[ittgenstein] to Basle, where Liszt had made a rendezvous with Wagner. You had written that you were coming to Carlsruhe via Basle, and would arrive there on Saturday. This was sufficient reason for me to come and meet you, and in addition to this you had asked me to address your letters to the *poste restante*. We spent two delightful days there. Liszt drank 'brotherhood' with me in 'Kirschwasser'. On Saturday at midday the Wittgensteins, Liszt, Wagner, Joachim, and I went to Strasburg (the cathedral made such an elevating, unique, and imposing impression on me that I am still happy when I think about it), from whence Joachim and I started on our return journey, first going to Baden-Baden, the others going for ten days to Paris. . . .[20]

It must not escape notice that this passage has Joachim – an adopted Meier-Wittgenstein directly filiated to Ludwig through Fanny Figdor, his grand-mother, travelling together with Princess Sayn-Wittgenstein, the hated adopted mother of Cosima Wagner. In 1843, then, the two Wittgenstein families most assuredly had connections with each other. Indeed, the Sayn-Wittgensteins and the Meier-Wittgensteins had connections to both Wagner and to each other of extraordinary historical importance.

The closeness of Joachim's relationship to Wagner is evident from what Moser then proceeds to reveal. He states that Liszt adopted the intimate 'Du' form of address when speaking with Joachim and continues:

> At Strasburg Richard Wagner read his text of the 'Ring of the Nibelungen' to the circle of Weimar friends. Joachim was so greatly struck with the grandeur of this poem, that in his keen enthusiasm for it he offered the master his services as leader of the violins at the first performance of this powerful work. Wagner, who had already heard of the musical attainments of the young man from Liszt and his friends, was very much taken with his striking personality, and he was now so touched at his offer that he also begged for permission to address him as 'Du'.[21]

The relationship, then, had been very warm, but in *My Life*[22] Wagner relates how the relationship cooled. Jacob Katz, the author of a study of Wagner's anti-Semitism, outlines its degeneration in the following passage, attributing it (as does Wagner) precisely to the effects of Wagner's famous article:

> The variability of Wagner's attitude toward Jews is particularly clear in his fluctuating relations with Joseph Joachim, the great violinist of Jewish origin and one of the most significant virtuosos and productive composers of his time. Joachim belonged to a group of musicians which, assisted by Franz Liszt and Hans von Bulow, had given a festive reception following Wagner's return from Italy to Basel in 1853. In the general liveliness of the gathering Wagner was struck by Joachim's reserve, whereupon Bulow explained to him that Joachim

was self-conscious on account of his 'opinions expressed in that famous article about Judaism'. Joachim had asked Bulow, Wagner wrote, 'at the presentation of one of his compositions . . . with a certain friendly anxiety, whether I [Wagner] would be able to note anything Jewish in that work'. Joachim was one of the Leipzig professors who had protested about the publication of Wagner's article. . . . Wagner for his part found in Joachim's supposed embarrassment a 'touching, indeed moving characteristic', and condescended to placate Joachim with 'particularly sympathetic parting words and a hearty embrace'. At this time Joachim, as an adherent of the Wagnerian artistic trend, was numbered among Wagner's 'exceptional Jews', a position that he completely forfeited with his later change of mind. . . .[23]

An outline of Joachim's career and relationship to Wagner is given in the *New Grove Dictionary of Music and Musicians*:[24]

After the formative years under Mendelssohn, Joachim grew to maturity with his first professional experience as Konzertmeister under Liszt in Weimar in 1850; he also instituted chamber music soirees there in 1851. Much as he admired Liszt and looked to him for guidance, his classical inclinations and training with Mendelssohn eventually led to a conflict of loyalties and, after his appointment in 1852 as violinist to King George V at Hanover, Joachim felt constrained to write to Liszt entirely dissociating himself from Liszt's conception of the new music and its followers. At this time he strengthened his intimate friendship with the Schumanns and formed another vital one with Brahms, who benefited immensely from his advice on orchestration and from hearing Joachim's excellent Hanover quartet play his early chamber works. Mutual admiration for each other's work together with an identity of artistic outlook confirmed their opposition to the new German School, but their famous letter protesting against the 'Music of the Future' merely served to polarize attitudes and distort their estimate of Wagner's music.[25]

What 'famous letter' is the Grove Dictionary referring to here? The 'new German School', of course, was typified by the music of Wagner and Liszt, and its chief opponents were Brahms and Joachim. Schumann had founded a paper, the *Neue Zeitschrift fur Musik* (the same that published Wagner's infamous article), which, under the editorship of Franz Brendel, had turned into a propaganda arm for Wagner, extolling the virtues of his musical romanticism. This journal, on its twenty-fifth anniversary in 1859, published an article claiming that every significant German musician supported the principles of this new German School. The article led to the celebrated letter of protest from Brahms and Joachim in 1860 referred to earlier. Their letter runs:

The undersigned have regretfully followed the aims of a certain faction whose journal is Brendel's *Zeitschrift fur Musik*.

The above-mentioned magazine continually states that serious musicians are basically in agreement with the cause it espouses, that they see work of artistic merit in the creations of the leaders of this faction and that, all in all, especially in North Germany, the arguments for and against the so-called 'music of the future' are settled in their favour.

The undersigned consider it their duty to protest against such falsification of the facts, and state that, as far as they are concerned, they do not recognize Brendel's cause and consider the products of the leaders and followers of the new German school, which partly uphold this cause and partly enforce new and unknown theories, to be contrary to the innermost spirit of music and to be strongly deplored and condemned.

Johannes Brahms
Joseph Joachim
Julius Otto Grimm
Bernhard Scholz[26]

This letter was published in the Berlin *Echo* and was the occasion of some derision, since the thirty-three-year-old Grimm was the only one of the four signatories out of his twenties. Perhaps as a result of this letter, Brahms was passed over for the conductorship of the Hamburg Philharmonic Society and he moved to Vienna in 1862.[27] In Vienna he was made welcome at the home of Karl Wittgenstein (Hermann's son and Ludwig's father) and some of his works were first performed there. The Wittgenstein hospitality extended to Joseph Joachim also. Indeed, Bartley writes:

> In prewar days, the Wittgensteins were prominent patrons of the arts. Gustav Mahler, Bruno Walter, Johannes Brahms, and Clara Schumann frequently visited the Palais Wittgenstein; Joseph Joachim and his quartet often played in its great salon.[28]

That is, Joseph Joachim, whom Wagner initially addressed as 'Du' and came to hate, knew – and was a relative of – the young Ludwig Wittgenstein, who attended school with Adolf Hitler.

Now most historical studies of Wagner and his famous anti-Semitic tract *Das Judenthum in der Musik* focus upon the Jewish composer Meyerbeer as Wagner's great *bête-noir*. Wagner's own words, however, indicate that his greatest hate was not Meyerbeer but rather Joseph Joachim. Thus Jacob Katz, in his study of this matter, writes:

> Wagner's tendency to evaluate men according to whether they were on his side or not is well known. He himself once enumerated the people who 'had deserted

him, such as Brockhausens, Karl Ritter, Willes, Laube, an immense number'. Whereas the accusation of disloyalty here affected only the persons concerned, the defection of Hiller and Joachim was connected with their Jewish origins: 'I am nevertheless glad that of the German musicians two Jews are the most repugnant to me: Hiller and Joachim. What was done to the latter, for example, that he should change from a rapturous enthusiast into a spiteful opponent?'[29]

What indeed? One must suspect that the cause was precisely Wagner's anti-Semitic article. Joachim had converted to Christianity circa 1854, but he felt concerned within himself whether his motive for conversion had been for spiritual or worldly advantage. This comes out in his fine and noble letter to Count Platen of 23 August 1864 in defence of a certain J. Grun, over whose anti-Semitic treatment by the Hanoverian authorities Joachim was to resign his livelihood in 1865:

> In accordance with your Excellency's wish I am writing to you with reference to the conversation concerning Herr Grun, which I had with your Excellency before the beginning of the holidays. I can say with absolute truth that since then I have thought the matter over frequently and conscientiously, as your Excellency recommended – without, however, being able to regard it in any other light.
>
> I could not possibly forget (and I beg to lay great stress on this) that Herr Grun was engaged on behalf of the management *through me*, with the express understanding that he should eventually succeed to the post then occupied by Herr Kompel. If Herr Grun, in spite of his excellent services and fidelity to duty, acknowledged by all his superiors, and after years of patient waiting, is not to be promoted after I have called attention to the matter, *because he is a Jew*, and if, for this reason, the promises made by me on behalf of a higher authority are not fulfilled, then according to my idea of honour and duty, I shall have no alter-native but to justify myself by retiring from my appointment at the same time as Herr Grun. If I remained in my present position after the rejection of Herr Grun I should never be able to get over the purely personal feeling that because I had become a member of the Christian Church I had gained worldly advan-tage and had obtained a privileged position in the Hanoverian Orchestra, whilst others of my race were forced into humiliating situations.[30]

Again, we see that like the devoutly Catholic Princess Wittgenstein, Joseph Joachim/Wittgenstein was an apostate Jew, a Catholic convert. Astonishingly, none of the individuals in the lead-up to the Holocaust we are tracing were Jewish, though they were all of Jewish descent. They might be best described – as was Ludwig Wittgenstein – as descendants, sometimes to the third and fourth generation, of Covenant-breaking fami-lies. It is this unlikely and paradoxical truth that has thrown historians off the scent of what really occurred. Holocaust investigators have focused upon the relation between Jews and the societies in which they lived in order to explain the Holocaust. The relations that really matter, however, concern not Jews, but rather what the societies saw as Jewish infiltration – Jews abandoning Jewishness and becoming indistinguishably part of the societies in question. Thus Hitler's complaint from *Mein Kampf*, quoted in the first chapter, 'Finally he needs only to have himself baptised to possess himself of all the possibilities and rights of the natives of the country. Not seldom he concludes this deal to the joy of the churches over the son they have won and of Israel over the successful swindle.' It is the apostate Jews who matter in this history – the Covenant-breakers – not the Jews themselves.

It is easy to document that Wagner's wife, Cosima, also hated Joachim. She thought of Joachim not just as an apostate Jew but as an apostate Wagnerite. Newman's biography of Wagner contains a passage describing her faint praise of the famous Jewish conductor (and Wagner interpreter) Hermann Levi following Levi's death in 1901, and continues:

> For so upright a Jewish artist as Joachim, however, she could never find a good word, for Joachim had not 'distinguished himself by his great fidelity to Bayreuth'. For Cosima he was always 'the Apostate' who had turned his back on Wagner and Liszt. In 1877, when in London, she saw Watts's masterly portrait of him. 'The whole biography of the excessively vile person,' she wrote, 'lies open to me in this portrait. The painter had no intention of this; and his artistic talent reveals itself precisely by the fact that he has represented the truth without being aware of it, while meaning, indeed, to express something splendid.' When, some years later, she met Joachim's daughters in Bayreuth, she could not fail to admit it as a good point in them that they were interested in Wagner, but still she could not help seeing their race in them: 'I cannot say,' she wrote to a friend, 'that they have anything Germanic about them, but in them the Oriental cast expresses itself in the most singular softness and submissiveness. When I thought of the connections of the father and then looked at these children I was deeply moved, particularly because it occurred to me that the vileness of the ancestors lay like a veil or a check upon the mind and the bent of the children.'[31]

The republication of Wagner's original 1850 tract against Jews was planned by Franz Brendel for 1867.[32] Wagner evidently had some misgivings, but he overcame them following Brendel's death and published the piece, now signed and with a Preface and an Afterword. Unlike his wife Cosima, Wagner did not criticize Joachim by name, but he was nevertheless the target of the Afterword. Katz writes on this:

Joachim's name was not mentioned in the afterword to *Judaism in Music*, but every reader had to know who was meant by 'the falling-away of a hitherto warmly devoted friend, a great violin virtuoso' who had renounced his disciple-ship with the development of the late Wagnerian music.[33]

Wagner's actual words in the passage of the Afterword focus upon the effect of the Brahms/Joachim letter on Franz Liszt, rather than himself, but in fact it was Wagner who had been the target. The 'ambushed enemy' Wagner refers to here are the Jews:

> ... you shall learn how matters went with my greatest friend and warmest advocate, Franz Liszt. Precisely through the splendid self-reliance which he shewed in all his doings, he furnished the ambushed enemy, ever alert for the puniest coign of vantage, with just the weapons they required. What the enemy so urgently wanted, the secreting of the to them so irksome Judaism–question, was quite agreeable to them [sic] as well; but naturally for the converse reason, namely to keep an embittering personal reference aloof from an honest art-dispute – whereas it was the other side's affair to keep concealed the motive of an honest fight, the key to all the calumnies launched-out on us. Thus the ferment of the whole commotion remained unmentioned by our side, too. On the contrary, it was a jovial inspiration of Liszt's, to accept the nickname fastened on us, of '*Zukunftsmusiker*' ('Musicians of the Future'), and adopt it in the sense once taken by the '*Gueux*' of the Netherlands. Clever strokes, like this of my friend's, were highly welcome to the enemy: on this point, then, they hardly needed any more to slander, and the title '*Zukunftsmusiker*' cut out a most convenient path for getting at the ardent, never-resting artist. With this falling-away of an erewhile cordially-devoted friend, a great violin-virtuoso on whom the Medusa-head would seem to have also worked at last, there began that seething agitation against Franz Liszt, who magnanimously heeded no attack, whence'er it came – that agitation which prepared for him the undeception and embitterment wherein at last he put an end for ever to his splendid efforts to found in Weimar a furthering home for Music.[34]

Wagner is saying explicitly here that Joachim's letter was a Jewish plot to get at Liszt and the 'Music of the Future'. Since by this stage of his career the 'Music of the Future' was identified overwhelmingly with Wagner rather than Liszt, Wagner is implying that the Medusa-headed Jewish musical conspiracy used a willing Joachim as its weapon against *him*. (Joachim, incidentally, had been the young leader of the Grand Ducal orchestra at Weimar.) Cosima Wagner's biographer refers to the musical celebrations following the great German victories of 1870 and the effect on Richard and Cosima:

Meanwhile the destiny of Germany was working itself out, and they both followed the progress of events with equal interest and delight. It was under the influence of these that he wrote his *Kaisermarsch*, which he had originally been commissioned to write as a coronation march, but which had taken hold of him more and more as he wrote it. It was certainly a disappointment to him afterwards when he heard what was going on in connexion with the so-called musical celebration of the peace in Berlin, for Joachim and others were at the head of it, and not only were they naturally in opposition to him, but they arranged a festival in which there was no place for him or his works.[35]

Joseph Joachim/Wittgenstein, then, had been sufficiently powerful to exclude Wagner from taking part in the celebration of the great German/Prussian victory over France! And his anti-Wagnerian influence was not something confined to musicians alone, nor even just to the 1870s. It extended to the general German musical public, for the conductor Bruno Walter (who was born in 1876) records of his training at the Berlin Conservatoire as a young man:

Johannes Brahms lived at some distance, in Vienna, but Joseph Joachim, his friend and adherent, was in Berlin. In him, wholly admirable though he was in every other respect, the reactionaries had their most influential representative. The nimbus that long years of masterful accomplishments on the violin and the splendid activity of his quartet had gained him was brightened further by the fame that his leadership had brought to Berlin's Royal Academy. His personal friendship with Schumann and, later, Brahms, and the enmity between him and Wagner clearly and effectively indicated his artistic inclinations. A large part of the musical public, especially the 'classically' minded Public described by me, reverently acknowledged his authority and adopted his likes and dislikes.

Apart from their reactionary tendency, the musical institutes mentioned above were of course deserving of the highest respect and appreciation. Their reputation was known all over the world. From other European countries and from America, a great many students, eager for a thorough musical education and for authentic interpretations and methods, were drawn to Germany which at that time was justly considered the 'mother-country of music'. I remember how interesting I found the babel of languages buzzing round my ear in the anterooms and corridors of the Conservatoire. My first experience of *Tristan* had wholly put me under the spell of Wagner, though I was still a boy at the time. I heard people speak against my ideal and cite Joachim as their authority.[36]

Joachim was *the* great German anti-Wagnerian. Katz, of course, in the passage quoted earlier, failed to draw attention to the Wittgenstein connection – after all, the Wittgensteins, from a Jewish perspective, were not Jews at all and, as a Catholic convert, Joachim's role could be seen as marginal.

But such an attitude is quite wrong. It is now abundantly clear that a specific individual – Joseph Joachim – non-Jewish, but still the target of Wagner's famous anti-Semitic diatribe, was closely connected to Ludwig Wittgenstein. Indeed, this man, acclaimed as the greatest violinist in the world, was his cousin – who grew up in the same house as did Ludwig's father in Leipzig and played music in Ludwig's Vienna home! Bruno Walter recounts his recollections of the Palais Wittgenstein:

Vienna 'society' as a whole saw but little of me. But I should not like to omit mention of the Wittgenstein Palace in Alleegasse. The Wittgensteins continued the noble tradition of those leading Vienna groups who considered it incumbent upon them to further art and the artists. But they were impelled not so much by a sense of duty imposed on them by their prominent social position as by their genuine enthusiasm for art. Brahms had been on friendly terms with the Wittgensteins, and Joachim and his quartet had frequently played at their house. Unless I am mistaken, Brahms's Clarinet Quintet had its first Viennese performance there, the magnificent clarinettist Mühlfeld being the assistant artist. The Wittgenstein house was frequented by musicians as well as by prominent painters and sculptors, and by the leading men from the world of science. Karl Wittgenstein was greatly interested in contemporary art. Klinger's *Beethoven* had found its way to his home from the Sezession Exhibition. Gustav Klimt among other modern painters, was prominently represented in one of the rooms. I was made happy by the fact that the Wittgenstein family had set their affection on me. There was Ludwig Wittgenstein, a brother, with whose extremely musical and charming wife I played music on a number of occasions. There was Clara, a sister, who had undertaken to further the destinies of the Soldat-Roeger Quartet. Whether I dropped in for a friendly visit or we played some chamber music in the *salon* hallowed by tradition I always enjoyed with gratification the all-pervading atmosphere of humanity and culture. Paul, Karl Wittgenstein's son, had lost an arm in the First World War. Nothing daunted, he had by means of assiduous study and energy trained himself until he became an exceptionally accomplished and highly though of one-arm pianist.[37]

The unnamed 'music-Jews' of whom Wagner complained, then, were these very Wittgensteins, who were in fact not Jews at all. Via Joachim, their musical writ ran from Leipzig and Berlin, through Weimar all the way to Vienna. Ludwig Wittgenstein did not merely come from a musical family – as his biographers acknowledge – he came from the very pinnacle of families arbitering German, and thus world, musical taste. And he was at school with Hitler when the role of Princess Wittgenstein in German music was notorious. The last volume of La Mara's collection of the Liszt-Wittgenstein correspondence had appeared in 1902. The scandal was topical. Liszt, Princess Wittgenstein's lover, had also had a well-known affair with Lola Montez, who was mistress of Louis I, king of Bavaria, and who brought about his forced abdication. The staid inhabitants of Linz, in fact, had been recovering, in their grandstand seats across the Bavarian border, from one of the great, and long-running, sexual scandals of the nineteenth century. Liszt, Princess Wittgenstein, Royalty, Romance and Music – what a heady combination!

At school, did Ludwig mention in music class that this Joseph Joachim, of the world-famous Berlin Royal Academy, who opposed the new musical conceptions of Richard Wagner and wrote joint letters with Brahms against Wagner and the 'Music of the Future', was his cousin, adopted uncle and the beneficiary of his family's charity? Did he let slip that Joachim played in his father's salon at home in Vienna and that he knew him? Did Hitler know that the man Wagner believed was the spearhead of the Medusa-headed Jewish musical conspiracy was an adopted Wittgenstein and a close blood relative of Ludwig? Or that Cosima Wagner thought this man to be a vile person and the daughters racially corrupted because Joachim was their father? The insidious corrupting influence that Wagner attributed to Jews had as its exemplar not Jews in general, but rather a Wittgenstein.

I argued earlier that Hitler's anti-Semitism arose, not, as many historians claim, through his reading anti-Semitic pamphlets in Vienna, but rather through a particular interaction with Ludwig Wittgenstein at school around 1904, about whose nature we can only speculate. If this hypothesis is correct, then Hitler's infatuation with Wagner might well have been sustained by a cause not suspected in the histories. I am suggesting, of course, that this cause was Hitler's (reasonable) belief that Wagner, too, hated Wittgensteins; that one at least of them was, in Wagner's own, indisputable words, 'most repugnant' to him. Hitler claimed an intimate acquaintance with Wagner's mental processes[38] and there is no doubt that he made an exhaustive study of his writings, not least the famous anti-Semitic tract. One wonders how many times the young Hitler's ambitions were stimulated by the following passage of the piece, which one can only read with a shudder:

> . . . on one thing I am clear: just as the influence which the Jews have gained upon our mental life – as displayed in the deflection and falsification of our highest culture-tendencies – just as this influence is no mere physiologic accident, so also must it be owned-to as definitive and past dispute. Whether the downfall of our Culture can be arrested by violent ejection of the destructive foreign element, I am unable to decide, since that would require forces with whose existence I am unacquainted.[39]

Hitler's fascination with Wagner, then, might involve the strong belief that Wagner had seen in another, adopted Wittgenstein relative – Joseph Joachim – something that he himself also had seen in Ludwig. The interest of what we have discovered in this investigation is that the murderous pathology of modern German anti-Semitism derives overwhelmingly not from Jews in general, but rather from the reaction of Wagner and Hitler to a single family.

It is now orthodoxy in Holocaust studies to trace the origins of the Holocaust to millennia of European anti-Semitism. It seems quite possible from our investigation, however, that historic anti-Semitism was not the only cause. What brought this general prejudice to a focus in Hitler's mind, what made it a life-long obsession and gave that obsession the emotional power to infect an entire nation, was something with very restricted and altogether different origins. That such a close connection in the objects of Wagner's and Hitler's hates could be dismissed as mere coincidence beggars belief. They were not simply parallel hates, directed at Jews in general, but rather a single entangled web of hatred woven tightly around a single non-Jewish family, whose characteristics were taken to be typical of Jews generally.

FOUR

The Twist of the Investigation

We can move now to deal with the crucially important question I raised in the introduction – Dr Knopfelmacher's hunch about there being a Jewish hand behind Nazi doctrine. Given that Wittgenstein ranks in the select group of very great philosophers (and theorizers about language) and Hitler in the select group of very great and effective ideologists (and users of language) is it possible that Wittgenstein's ideas had some effect upon Hitler as source?

Wittgenstein was beyond doubt a great thinker. While still in his early twenties he was impressing Bertrand Russell – at this stage the world's ranking analytical philosopher – as Russell's superior. We know from the book *Culture and Value* that Wittgenstein thought of himself as one of the greatest of Jewish thinkers and even that he thought the questions that he raised in his philosophizing were 'of a different racial origin, as it were'. This comment about the different racial origin of his philosophical questions was recorded as late as 1948 or 1949 in his *Last Writings on the Philosophy of Psychology*.[1] For a Viennese of Jewish descent to talk of the racial origin of his questions unmindful of Nazi doctrine and the recent extermination of the Jews of Vienna is quite unthinkable. Wittgenstein clearly thought of himself as Jewish (as we know from other sources) but also saw his philosophical method as being distinctively Jewish. To Drury, in 1949, he insisted, 'my thoughts are one hundred percent Hebraic'.[2] Wittgenstein certainly flowered early, and, at least in his own view, the thoughts that constituted this flowering were connected to his Jewish origins; to a mode of thinking that is distinctively Jewish.

We know from *Mein Kampf* two important features of Hitler's thought: first that he hated a 'Jewish doctrine that does away with the personality', and secondly that he had made a great discovery while at the *Realschule*. That great discovery was that 'I learned to understand and grasp the meaning of history.'[3] This appears not to have been just a throwaway line of Hitlerian bombast, for when he was later asked by an intimate about which of the many statements he made in *Mein Kampf* was the most self-revealing, he replied at once: 'A short sentence at the very beginning of the book in which I say that as a youth I learned the meaning of history.'[4] We shall see that Wittgenstein's philosophy of Mind leads naturally and inevitably to an ultra-radical account both of communication and of history. Its exact nature and antecedents have been widely misunderstood, but it was this – Wittgenstein's early insight into the nature of the Mind – that was the source of Hitler's claim to have discovered the meaning of history. And Wittgenstein's theory has quite unappreciated practical consequences which Hitler manipulated in order to seize power. Hitler, I think, in reporting his great discovery, was in this case not being bombastic, but simply stating the truth – as he saw it – about what he had stumbled across. We also know, as we shall see later, that both Hitler and Wittgenstein were strongly affected by Schopenhauer.

Now the currently received account of Hitler's statements in *Mein Kampf* is that the 'Jewish doctrine that does away with the personality', of which he complained, was simply Bolshevism, which Hitler, of course, saw as a Jewish plot. His own 'National Socialism' is interpreted as a racial – and restricted – variation of this universalist doctrine, with certainly Jews but also many other races excluded as well. And his 'discovery of the meaning of history' is interpreted as the view that history is essentially just the struggle of races, with the Jews as parasites upon the heroic Aryan participants.

What I am going to propose here is a quite different interpretation. What is critical for understanding Hitlerian doctrines, I think, is that they are altered – warped – presentations of the thoughts of another man. These original thoughts derive from what has been described – and legitimately described – as a 'mystical experience' of the young Ludwig Wittgenstein. Once the true nature of this mystical experience is divined, I believe, both Wittgenstein's philosophy and the origins of Nazi doctrine lie unveiled before us.

Wittgenstein, late in 1948, said to Drury, 'My fundamental ideas came to me very early in life.'[5] If he described them as 'fundamental ideas' then one must expect them to feature in both his early work and his later work. Wittgensteinian commentators present Wittgenstein's later work as a wholesale rejection of the philosophy that he had developed as a young man and published in the *Tractatus*. But whatever Wittgenstein described in 1948 as his 'fundamental ideas' must have endured until then from the time of their discovery 'very early in life'. Whatever Wittgenstein had in mind, he did not describe them as his 'early errors' but as 'fundamental ideas'.

Is there any doctrine that endured unchanged from his early work before the Great War through to his last writings in the 1950s? There is at least one unvarying feature of Wittgenstein's philosophy: it concerns his account of the self – the subject of experience. Here is his view of the self from before the Great War: 'The thinking, presenting subject; there is no such thing . . . in an important sense there is no subject.'[6] In the 1930s he is known to have espoused what Sir Peter Strawson has called the 'no-ownership theory' of the mind. Exactly what this involves will be shown later, but in essence – and like his view in the *Tractatus* – it denies the existence of multiple individual subjects of experience. The common-sense view is that each person has a mind, so the number of minds is the same as the number of people. The 'no-ownership' theory denies this. I shall document later that this same 'no-ownership' view is still present in Wittgenstein's last writings. Experiences are not private, so goes the fundamental doctrine of his later work, just because there are no multiple minds.

If the argument I shall present holds good, then throughout Wittgenstein's life he adhered to a view on which the individual subject of experience – the isolated consciousness – was somehow done away with. This does sound a little, does it not, like Hitler's complaint about a Jewish doctrine that does away with the personality?

I shall argue that Hitler took this early philosophical idea of Wittgenstein's and modified it so as to exclude Wittgenstein and all those like him – i.e. Jews. Nazi metaphysics, as discernible in Hitler's writings, I shall suggest, is nothing but Wittgenstein's theory of the mind modified so as to exclude the race of its inventor. In the Nazi mutation, there is not one, universal, unowned mind for all human beings; there is, however, a single Aryan mind, shared by all of the correct race. I am not suggesting that Hitler adhered to the doctrine on intellectual grounds or that he might have been able to defend it in, say, a Cambridge philosophy seminar. But Hitler, I think, shared the mystical insight of the early Wittgenstein, which Wittgenstein clothed in its logical shrouds only later. The logical shrouds are not the doctrine and they serve only to obscure it. If Wittgenstein's thought really was 'one hundred percent Hebraic' as he said, and the complaint of history's greatest Jew-killer was against a Jewish doctrine that does away with the personality, then its possible origins at the *Realschule* must be investigated.

I shall be arguing that National Socialism was not a restricted, racial variant of Bolshevism; it was a restricted, racial version of what one might call Mental Socialism – that is, of Wittgenstein's no-ownership theory of the mind.

Let us begin our labour with the German philosopher Arthur Schopenhauer, who was the first philosophical influence upon

Wittgenstein and from whom Hitler admitted that he 'learned a great deal'. With Schopenhauer, we see a rudimentary form of Wittgenstein's doctrine: the Will is universal and unowned. (For Wittgenstein, *all* mental faculties are unowned; the attack on the idea of 'mental privacy' being virtually his philosophical life's work.)

In the preface to the first edition of *The World as Will and Idea*, Schopenhauer wrote the following:

> I propose to state here how this book is to be read, in order that it may be thoroughly understood. What is to be imparted by it is a single thought. Yet in spite of all my efforts, I have not been able to find a shorter way of imparting that thought than the whole of this book. I consider this thought to be that which has been sought for a very long time under the name of philosophy, and that whose discovery is for this very reason regarded by those versed in history as just as impossible as the discovery of the philosopher's stone, although Pliny had already said to them: How many things are considered impossible until they are actually done![7]

I have chosen this quote from Schopenhauer because, despite its enormous presumption, it asserts something that I believe might well be true. That is, that there is a single thought, the grasping of which is the key to all philosophical problems. I mean this quite literally, in just the sense that a physicist might say that Newton's inverse square law is the thought that unlocks the secrets of celestial motion, or a biologist that the way to understand inheritance is via the structure of DNA. It is not that the inverse square law or DNA's molecular structure of themselves answer any cosmological or genetic question, but in each field these are the root concepts, whose application does answer these questions, often routinely. This 'single thought' was worked upon, and its explanatory power outlined, by Schopenhauer over the course of his adult life. He convinced, among others, Richard Wagner, who adopted Schopenhauer's philosophy as his own.

Schopenhauer applied this thought to account for a wide variety of phenomena. And he wrote that it had two aspects; theoretical and practical. As we shall see, the theoretical aspect was what Wittgenstein developed and extended. The practical aspect was seized upon by Hitler.

Hitler is on record as saying, 'I carried Schopenhauer's works with me throughout the whole of the First World War. From him I learned a great deal.'[8] Hitler's secretary reported after the Second World War that he quoted Schopenhauer from memory 'by the page'. Maser records:

During the latter part of 1913 his landlord Josef Popp often found him reading the works of Schopenhauer and Plato, the former being the philosopher to whom Hitler is known to have referred more often than to any other. He would praise his style, knew by heart passages from his writings and would sometimes quote them without any indication of their provenance. According to Hans Frank, Hitler told him that even during the First World War he had never been without the Reclam pocket edition of *The World as Will and Idea*. This story would seem to be corroborated by the statement of a fellow-soldier, Hans Mend, to the effect that Hitler spent a great deal of time reading Reclam books during off-duty periods in the line.[9]

It is not any part of Hitler's public image now to think of him as philo-sophically literate. He is regarded as essentially just an evil, mountebank mob-orator, with a very limited intellect. But the following thought must strike the reflective reader: How many of our contemporary politicians could quote pages of Schopenhauer, or indeed, any philosopher, off by heart? Are there any? And perhaps the further thought might then come: How many professors of Philosophy could do it? Knowing something by rote is no guarantee of understanding, of course, but on the other hand, it is certainly evidence of understanding, particularly in an adult. Hitler was evidently so struck by Schopenhauer's philosophy that he committed pages of it to memory. My own bet is that Hitler had as deep an understanding of Schopenhauer's philosophy as any man alive. Hitler knew his Schopenhauer, and I suspect, had also learned something very important from Wittgenstein.

But what, in Schopenhauer's wide-ranging writings, was Hitler's specific interest? He quotes Schopenhauer's anti-Semitic statements, of course (as he does those of Luther and others), but these hardly amount to more than a few paragraphs in total. Quite certainly Hitler had an interest in Schopenhauer's metaphysics of the Will. But it seems to me to be a more likely hypothesis (which I shall attempt to justify in the course of what follows) that Hitler's prime interest in Schopenhauer's writings was not the philosophy so much, but rather in how the theory of the Will underpinned Schopenhauer's account of the occult.

Schopenhauer used his 'single thought' not just to expound the nature of philosophy: he also used it to expound the nature of magic (which he believed was efficacious) in the chapter 'Animal Magnetism and Magic' of his work *On the Will in Nature*.[10] Now Hitler, too, had a more than passing interest in the occult. This can be documented from many sources, but I offer in particular support a remarkable poem by him, dating to the Great War:

I often go on bitter nights
To Wotan's oak in the quiet glade
With dark powers to weave a union –
The runic letters the moon makes with its magic spell
And all who are full of impudence during the day
Are made small by the magic formula!
They draw shining steel – but instead of going into combat
They solidify into stalagmites.
So the false ones part from the real ones –
I reach into the nest of words
And then give to the good and just
With my formula blessings and prosperity.[11]

This remarkable and disturbing poem – if it is genuinely Hitler's own – indicates some level of familiarity with rune magic. The poet reports reading runes in the pattern of moonlight through the oak foliage – perhaps in shadows on the ground. It would be natural for a poet with such interests to concern himself with how Schopenhauer dealt with the occult.

Schopenhauer's philosophy, then, has a sort of flip side, that is ignored by his modern expositors.[12] He thought that, in accounting for the Will, he thereby also had stumbled across the correct account of occult phenomena. I shall show that both Hitler's ideology and Wittgenstein's philosophy stem from Schopenhauer's doctrine of the Will, but whereas Wittgenstein's use of Schopenhauer's insight was theoretical, Hitler's use was of this practical flip side. Indeed Schopenhauer even explains his use of the words 'practical metaphysics' by giving the designation:

. . . *practical metaphysics*, the term which Bacon in his classification of the sciences (*Instauratio Magna* L. III) used to designate magic: it is empirical or experimental metaphysics.[13]

Whichever use we consider, whether theoretical or practical, and whatever our beliefs about the efficacy of magic, the effects of Schopenhauer's thought upon us all have been profound.

Wittgenstein, from his early days a Schopenhaurian, returned to Cambridge, and philosophy, in 1929. He informed his Cambridge pupils that he had made a great discovery of a new 'method of doing philosophy'. He continued by saying that the 'nimbus of philosophy, had been lost and that

there was now, in philosophy, a 'kink' in 'the development of human thought', comparable to that which occurred when Galileo and his contemporaries invented dynamics; that a 'new method' had been discovered, as had happened when 'chemistry was developed out of alchemy'; and that it was now possible for the first time that there should be 'skilful' philosophers, though of course there had in the past been 'great' philosophers.[14]

My account of the relation between Schopenhauer and Wittgenstein is that Wittgenstein's philosophy of mind (the 'no-ownership theory' described in the young Peter Strawson's book, *Individuals*)[15] is an application to all mental phenomena of the way that Schopenhauer treated the Will – as unitary and undivided throughout space and time; not multiplied according to the number of men, each of whom exercises his own will – and hence not 'private'. It is the working out of Schopenhauer's 'single thought' – indeed it *is* Schopenhauer's 'single thought'. For just as in Schopenhauer the Will is not 'private', so in Wittgenstein no mental phenomenon at all is 'private'. On the face of it, Wittgenstein's position does sound like a generalization of Schopenhauer's own, does it not?

The idea occurs in Emerson's *Essays*. McGuinness, Wittgenstein's biographer, remarks that while these days the *Essays* are read for style, Wittgenstein read them for their content, and that they open with a favourite thought of Wittgenstein's early days, that

> There is one mind common to all individual men. Every man is an inlet to the same and to all of the same.[16]

Now Emerson's essay is of particular interest for us because it ties together a no-ownership theory of the mind ('one mind common to all individual men') with a quite peculiar philosophy of history. We, of course, are on notice to look for any such link because of Hitler's claim about his discovery of the meaning of history at the *Realschule*.

Something like a no-ownership theory of mind might lie behind a remark Hitler made during a table conversation of 13 December 1941, that 'mind and soul undoubtedly return . . . to a general reservoir. Thus we are the basic material that fertilizes the stock from which new life springs.'[17] Maser comments that 'Hitler's "stock from which new life springs" corresponds to Plato's "world soul". The principle that moves the universe, the power that moves all things, the ideal entity and world-consciousness.' It does indeed seem to correspond to Plato, but there is another, modern philosopher, who is at least as likely a source here as Plato, for Wittgenstein was also concerned with the 'world soul'. He referred to this 'world soul' – the *anima mundi* – in his *Notebooks*:

There really is only one world soul, which I for preference call *my* soul and as which alone I conceive what I call the souls of others.[18]

What else did Emerson have to say on this world soul – the common mind? He had rather a lot to say, but the core of what he says is that whoever has access to this common mind is alone able to read the riddle of history. Here is the continuation of the brief extract from Emerson's paper that McGuinness quoted:

> There is one mind common to all individual men. Every man is an inlet to the same and to all of the same. He that is once admitted to the right of reason is made a freeman of the whole estate. What Plato has thought he may think; what a saint has felt he may feel; what at any time has befallen any man, he can under-stand. Who hath access to this universal mind is a party to all that is or can be done, for this is the only and sovereign agent.
> Of the works of this mind history is the record. . . .
> This human mind wrote history, and this must read it. The Sphinx must solve her own riddle. If the whole of history is in one man, it is all to be explained from individual experience. . . .
> Of the universal mind each man is one more incarnation.[19]

We shall find this idea of a universal, unowned mind to be curiously recurrent in human history. There is no doubt, judging from the Hindu scriptures, that it was the original religious doctrine of the early Aryans. In Judaism, on the other hand, while God might speak through the prophets, the prophets do not become God, and indeed the idea that a man could be God is an abomination. In Indian – i.e. Aryan – religions, on the contrary, realization of the identity between the individual and the Divine is the very goal of religious practice. What the Aryan aspires to, the Jew abhors as the supreme impiety. And even today, this ancient Aryan doctrine issues forth from the mouths of anti-Semites.

Here is this doctrine as it occurs in a lecture given by the mathematician I. R. Shafarevitch (a leading Soviet dissident during the Brezhnev repres-sions and Russia's most prominent anti-Semite), on his receiving a prize from the Gottingen Academy of Science:

> A superficial glance at mathematics may give an impression that it is a result of separate individual efforts of many scientists scattered about in continents and in ages. However, the inner logic of its development reminds one much more of the work of a single intellect, developing its thought systematically and consis-tently using the variety of human individualities only as a means. It resembles an orchestra performing a symphony composed by someone. A theme passes

from one instrument to another, and when one of the participants is bound to drop his part, it is taken up by another and performed with irreproachable precision.

This is by no means a figure of speech. The history of mathematics has known many cases when a discovery made by one scientist remains unknown until it is later reproduced by another with striking precision. In the letter written on the eve of his fatal duel, Galois made several assertions of paramount importance concerning integrals of algebraic functions. More than twenty years later Riemann, who undoubtedly knew nothing about the letter of Galois, found anew and proved exactly the same assertions. Another example: after Lobachevski and Bolyai laid the foundation of non-Euclidean geometry independently of one another, it became known that two other men, Gauss and Schweikart, also working independently, had both come to the same results ten years before. One is overwhelmed by a curious feeling when one sees the same designs as if drawn by a single hand in the work done by four scientists quite independently of one another.[20]

What Shafarevitch says here about mathematics, as the product of a single intellect expressing itself through a variety of human instruments, is, as I shall demonstrate, Wittgenstein's idea of language in general. In Wittgenstein's philosophy, language (not merely the Will) uses its human instruments as vehicles for its own expression. It is not, as we naively think, a person who says something, but rather the proposition – language itself – that says something, through the mouth of a person. Anglo-Saxon readers, doubtful that Shafarevitch counts as a respectable lineage for the doctrine, might be surprised to find Coleridge expressing the same idea:

> And what if all of animated nature
> Be but organic harps diversely fram'd,
> That tremble into thought, as o'er them sweeps
> Plastic and vast, one intellectual breeze,
> At once the Soul of each and God of all?[21]

Now despite Wittgenstein claiming that his thought was one hundred per cent Hebraic, on this one crucial issue his thought was one hundred per cent *non*-Hebraic, for via Schopenhauer, he adopted this ancient Aryan doctrine – the supreme Jewish blasphemy – as his own.[22] In Hitler, as I shall demonstrate, the unitary Will of Schopenhauer is split on racial lines – he thought there really was a single Aryan racial will, whose self-conscious realization of its own nature was in himself. He feared that this original Aryan doctrine of a single racial will was being parasitized by Jewish internationalism – externally the doctrine of the brotherhood of man, but metaphysically the no–ownership theory. And his discovery of the Aryan racial mind and its relation to history, philosophy and race was made while he was attending the *Realschule* with Wittgenstein. What, then, is this strange and obscure doctrine I am claiming Wittgenstein expounded? Surprisingly, it is best approached through the religions of the Aryan invaders of India, who gave us both a mystical doctrine of the nature of the self and the Swastika.

FIVE

Mystical Experience and the Self

Wagner's intended last opera – *The Victors* – was to have been on the life of Buddha, interpreted from the perspective of Schopenhauer's philosophy. Schopenhauer propounded the curious idea that Buddhism, rather than Judaism, was the original source of Christianity, and he outlined a sort of Aryan Christianity, whose nature Paul Rose presents as follows:

> . . . there is one important idea in his revolutionary approach to religion that was to resound in the writings of Wagner and other racial determinists. This is the idea of a restored 'Aryan Christianity' – the original Christianity having been distortedly associated with Judaism in the course of history. In one essay, Schopenhauer remarks that, except for its attitude to animals, Christian morality comes close to his adored Buddhism: 'We can scarcely doubt that like the idea of a god become man, the Christian morality originates from India and may have come to Judaea by way of Egypt so that Christianity would be a reflected splendour of the primordial light of India from the ruins of Egypt – but unfortunately it fell on Jewish soil. . . .
>
> For Schopenhauer, the only authentically Jewish religious ideas are the pernicious ones of optimism, rationalism and free will; anything positive had been filched by the Jews from others. For instance, the nobly pessimistic concept of the Fall was taken from the Persians. In fact, 'Judaism' proper, he asserts, was invented only after Cyrus had liberated the Judean captives of Babylon: previously the Jews had worshipped Baal and Moloch! Christianity, however, is Aryan in origin and has nothing in common with the (Semitic) delusions of the Jews: 'The New Testament, on the other hand, must somehow be of Indian origin. . . . Christ's teaching sprung from Indian wisdom has covered the old and quite different trunk of Judaism. . . . Everything that is true in Christianity is found also in Buddhism and Brahminism.' Any actual historical connection of the Jews with the origins of Christianity is explained away thus: 'We should have to assume that the religious and moral elements in Christianity were put together by Alexandrian Jews acquainted with Indian and Buddhist doctrines.'

The impact of Schopenhauer's metaphysical revolutionary anti–Semitism on Wagner was immediate, and Wagner's correspondence of the 1850s shows that he grasped the anti-Jewish potential of the whole Schopenhauerian system, especially its conception of a de-Judaized 'Aryan Christianity'. This rapid recognition of Schopenhauer's genius was made easier by the fact, as he himself explained, that his idol was expressing coherently notions that he himself had long intuited. One detailed example was the idea of the Christian Grail, which Wagner had already adduced in his 'Wibelungen' essay of 1849 as an allegory of the racial Aryan character of Christianity.[1]

Such was 'Aryan Christianity' – anti-Semitic in the extreme and totally in accord with the unsustainable doctrine of Houston Stewart Chamberlain that Jesus was not a Jew. Rose continues, some pages later, with a further outline:

The Schopenhauerian complex of ardently anti-Jewish notions – Aryan Christianity, Jewish cruelty to animals, the need for a renouncing Mitleid to redeem men from Jewish materialism and egoism – rapidly found artistic expression in Wagner's operatic plans of the 1850s, not only in *Tristan* but also in the drafts for *The Conquerors* (*Die Sieger*) and *Parsifal*, and even in the seemingly Teutonic *Götterdämmerung*. These works were all sketched out or developed conflatedly during 1856-8 in the aftermath of Wagner's exposure to Schopenhauer. *The Conquerors* told a story of the Buddha in terms of renunciation and reincarnation – the fundamentals of Aryan Christianity. This subject was closely bound up with the first scenario of *Parsifal*. Wagner had been struck by the medieval Christian poem in 1845 but it was only the Schopenhauerian revelation of Buddhist sympathy for animals that gave him the inspiration for his own individual treatment of the theme in 1857: the Buddhist/Aryan Parsifal 'takes the animals' incomplete existence upon himself and becomes the world's redeemer' – this was Wagner's novel explanation of what became the Good Friday Music in the finished opera. Kundry's peculiar history of transformations in the opera may also be read as a case of reincarnations, while Parsifal's ritual of the Grail stems not from the Eucharist of 'Jewish' Christianity but from a purer Aryan Christian source. As to *Götterdämmerung*, Wagner placed his thoughts on changing its ending to a more Schopenhauerian 'renunciatory' one in the same notebook in which he jotted down *The Conquerors* in May 1856. Of course, the Jews *per se* are not mentioned in these drafts and finished works. As with *Jesus of Nazareth*, they do not need to be attacked directly since the anti-Jewish message impregnates the entire conception of the drama. Buddhism and Aryan Christianity, renunciation and self-destruction, were by definition non-Jewish, and any opera on these subjects was *ipso facto* a repudiation of Judaism. . . .[2]

We can imagine that the climactic moment of *The Victors* would have been the Enlightenment, following the night's meditation which Buddha

entered upon with his hand touching the earth as a visible sign of his resolution to succeed in his great endeavour. The musical build-up to this
through the meditative night, and its musical resolution in the Great
Enlightenment, might have rivalled the famous chord in *Tristan und Isolde*
– who knows? The theme is certainly worthy material for a great opera. It
was never written, but Wagner chose the theme because of his reading of
Schopenhauer, who strongly endorsed what he understood to be the metaphysics of self-transcendence behind Buddhism.

What exactly was this metaphysics? Whatever it was, it was no mere end-
of-life conversion for Wagner. As is clear from his prose writings about
Schopenhauer, it is discernible in other of his operas. Michael Tanner, for
example, identifies it in *Tristan und Isolde*, and expounds Wagner's
Schopenhaurian metaphysics as follows:

> In the centre of the work, at the climax of the most famous part of the so-called
> love duet, 'O sink hernieder, Nacht der Lieb' (Oh sink upon us, night of love),
> the lovers sing together, 'selbst dann bin ich die Welt' (then I myself am the
> world), an astoundingly audacious claim, which means that they have expanded
> to embrace everything, or everything has contracted to satisfy their joint solip-
> sism. One might have expected, given that they were going to be so extravagant,
> that they would say 'we' rather than 'I', and if they were only a little less extra-
> ordinary that is what they would have said. But Wagner gives them the logic of
> their convictions: if each of them is the world, then they are one another. That,
> too, is something from which they don't flinch, as they move on to the final
> stretch of the duet, and do indeed exchange names, that is identities, building
> up on wave after wave of orchestral sound, in what is without competition as the
> longest, most extreme climax in music. . . .[3]

That is, the lovers sing together 'selbst dann bin ich die Welt' (then I
myself am the world).[4] We have here a statement in song of
Schopenhauer's metaphysics – as interpreted by Wagner – in which the
individual self falls away. How might this tie in, as Wagner thought it did,
to Buddhist ideas of renunciation?

The great doctrine revealed by Buddha after the Enlightenment was the
means to deliverance from suffering; and its essence – the Anatta doctrine
– involved some sort of realization that the subject of experience – the self
– did not exist. We have already noted a similar-sounding doctrine in the
first book of the young Wittgenstein, the *Tractatus*. And the last sections of
the *Tractatus* are shot through with a very strange logical mysticism,
perhaps the most striking feature of the book. We read there about the Self,
for example, the vatic pronouncements that

5.621   The world and life are one.

5.63   I am my world. (The microcosm.)

5.631   The thinking, presenting subject; there is no such thing.

If I wrote a book 'The world as I found it', I should also have therein to report on my body and say which members obey my will and which do not, etc. This then would be a method of isolating the subject or rather of showing that in an important sense there is no subject: that is to say, of it alone in this book mention could *not* be made.

5.632   The subject does not belong to the world but it is a limit of the world.

5.633   *Where in* the world is a metaphysical subject to be noted?

You say that this case is altogether like that of the eye and the field of sight. But you do *not* really see the eye.

And from nothing *in the field of sight* can it be concluded that it is seen from an eye.

5.6331   For the field of sight has not a form like this:[5]

And in the next comment but one, we read, 'Here we see that solipsism strictly carried out coincides with pure realism. The I in solipsism shrinks to an extensionless point and there remains the reality co-ordinated with it.' This, and Wittgenstein's earlier comment 'I am my world', sounds, of course, very like the lovers of Wagner's opera singing, in the insight that love has brought them, 'selbst dann bin ich die Welt'. In fact the doctrine here does not merely sound the same; it is, I am arguing, the very same doctrine, traceable in both Wagner and Wittgenstein, through their joint philosophical source Schopenhauer – and thus to oriental mysticism as interpreted by Schopenhauer. Wittgenstein even recorded the following archetypically Indian thought on 23 May 1915, in his *Notebooks*: 'There really is only one world soul, which I for preference call *my* soul. . . .' That Wittgenstein's interest in these matters was no mere flash-in-the-pan youthful infatuation with Schopenhauer is also clear, for it is clearly expressed in many of the comments faithfully recorded in the late 1920s by notables of the Vienna Circle such as Moritz Schlick. The Vienna Circle was largely composed of logical positivists of left-wing political orientation and its entirely negative view of 'bourgeois mysticism' followed the Communist Party line. Ray Monk's biography of Wittgenstein offers the following, on the reception of Wittgenstein and his *Tractatus* by the mysticism-hating Vienna Circle, quoting the philosopher Rudolf Carnap:

> . . . I had erroneously believed that his attitude to metaphysics was similar to ours. I had not paid sufficient attention to the statements in his book about the mystical, because his feeling and thoughts in this area were too divergent from mine. Only personal contact with him helped me to see more clearly his attitude at this point.[6]

Sometimes, Monk says, Wittgenstein would turn his back on the Positivists and read them the poetry of Rabindranath Tagore, the Bengali mystic, whose play, *King of the Dark Chamber*, proved sufficient inspiration to later have Wittgenstein and his student, Yorick Smythies, produce their own version in colloquial English.[7]

Wittgenstein saw Tagore's poetry as directly related in content to the central themes of the *Tractatus*. Tagore, of course, was a devout Hindu, and his work is permeated by Hindu mysticism, in which the goal of religious practice is to realize the identity of the individual soul with the world soul, the same idea that Wittgenstein had written in the *Notebooks* on 23 May 1915. In Hinduism, the individual Atman turns out, at the moment of supreme religious realization, to be identical with Brahman. In the other great oriental religion, Buddhism, the supreme realization is presented slightly differently as discovery of the non-existence of the Atman – the individual soul – in the first place. The denial of the existence of the Atman is in fact a defining doctrine of the Buddhist faith, described (from the Pali language of Ceylon, in which the earliest Buddhist scriptures have been preserved) as the Anatta (no Atman) doctrine. Since Wagner's own focus was Buddhism, rather than Hinduism, we shall attend a little more closely to mysticism and the Anatta doctrine.

The goal of Buddhist practice is a state known as 'enlightenment' or 'illumination'. It is clearly describable as a 'mystical' experience and it is intimately connected with a belief in the non-existence of the individual self. Descriptions of exactly what enlightenment is – as opposed to what it is not – are extremely rare in the modern literature,[8] but there is a flourishing literature on the meditative practices that are necessary for its production. English translations of Buddhist texts have tended to describe these meditative states by the word 'trance', with all its connotations of hypnosis, passivity and lack of full awareness. In both Buddhist and Hindu texts, however, these states are not viewed like that at all.

Two of the original Sanscrit terms applied here are *dhyana* and *samadhi*, each with a quite precise application, and neither really cognate to the English 'trance'.[9] In English, one thinks of a trance as involving a dulling of consciousness, or of a state akin to hypnosis. It is clear from the oriental scriptures, however, that *dhyana* and *samadhi* are intended to cover what we might metaphorically call *super*-conscious states. With these terms, we appear to have the beginnings of a classification or typology of the intense and clear focusing of the mind that is alleged to arise from meditative practices. In the Japanese Zen tradition, the goal of meditative practice is labelled *satori* where *satori*, from its descriptions in English translation, would appear to be some sort of momentary revelatory ecstasy. (The very word 'Zen' is a translation, via a Chinese equivalent, of this Sanscrit word *dhyana*.)[10] At least one reputable Buddhist writer has portrayed dhyana and *satori* as an experience of unity both with what one is perceiving and with the world, in which one has no feeling of being a separate subject in a world of objects. Thus Suzuki: '. . . there is in satori no differentiation of subject and object'.[11]

What this might mean is none too clear, but similar-sounding descriptions are not unknown in the West. Graham Reed, for example, writes of a schizophrenic, who, on observing a carpet being beaten, asked, 'Why are they beating me?'[12] And Masters and Houston quote a participant in a psychedelic drug experiment reporting afterwards that

> The world is experienced as a physical extension of oneself, of one's own nervous system. Consequently I felt the blows of pick axes wielded by construction men tearing up the street. . . .[13]

Clearly something very odd is being reported about the subject/object link here: neither subject had any sense of being confined within his skin. In another experiment, this time with psilocybin, one of the subjects reported:

> There was no duality between myself and what I experienced. Rather I *was* these feelings . . . At this time it seemed I was not M.R. listening to a recording, but paradoxically was the music itself.[14]

A reader versed in the literature of comparative mysticism might doubt (probably too quickly) that the experiences reported here have anything to do with oriental mysticism. A jaundiced reader might even dismiss the subjects in these cases as either mad or deranged by drugs. But non-pathological descriptions of similar-sounding experiences are quite easy to find. The poet T. S. Eliot, for example, after writing of the apprehension of reality granted to the saints, regrets that

> For most of us, there is only the unattended
> Moment, the moment in and out of time,
> The distraction fit, lost in a shaft of sunlight,
> The wild thyme unseen, or the winter lightning
> Or the waterfall, or music heard so deeply
> That it is not heard at all, but you are the music
> While the music lasts.[15]

For Eliot, unity with the heard sound is attributed to the listener being somehow lost in listening, other things being unable to intrude upon the depth of contemplative rapture. The state is well enough known to have been given its own label in at least one European language, the Germans calling it *Einfühlung*.[16] Eliot was far from being alone in English literature in writing of the experience. Indeed, this theme, often allied with an unsystematized nature mysticism, is so common in Romantic poetry that it might be said almost to infest it.[17] Abrams, in describing this characteristic of Romantic poetry, stresses

> the extraordinary weight that other romantic poets, as well as Coleridge and Wordsworth, placed on the experience of *Einfühlung*, or loss of distinction between self and external scene. E.g. Shelley, 'On Life', *Literary and Philosophical Criticism*, p. 56: 'Those who are subject to the state called reverie, feel as if their nature were dissolved into the surrounding universe, or as if the surrounding universe were absorbed into their being. They are conscious of no distinction.'[18]

Indeed not. Here is the idea as it expresses itself through Byron:

> My altars are the mountains and the Ocean,
> Earth – air – stars, – all that springs from the great Whole,
> Who hath produced, and will receive the Soul.[19]

In Byron, this theme of unity with the universe – as it informs *Childe Harolde* in particular – becomes something oceanic, as in the following:

> I live not in myself, but I become
> Portion of that around me; and to me

> High mountains are a feeling, but the hum
> Of human cities torture: I can see
> Nothing to loathe in nature, save to be
> A link reluctant in a fleshly chain,
> Class'd among creatures, when the soul can flee,
> And with the sky, the peak, the heaving plain
> Of ocean, or the stars, mingle, and not in vain
>
> And thus I am absorb'd. . . .[20]

And again:

> Are not the mountains, waves and skies
> a part of me and of my soul, as I of them?[21]

Or yet again

> . . . I steal
> From all I may be, or have been before,
> To mingle with the Universe.[22]

Byron's lines are of importance to us because both Wittgenstein and Hitler came across them, quoted for their descriptive, explanatory power, when they read Schopenhauer's *World as Will and Idea*.[23] In a little while we will have cause to re-examine the crucial section 34 of Schopenhauer's book.

Now various passages in Wittgenstein's early work convey this very thought of Schopenhauer's.[24] In these passages, the subject is not seen as confined to a body. Thus:

> The philosophical I is not the human being, not the human body or the human soul with the psychological properties, but the metaphysical subject, the boundary (not a part) of the world. The human body, however, my body in particular, is a part of the world among others, among animals, plants, stones, etc, etc.
>
> Whoever realizes this will not want to procure a pre-eminent place for his own body. . . .[25]

Wittgenstein is saying here that the 'philosophical I', unlike the body, is not one 'among others'. Let me now juxtapose two quotations, one from Schopenhauer (the same section 34 from which Byron's lines were taken) and one from a lecture by L. E. J. Brouwer, the great twentieth-century Dutch philosopher/mathematician. Schopenhauer writes that it is possible to so perceive things that we devote the whole power of our mind to perception, sink ourselves completely therein, and let our whole consciousness be filled by the calm contemplation of the natural object actually present, whether it be a landscape, a tree, a rock, a crag, a building, or anything else. We *lose* ourselves entirely in the object, to use a pregnant expression; in other words, we forget our individuality, our will, and continue to exist only as pure subject, as clear mirror of the object, so that it is as though the object alone existed without anyone to perceive it, and thus we are no longer able to separate the perceiver from the perception, but the two have become one, since the entire consciousness is filled and occupied by a single image of perception.[26]

This is a description by a Western writer (who would appear to have experienced it) of a contemplative state that sounds, in its consequences for the subject/object link, very much like what the orientals call *dhyana*. Whether we call it *dhyana* or *Einfühlung* does not really matter, since its nature is clear. I am not arguing here that these variously named states are identical in all respects. I am simply using descriptions from the considerable literature on them to outline what seems to be common in states that transcend or obliterate the subject/object distinction. The point is that in Schopenhauer's description we are dealing with a report of a subject/object-transcending experience that is central in his philosophy – his own experimental evidence for it, as it were. It would appear to be more than just a bit of florid prose that Schopenhauer dashed off while in an extravagant mood.[27] He was on to something important about the mind that these states appear to make evident. The relevance of this to the previous quotes from Eliot, etc is in any case apparent and of itself justifies further examination. Now compare this with Brouwer:

> . . . it is possible at will either to sink into a reverie, taking no stand in time and making no separation between self and the eternal world, or else to effect such a separation by one's own effort. . . .[28]

Why are these two quotes significant? Of course they express the same idea; the idea of a unification of subject and object that I have been labouring to convince the reader is important. But the claim in Brouwer's case was made in one of his lectures in Vienna that Wittgenstein attended on 10 March 1928, along with the Vienna Circle philosophers, Herbert Feigl and Friedrich Waismann. At this stage Wittgenstein had been away from academic philosophy since his time in Cambridge before the Great War – some fifteen years. But Feigl tells us that Wittgenstein came forth from the lecture on fire, in a fever of intellectual excitement.[29] In Feigl's opinion, this lecture of Brouwer's marked the return of Wittgenstein to philosophical activities. But why should Wittgenstein have been so excited? Certainly there was the anticipation of Brouwer's remark in Schopenhauer's work, which Wittgenstein knew, but why should what Brouwer said in this lecture have been so important?

He was excited because he had had this experience himself. In fact he had based his philosophy upon it.[30] This was the fundamental insight he spoke of to Drury – the one that he said came to him very early in life.[31] It sounds identical with the youthful experience of Wordsworth that inspired the *Prelude* and that was the concern of Coleridge and of so many other English poets. It was the great concern of Schopenhauer. It was the great concern of Wagner. And it is the Rosetta Stone that unlocks the secrets of Nazism. What Wittgenstein glimpsed was, I believe, shared with, accepted, but perverted, by Adolf Hitler.

The pioneer studies of Wittgenstein's early mysticism were made by Erich Heller in *Encounter* and by Wittgenstein's biographer, Brian McGuinness, in a paper in the *Philosophical Review*.[32] McGuinness convincingly documents that Wittgenstein underwent the unitive experience we have been considering. That he did follows in any case as a reasonable deduction from Wittgenstein's own words. McGuinness informs us that the trigger for Wittgenstein's experience of unity appears to have been a scene in a play he saw. In this play (*Die Kreuzelschreiber* by Ludwig Anzengreuber) a character, after being depressed and falling asleep, wakes up with unreasoning happiness and exults:

> Nothing can happen to you! The worst sufferings count for nothing once they're over. Whether you're six feet under the grass or know that you've got to face it all thousands of times more – nothing can happen to you! – *you're part of everything and everything's part of you.* [my emphasis] Nothing can happen to you![33]

The crux here, of course, is the line 'You're part of everything and everything's part of you.' It is the one continuous thread that links together Byron, Emerson, Schopenhauer, Wagner, Brouwer and Wittgenstein – and thinkers further east. There is perhaps a reference to this experience in a remark of Wittgenstein's that can be dated to around 1942, and that was printed in 1956 on p 123 of the *Remarks on the Foundations of Mathematics* – over thirty years on.[34] After a discussion of the phenomenon of sudden realization, he adds intriguingly and quite out of the blue: 'Cannot watching a play lead me to something?'

Direct evidence that Wittgenstein had undergone the unitive experience expressed by the lines of the play occurs in his *Lecture on Ethics*.[35] Writing of this feeling of safety that was expressed by the character in

Anzengreuber's play, he said explicitly that he knew it. Wittgenstein had been trying to convey what he thought of when he considered the meaning of 'excellence':

> ... the best way of describing it is to say that when I have it I wonder at the existence of the world. And I am then inclined to use such phrases as 'How extraordinary that anything should exist.' I will mention another experience *which I also know* [my emphasis] and which others of you might be acquainted with; it is what one might call, the experience of being absolutely safe. I mean the state of mind in which one is inclined to say 'I am safe, nothing can injure me whatever happens.'

The trigger for Wittgenstein's feeling of absolute safety (the one that he 'also knew') was, I am urging, precisely the man in the play expressing his feeling reciprocally a part of everything, which feeling I am identifying with the state of *dhyana*. After all, if *dhyana* is perception without consciousness of the subject – self-abandoned perception, as it were – what could someone experiencing it feel there was to be hurt? It is precisely 'the self' that is gone, lost in the experience and thus also the possibility of damage to the self. And I repeat, Wittgenstein said that he 'knew it'.[36]

There is also the following conversation recorded by Drury, presumably referring to Julian Bell or John Cornford (the emphasis is mine):

> On the way home we mentioned a student we had both known in Cambridge, who had been killed fighting with the International Brigade in Spain. Some of his friends had said to Wittgenstein, 'What a relief to know that this was the end of his sufferings and that we don't have to think of a "future life".' Wittgenstein said he was shocked at their speaking in this way. I tried to explain to him that for me the only perfect moments in my life were *when I had been so absorbed in the object – nature or music – that all self-consciousness was abolished. The 'I' had ceased to be.*
> WITTGENSTEIN: And you think of death as the gateway to a permanent state of mind such as that.
> DRURY: Yes, that is how I think of a future life.[37]

Wittgenstein, according to Drury, was 'disinclined to continue the conversation'. But it is quite clear from all the evidence I have assembled that this experience of 'losing of the self in contemplation' was well known to him – from other works he had read (Emerson,[38] Schopenhauer, James), from lectures (as with Brouwer), from conversation (as with Drury), and in his own experience. I have stressed that disappearance of the self/other distinction appears to be a common feature of the experiences labelled in the mystical literature as *dhyana*, *Einfühlung*, reverie, *satori* or self-loss-in-contemplation. What is important for the moment is not the labelling – or even if these variously described states are identical in all respects – but correctly understanding the nature of what Wittgenstein appears to have experienced. This experience is the one that Wittgenstein fixed on when he wanted to focus on 'absolute value'; his experience *'par excellence'*. And it, or something very like it, forms part of the meditative practice of the two major oriental religions.

Now the cardinal point to note here is that important philosophical consequences about the nature of the mind are said to follow from it. The claim of Buddhism in the Anatta doctrine proclaimed by its founder is that when, through arduous meditative practice, the world is seen aright, the self (Atman) is realized not to exist. In the case of Wittgenstein,[39] we know that the philosophy of mind he espoused in the thirties (labelled by the young Peter Strawson the 'no-ownership theory') also found no room for a multiplicity of subjects of experience. That he held a similar view in his *Tractatus* period is clear from *Tractatus* 5.5421 where we read:

... there is no such thing as the soul – the subject, etc. – as it is conceived in the superficial psychology of the present day.

And even more uncompromisingly in *Tractatus* 5.631:

There is no such thing as the subject that thinks or entertains ideas.

We know that he thought the truth of the matter lay with a philosophy on the far side of solipsism. Discussing the idea that the world is idea, he said:

... here solipsism teaches us a lesson. It is that thought which is on the way to destroy this error. For if the world is idea, it isn't any person's idea. (Solipsism stop short of this and says that it is my idea.)[40]

In later chapters I shall show that this was no aberration of the thirties; he held a consistent philosophy of mind from the *Tractatus* days to his death. In any case, however, the important question to ask is this: Towards what philosophy of mind would we expect such experiences to incline a philosopher? Do they help us to understand Wittgenstein? I claim not merely that they do help us: I claim also that he cannot be understood without them, and that commentary ignorant of their role is just a waste of time.[41] I claim further that they shed light on the causes of the Holocaust, for these unitive experiences whose ultimate direction is towards a sense of oneness with – indeed mystical identity with – God are archetypally forbidden to Jews. There is a strong Jewish mystical tradition, of course, and in its higher flights the blessed Jewish mystic might even rapturously contemplate the Divine Throne. But that he might aspire to become the Holy One himself is not only a possibility not to be contemplated, but something to be fled from as an abomination. In the early Aryan religions of the Indian sub-continent, however, the means to these unificatory experiences – meditation, yoga, chanting, etc – were sought out and culti-vated with an ardour that has survived even to the present day. With these, the divinization that is forbidden in the Semitic religions is the very goal.

I shall therefore develop the philosophy of mind these experiences presuppose and use it to expound Wittgenstein's aphorisms and make their background clear. Their background is Schopenhauer and, through Schopenhauer, early Aryan religion.

This background is particularly worth investigating in view of the philosophy of Wittgenstein's first musical love, Richard Wagner. For here is Wagner on the *Artwork of the Future*, discussing the *modus operandi* of the musician in terms of this very unificatory experience. (The reader can take it for granted that the future Führer devoured this passage many times.) It is pure Schopenhauer and written with a passion that almost approaches an invocation:

We can but take it that the *individual will*, silenced in the plastic artist through pure beholding, awakes in the musician as the *universal will*, and – above and beyond all power of vision – now recognizes itself as such in full self-consciousness. Hence the great difference in the mental state of the concipient musician and the designing artist; hence the radically diverse effects of music and of painting: here profoundest stilling, there utmost excitation of the will. In other words we here have the will in the individual as such, the will imprisoned by the fancy of its difference from the essence of things outside, and unable to lift itself above its barriers save in the purely disinterested beholding of objects: whilst there, in the musician's case, the will feels *one* forthwith, above all grounds of individuality: for hearing has opened it the gate through which the world thrusts home to it, it to the world.

This prodigious breaking down the floodgates of appearance must neces-sarily call forth in the inspired musician a state of ecstasy wherewith no other can compare: in it the will perceives itself the almighty will of all things.[42]

We are investigating, then, Wittgenstein's philosophy and the Holocaust, from a perspective that has been lamentably ignored and that is crucially important. We shall see that understanding National Socialism (even the Nazi theory of art) demands a certain taxonomy of a particular mysticism that is best expounded through Schopenhauer, oriental religions, Wagner, Wittgenstein and Hitler. I shall try to establish that that which in Wittgenstein's philosophy is unowned and not private – language itself, or the unowned Universal Mind – was in Hitler's nationalist perversion of this doctrine transformed into the Mind of the Master Race – the 'German Idea'. From participation in this, Jews were excluded by the essential nature of Judaism – which alone of the great theistic religions rules out any sort of mystical union. Jewish exclusion was thus for mystical reasons and the ground – the field of battle – was set for the great struggle between Yahweh and Odin that raged from 1933 to 1945.[43]

SIX

Schopenhauer, Rosenberg and Race Theory

In his *Biographical Sketch* of Wittgenstein, Von Wright states bluntly that Wittgenstein appears to have had no historical predecessors in philosophy.[1] This is certainly a tribute to Wittgenstein's originality, but by now the reader ought to have developed some doubts that it might be so. My own belief is that, through Schopenhauer, his predecessors occupy a greater historical and geographical spread than do those of any other Western philosopher.

Wittgenstein's philosophy of mind has an ancient and curiously split pedigree. Some of its lineage goes back through Schopenhauer to Kant. But its apparent novelty is due to the other branch that goes back through Schopenhauer. It is basically Indian, in just the sense that Schopenhauer's philosophy of mind is Indian. This is not to say that the source was necessarily Indian. But Wittgenstein's doctrines have (as Schopenhauer acknowledged of his own philosophy) an Indian character, a discernible Indian 'smell'. Western philosophers such as Von Wright, unused to seeing modern philosophical issues in Indian religious doctrines, are thus unlikely to detect their eruption in the work of the most original philosopher this century.

It is also possible that the source of this Indian smell, certainly in Schopenhauer's philosophy and therefore possibly in Wittgenstein's also, really was India after all. We shall examine some of the internal evidence in Schopenhauer's works in a moment. The trail is hardly over virgin ground, for details of Schopenhauer's abiding interest in Indian thought have been recorded already, most recently by Wilhelm Halbfass:

> Schopenhauer's interest in India was awakened early by the Orientalist F. Majer,[2] who was effective as a recruiter for India among the Romantics. . . .[3]

Halbfass also quotes Schopenhauer's own words of 1816, written during the production of the first volume of *The World as Will and Representation*:

By the way, I admit that I do not believe that my doctrine could have ever been formulated before the Upanishads, Plato, and Kant were able to all cast their light simultaneously on to a human mind.[4]

What was the 'harmony' that Schopenhauer discerned between his own and Indian thought? Halbfass continues:

His approach to Indian philosophy was, so to speak, that of a 'recognitive historiography of philosophy' ('wiedererkennende Philosophiegeschichte') which remained open to the possibility of finding the same insights in the most diverse historical contexts. Schopenhauer felt that the basic ideas of his philosophy, viz., the doctrine of the 'world as will and representation', of a fundamental unity of reality and an apparent projection into spatio-temporal multiplicity, could be found among the Indians, and not just in the form of historical antecedents, but in a sense of truth which knows no historical and geographical restrictions.[5]

This approach is exactly the one we have been following in our interpretation of Wittgenstein in the light of Schopenhauer. And we shall try to bring out the relevance of the doctrines 'found among the Indians' to both Schopenhauer and Wittgenstein, again 'in a sense of truth which knows no historical and geographical restrictions'. The reader must note that these doctrines found among the Indians are the only surviving examples of the religious beliefs of the early Aryans. We shall see soon what the Nazi race theorists were to make of these Aryan doctrines. Suffice to say that, they present a theory of the mind that is fundamentally at odds with the Jewish doctrine of the 'otherness' of Yahweh. For these early Aryans, the Divine Mind *is* the individual mind, if only the individual mind could purge itself of the errors that prevent it from discerning this fact.

Modern commentators on Schopenhauer tend to downplay the significance of the Indian connection. There appears to be a feeling that his interpretation of Indian religious doctrines was idiosyncratic and quite certainly wrong; even that Schopenhauer was somewhat of a crank. The commentators might be right about this, but it is foolishness to ignore the beliefs of influential cranks. Schopenhauer's ideas infected Nietszche, Wagner, Wittgenstein and Hitler. It is therefore important to bring out what Schopenhauer thought was significant about Indian religious doctrines, for he had no doubts at all about their value. He was rather contemptuous of Anglican missionaries in particular and wrote:

We, on the contrary, now send to the Brahmans English clergymen and evangelical linen-weavers, in order out of sympathy to put them right, and to point out to them that they are created out of nothing, and that they ought to be grateful and pleased about it. But it is just the same as if we fired a bullet at a cliff. In India our religions will never at any time take root; the ancient wisdom of the human race will not be supplanted by the events in Galilee. On the contrary, Indian wisdom flows back to Europe, and will produce a fundamental change in our knowledge and thought.[6]

It certainly did have a role to play in changing Schopenhauer's thought. Halbfass isolates an idea of Schopenhauer's which became central to Wittgenstein's own philosophy and continues:

Schopenhauer often invoked Indian thought when he wished to illustrate what he saw as the central relationship between ethics and metaphysics. As early as 1813, while working on his doctoral dissertation, he formulated his principle of 'a philosophy which should be at once ethics and metaphysics'. He attempted to achieve such a unified system of thought by anchoring the fundamental ethical phenomenon of compassion in a metaphysics of identity which he found exemplified in the Vedanta. He repeatedly explained that for him, 'the foundation of morals ultimately rests upon that truth' which was expressed in the Upanisadic formula tat tvam asi ('that art thou').[7]

For Wittgenstein there was no doubt at all that logic and ethics hang together. And the key to this unity, in Wittgenstein also, was the identity of all subjects; not, as in Schopenhauer, with 'the pure subject of knowing', but with common language; with the one proposition articulated through millions of mouths, showing the true nature, the mystical nature, of the mysterious 'I'.[8] He might even have known Kabir's expression of it via the translations of Rabindranath Tagore, whom he greatly admired:

No one knows this ineffable movement.
How could one tongue describe it?
If any man has a million mouths and tongues,
let that great one speak.[9]

The proposition speaks, contingently through this or that mouth, while remaining the numerically one proposition; not 'private' but public: expressed through 'a million mouths and tongues'. This is the 'great one' that speaks, and full recognition of its (= 'one's own') nature is the ineffable movement, that is, divinization. In Schopenhauer, the Will expresses itself contingently via this or that creature while in itself remaining numerically one. In Hinduism, the apparently many individual Atmans are in truth one Brahman. In Buddhism, the whole idea of the individualized Atman is simply swept aside as the root cause of the ignorance from which Buddha offered deliverance. But the reasoning behind the move in each case is apparent: it was first recorded in India and only later repeated in Schopenhauer and Wittgenstein. The Indians – the early Aryan invaders of the sub-continent – therefore have inventor's rights, and justify my use of 'Indian' in describing the doctrine.

Schopenhauer's philosophy and his attribution of its core to Indian origins, crankish or not, was accepted by a number of European thinkers, and they were to prove enormously influential. The most important of them, for our purpose, was the composer Richard Wagner, and from Wagner, the idea percolated through the mind of Adolf Hitler to become incorporated into Nazi race theory. What is fascinating in this transformation is that these Indian doctrines were held to be acceptable provided they were restricted to Aryans only.

Alfred Rosenberg, the chief Nazi race theoretician, who, in his capacity as Reich Minister for the Occupied Eastern Territories, was deservedly hanged in 1946, incorporated this theme from the Schopenhauer/Wagner view of Indian religions into the very core of Nazi racial theories. It is clear from Rosenberg's writings that the Atman/Brahman identity was seen as a central insight of Aryan philosophy. The fault of the Hindu branch of the Aryans, however, was that this insight, due to 'bastardization', lost its racial base. It is perhaps not clear to a reader how race can enter into apprehension of a philosophical idea, but the following turgid prose from Rosenberg illustrates how the official Nazi race theorist saw it:

The Indian, as a born master, felt his soul expand to be a breath of life which filled the entire universe. At the same time he felt the world throb within his bosom. Even Nature herself, mysterious, rich and all-generous, could not entice him out of this metaphysical profundity. A life of action which had been recognized by the old teachings of the Upanishads as being an indispensable precondition for even the ascetic thinker, began, before the wanderer's eyes, to fade into the universe of the soul; and this course from variegated colour to the white light of knowledge led to the most grandiose of attempts to overthrow nature through reason. No doubt, at that time many exceptional or aristocratic Indians succeeded in surmounting the mundane world. However, later Indians were bequeathed only the teachings, not their vital, living, racial preconditions. Gradually they lost all understanding of the blood–colour sense of Varna.[10] Today, the application of Varna to the area of technical division of labour represents the most hideous mockery of one of the world's wisest insights. The later Indian did not know of Blood, Ego and All, but only of the last two entities. The vital attempt to grasp Ego in itself died within him. The Indian fell heir to a race-crime whose offspring can be seen today as the

spiritually impoverished bastards who seek to cure their crippled being in the
waters of the Ganges. . . .[11]

Rosenberg granted, then, that exceptional or aristocratic individuals among
the early Aryans in India attained to metaphysical insights through knowledge of the Atman/Brahman identity. The problem was that these insights
were vitiated by racial admixture as the Aryans interbred with the
aboriginal inhabitants of India. Thus Rosenberg continues:

> The Indian monist, even after he had 'overcome', through rational decision, the
> spiritual polarity of Ego/All in favour of the latter pole . . . was therefore not
> inclined to consider race and personality as concepts which possessed a high
> value. . . . All that is real is embodied in the world-soul (Brahman) and in its
> eternal rebirth in individualities (Atman). Above all, there resulted from this
> turning away from nature a continuous weakening of the earlier clear represen-
> tation and conception of race. Instinct was enticed from its earthly kingdom by
> dogmatic-philosophical perception. If the world-soul is all that exists and
> Atman is its essence, then the idea of personality has to disappear. The shape-
> less All/One has been attained.[12]

The Atman/Brahman identity, then, while perfectly acceptable to exceptional, racially pure Aryans, had, because of the all-inclusive universality of
the doctrine, permitted miscegenation. This miscegenation had destroyed
the conditions that had created individuals capable of realizing the truth of
the doctrine in the first place. Those aspiring to Aryan metaphysical
knowledge were now different – no longer Aryan. The sublime Aryan
metaphysics had changed as the race of those professing it changed. Thus
Rosenberg continues:

> When this occurred, the Indian ceased to be creative; the dark, foreign blood of
> the Sudras – who were considered equal because of Atman – flowed in, annihi-
> lated the original concept of caste or race, and bastardization began. Snake and
> phallus cults began to fester among the natives. The symbolic expression of
> one-hundred-armed Siva became realistically represented as a fearful bastard-
> art developed in the primeval jungles. The old heroic odes were remembered
> only at the imperial court; only there could be found the lyrics of Kalidasa and
> other, mostly unknown, great poets. Cankara attempted to create Indian philos-
> ophy anew. It was in vain: the arteries of the race-body had been severed, and
> the Aryan–Indian blood flowed out, only here and there fertilizing the perme-
> able soil of ancient India. Only a philosophical-technical doctrine was left
> behind for later life; and in its subsequent insanely distorted form this domi-
> nates contemporary Hindu life. We must not intolerantly maintain that the
> Indian gave up or perverted first his race and then his personality. Much more

to the point is the metaphysical occurrence that was reflected in the passionate demand for the overthrow of the phenomenon of dualism, as well as the reciprocally-conditioning lower forms of this polarity.

Seen from the outside, philosophical recognition of the great equality of Atman-Brahman led to racial decline. In other lands such a phenomenon did not signify the solidification of a philosophical idea but was, rather, the consequence of uninterrupted miscegenation between two or many opposing races, whose respective capacities were neither elevated nor complemented by this process, but subjected to mutual annihilation.

Nazi race-theory, in other words, held that philosophical recognition of the Atman/Brahman identity – or rather admitting other races into knowledge of it and thus miscegenation – 'led to racial decline'. Is this not extraordinary? And yet, if our considerations of the previous chapters arc correct, something very like the Atman/Brahman identity lies at the heart of Wittgenstein's philosophy! It is therefore a genuine possibility that when Hitler railed against the 'Jewish doctrine that does away with the personality', it was just this that he was referring to. The doctrines Hitler attributed to Jews, in fact, would be rejected by any pious Jews at all. We know, however, that a certain twentieth-century philosopher of Jewish descent propounded just such doctrines under another guise at Trinity College, Cambridge, not just in the 1930s, but quite certainly as early as before the Great War and just possibly when he was attending school with Hitler.

Rosenberg was no one-off in expounding Nazi philosophy in this wise. Heinrich Himmler, the SS leader, said of astrology:

We cannot permit any astrologers to follow their calling except those who are working for us. In the National Socialist state astrology must remain a *privilegium singulorum*. It is not for the broad masses. . . . We base our attitude on the fact that astrology, as a universalist doctrine, is diametrically opposed to our own philosophical view of the world. . . . A doctrine which is meant to apply in equal measure to Negroes, Indians, Chinese, and Aryans is in opposition to our conception of the racial soul. Each one of the peoples I have named has its own specific racial soul. . . .[13]

Aryans have a 'racial soul'! Remarkable, is it not? Let us now consider an hypothesis that draws together the various factors .

Hitler and Wittgenstein, as we saw, had some sort of interaction around 1904. Wittgenstein's personality even then – forceful and used to commanding servants and expressing itself in High German – had a profound effect upon the young Hitler. Somehow, Hitler came to a knowledge of Wittgenstein's youthful *Einfühlung* experience and of what it purported to show about the nature of the subject of experience: to wit, that Aryan, Jew, Negro or Chinese, we all share the one mind. (None of this is outside the bounds of possibility for intelligent teenage boys.) For some unknown but historically crucial reason, they fell out. Hitler came to find repellent belief in a common, universal mind that included Jews. He came to see the doctrine as a means by which Jews could preach internationalism and the brotherhood of man, while weakening Aryan solidarity against the Jews. While Wittgenstein presented himself as an 'international seeker after truth', his family was exploiting Austrian Germans through its control of the empire's economy. The solution Hitler arrived at was to fight against the universal aspect of Wittgenstein's doctrine and restrict the common mind to those of pure Aryan race alone; that is, to restrict it to Aryans and rule out the Jews. There was indeed a 'racial mind', as the Aryans had believed, but only Aryans could attain to it.

In the extract from Rosenberg's writings I presented earlier, we see precisely this hypothesis I have presented about Jews in Europe transferred to the Sudras in India. Rosenberg writes that 'If the world-soul is all that exists then the idea of personality has to disappear.' Certainly in Wittgenstein's writings, as I shall show, there are no individual minds. Rosenberg then writes that 'when this occurred . . . the dark, foreign blood of the Sudras [read 'Jews'] – who were considered equal because of Atman [read 'because of a common consciousness'] – flowed in, annihilated the original concept of caste or race, and bastardization began.' In Europe, of course, the Nazi protest against 'Jewish internationalism' was indeed that it led to overthrow of purity of race, to 'the arteries of the race-body' being severed. Hitler's protest in *Mein Kampf* was that he saw this process taking place in the Vienna of his youth: legal equality of the races under the Habsburgs leading to racial degeneration through 'bastardization'. He complained to Hermann Rauschning about Vienna that 'Austria is rotten with Jews. Vienna is no longer a German city. Slav mestizos have overrun the place.'[14] Slav mestizos? Who were these 'Slav mestizos'? Given that an earlier Ludwig Wittgenstein had been prince of Russia, the description 'Slav mestizos' is, I think, obvious. The foreign blood that was flowing into Austria – like the Sudra blood that allegedly corrupted India through unrestricted application to other races of Aryan metaphysics – was, in the first instance, the Slav/Jewish blood of the Wittgensteins.

There is also another interesting way in which the thought of the Cambridge philosopher connects with that of the Nazi leader. It is a characteristic of the no-ownership theory of mind that it sees thoughts and ideas not as the activities of particular thinkers which vanish when the thinkers die, but rather as eternal forms which can connect to us in the present. It is therefore of compelling interest that Hitler explained the 'meaning of history' in terms of forms also. His vision was of a universal mental community of Aryans in conflict with an external threat whose most dangerous weapon was precisely the internationalism flowing from *Einfühlung*. This threat was 'the Jew', considered not as an individual human being, but rather as a form, as something eternal; Ludwig Wittgenstein objectified into the eternal Jew. Thus in *Mein Kampf*, Hitler writes:

> His traits of character have remained the same, whether two thousand years ago as a grain dealer in Ostia, speaking Roman, or whether as a flour profiteer of today, jabbering German with a Jewish accent. It is always the same Jew.[15]

'It is always the same Jew.' What we see here is 'the Jew' as eternal form not as individual and whose nature it is to be separate, to 'jabber German'.

In missing the universal nature of the Mind, however, Hitler came to see the publicity of thought as making possible contact with the minds of deceased Aryan individuals – Frederick the Great or Frederick Barbarossa. What should have been understanding of the nature of the living, immortal Mind became instead a sort of occult communion with what had to be seen as the souls of the dead. Hitler committed suicide, yet looked for the coming of another 'genius' in a hundred years or so. Who did he conceive this future genius to be? I suggest that the individual he had in mind was none other than himself, again conceived of as an eternal form. He lamented before his suicide, 'What an artist dies in me!' echoing the last words of another great persecutor of the Jew, the Roman Emperor Nero. Just as 'the Jew' was described in *Mein Kampf* as a form, so the persecutor of Jews was a form. Hitler was indifferently Nero, Hitler and the persecutor to come. And his struggle – *Mein Kampf* – was likewise something eternal.

The occult communication with the souls of the great departed German heroes that Himmler had the SS engage in at Wewelsburg Castle, near Padersborn in Westphalia, can also be interpreted from a no–ownership perspective:

> He was also a convinced believer in reincarnation – in a speech to high-ranking SS officers, delivered at Dachau in 1936, he told them that they had all been with each other somewhere before and that they would all meet again after their present lives had ended. He believed that he himself was the reincarnation of Heinrich the Fowler (875-936), the monarch who had founded the Saxon royal house, had driven the Poles eastward, and whose memory he held in peculiar veneration. On the thousandth anniversary of Heinrich's death he swore an oath to continue the king's 'civilizing mission in the east' and each year thereafter he

spent some time in silent meditation before the dead monarch's tomb which, so he said, was 'a sacred spot to which we Germans make pilgrimage'. It is somewhat difficult to reconcile Himmler's belief that he was the reincarnation of Heinrich the Fowler with his simultaneous belief, confided to his masseur Felix Kersten during the war, that in the silences of the night he held long conversations with the dead man's spirit – perhaps he meant that he retreated into the inmost recesses of his own soul, perhaps that he was in the habit of talking to himself.

It is to be presumed that Himmler believed himself to be a descendant of Heinrich the Fowler, for the particular form of the theory of reincarnation to which he gave his assent was that advocated by Karl Eckhart, who argued that each man was reborn in the body of one of his descendants, that we are all, in a sense, our own ancestors.[16]

Himmler was not 'in the habit of talking to himself'. What he was doing was quite different: he was linking himself to Heinrich's thoughts; becoming Heinrich through this very meditation technique. Heinrich the Fowler was contactable via re-enactment and expression of his characteristic mental processes through the vehicle of Heinrich Himmler's body. We have, then, in the no-ownership theory of mind, a model for understanding one characteristic occult practice; communication with the mental processes of the dead. That this practice is discernible in so high-ranking a Nazi as Himmler (and one so close to Hitler) forces us to examine how the no-ownership theory relates to magic and the occult.

As we shall see in the next chapter, there is not one single no-ownership account of magic and its mode of operation, but three. None of these dispute the efficacy of magic. These accounts were presented by Schopenhauer, the Oxford philosopher Collingwood, and Wittgenstein. Certainly Schopenhauer believed magic had its own mode of operation. Wittgenstein devoted one of his substantial works to an examination of how magic, like language, could represent, as in, say, a curse. And Collingwood presented virtually an entire chapter on the topic in developing his theory of art. Hitler's life, of course, reeks of magic and the occult. Comprehension of the Schopenhauerian account of magic goes a long way to help us understand exactly what it was that Hitler wrought and how he was able to bring it about.

SEVEN

Magic, Sorcery and Hitler

The Magus © Bayerische Staatsbildiothek

To many, Cambridge and Oxford universities come paired with images of something distinctively and gloriously English: dreaming spires and reflective civilization. To others come thoughts of triumphant intellectual progress: the great scientific discoveries in physics and biology, the philosophical work of Russell, Moore and Wittgenstein, or the economic theories of Keynes. At various times over the century past, however, a number of Oxbridge no-ownership academics and students concerned themselves not with the humanities or the sciences, but with the hermetic mysteries of magic and the occult. In this they followed the same path as the

Alexandrine neo-Platonists, who also moved from a theory of a single soul with Plotinus to ritual magic with Iamblichus.[1]

Some of these no-ownership theorists studied magic as object, and produced very clever philosophical/anthropological observations on its role and mode of operation. In this category I include Collingwood and Wittgenstein. Some, however, devoted themselves to the practice of magic. Into this category come Aleister Crowley, Walter Duranty and a number of others. One aspect of this hermetic involvement of interest for our purposes is its repercussions, for via Crowley, Dennis Wheatley and Maxwell Knight, it was to penetrate the British security agencies. Those in positions of authority were not religious men and so did not view Crowley's advice askance. They used this advice to their own purpose, to help engineer, for example, the Hess defection.[2] It appears that some of them even apprenticed themselves to Crowley, though this astonishing fact and its consequences are properly the concern of another book. Our prime concern here is not to demonstrate the existence of a coven within the British security agencies, but rather in how magic – which Schopenhauer called 'practical metaphysics' – connects to the no-ownership theory of mind. We shall also be looking at Hitler's beliefs about magic and how they influenced his life.

Schopenhauer remarked upon occult phenomena in various works and in two he discussed them in depth. These two are the chapter 'Animal Magnetism and Magic' in *On the Will in Nature* and the essay 'On Spirit Seeing' in *Parerga and Paralipomena*.[3] Modern expositors of Schopenhauer's thought omit these essays entirely, as something of a scandal, much as historians neglected the alchemical writings of Sir Isaac Newton. They quite overlook their historical importance, and present Schopenhauer as a rationalist philosopher in the same mould as Kant. Schopenhauer, however, developed his own theory of occult phenomena, intrinsically tied to his own account of the Will. It was Schopenhauer's ideas here that were to resonate in the musical mind of Richard Wagner. Wagner, for example, writes approvingly of Schopenhauer that he 'has also given us the best of guides through his profound hypothesis concerning the physiologic phenomenon of clairvoyance. . . .'[4] There is little doubt that Hitler had read the relevant sections of both Wagner and Schopenhauer.

Schopenhauer had no doubt that the reported phenomena really occurred, but thought their standard magical explanation in terms of spirits to be so much claptrap. He offered an account of the nature of magic that was original with him and that has not, so far as I am aware, been presented elsewhere, although a variant that might be Schopenhauer's is discernible in Crowley's writings on magic, with their emphasis on the Will. I do not propose to investigate Crowley's writings here, nor do I commend them to the reader. Reading Crowley is like dipping one's hand into a bag full of lice and leeches.

To approach Schopenhauer's theory, we must consider first the question of the efficacy of magic. Readers of a rationalist persuasion will take it for granted that magic is not casually efficacious; but on the question of whether magical phenomena really occur, the assumption of what follows is that some of them really do. Australian and South African readers are probably less sceptical than English and European readers in this regard. I well remember newspaper articles from my youth in Western Australia, recording cases of tribal aborigines brought to Perth hospitals following malevolent tribal sorcery. In some cases the victims died. Rather than document what I say here, I refer the doubtful reader to the anthropological literature. Analogues of 'pointing the bone' or 'singing to death' ceremonies exist in many human groups, but the Australian aboriginal practice is as well documented as any – as is the fact that there are deaths to its account.

Sceptics dismiss such cases by saying that the victims simply died of fright and that the magical means employed were not efficacious as magic, but worked their effect through other means – perhaps via a pre-disposing fear. The point, however, is that whatever these other means are, we are ignorant of them: I cannot kill an aborigine by pointing a bone or by 'singing him to death', nor, I believe, can any Western psychologist or anthropologist; yet for all that, the tribal sorcery worked. It is therefore no explanation of the death by sorcery cases to say that the poor victims 'died of fright' since the truth is that we have not even the beginnings of a comprehensive theory that might account for deaths of this nature. Indeed, I understand that the aboriginal sorcery victims typically did not appear afraid at all, but instead accepted the inevitability of their fate with resignation. The normal rationalist response, therefore, is simply too quick. Sorcery – like hypnosis, which is itself a quasi-magical technique, at least historically – quite certainly does work sometimes. How it works we simply do not yet know.

On this dismissive, 'rationalist response', I can do no better than quote Collingwood's criticism of Sir James Frazer's account in *The Golden Bough* of another magical phenomenon concerning nail-clippings:

> . . . the theory does not fit the facts it was devised to explain . . .
> The observed fact is that the 'savage' destroys his own nail-clippings. The theory is that he believes in a 'mystical' connexion (to use the French adjective) between these nail-clippings and his own body, such that their destruction is

injurious to himself. But, if he believed this, he would regard his own destruction of his nail-clippings as suicide. He does not so regard it; therefore he does not believe in the alleged 'mystical' connexion and the grounds on which he has been credited with a 'primitive mentality' disappear.

Simple though it is, the blunder is not innocent. It masks a half-conscious conspiracy to bring into ridicule and contempt civilizations different from our own; and, in particular, civilizations in which magic is openly recognized. Anthropologists would of course indignantly deny this; but under cross-examination their denials would break down. The theory from which we started was that a 'savage' destroys his nail-clippings to prevent an enemy from destroying them with certain magical ceremonies. The anthropologist next says to himself: 'My informant tells me he is afraid of some one's doing two things simultaneously: destroying these nail-clippings, and performing certain ceremonies. Now he must know as well as I do that the ceremonies are mere hocus-pocus. There is nothing to be afraid of there. Consequently he must be afraid of the destruction of the nail-clippings.' Some such work as this must have been going on in the anthropologist's mind; for if it had not, he would not have based his theory on a pseudo fact (fear of the destruction of nail-clippings as such) instead of basing on the genuine fact which he had correctly observed (fear of that destruction when, and only when, accompanied by magical ceremonies). The motive power behind this substitution is the anthropologist's conviction that the ceremonies which would accompany the destruction of the nail-clippings are 'mere hocus-pocus' and could not possibly hurt anyone. But these ceremonies are the one and only magical part of the whole business. The alleged theory of magic has been constructed by manipulating the facts so that all magical elements are left out of them. In other words, the theory is a thinly disguised refusal to study magic at all.[5]

Collingwood had no doubt that magic was efficacious, but his account of its efficacy – as one would expect from an Oxford philosopher/historian – was not a supernatural one. He saw magic as resting essentially upon little-known facts of human psychology and suggested that our difficulties in theorizing about it derive, not from these facts, but rather from deep-seated fear, from the fact that we are so terrified of magic that we simply dare not think straight about it. 'Let us note here that the occult in general is a staple of Hollywood horror films. The reason it features in such popular films is not because of its comic effects, but because the occult really is profoundly frightening. So what Collingwood suggests about our 'very strong disinclination to think about the subject in a cool and logical manner' might very well be true, though his own theory of 'What Magic Is' is not in itself particularly frightening. In stating it, he emphasizes the representative role of magic, exactly as did Wittgenstein in his *Remarks on Frazer's Golden Bough*. Schopenhauer had asked, 'How can the Will act magically?' The question Wittgenstein and Collingwood raised was the non-causal one, 'How can Magic serve to represent – or give expression to – the desires of its practitioners?' These are not totally unrelated ways of investigating the matter. Here, first, is Collingwood on magic in the abstract:

The only profitable way of theorizing about magic is to approach it from the side of art. The similarities between magic and applied science, on which the Tylor-Frazer theory rests, are very slight, and the dissimilarities are great. The magician as such is not a scientist; and if we admit this, and call him a bad scientist, we are merely finding a term of abuse for the characteristics that differentiate him from a scientist, without troubling to analyse those characteristics . . . the similarities between magic and art are both strong and intimate. Magical practices invariably contain, not as peripheral elements but as central elements, artistic activities like dances, songs, drawing, or modelling. Moreover these elements have a function which in two ways resembles the function of amusement.

(i) They are means to a preconceived end, and are therefore not art proper but craft.

(ii) This end is the arousing of emotion.

(i) That magic is essentially means to a preconceived end is, I think, obvious; and equally obvious that what is thus used as means is always something artistic, or rather (since, being used as means to an end, it cannot be art proper) quasi-artistic.

(ii) That the end of magic is always and solely arousing of certain emotions is less obvious; but every one will admit that this is at least sometimes and partially its end. The use of the bull-roarer in Australian initiation-ceremonies is intended, partly at least, to arouse certain emotions in the candidates for initiation and certain others in uninitiated persons who may happen to overhear it. A tribe which dances a war-dance before going to fight its neighbours is working up its warlike emotions. The warriors are dancing themselves into a conviction of their own invincibility. The various and complicated magic which surrounds and accompanies the agriculture of a peasant society expresses that society's emotions towards its flocks and herds, its crops and the instruments of its labour; or rather, evokes in its members at each critical point in the calendar that emotion, from among all these, which is appropriate to the corresponding phase of its annual work.

But although magic arouses emotion, it does this in quite another way than amusement. Emotions aroused by magical acts are not discharged by those acts. It is important for the practical life of the people concerned that this should not happen; and magical practices are magical precisely because they have been so designed that it shall not happen. The contrary is what happens: these emotions are focused and crystallized, consolidated into effective agents in practical life. The process is the exact opposite of a catharsis. There the emotion is discharged so that it shall not interfere with practical life; here it is canalized and directed upon practical life.[7]

Collingwood defends no supernatural account of such alleged phenomena as levitation or materialization. And what he says might indeed work as an outline account of the effect of spells or curses, etc. He is sketching how magic can have an effect upon someone, but he denies that magic can work directly upon inanimate objects. Thus we read further:

> I am suggesting that these emotional effects, partly on the performers themselves, partly on others favourably or unfavourably affected by the performance, are the only effects which magic can produce, and the only ones which, when intelligently performed, it is meant to produce. The primary function of all magical acts, I am suggesting, is to generate in the agent or agents certain emotions that are considered necessary or useful for the work of living; their secondary function is to generate in others, friends or enemies of the agent, emotions useful or detrimental to lives of these others.
>
> To any one with sufficient psychological knowledge to understand the effect which our emotions have on the success or failure of our enterprises, and in the production or cure of diseases, it will be clear that this theory of magic amply accounts for its ordinary everyday employment in connexion with the ordinary everyday activities of the people who believe in it. Such a person thinks, for example, that a war undertaken without the proper dances would end in defeat; or that if he took his axe to the forest without doing the proper magic first, he would not succeed in cutting down a tree. But this belief does not imply that the enemy is defeated or the tree felled by the power of the magic distinct from the labour of the 'savage'. It means that warfare or woodcraft, nothing can be done without morale; and the function of magic is to develop and conserve morale; or to damage it. For example, if an enemy spied upon our war-dance and saw how magnificently we did it, might he not slink away and beg his friends to submit without a battle? Where the purpose of magic is to screw our courage up to the point of attacking, not a rock or a tree, but a human enemy, the enemy's will to encounter us may be fatally weakened by the magic alone. How far this negative emotional effect might produce diseases of various kinds or even death is a question about which no student of medical psychology will wish to dogmatize.

Collingwood, then, saw magical techniques as essentially designed to work upon morale, for good or ill, but he was also quite open about how far the power of these techniques might extend. Even today, of course, we are still profoundly ignorant. And what Collingwood is saying here might be worth rephrasing as we bear in mind the terrible events of the 1930s. We read in Collingwood that 'the enemy's will to encounter us may be fatally weakened by the magic alone'. If we substitute the word 'propaganda' for 'magic' here, we recognize an exact description of Hitler's policies in the thirties: gatherings at night in Nuremberg and mass affirmation of the will to win in the midst of occult symbols from pre-Christian Germanic mythology. What Collingwood wrote, apparently only of savage tribes, has an obvious twentieth-century application to the effects of the Nuremberg Rallies. Foreign observers did see them and justifiably went away afraid to their very bowels.

There is perhaps a resistance to applying a word like 'magic' to activities such as these. We are more accustomed to bundle them under the labels 'morale-building' or 'propaganda'. It certainly sounds more objective, more scientific. But this resistance to calling it 'magic' seems to me to do nothing but cloud clear perception of what Hitler was doing. More importantly, as we shall see, it clouds clear perception of what Hitler thought he was doing. It is not that I am advising the reader to simply substitute the word 'magic' for 'mass political propaganda'. It is rather that if we insist upon calling what are clearly magical activities 'mass political propaganda' we will fail to understand what was really going on.

What Hitler managed to bring about with these rallies perfectly fits Collingwood's description of magical effects. And if we are open-minded, we can discern in the rallies an exact twentieth-century counterpart of what Collingwood is describing as magic amongst savages. Should the reader still reject the 'magic' label here for the various Nazi mass phenomena, it is obviously of relevance that their originator saw them as involving hypnosis and magic. We have a number of records of Hitler describing the psychology of the mass rallies in terms of the suggestions implanted under hypnosis – that is, a quasi-magical technique.[8] And Hitler's description raises a further feature of coming together in groups that Collingwood passed over; the idea of the group mind, the shared mind, the unowned mind:

'My success in initiating the greatest people's movement of all time is due to my never having done anything in violation of the vital laws and the feelings of the mass. These feelings may be primitive, but they have the resistance and indestructibility of natural qualities. . . . It is only because I take their vital laws into consideration that I can rule them. . . .'

He had made the masses fanatic, he explained, in order to fashion them into the instruments of his policy. He had awakened the masses. He had lifted them out of themselves, and given them meaning and a function. He had been reproached with appealing to their lowest instincts. Actually, he was doing something quite different. If he were to go to the masses with reasonable deliberations, they would not understand him. But if he awakened corresponding feelings in them, they followed the simple slogans he presented to them.

'At a mass meeting,' he cried, 'thought is eliminated. And because this is the state of mind I require, because it secures to me the best sounding-board for my speeches, I order everyone to attend the meetings, where they become part of the mass whether they like it or not, "intellectuals" and *bourgeois* as well as workers. I mingle the people. I speak to them only as the mass.'

He paused to reflect for a moment. Then he resumed with increased eagerness:

'I am conscious that I have no equal in the art of swaying the masses, not even Goebbels. Everything that can be learnt with the intelligence, everything that can be achieved by the aid of clever ideas, Goebbels can do, but real leadership of the masses cannot be learnt. And remember this: the bigger the crowd, the more easily is it swayed. Also, the more you mingle the classes – peasants, workers, black-coated workers – the more surely will you achieve the typical mass character. Don't waste time over "intellectual" meetings and groups drawn together by mutual interests. Anything you may achieve with such folk today by means of reasonable explanation may be erased to-morrow by an opposite explanation. But what you tell the people in the mass, in a receptive state of fanatic devotion, will remain like words received under an hypnotic influence, ineradicable, and impervious to every reasonable explanation. . . .'

Hitler then began to discuss the use of propaganda to defeat opponents – a problem, he strongly emphasised, that was quite distinct from the previous one. The two must on no account be confused. He had been discussing the mastery of the masses, but propaganda meant the defeat of opponents. The two had one thing in common: both must eschew all discussion of reasons, all refutation of opinions – in short, there must be no debating or doubting. But apart from this, the aim of a propaganda battle with one's opponents was quite a different one.

'Mastery always means the transmission of a stronger will to a weaker one. How shall I press my will upon my opponent? By first splitting and paralysing his will, putting him at loggerheads with himself, throwing him into confusion.'

He conceived the transmission of the will, he said, as something in the nature of a physical and biological process. Foreign bodies penetrated the circulation of the enemy, gained a foothold, and gave rise to disease and infirmity till he was ready to surrender. The instrument of terrorism was indispensable, less for its direct effects than for its undermining of the opposing will.

Sceptics about magic will insist that there is no warrant in any of this to support the view that Hitler was consciously using magic and that the effect of the rallies is better understood via disciplines such as psychology or mass marketing. Ignoring the point that to some extent these disciplines have simply relabelled magical concepts to sound scientific ('spell' = 'post-hypnotic suggestion'), such sceptics are quite overlooking the intellectual background from which Hitler was proceeding. What, for example, was the importance of achieving a state in which thought was eliminated? Where did Hitler get the idea from in the first place? Did he have intellectual precursors?

Hitler's pioneer predecessors of this idea were Arthur Schopenhauer and Richard Wagner, both of whom were emphatic that suspension of thought was a precondition for action by the unowned, universal Will. Wagner consciously strove to bring this state about by his music and produced lengthy prose accounts describing what then ensued.[9] It was the very point of his music. Schopenhauer we shall consider in a moment.

Rauschning recorded a further conversation he had with Hitler in which Hitler outlined his intellectual forebears, stating that besides Lenin, Trotsky and the infamous anti-Semitic forgery *The Protocols of the Elders of Zion*, he had 'got illumination and ideas from the Catholic Church, and from the Freemasons, that I could never have obtained from other sources'. When queried by Rauschning what he had learned from the Freemasons, Hitler replied:

> 'That's simple. Needless to say, I don't seriously believe in the abysmal evilness and noxiousness of these people. . . . But there is one dangerous element, and that is the element I have copied from them. They form a sort of priestly nobility. They have developed an esoteric doctrine, not merely formulated, but imparted through the medium of symbols and mysterious rites in degrees of initiation. The hierarchical organisation and the initiation through symbolic rites, that is to say without bothering the brains but by working on the imagination through magic and the symbols of a cult – all this is the dangerous element and the element that I have taken over. Don't you see that our party must be of this character?'
>
> He banged the table.
>
> 'An Order, that is what it has to be – an Order, the hierarchical Order of a secular priesthood.'

If Rauschning is an accurate reporter – and he claims to have written down each conversation soon after having it – then Hitler deliberately worked upon the imagination through magic.

To those who doubt the causal efficacy of magic altogether, even on the Collingwood model, the enterprise on which we have embarked is still not something to be dismissed as unimportant or misguided. It might be that magical practice explains at the very least what Hitler *thought* he was doing, whether or not it actually explains what he actually brought to pass. In similar fashion, no historian can pretend to understand the Crusades in ignorance of the religious beliefs of the Crusaders. The historian might deny that divine help brought about the capture of Jerusalem, while granting that *belief* in divine help had an effect upon Crusader morale that made the capture possible. Equally, an historian might deny that magic is efficacious, while granting that the techniques Hitler developed on the basis of his belief that magic is efficacious, did indeed work. Now whatever the scoffing of the sceptics about magic – and about whether what I am characterizing as magic is legitimately so characterized – the technique, as Hitler applied it, did work. Hitler's successes from 1920 to 1940 have a claim to rank amongst the most astounding by any individual in the history of the world. A lone, gas-affected war veteran – an Austrian foreigner – arose from nothing to leadership of a great nation. He created millions of jobs and rescued the country from destitution. Nation after nation fell to him bloodlessly. And when it did come to blood, France fell within a matter of weeks to a militarily inferior opponent. Hitler's own career, then, is the experimental evidence that magic – as characterized by Collingwood – really is causally efficacious after all. In the phenomenon of Nazism, it was subjected to sustained experimental testing and it worked.[10]

What then of the alleged supernatural effects of magic, those that concern not morale, but allegedly violate the laws of nature? Unlike Schopenhauer, Collingwood denied this possibility. He restricted himself to a sphere of efficacious magic concerned with human morale and contrasted this with a sphere of bogus magic, of alleged effects in violation of the laws of nature, which he did not believe were possible. The distinction is necessary if we are to take Collingwood, Schopenhauer and Wittgenstein seriously. And this now brings us to focus upon the question of how this efficacious magic produces its effects. Here we come to the essence of the problem and the connection between what Collingwood has to say on the matter and what Wittgenstein wrote. (We shall see later that Schopenhauer's account of the means by which magic works is rather different.)

If we ask how magic produces these emotional effects, the answer is easy. It is done by representation. A situation is created (the warriors brandish their spears, the peasant gets out his plough, and so forth, when no battle is being fought and no seed is being sown) representing the practical situation upon which emotion is to be directed. It is essential to the magical efficacy of the act that the agent shall be conscious of this relation, and shall recognize what he is doing as a war-dance, a plough-ritual, or the like. This is why, on first approaching the ritual, he must have it explained to him, either by word of mouth (which may take the form of initiatory instruction, or of an explanatory speech or song forming part of the ritual itself) or by such close mimicry that mistake is impossible.

Magic is a representation where the emotion evoked is an emotion valued on account of its function in practical life, evoked in order that it may discharge that function, and fed by the generative or focusing magical activity into the practical life that needs it. Magical activity is a kind of dynamo supplying the mechanism of practical life with the emotional current that drives it. Hence magic is a necessity for every sort and condition of man, and is actually found in every healthy society. A society which thinks, as our own thinks, that it has outlived the need for magic, is either mistaken in that opinion, or else it is a dying society, perishing for lack of interest in its own maintenance.[11]

Collingwood's account of magic, while dismissive of the rationalist Frazer account (which Wittgenstein also criticized), is also one to which no rationalist will take exception, for it is a naturalistic account of magic. For Collingwood, a successful magical spell is in no way different from a college basketball team being sufficiently inspired by its supporters chanting 'Rah! Rah! Rah!' to go on and win the game. A spell is effective just as this chant can be effective.[12] Collingwood's point is that we know very little either about how magic works or about its possible ramifications within the psyche, and that this ignorance ought not to be used dismissively to dispose of a human practice that really is efficacious after all.

Collingwood's is clearly a possible account of magic, in the sense that there are no obvious flaws of logic in its presentation. I have called it a no-ownership account because Collingwood was a no-ownership theorist, but he did not tie his presentation of magical phenomena explicitly to his no-ownership theory of the mind. (The reader must suspect that as a salaried Oxford professor, Collingwood was unduly constrained in publicly expressing just how radical his ideas really were.) His theory of magic might even be defended by critics of the no-ownership philosophy. Collingwood's philosophy of magic, however, is our entrée into the subject and I hope that its presentation has convinced the reader that the question of the efficacy of magic is not something to be dismissed as an atavism, and that there might indeed be some point to considering Nazism as a magical phenomenon based upon the no-ownership theory of mind.

From Collingwood's account of magic – essentially as morale-building or morale-destroying – we now turn to consider another no-ownership theory of magic. Unlike Collingwood, Schopenhauer explicitly presents the technique whereby magical effects are to be induced. Before presenting it, let me focus upon why we are bothering to investigate the Nazi phenomenon from this perspective.

To my sensibilities – and I am far from the first to suffer this impression – Nazism positively reeks of the occult. Hitler's public performances and gestures; his flashing eyes and rough, guttural, at times incomprehensible voice, the background use of colours, runes and the death's head symbols on the guards close to him, call to mind nothing so much as a sorcerer acting in full and conscious cooperation with whatever powers are using his human form as vehicle. The Hoffmann photographs of Hitler rehearsing a speech might have served equally to represent a warlock in full-flight magical invocation. If this idea is not just fanciful, then we should expect Hitler to have exhibited some of the powers popularly attributed to mediums. Do we have any evidence that he did?

In fact there is a great deal of evidence that he did, from reporters with no obvious axe to grind. Perhaps they were simply gullible, but we must surely consider what they had to say first, without prematurely dismissing the whole matter as simply *a priori* impossible.

First, Hitler is alleged to have had premonitory powers, and, if his photographer is to be believed, avoided several assassination attempts solely by that means. Here, for example, is Heinrich Hoffmann's by no means slavishly devoted account of his time with Hitler, published after the war was over and Hitler was dead. Hoffmann was a long-time Hitler associate. His employee, Eva Braun, was to marry Hitler and his daughter was the wife of Baldur von Schirach, the leader of the Hitler Youth. We read first of Hitler's attitude towards the supernatural:

> Often, when he was hesitant over some decision, he would take a coin and toss for it; and though he would laugh at his own stupidity in appealing thus to Fate, he was always obviously delighted when the toss fell the way he hoped it would.
>
> He believed firmly in the chronological repetition and faithful reproduction of certain historical events. For him November was the Month of Revolution; May was a propitious month for any undertaking, even when eventual success followed but later.
>
> In 1922 he read a prophecy in an astrological calendar which exactly fitted the events of the putsch of November, 1923, and for years afterwards he used to talk about it. Even though he would never admit it, this prophecy undoubtedly made a lasting and profound impression on him.
>
> During the course of our twenty-five years of association I had numberless opportunities of seeing how prone he was to premonitions. Quite suddenly and for no reason which he could explain, he would become uneasy. On the occasion of the Bürgerbräukeller attempt, too, he had this mysterious, impelling feeling that there was something in the air, that something was wrong, and he altered all his plans, without really having the least idea why he did so. . . .[13]
>
> I shall never forget the disconcerted expression on Hitler's face when he was laying the foundation stone of the Haus der Deutschen Kunst in Munich in 1933. At the symbolic stroke, the silver hammer in his hand broke in two. Very few people noticed it, and Hitler immediately ordered that no public mention was to be made of the untoward incident. 'The people are superstitious,' he declared, 'and might well see in this ridiculous little misfortune an omen of evil.' But looking at him, I realised how taken aback he was; it was not of the people, but of himself that he was thinking!
>
> Such little incidents invariably left an unpleasant impression on him. We

never mentioned them again, for fear of depressing him.

Once – after Hitler had come to power – someone in our intimate circle started to talk about the centuries, the prophecies of the famous astrologer, Nostradamus. Hitler was very interested, and told one of his officials to get the books for him from the State Library, but on no account to say for whom he was getting them. As it was, a deposit of three thousand marks had to be put down before the Library would give him the books.

In the prophecies mention is made of a mighty mountain, over which a great eagle is sweeping, and Hitler compared the mountain to Germany and the eagle to himself. He went through the prophecies sentence by sentence, and said that although he could not claim that they all had direct bearing on himself, he did feel that they constituted an inexplicable phenomenon; and in this connection, he quoted Hamlet: 'There are more things in Heaven and earth. . . .'[14]

Hoffmann continues his narrative by describing a number of incidents he witnessed in which Hitler's premonitory sense enabled him to avert assassination attempts and accidents. In one, involving Hitler's train, twenty-two people died. In another, Hitler escaped an assassin who fired three shots. It is difficult, sixty years onwards, to determine to what extent Hoffmann might have embellished the details of these events, but he himself clearly believed in Hitler's premonitory powers. His testimony sounds neither contrived nor slavishly worshipful; it is even mildly disapproving in its record of Hitler's superstition when the silver hammer broke.

Whatever one thinks of this, there is the well-attested matter of Hitler's compelling personal magnetism to take into account. References to it are not confined to the fringe literature. One cannot read any substantial biography of Hitler or of the events of 1933-45 without coming across references to it. Albert Speer, the German generals and many, many others experienced a mesmeric power in Hitler's presence so compelling as to be almost palpable. With Germany facing utter ruin, front-line officers who entered Hitler's presence determined to tell him that the military situation was hopeless, emerged from the bunker with complete confidence in ultimate victory. Even Winston Churchill recognized it, as early as 1932. After the war, he recalled his German trip of 1932 and of a discussion he had had with Hitler's then secretary, Ernst Hanfstaengl, in order to arrange a meeting with Hitler. Churchill gave Hitler's mesmeric powers as the reason for not proceeding with it. He wrote: 'There is no doubt that Hitler had a power of fascinating men, and the sense of force and authority is apt to assert itself unduly upon the tourist.'[15] If one so perspicacious and eminent as Winston Churchill recognized what we in any case have a vast number of reports concerning, then we are justified in pursuing our line of inquiry rather further than we otherwise might have inclined. To an extraordinary degree, Hitler did have a power to fascinate and hypnotize. When, where and how did he acquire this power? The question is obviously of fundamental importance in explaining his dominance over other NSDAP officials and his rise to leadership. It is foolishness in the extreme to think Hitler was passively carried along by events. Without an understanding of how he did it, the possibility must be open that someone else might rediscover whatever it was and precipitate something similarly dreadful again. There appears to be no comprehensive study of it, however, and what information we have exists only in snippets. Lord Bullock's biography of Hitler notes of his Vienna days that

> He spent much time in the public library, but his reading was indiscriminate and unsystematic. Ancient Rome, the Eastern Religions, Yoga, Occultism, Hypnotism, Astrology, Protestantism, each in turn excited his interest for a moment.[16]

Lord Bullock's judgement that Hitler's reading 'was indiscriminate and unsystematic' is clearly quite unsupported. It seems to me very likely that there was some connecting theme here that has not yet been divined.

It is a universal failing of writers on Hitler to assume that there is nothing mysterious or difficult to understand about him. Yet if we ignore the moral dimension of what he wrought – its overwhelming wickedness – then it seems to me that Hitler has a claim to rank as the most extraordinary man the continent of Europe has ever produced. What did he discover that allowed him to do what he did? The truth is that no one has any idea, but he certainly discovered something and used it to manipulate first the NSDAP and then Germany. It is obviously difficult to see, for no one, thank God, has even come close to duplicating what he did.

The working hypothesis of this work is that the ultimate secret of Hitler's powers, and perhaps the unifying theme behind the books he chose to read, was an applied philosophy. It was this philosophy – a racially restricted Aryan version of Wittgenstein's no-ownership theory – that determined which books he chose to read. Like Wittgenstein, with *his* compelling personal power, Hitler's *mana* derived from the very same philosophy of how the Mind works and how Language represents. Its ultimate source, I believe, was Schopenhauer via the young Wittgenstein. Let us venture into deeper waters.

The great point Schopenhauer thought he had established with his philosophy was that the Will lies outside the causal order of the natural world. In fact he claimed further that the world is simply the Will as perceived by the senses. This Will 'objectifies' itself in the various objects that we see, touch, hear, smell and taste – each object representing a 'grade' of the will. The granite hills we see are the visible form of the will to permanence; the sport of the ephemeral clouds the will to impermanence and so on. This is what they – and the Will – are, in their essence. We can touch the Will as it disports itself for us, for it has created the world, not as a remote and transcendent cause, but as something profoundly immanent. The cliffs, the clouds, these are the visible, object form of what we know in another way within ourselves as subject. That is, the self-same will which has come to expression in the body of the reader also has presented itself visibly in the appearance of objects in the world.

What Schopenhauer further outlined on the basis of his theory of the will was a realm of metaphysical causality, whose particular feature is that it is not subject to the categories of space and time, but, rather outside the natural causal order altogether. The Will acts, as it were, directly.

Now as we have recognized the *will* to be this thing-in-itself, this enables us to suppose that perhaps such a will underlies both spirit and bodily phenomena. All previous explanations of spirit phenomena have been *spiritualistic*; precisely as such, they are the subject of Kant's criticism in the first part of his *Träume eines Geistersehers*. Here I am attempting an *idealistic* explanation.[17]

It must come as no surprise that the explanation of spirit phenomena Schopenhauer invoked was the no-ownership theory of the common will. Here is his outline of how he saw magic as operating:

. . . one is astonished at the steadfastness with which humanity everywhere and at all times, in spite of so many failures, has pursued the idea of magic, and from this we shall conclude that it must have a deep foundation, at least in the nature of human beings, if not of things generally, and that it cannot be an arbitrarily devised notion. Although the writers on the subject differ in the definition of *magic*, the fundamental idea is everywhere unmistakable. Namely, at all times and in all countries the opinion has been held that besides the regular way of producing changes in the world by means of the causal nexus of bodies, there must be another quite different way that does not rest on the causal nexus at all. Hence, too, its means obviously appeared to be absurd when they were viewed in the light of that first way, in that the unsuitability of the applied cause to the intended effect was obvious, and the causal nexus between the two was impossible. But the presupposition was made in this case that besides the external connection establishing the *nexus physicus* between the phenomena of this world there must be another passing through the essence-in-itself of all things, a subterranean connection, so to speak, in virtue of which an immediate effect was possible from *one* point of the appearance to every other, through a *nexus metaphysicus*. Accordingly, it was thought that an effect must be possible on

things from within instead of the usual one from without, an effect of phenomenon on phenomenon, by virtue of the essence-in-itself which is one and the
same in all appearances; that, just as we act causally as *natura naturata* [created
nature], we could probably also be capable of acting as *natura naturans* [creating
nature], and of making the microcosm assert itself for a moment as the macro-
cosm; that solid as the partitions of individuation and separation may be, they
might occasionally permit a communication, behind the scenes as it were, or like
a secret game under the table; and that, just as in somnambulist clairvoyance,
there is an annulment of the individual isolation of *knowledge*, there can be also
one of the individual isolation of the *will*. Such an idea cannot have arisen
empirically, nor can it be the confirmation through experience that has
preserved it through all ages and in all countries, for in most cases experience
was bound to prove entirely opposed to it. I am therefore of the opinion that we
must seek at a very great depth the origin of this idea that is so universal with
the whole of humanity and is ineradicable in spite of so much experience to the
contrary and of ordinary common sense. Namely, we must seek it in the inner
feeling of the omnipotence of the will-in-itself, of that will which is the inner
being of human beings and at the same time of the whole of nature and in the
connected presupposition that that omnipotence might well make itself felt for
once, in some way or the other, even as issuing out from the individual. One was
not capable of investigating and separating what might be possible to that will
as thing-in-itself, on the one hand, and its individual manifestation on the other.
No, it was simply assumed that in certain circumstances the will was able to
break through the barrier of individuation.[18]

Schopenhauer's conception of magic, then, is of a causality acting 'under
the table', which becomes actualizable when the will is 'able to break
through the barrier of individuation'.[19] That is, the will can act magically
when it is seen in its true nature; not as 'my will' or 'your will' but as the
unitary will behind all phenomena. This is an extraordinary doctrine, and
rather difficult to test empirically, for it is not clear how one can act, as an
individual, to bring it about that the universal will magically achieves a
certain result. And if a scientific test of magic fails, the magician can always
retort, 'No, I wasn't able to act as a vehicle of *the* will; I was sadly only
acting inefficaciously with my paltry individual will.'[20] Schopenhauer, in
fact, does suggest a means by which the universal will can, in full
consciousness of its nature, act through an individual; but this is to anticipate what Hitler discovered, and we still have considerable ground to cover
before we approach it. Here is Schopenhauer's account of the phenomenon
described as 'communication with the souls of the dead':

Finally, when explaining spirit apparitions, we might still refer to the fact that
the difference between those who were formerly alive and those now alive is not

absolute, but that one and the same will-to-live appears in both. In this way, a living man, going back far enough, might bring to light reminiscences that appear as the communications of one who is dead.[21]

This passage – together with what we know of, say, Himmler's occult activities – should alert us to how the no-ownership theory lends itself to a doctrine of communication with what might seem to be disembodied entities. For on the no-ownership account, of course, these reminiscences do not merely appear as being communications of the dead; they are the very mental processes of the dead, the activities of the self-same Mind that is past, passing and yet to come, abiding in eternity, outside the time-stream altogether. The very conscious thinking of long-dead Pythagoras expresses itself totally unchanged both through Pythagoras's body and through the body of the geometrically inclined reader. History, as Collingwood put it, in the title of his essay, is just the recollection of past experience; the thoughts of the deceased personages recorded in history come to life in us. Hence Hitler's discovery of the meaning of history and hence his reverence for such figures as Frederick the Great and Frederick Barbarossa. The occult starts when these timeless thoughts are seen, not as unowned, but as belonging to other, perhaps disembodied, entities.

Schopenhauer's account of the nature of intercourse with demons is of great interest, for he saw the essence of all of the means of bringing about occult effects as a fixation of the Will and nothing else:

According to the fundamental idea just presented, we find that in all attempts at magic the physical means employed was always taken to be merely the vehicle of something metaphysical, in that otherwise it could obviously have no relation to the intended effect. Such were foreign words, symbolic actions, drawn figures, images in wax, and so on. And according to that original feeling, we see that what was borne by such a vehicle was ultimately always an act of the *will* that one connected with it. The very natural inducement to do this was the fact that in the movements of one's own body one became aware every moment of a wholly inexplicable and hence evidently metaphysical influence of the will. Ought it not to be possible, one thought, for such an influence to be extended to other bodies as well? To discover the way of eliminating the isolation in which the will finds itself in every individual, and to gain an increase in the immediate sphere of the will beyond the body of the person who wills – that was the task of magic.

Yet this fundamental idea from which magic really seems to have sprung, was far from passing at once into distinct consciousness and from being known *in abstracto*; and magic was a long way from understanding itself. Only in a few reflecting and scholarly authors of earlier centuries, as I shall show in a moment from quotations, do we find the distinct idea that magic power lies in the *will* itself, and that the extravagant signs and acts, together with the senseless words accompanying them, which passed for the means of exorcising and binding the demons, are merely vehicles and means-for-fixing of the *will*. In this way the act of will, which is to operate magically, ceases to be a mere wish and becomes the deed; it receives a *corpus* (as Paracelsus says), and to a certain extent the individual will proclaims that it is now asserting itself as general will, as will-in-itself.

The 'general will' or 'will-in-itself' that Schopenhauer is referring to here, of course, is the will as conceived by the no-ownership theory. On this theory, what Schopenhauer describes as the goal of magic in fact happens all the time, but unknowingly. The unitary will to perform any particular act expresses itself through my body and the bodies of countless others simultaneously, throughout space and time. But how, for Schopenhauer, does this will come to act knowingly, so that an individual can, as an individual, act to bring about magical effects? What was his account of the mechanism of magic?

First, he was emphatic that the trappings of magic – wax images, amulets, etc – did not function of themselves. And he thought that polytheism was particularly suited to magical practices because the polytheistic gods are personifications of natural forces. What had caused the problems for magical practice – what had forced it underground – was Judaism and the religions derived from it. From the time of Moses, Jews were barred from practising any form of divination or magic:

> There shall not be found among you any one . . . who practises divination, a soothsayer, or an augur, or a sorcerer, or a charmer, or a medium, or a wizard, or a necromancer. For whoever does these things is an abomination. . . .[22]

But what was the practice that Yahweh forbade? What did these diviners, soothsayers, augurers, sorcerers, mediums, wizards and necromancers actually do in order to qualify as abominable? According to Schopenhauer, in the light of his metaphysics, they used means whose nature they misunderstood to focus the universal will and thereby attain absolute mastery over nature. They mistakenly attributed the cause of magical effects not to the unowned almighty will, but to the means by which they focused the will, that is, by using wax images and dolls, or by invoking the aid of supernatural beings – angels, cherubim, demons, personifications of elemental forces and so on. But these external actions are

> not really what is essential, but the vehicle, that whereby the will, the only real agent, obtains its direction and fixation in the material world, and goes over into

reality; and so, as a rule, it is indispensable. With the remaining authors of those times, in keeping with that fundamental idea of magic, nothing is established but the aims arbitrarily to exert absolute mastery over nature. Yet they could not rise to the idea that such a mastery must be immediate, but conceived it as being altogether *mediate*. For the religions of all countries had put nature under the dominion of gods and demons. So it was the endeavour of the magician to direct these in accordance with his will, to induce, indeed to compel them to serve him. He ascribed to them anything in which he was successful, just as Mesmer to begin with attributed the success of his magnetizing to the bar magnets he held in his hands, instead of to his will, which was the real agent.

These gods and demons of the polytheistic peoples were, for Schopenhauer (just as for Wagner), representations of metaphysical principles. How do they affect people? It is striking that Schopenhauer mentions hypnosis in support of what he claims. He was writing when the hypnotic phenomena that Mesmer demonstrated were seen as but little removed from magic and when it was considered possible that a science might emerge from magic as chemistry had emerged from – and developed the techniques of – alchemy. Schopenhauer saw his own contribution as explaining how magical concepts might have been not mere superstition, but really have had application. We read of gods and demons, for example, that

demons and gods of every kind are always hypostases, by means of which the faithful of every colour and sect make understandable to themselves the *metaphysical*, that which lies *behind* nature, that which gives it existence and stability and thus controls it. And so when it is said that magic acts through the help of demons, the meaning at bottom is always that it is an acting not on a physical but on a *metaphysical* path, not natural but supernatural. But if now in the few facts that speak in favour of the reality of magic, namely, animal magnetism and sympathetic cures, we recognize nothing but an immediate working of the will, which here manifests its direct power without, as it otherwise does only within, the individual that wills, and if we see, as I shall document by decisive, unequivocal quotations, that those more deeply initiated in ancient magic derive all its effects solely from the *will*, of the person who practices it, then this is indeed a strong empirical instance of my doctrine that the metaphysical in general, that which alone still exists outside the representation, the thing-in-itself of the world, is nothing but what we recognize in ourselves as *will*.

Schopenhauer is accounting for magical activity as a function solely of the will of the magical practitioner, with the invocation of gods or demons being the means by which this will is brought to representation. The magician thus invokes Poseidon in dealing with horses, earthquakes or the sea, where a common form is recognized in the god's domain.[23]

Schopenhauer then attributed the apparent need of these gods, demons, images, etc in magical practice to 'false notions of the intellect' which are not the sovereign agent, though they give the illusion that they are. He emphasises, however, their role as akin to the placebo effect, to 'the medicine, often quite useless, given to many gullible patients'. That is, the will works as the sovereign magical agent *despite* the magical paraphernalia

> Now if those magicians conceived of the direct authority that the will may occasionally exercise over nature as merely indirect through the help of demons, this could not prevent its acting, whenever and wherever such may have taken place. For just because in things of this kind the will-in-itself is active in its original nature and is therefore separated from the representation, false notions of the intellect cannot frustrate its action, but theory and practice are very far apart here: the falseness of the former does not stand in the way of the latter, and the correct theory does not qualify for practice. . . . I knew a landowner whose peasants had long been accustomed to have their attacks of fever dispelled by their master's magic words. Although he considered himself to be fully convinced of the impossibility of all such things, out of good nature he did the peasants' will in the traditional manner, and often with a favorable result. He attributed this to their firm confidence, without considering that this must also render effective the medicine, often quite useless, given to many gullible patients.

The emphasis here is that it is *not* the bar magnets that induce hypnosis, just as it is not the wax images that bring about the magical effects. Nonetheless, by the practitioner using them as a *corpus*, the effect is brought about. Schopenhauer attributes the lack of knowledge about the true means of bringing about magical effects via the focused will to hostile authorities, who have been the filter through which has had to pass those of the ancient Hermetic books we possess. Thus

> Now if theurgy and demonomagic, as previously described, were the mere interpretation and expression of the matter, the mere husk beyond which however most people did not go, still there was no lack of those who, looking inward, well recognized that what was acting in occasional magical influences was nothing but the will. However, we must not look for these people of deeper insight among those who approached magic as strangers or even enemies, and it is precisely by such people that most of the books on the subject have been written. They know magic merely from law courts and the examination of witnesses, and hence describe only its exterior. Indeed, they cautiously pass over in silence the actual proceedings where such have perhaps come to their knowledge through confessions, in order not to spread the terrible vice of sorcery.

It is here that Schopenhauer begins his presentation of his researches in the

Hermetic literature in support of his claim that his own theory of the will explained what magicians had been doing all along. He quotes Roger Bacon, Paracelsus and Vanini and emphasizes that for magical effects to occur, the will needs a *corpus*. That is, it is not enough to merely wish for something to happen; magical effects require that the will attains to representation. The unitary form of the desired event must be present also in the magical working. One thinks of pins pushed into dolls to magically represent harm being done to someone, or of Mesmer using magnets in passes to induce hypnosis. In all these cases, Schopenhauer thought, what was really going on was one-pointed fixation of the intent will and that the role of magical representing was so to 'focus' the will that action followed. Schopenhauer first tried to demonstrate from the ancient European Hermetica that authorities had already suggested his own account. Thus he writes:

> . . . it is the philosophers and investigators of nature who lived in those times of the prevailing superstition that we have to ask for information concerning the real essence of the matter. From their statements it appears most clearly that in magic, precisely as in animal magnetism, the agent proper is nothing but the will. To document this I must give a few quotations. Thus Roger Bacon in the thirteenth century said: 'When an evil-minded man resolutely thinks of injuring another, when he passionately desires this and intends to do so with determination, and is firmly convinced that he can injure him, then there is no doubt that nature will obey the intentions of his will.' (*Opus Majus*, London, 1733, p 252). But it is Theophrastus Paracelsus in particular who gives more information about the inner nature of magic than I think anyone else, and who is even not afraid to give an exact description of its processes, occurring especially in Volume I, pages 91, 353 *seqq*., and 789; Volume II, pages 362 and 496 (according to the Strassburg edition of his works in two folio volumes, 1903). In the first volume he says:

> > Observe the following concerning images of wax; if in my will I bear hostility to another, this must be carried out through a *medium*, i.e., a corpus. Thus it is possible for my spirit, without the help of my body using a sword, to stab or wound another through my *ardent desire*. Thus it is also possible for me to bring my opponent's spirit into the image by my will, and then to bend or paralyse it as I please. You should know that the effect of the *will* is a great point in medicine. For if a man grudges another everything good and hates him, it is possible that, if he curses him, the curse may come about.[24]

Now the effect of the will quite certainly is a great point in medicine. What its full extent or limits are, we still don't know. Paracelsus was simply stating what twentieth-century research has demonstrated to be the case with sophisticated statistical analysis. Patients who believe they are being treated with medicine – even if it is only sugar – recover faster than do members of a control group taking sugar alone. This is the famous 'placebo effect'. Given the known validity of the placebo effect, it seems not impossible that it might exist in negative form. That is, that just as a man can be cured by the belief that he is receiving medicine, even when he is not receiving medicine, so a man might sicken from the belief that he is being poisoned, even when he is not being poisoned. And further, he might sicken if he believes the harm being done to him comes not from material poison but from an immaterial, magical attack. That is; a curse might well function to cause someone to sicken or perhaps die. The mechanism by which the curse worked would be quite opaque to a mechanist, just as the mechanism involved in the placebo effect is still opaque even to biochemists. For all that, the placebo effect is real and so, I am suggesting, are magical techniques when used by those versed in the art. They certainly worked amongst Australian aborigines.

Besides the *corpus* that is required to focus the will and the necessary belief that the magic will be effective, however, Schopenhauer identified in the occult literature a further element necessary for the will to act magically. By means of this element, rational thought is overcome and the mind is able to act according to its instincts. This element is the 'violent and immoderate excitement of the soul itself'. Thus Schopenhauer quotes from the first book of *De occulta Philosophia* by Agrippa v. Nettesheim that 'All that is dictated by the spirit of one who feels intense hatred has the effect of damaging and destroying; and it is much the same with everything that the spirit does and dictates by means of written characters, figures, words (conversations), gestures, and the like, all this supports the desire of the soul and obtains certain extraordinary powers. . . .' He also quotes Vanini saying that 'a vivid imagination, obeyed by blood and spirit, can really affect a thing that is conceived in the mind not only inwardly but also outwardly'.[25]

Schopenhauer's concluding summary on his survey of the Hermetic writings runs:

> The agreement of all these authors not only with one another but with the convictions to which animal magnetism has led in recent times, and finally too with what might be inferred in this respect from my speculative teaching, is truly a phenomenon to be carefully considered. This much is certain, that an anticipation of my metaphysics underlies all attempts at magic that have ever been made, whether successful or unsuccessful: in them the consciousness was expressed that the law of causality is merely the bond of appearances, but the essence-in-itself of things remains independent of it, and that if, from this

essence and hence from within, an immediate effect on nature were possible, that effect could be brought about only through the will itself. But if we wished to set up magic as practical metaphysics in accordance with Bacon's classification, then it is certain that the theoretical metaphysics correctly related to it could be no other than my resolution of the world into will and representation.

What is to be concluded from Schopenhauer's reading of the Hermetic tradition? Perhaps we should simply shake our heads with the sceptics at this monument to centuries of human gullibility. On the other hand, perhaps it is a clue to something of extraordinary significance.

We know that Hitler believed in the efficacy of magic. We know that he convinced some people that he possessed premonitory powers and he quite definitely had the power to fascinate. According to Hermann Rauschning, he believed that his own advance was attributable to magical insights. Rauschning was a confidant of sorts, before Hitler and he fell out, and his record of conversations with Hitler in the thirties is particularly engrossing for what it reveals about Hitler's thought processes. He recounts one particular talk:

We had come to a turning-point in world history – that was his constant theme. We uninstructed persons, it was clear, had no conception of the scale of the revolution that was to take place in all life. At these times Hitler spoke as a seer, as one of the initiated. His inspired pronouncements were based on a biological mysticism – or shall we call it a mystical biology? The pursuit of the 'random path of the intelligence', we learned, was the real defection of man from his divine mission. To have 'magic insight' was apparently Hitler's idea of the goal of human progress. He himself felt that he already had the rudiments of this gift. He attributed to it his successes and his future eminence. . . .

He saw his own remarkable career as a confirmation of hidden powers. He saw himself as chosen for superhuman tasks, as the prophet of the rebirth of man in a new form. Humanity, he proclaimed, was in the throes of a vast metamorphosis. A process of change that had lasted literally for thousands of years was approaching its completion. Man's solar period was coming to its end. The coming age was revealing itself in the first great human figures of a new type. Just as, according to the imperishable prophecies of the old Nordic peoples, the world has continually to renew itself, the old order perishing with its gods, just as the Nordic peoples took the sun's passing of the solstices as a figure of the rhythm of life, which proceeds not in a straight line of eternal progress but in a spiral, so must man now, apparently, turn back in order to attain a higher stage. . . .

He is capable of entertaining the most incompatible ideas in association with one another. One thing is certain – Hitler has the spirit of the prophet. He is not content to be a mere politician.

In our talks he put these ideas before me in a rather more materialistic form.

'Creation is not yet at an end,' he said. 'At all events, not so far as the creature Man is concerned. Biologically regarded, man has clearly arrived at a turning-point. A new variety of man is beginning to separate out. A mutation, precisely in the scientific sense. The existing type of man is passing, in consequence, inescapably into the biological stage of atrophy. The old type of man will have but a stunted existence. All creative energy will be concentrated in the new one. The two types will rapidly diverge from one another. One will sink to a sub-human race and the other rise far above the man of to-day. I might call the two varieties the god-man and the mass-animal.'

That, I commented, was very reminiscent of Nietzsche and his superman. But I had always taken all this as metaphorical.

'Yes,' Hitler continued, 'man has to be passed and surpassed. Nietzsche did, it is true, realise something of this, in his way. He went so far as to recognise the superman as a new biological variety. But he was not too sure of it. Man is becoming God – that is the simple fact. Man is God in the making. Man has eternally to strain at his limitations. The moment he relaxes and contents himself with them, he decays and falls below the human level. He becomes a quasi-beast. Gods and beasts, that is what our world is made of.

'And how simple, how elementary it all becomes! It is constantly the same decision that has to be made, whether I am faced with new political decisions to be made or with problems of the reordering of our social system. All those who cut themselves off from our movement, who cling to the old order, die away and are doomed. But those who listen to the immemorial message of man, who devote themselves to our eternal movement, are called to a new humanity. Do you now appreciate the depth of our National Socialist movement? Can there be anything greater and more all-comprehending? Those who see in National Socialism nothing more than a political movement know scarcely anything of it. It is more even than a religion: it is the will to create mankind anew. . . .

'The new man is among us! He is here!' exclaimed Hitler triumphantly. 'Now are you satisfied? I will tell you a secret. I have seen the vision of the new man – fearless and formidable. I shrank from him!'[26]

If Rauschning's report is trustworthy, then Hitler appears to have had as his goal the conscious breeding of magically sensitive individuals – mediums – presumably either prone to suffer the same vision from which he shrank, or else themselves the object of this fearful vision taken flesh. That this was the case is supported by some writings of Georg Lanz von Liebenfels, the Austrian from whose anti-Semitic journal *Ostara* Hitler purloined many of his ideas. Von Liebenfels saw the production of a race in tune with magic as the very *raison d'être* of the racial breeding programme. It is now generally accepted that the 'anti-Semitic pamphlets' that Hitler read in Vienna, and which *Mein Kampf* tells us informed him on the Jewish question, were from this very journal. Werner Maser's summary of the ideas in *Ostara* is very interesting when read in tandem with the extracts from Rauschning's book that we have just considered:

No. 29 (autumn 1908), after calling attention to statements of policy in previous issues, goes on to define the publication's task as follows: 'The *Ostara* is the first and only periodical devoted to investigating and cultivating heroic racial characteristics and the law of man in such a way that, by actually applying the discoveries of ethnology, we may through systematic eugenics . . . preserve the heroic and noble race from destruction by socialist and feminist revolutionaries.' This extract speaks for itself. In 1905 Lanz von Liebenfels founded the 'Order of the New Temple' whose membership was restricted to fair-haired, blue-eyed men, all of whom were pledged to marry fair-haired, blue-eyed women. In 1908 Liebenfels, an uncommonly prolific journalist, produced his *magnum opus*, which was reprinted in the *Ostara* between 1928 and 1930, in the form of a pamphlet entitled *Theozoology or the Science of Sodom's Apelings and the Divine Electron. An Introduction to the Earliest and Most Recent World View and a Vindication of Royalty and the Nobility*. 'Sodom's apelings' were the dark-skinned, 'inferior races' whom Liebenfels described as the 'bungled handiwork' of demons in contrast to the blue-eyed, fair-haired 'Aryo-heroes', the masterpiece of the gods. These latter beings were equipped with electric bodily organs and built in electric transmitting and power stations. They were the archetypes of the human species and the human race. By means of 'purifying eugenics' he proposed to awaken the gods who, he alleged, continued to slumber in the 'fleshy coffins of men's bodies'. At the same time he proposed to help the new human race, about to emerge out of the Aryo-heroic race, to regain their former divine 'electro-magnetic-radiological' organs and, thus equipped, to become 'all-knowing, all-wise and all-powerful' as in the primeval era of the gods.[27]

This was the goal of the Nazi breeding programmes that Hitler set in train. The key to understanding it all is magic – a theurgy to awaken the gods by selective breeding.

How was this to be brought about? In the work of a philosopher from whom Hitler acknowledged he had learnt a lot, and from whom he could quote by the page, he would have found a detailed survey of the Hermetic literature including instructions on the means by which magical effects could be brought about. These instructions fundamentally presuppose the no-ownership theory of the mind, a uniting of the individual will with something supra-personal that can identically unite with other personal wills.

Now Hitler's cultured, Schopenhauer-reading school-fellow of 1904 – Ludwig Wittgenstein – adhered to a generalized no-ownership theory as far back as we have recorded information and stated that his very first philosophy was 'a Schopenhaurean Idealism'. This school-fellow, as we have deduced, was the most likely target of the young Hitler's very first recorded anti-Semitic epithet, '*Saujud*!' Hitler hated this school=fellow for his perceived Jewishness.

And hatred was the key. Magical effects can be brought about, quotes Schopenhauer from the Hermetica, by 'violent and immoderate excitation of the emotions'. Hitler excited his emotions – presumably to the immoderate degree required – by continual cultivation of Jew-hatred. Rauschning tells us that 'The extent to which he was obsessed by his hatred of the Jews was shown by the way he could scarcely speak without bringing in sooner or later at least one scathing reference to them.'[28] Here is a report of a conversation with Hitler from the early twenties, made by Josef Hell, the editor of the Munich weekly magazine *Der Gerade Weg*:

> While up until now Hitler had spoken comparatively calmly and moderately, his nature now changed completely. He no longer looked at me, rather above and beyond me into the distance and made his following statements with rising vocal effort, so that he fell into a kind of paroxysm and finally screamed at me as if I were an entire nationalist gathering: 'When I really am in power, then the annihilation of the Jews will be my first and most important task. As soon as I have the power to do it I shall, for example, have erected in the Marienplatz in Munich gallows and more gallows, as many as can be fitted in without stopping the traffic. Then the Jews will be hanged, one after another, and they will stay hanging, until they stink. They will hang as long as the principles of hygiene permit. As soon as they have been taken down, the next ones will be strung up, and this will continue until the last Jew in Munich is destroyed. The same thing will happen in the other cities until Germany is cleansed of the last Jews.'[29]

This certainly must count as 'immoderate'. And in hating Jews, he was hating a people whose religion forbade the practice of magic and which implicitly rejected the no-ownership theory of the Will as a great impiety. I am suggesting that the secret of Hitler's success was a profound knowledge of magical causes occasioned by his reading of Schopenhauer's account of the European Hermetic literature; and the intellectual attraction of Schopenhauer was the no-ownership theory which he had already acquired from the young Wittgenstein. His anti-Semitism was directed at the race of the apostate Jew who introduced him to the no-ownership theory and it was the anti-Semitism – the hate – that made possible magical means of action against that race. He used it to win power over Germans through the incantations of his voice. Anti-Semitism was not incidental to Hitler's rise to power. It was the very essence of it – that is, there was an internal connection between Hitler's Jew-hatred and his success.

There is one final connection between Hitler's anti-Semitism, the occult and the Wittgensteins in particular to which I draw to the reader's attention. Here is Rauschning's account of Hitler's final words to him on 'the Jew':

'But we have been speaking,' said Hitler, 'of the Jew only as the ruler of the economic world empire. We have been speaking of him as our political opponent. Where does he stand in the deeper struggle for the new world era?'

I confessed that I had no notion.

'There cannot be two Chosen People. We are God's People. Does not that fully answer the question?'

'That is to be understood symbolically?'

Again he banged the table.

'Symbolically? No! It's the sheer simple undiluted truth. Two worlds face one another – the men of God and the men of Satan! The Jew is the anti-man, the creature of another god. He must have come from another root of the human race. I set the Aryan and the Jew over against each other; and if I call one of them a human being I must call the other something else. The two are as widely separated as man and beast. Not that I would call the Jew a beast. He is much further from the beasts than we Aryans. He is a creature outside nature and alien to nature.'

Hitler seemed to have more to say. But words failed him amid the onrush of his surging thoughts. His face was distorted and working. He snapped his fingers in his excitement. 'It's an endless subject,' he spluttered.[30]

To anyone who has wasted his or her time becoming familiar with the occult literature, talk of 'another root of the human race' strikes a very familiar chord. The doctrine of 'Root Races' is associated with the Theosophical Society and its founder, the nineteenth-century occultist Helena Petrovna Blavatsky. Madame Blavatsky's *Secret Doctrine*, which appeared in 1888, sketched out an occult theory of the evolution of Man. Aryans formed 'the Fifth Root Race'. Jews, on the other hand, were an abnormal and unnatural link between the Fourth and Fifth Root Races. The 'Fourth Root Race' had lived in Atlantis and been ruled by black magicians. Writers interested in establishing that Hitler knew Blavatsky's race doctrines have focused upon his days in Vienna or in Munich and upon the apostate German Theosophist Rudolf Steiner.[31] But there is a possible link of very much greater significance for our purposes, because it goes back considerably earlier and might even have been communicated to Hitler while at the *Realschule*.

Consider this striking passage from Peter Washington's book *Madame*

Blavatsky's Baboon concerning the alleged sexual life of Madame Blavatsky:

> She may or may not have had lovers, including the German baron Meyendorf, the Polish Prince Wittgenstein and a Hungarian opera singer, Agardi Metrovitch. All these names were linked to hers, though she sometimes denied the liaisons and sometimes hinted that they were true.[32]

If 'the Polish Prince Wittgenstein' were indeed Madame Blavatsky's lover, or close family acquaintance, then it would be no surprise to find that Madame Blavatsky's ideas (which took firm root in London, New York, Sydney and India) were also particularly well known in the Wittgenstein family. It seems clear, from Madame Blavatsky's own words, that Prince Wittgenstein was indeed a close acquaintance. Thus Marion Meade, in her now standard Blavatsky biography, writes of the attack on Madame Blavatsky in the *New York Sun* of 20 July 1890:

> Not only did the *Sun* name names, it accused her of having been a member of the Paris demimonde during 1857-1858, and of having had 'a liaison with the Prince Emile de Wittgenstein. . . .'
>   Helena immediately instructed Judge to file suit for libel against the *Sun*. . . . Ignoring all of the charges, she dismissed the demimonde accusation as 'so ridiculous as to rouse laughter' and concentrated on the aspersion against Prince Wittgenstein 'now dead . . . an old friend of my family whom I saw for the last time when I was 18 years old . . . He was a cousin of the late Empress of Russia and little thought that upon his grave would be thrown the filth of a modern New York newspaper. The insult to him and to me I am bound by all the dictates of my duty to reply.'[33]

Meade's biography demonstrates that Madame Blavatsky was undoubtedly a liar about many things, but on this crucial matter about a long-standing family link to the Wittgensteins, she appears to have been telling the truth. Marion Meade believes that Wittgenstein had probably not been her lover, but there was a link, and it involved not just a family friendship, but rather a sharing of the very same occult interests as Madame Blavatsky. The historian of the Theosophical Society writes that in 1873 the 'British National Association of Spiritualists' was formed, amongst whose Honorary or Corresponding members was Prince Emile de Sayn-Wittgenstein.[34] Prince Wittgenstein wrote a letter to *The Spiritualist* in 1878, describing how he was shielded from danger during the war with Turkey by one of the 'leading Brethren of the Society', whom Madame Blavatsky explained in *The Theosophist* of March 1883 was the Master

Morya, one of the gurus of the Theosophical Society, to whom she alone appears to have had communicatory access.[35] Josephine Ransom, the Theosophical Society historian, names Prince Wittgenstein as a Fellow of the Theosophical Society, and continues:

> Another student of Spiritualism in Russia, and an old friend of H.P.B.'s family, was Prince Emile de Sayn Wittgenstein (F.T.S.), cousin of the Empress and aide-de-camp to the Emperor, whose confidence he enjoyed. He assisted the Emperor to acquire a most complete library of Spiritualist books.[36]

So Madame Blavatsky – the font of a doctrine according to which Jews were, as Hitler said, 'from another root of the human race' – had connections to the Wittgenstein family and had been born near the Wittgenstein estate in the Ukraine.[37] Emile Wittgenstein was the brother of the man whom Franz Liszt cuckolded; the brother-in-law of Princess Carolyne Wittgenstein whom Cosima Wagner hated for her Jewishness. Madame Blavatsky would therefore have known something of the events concerning the great and newsworthy Wittgenstein elopement.[38]

Hitler's reference to the Jew as 'from another root of the human race' is thus particularly striking in the context of our own investigation. It is clearly possible that Madame Blavatsky's pernicious influence was working in the mind of Hitler in 1904, nearly a decade earlier than anyone has dreamed possible. I am not claiming here that there definitely was a Blavatsky connection (via Ludwig through Blavatsky's Prince Emile Wittgenstein), but the mere fact that this suggestion cannot now be just dismissed out of hand must open up yet a further new road for research into the Holocaust. Madame Blavatsky gives a potted history of the Jews. They

> are a tribe descended from the Chandâlas of India, the outcasts, many of them ex-Brâhmans, who sought refuge in Chaldaea, in Scinde, and Aria (Iran), and were truly born from their father A-Bram (No-Brâhman) some 8,000 years B.C.[39]

Her etymology of 'Abraham', while linguistically simply silly, fits strangely well with the results of our investigation into the common mind of Aryan mysticism – that is, Brahman – and its rejection by Judaism.

We have considered Collingwood, Schopenhauer, Madame Blavatsky and Hitler. But what were Wittgenstein's views on magic? Many students of Wittgenstein still associate him with the Vienna scientific positivists. They take him to have been an opponent of magical modes of thinking. It is now well known, from his *Remarks on Frazer's Golden Bough*, that quite to the contrary, he defended an account of magic and thought it to reflect something very deep in human beings connected with the nature of representation. And exactly as did Hitler, he also dismissed attempts to explain the practice in terms of anything other than itself. Talking of the killing of the priest-king at Nemi – the case which concerned Frazer – he wrote 'Even the idea of trying to explain the practice – say the killing of the priest-king – seems to me wrong-headed.' Wittgenstein's thoughts on the nature of magic, however, went considerably beyond this. What is not appreciated by readers of Wittgenstein is that he saw his own activity as essentially a magical practice. We read, for example (the italics are in the original):

I now believe that it would be right to begin my book with remarks about metaphysics as a kind of magic.

But in doing this I must not make a case for magic nor may I make fun of it.

The depth of magic should be preserved.

Indeed, here the elimination of magic has itself the character of magic.

For, back then, when I began talking about the 'world' (and not about this tree or table), what else did I want but to keep something higher spellbound in my words?[40]

We can deduce further from these remarks that Wittgenstein recognized some identity between the ideas behind magic and those that inspired the philosophy he presented in the *Tractatus*. In exorcizing the grip of metaphysics upon the mind of the aspirant philosopher, he was engaging in just that: an exorcism, leaving behind only silent, inexpressible insight from the realm of the Mystical – the unified whole seen *sub specie aeternitatis* which is what is left when the everyday mind goes. His own words – the staccato aphorisms of the *Tractatus* – were the invocation of 'something higher', the attempt, as he described it, to keep it spellbound by logical means. The *Tractatus* was the spell.

Modern interpretations of Wittgenstein's work treat him simply as a logician with a mystical bent. It is clearly time to see him rather differently. The ultimate goal of his philosophy was Mystical illumination; to be obtained by transformation of the soul of the aspirant into the Universal Soul. In the *Notebooks*, he referred to his metaphysical 'I' as the 'Godhead'.[41] And we have seen his own words describing how the role of the *Tractatus* was nothing less than to be the spell, understanding of which would bind this Godhead; and bring it forth in the mind of the enlightened philosopher.

Part III

EIGHT

The Key to the Mind

I hope that what I have written so far will have convinced the reader that there is at least the possibility of a connection between the philosophy of Wittgenstein and the doctrines of Nazism – a possibility strong enough to warrant further serious investigation. However far apart the cool, enigmatic pronouncements of the logician may seem from the crude rantings of Hitler's public harangues, there is a single vital idea which underlies both of them, though perverted by Hitler to suit his racial beliefs. That idea is the no-ownership theory of mind. In this section of the book we shall be looking in more detail at that theory, its history and the criticism to which it has been subjected.

The first point to note is that it is at bottom a religious concept. This is true of Wittgenstein's reference to his metaphysical 'I' as the 'Godhead'. It is also true of Hitler's sanctification of racial purity and the mystical brotherhood of the New Man he claimed to be creating.

The essence of the no-ownership theory was expressed by Emerson in his restatement of the original Aryan doctrine of consciousness: '. . . the act of seeing and the thing seen, the seer and the spectacle, the subject and the object, is one'.[1] That this was indeed Wittgenstein's view is clear from some contemporary reports of what he said.

The Trinity College philosopher G. E. Moore, in his report of Wittgenstein's 1930-3 lectures, wrote that like so many philosophers, 'he seemed not to distinguish between "what I see" and "my seeing of it"'.[2] There is a natural – almost inescapable – view to take in accounting for what occurs when a subject is conscious of something. This is that when someone is conscious of, say, a table, there are three elements involved: the person, the table and an immensely puzzling relation between them – awareness. It seems, likewise, that when a person thinks a thought, there must be a person, a thought and consciousness of that thought. This was the view of the Trinity College philosophers Bertrand Russell and G. E. Moore. We know, however, that Wittgenstein thought views like Moore's and Russell's, though 'superficially attractive', were mistaken.[3] Explaining the logical form of expressions such as 'A believes that p', he wrote:

> . . . if these are considered superficially, it looks as if the proposition p stood in some kind of relation to an object A.
> (And in modern theory of knowledge (Russell, Moore, etc.) these propositions have actually been construed in this way.)[4]

In the next remark he continues:

> It is clear, however, that 'A believes that p', 'A has the thought p', and 'A says p' are of the form ' "p" says p': and this does not involve a correlation of a fact with an object. . . .

Finally, we read his conclusion from the foregoing:

> This shows that there is no such thing as the soul – the subject, etc. – as it is conceived in the superficial psychology of the present day.[5]

It seems reasonably clear what Wittgenstein was opposing: any analysis on which consciousness is construed as a relation between a subject and an object. But what was his alternative analysis? The short answer is that nobody appears to know. There is certainly no consensus. It lies hidden away in the numbered propositions of the *Tractatus* like a mystery of the Kabbala. But we can hypothesize.

So far as thought is concerned, he seems to be saying that it is the *proposition* that says something, all by itself. It works through an expressing vehicle (the person from whose mouth or pen the proposition emerges) but that person is not truly the author of the proposition. The proposition expresses itself: 'p' says p. It follows that there is not a person there making propositions, thinking thoughts; there is therefore no such thing as the individual human soul.

But why did Wittgenstein oppose the Moore/Russell analysis of consciousness? What hinges upon the issue? What Wittgenstein says 'is clear' is anything but clear. His two or three remarks here have sustained an academic industry for seventy years, whose product has served only to muddy further the already opaque waters.

Moore's own view of consciousness has been much quoted in the philosophical literature, and rightly so. For what he says here is well worth pondering: there does seem to be more involved in being aware of something than just the something we are aware of. The problem, however, is that whatever this other element might be (the one that Moore called 'consciousness'), it is not itself an object of consciousness, and therefore it cannot be something of which we are aware. We cannot scrutinise it. It is that by which we have our mental life, not an object *for* our mental life.

Some of us of a contemplative bent, however, might have attempted to come across this mysterious 'unalloyed consciousness' through meditative techniques – we sit down and resolve that *this* time we shall grasp it. We notice bodily sensations, traffic noise, light on our eyelids, etc, and think to ourselves, 'It's not *these*, these are objects of consciousness, not the thing itself.' Perhaps, if we persist, we even lose awareness of these and become absorbed in some one meditative object. But the goal of the pure essence remains as far distant as ever. Moore sensed the difficulty himself. He wrote that

> the moment we try to fix our attention upon consciousness and to see what, distinctly, it is, it seems to vanish: it seems as if we had before us a mere emptiness. When we try to introspect the sensation of blue, all we can see is the blue: the other element is as if it were diaphanous.[6]

In the very next line, however, Moore claims that this diaphanous element – consciousness – *can* be distinguished if only we look closely enough. This would mean that the contemplating meditative consciousness really is capable of being aware of itself. But what is this consciousness (of which it is aware) conscious *of*? It is conscious of being aware of itself. So our consciousness is aware of itself being aware of itself. Ask the same question again and the answer is that it is aware of itself being aware of itself being aware of itself . . . and so on for ever. Therefore out consciousness is having to perform an infinite number of acts of awareness simultaneously – an obvious impossibility. It follows that trying to isolate pure consciousness as something examinable, as something experienceable, has to be impossible.

Schopenhauer, Emerson and the others claimed on the contrary that subject, act and object *cannot* be distinguished. This sounds more akin to what Wittgenstein appears to be claiming and we have McGuinness's testimony that Wittgenstein read Schopenhauer and Emerson favourably.

Why, though, have I taken an issue of modern philosophical psychology and tried to relate it to obscure early Aryan doctrine going back at least two and a half millennia? The reason is that I think we are dealing with the same issue. However doubtful the reader might feel at this stage, the doubt will be considerably lessened by reading the remainder of this work. It is clear in any case that Wittgenstein's mentor Schopenhauer thought they were the same issue, for he seized upon the early Aryan texts to expound his own philosophy of the unowned will, just as did Hitler's hero, Richard Wagner. Thus Wagner, in a passage just prior to an anti-Jewish diatribe, writes of the Aryan philosophy of mind in the Hindu Upanishads:

> How totally these lessons of ancestral wisdom had been lost to us, we may judge by their having to be re-discovered after tens of centuries by Schopenhauer. . . .[7]

As avid readers of Schopenhauer's philosophy, both Wittgenstein and Hitler also were aware of 'these lessons of ancestral wisdom'. In India they are associated with arduous meditative practices – yoga and so on – leading to unification; that is, the individual soul realizing *tat tvam asi*; its essential identity with this All. In this 'ancestral wisdom' there are no multiple subjects for the Moore/Russell view to apply *to*.

Wittgenstein evidently stumbled spontaneously into one of these meditative states – the unificatory experience we considered earlier – at an early age. I shall argue that he incorporated the insight he gained from it into his philosophy. This insight, as we shall see, is absolutely radical, though its full presentation must wait a little while yet. Let us note, for the moment, that Wittgenstein held that awareness of an object lacks components and is not to be analysed along the subject/art/object lines of Moore and Russell and 'the superficial psychology of the present day'. It is a doctrine of consciousness that, if Emerson and Schopenhauer can be believed, is legitimately described as 'Aryan'. It is intimately bound up with a mystical doctrine of the nature of the self, and it is very, very old.

There is an apparent contradiction in expositions of Wittgenstein's thought on this matter. The philosopher David Shwayder expounds the *Tractatus* account of thought[8] in terms of an identity between thinking and thought – a thought *is* a thinking that such and such; i.e. there is not a thought as object *and* an act of thinking it.[9] Expounding Wittgenstein, Shwayder continues:

> It is not, as with Frege, the *Sinn* thought. Nor is it what Moore calls a proposition, and even less is it a sentence. Wittgenstein, in a letter to Russell, made it entirely explicit that a thought was something psychological. A picture is a mental act . . . of thinking that such and such is the case.

Picturing, which is the *Tractatus* account of thought, would seem to be, on this interpretation, something private. After all, it is an act; not an object.[10]

Now compare Shwayder's account of what Wittgenstein says about thought (that it is an *act*) with the following extract from a paper by the philosopher Jaakko Hintikka. Hintikka, following Frege and in seeming opposition to Shwayder, writes:

> There is . . . nothing private and nothing psychological about Wittgenstein's notion of a thought. Like Frege's *Gedanke*, it can be shared by different people.[11]

Shwayder, as we have seen, interprets Wittgenstein's notion of a thought as a mental act. Hintikka is claiming in the above passage that a thought is something shareable. On the face of it, there certainly appears to be a conflict here.

Now resolution of this conflict leads to a philosophy of mind that has not been considered by mainstream academic philosophers because their (mistaken) instinctive reaction is that it is obviously false. It is this position that I believe was espoused by Wittgenstein throughout his life and, in a perverted variant, by Adolf Hitler.

Unlikely as it appears, Shwayder and Hintikka are both correct in their interpretation of Wittgenstein. A thought, in the *Tractatus* (indeed throughout Wittgenstein's philosophy), is construed in a philosophically ultra-radical fashion as a shareable act of thinking. The mouth through which it expresses itself is incidental to it. This can be modelled on the analogy of instruments of an orchestra taking up a theme, which we saw Shafaravich use earlier in accounting for the development of mathematics. The proposition corresponds to the theme, which can indifferently issue from this violin or that one, just as Pythagoras's Theorem can be thought by this man or that one. When two individuals think the same thought there are not two acts of thinking and a common content: there is a single act of thinking in which, so far as consciousness is concerned, the two individuals intersect. The apparent conflict between Shwayder and Hintikka in interpreting Wittgenstein is resolved if mental acts of consciousness are public; if individual token thinkings in consciousness are performable by more than one mind.[12] They are both mental acts *and* shareable. Hintikka is correct in seeing them as public, but mistakenly equates them with Fregean contents; Shwayder is correct in seeing them as acts, but fails to remark on their publicity. Both fail to see how Wittgenstein's account of thought squares with his account of the self as something supra-personal.

What I am presenting as Wittgenstein's account of the mind requires internal documentation from his work, of course. It is not a doctrine whose ramifications are easily grasped, but it seems clear that, for Wittgenstein, a thought is not a separable proposition upon which the searchlight of consciousness focuses in the act of thinking, thereby linking it to a subject.

The triad: subject, mental act and object is, on this account, a mistaken analysis of cognition.

It seems, however, that it lies open to the criticism Moore made of Wittgenstein's 1930s lectures, that no distinction is made between act and object of consciousness. If a thought *is* a thinking that such and such, as Shwayder correctly characterizes the *Tractatus* view, then thought and thinking collapse into one. Moore's objection – that he failed to distinguish between act and object – seems valid. How can it be resolved? Clearly the issues are ancient, important and unresolved. Let us see, on the Wittgensteinian account, how it is that multiple acts of having, say, a toothache, can come about.

Just as two objects have different colours if one is red and one is green, so two people have different pains if one has toothache and the other heartburn. And just as two objects have the same colour if they are both red or both blue, so two people have the same pain if they both have toothache or both have heartburn. Were this not the case, we could never say, as we manifestly do, that two people have the same pain. We equally would have to deny that two post-boxes could ever have the same colour. 'After all,' we might reason, 'even if they are both scarlet, they can't have the same colour for there are two of them. They must really only have similar colours.' Now such an assertion is the line most academic philosophers take.[13] They deny that two people can ever have the same (identical, numerically one) pain, thought, etc, and claim that 'properly speaking' two people can have only 'similar' pains, never the same pain.

They can only say this, however, by doing violence to the concept of similarity. Let us reconsider colour. In the case of colour it is clear that vermilion is similar to scarlet; they are colours of the same kind; similar shades. Two objects have similar shades of colour if one is vermilion and one is scarlet. Analogously, angina is similar to rheumatic pain in the chest; they are pains of the same kind. Two people therefore have similar though not identical pain if one has angina and the other thoracic rheumatic pain. If the other has toothache, however, the pains are not similar but totally different.

Thus there are three possibilities: the pains of two people can be *different*, they can be *similar* (differing in some small respect) or they can be the *same*. So the philosopher who says that two people's pains can only ever be similar and never the same, is making an enormous claim. It is far from being the simple deliverance of reason it is assumed to be. It is, in fact, contrary to what people say every day.

Consider in this regard an unfinished story recounted by Wittgenstein. Wittgenstein had been making commonplace observations, similar to the preceding, in order to show the falsity of such claims as 'Another person can't have *my* pains.' Evidently some die-hard defender of this position struck himself on the breast and exclaimed, 'But surely another person can't have *this* pain.' Wittgenstein wrote in answer to this:

> One does not define a criterion of identity by emphatic stressing of the word 'this'. Rather, what the emphasis does is to suggest the case in which we are conversant with such a criterion of identity, but have to be reminded of it.[16]

What Wittgenstein says here is perfectly true, but the point is not clear. So let us imaginatively continue the dialogue.

Wittgenstein might have shown the man his error by similarly striking his own breast and replying, 'Of course they can! I felt it here,' pointing to where he had struck himself. The dialogue might go: 'But look, Wittgenstein, I feel a dull ache which is throbbing a bit, but lessening slightly. Surely you can't have *that* pain?' And the reply to this might be either 'Yes, that's the very pain I feel,' or perhaps 'No, I was mistaken, mine is much more of a sharp shooting sensation – it's not even similar, let alone the same!'

The point of the dialogue is that when Wittgenstein *does* feel the same pain, it's simply false to say that he only feels a 'similar' though not identical pain. Of course it is possible for two people to have only similar though not the same pains – as in the angina/rheumatic pain example – but it is a mistake to say that this must be so in all cases. Two different people can indeed suffer the same pain.

The point is clear enough. But when competent philosophers adopt a position that sounds absurd, a critic should explain why they might have felt driven to adopt it. Remarkably, they don't see the absurdity; they even see the proposition 'No one can have the same pain as another' as necessarily true! They forget that a doctor might say of two of his patients that they suffer the same pain from gout, while a third patient (with the same uric acid level) suffers only minor discomfort. How comes it that such everyday expressions are overlooked?

One reason is that there are two *places* of pain involved in Wittgenstein's example. Because of this we might think, 'Ah yes, I have a pain in my breast and Wittgenstein has one in his breast, so there must be two of these things.' And here we fall into our first logical error: we treat pains as being like particular objects rather than as universals. But pains aren't things; they are properties of creatures. If we mistakenly think of pain not as a property of creatures, but as a sort of thing – a private object – then the two spatial locations involved incline us to think that there must be two of these 'private objects' involved here. We quite forget that if we applied the same argument to the colours of post-boxes, the absurdity would force itself to our attention at once – 'No two post-boxes can have the same colour, one colour is here and the other is there!'

Another source of the view that another can't have my pains is connected with this. It arises from the tendency, remarked upon earlier, to run together the act and the object – the having of the pain and the pain that is had, so that we end up with two private objects individuated by their havers, rather than with one common property. This was the position of the young Peter Strawson:

> . . . experiences . . . owe their identity as particulars to the identity of the person whose . . . experiences they are.[15]

But as we have seen, it is not the *experience* that owes its identity as a particular to the experiencer – it is the *having of* this experience by an experiencer that owes its identity as a particular event to the experiencer. The particular pain of heartburn, unfortunately, is something we all can share. Your suffering it, however, is distinguished from my suffering it via you and me.

If this act/object distinction is overlooked or drawn mistakenly, as in Strawson, we end in absurdity. Consider, for example, this further quote from Strawson:

> . . . it does not seem to make sense to suggest, for example, that the identical pain which was in fact one's own might have been another's.[16]

What can he have meant by this? If 'the identical pain that is in fact one's own' happens to be heartburn, are we to conclude that no one else can ever have heartburn?

The point is that we can't argue that two people can't have the same pain because they are different people – 'You can't have my pain because I'm me and you're you' – for it is precisely a feature of a property that it can occur in many places. And since pain is a property of creatures (it can't exist independently, without a bearer), it can occur unchanged to many different creatures and at many different times. If this were not the case, how could we understand a prescription instructing us to take a pill when a certain pain recurs? A consistent Strawsonian must amend the prescription to read 'when a similar pain recurs' – but this, though it is indeed a possible prescription label, would be a different instruction from that of the original label.

These quotations I have presented from Strawson's book occur in the section of *Individuals* where popular philosophical opinion believes the no-ownership account of the mind to have been definitively refuted. I hope that the reader has developed a suspicion by now that all might not be well with the refutation.

Philosophers quite promiscuously run together the had and the having wherever the topic of properties arises. In discussion, I have heard philosophers express wonderment that anyone might dispute that two pieces of A4 paper are 'two instances of white'.[17] The philosophers, however, tend to confuse the colour with the colour patch.

Of course, if the two pieces of paper are different shades of white (i.e. different whites) then we do have two instances of white. But otherwise, they are quite clearly just the *same* instance of white! Something quite peculiar is going on when it is claimed that the two pieces of paper display 'two instances of white', on no other grounds than that there are two pieces of paper there! The essential conjuring trick of the orthodox position is the false claim that colours can vary in some way other than as colours; that is, that they can vary as colours by varying in position.

The colour is not the colour patch, although one might point to a colour patch in pointing to the instance of the colour. One instance of red is vermilion, another is scarlet, another is magenta, etc. The instance is not the vermilion patch on the rug or the scarlet flag or the magenta stamp. Similarly, lumbago is one instance of rheumatic pain, not Jones's having that particular lumbago. And while it is true that one can say correctly that Jones's lumbago is a particular instance of rheumatism, that does not prevent Smith from suffering that identical instance of rheumatism – i.e. Jones and Smith might both be suffering the same lumbago.

To put this point yet again, it is not necessary for the individuation of a particular property or instance of a property that its bearer also be individuated, and in particular, it is not necessary for the individuation of a pain that one also individuate its subject.

This point is absolutely crucial to appreciating Wittgenstein's philosophy of mind. It can be expressed by saying that the subject of pain is not a feature of the pain the subject has, or as Wittgenstein more memorably put it, that the data of immediate experience have no owner.[18]

So far the discussion has been couched in terms of pain, but the same logical points clearly apply to anything mental at all. For just as no particular pain is necessarily uniquely mine, so no thought, dream, after-image, emotion, expectation, etc is necessarily uniquely mine. As Frege put it about the thinker:

'He is the owner of the thinking, not of the thought.'[23]

If thoughts were necessarily private possessions – if no one but me could have my thoughts (that it's hot today, say) – then how could communication be possible at all? Thoughts are precisely that which is communicated and so, *a fortiori*, must be accessible to more than one mind. Indeed, the very first words of Wittgenstein's first publication run:

> . . . this book will be understood only by someone who has himself already had the thoughts expressed in it.[20]

Now what Wittgenstein wrote makes sense, so what he says must not be impossible. And this alone suffices to show that thoughts admit of publicity.

In general, there is no property of 'being-had-by-me-ness' in any of my mental states. This is clear from the preceding discussion and from everyday locutions: 'At that moment the same thought struck us both', etc. But a further argument was developed by Wittgenstein in *Philosophical Remarks*:

> What distinguishes his toothache from mine? . . . How are toothaches to be distinguished from one another? By intensity and similar characteristics. . . . But suppose these are the same in the two cases? But if it is objected that the distinction is simply that in the one case *I* have it, in the other *he*; then the owner is a defining mark of the toothache itself; but then what does the proposition 'I have toothache' (or someone else does) assert? Nothing at all.
>
> If the word 'toothache' has the same meaning in both cases, then we must be able to compare the toothaches of the two people; and if their intensities etc. coincide, they're the same. Just as two suits have the same colour, if they match one another in brightness, saturation etc.
>
> Equally, it's nonsense to say that two people can't have the same sense-datum, if by 'sense-datum', what is *primary* is really intended.[21]

Wittgenstein's argument here runs as follows: If a particular pain is distinguished (given the 'defining mark') as being one felt by a certain subject (John's pain), then to say that John feels this pain is as meaningless as saying that John owns John's suit. It follows that the ownership of a pain cannot be a feature of the pain itself, so that it is legitimate to speak of John's toothache and Jane's toothache as being the *same* pain, provided what they feel is pain of the same intensity, etc.

Wittgenstein applies this to all forms of primary sense-data, these being traditionally the items directly given to consciousness in perception and about whose nature no doubt is possible.

Let us now apply our findings to an example invented by Wittgenstein. This will be our lead into the whole idea of a common mind. Wittgenstein asks us to imagine that he and someone else share a part of their body in common, as with Siamese twins; say a hand. He continues:

> Imagine the nerves and tendons of my arm and A's connected to this hand by an operation. Now imagine the hand stung by a wasp. Both of us cry, contort our faces, give the same description of the pain etc.[22]

We are to imagine that the pain felt is the same. This leads immediately to the question Wittgeastein now raises: Are we to say in such a case that there is one pain involved or rather two distinct pains that by chance happen to have the same properties? And if the latter, in virtue of what can one count them as two? Is it a case of something unitary shared by both or rather of two distinguishable items with a common form, as with, say, the pans of a balance?

Wittgenstein invented the case to focus on the possibility of shared experience and he thought that the case qualified as a clear example of a breach of mental privacy. The idea behind it, of course, is that Wittgenstein and the other fellow meet as subjects in the pain, their minds overlapping and intersecting in the common object of experience; so that, so far as just the phenomenology of the example is concerned (neglecting expressions of pain through the two mouths), only one event takes place. The Siamese twins share not just a hand, but a single experience.

Now are there any considerations that might incline us to think that this way of looking at things has to be mistaken? Is there any argument that forces rejection of the possibility the case raises?

Well, in virtue of what might we be forced to conclude that there must be two mental events when the wasp causes the pain? One philosopher with whom I discussed the matter as an undergraduate exclaimed, 'Because there are two people screaming!' – as if this settled things. But it doesn't at all, any more than we could argue from the fact that one thunderclap can cause effects in two different places that therefore there must have been two thunderclaps. Like the thunderclap, the pain in Wittgenstein's example is a unitary cause. It is the one pain, in the shared hand, which happens to cause multiple screams.

Other philosophers have argued that two pains can be located in this example via the two brain processes causally necessary for the pain to be had by each. This is not so, however. Consider this analogy: A stage has a spot on it if a searchlight shines on it. If two beams shine on it, it has two spots (if the beams don't coincide). But when the spots do coincide, we can't argue from the fact that various causal mechanisms in the searchlights are necessary to shine two beams on the spot that therefore the stage has two spots. There is one having of one spot by the stage. Likewise in Wittgenstein's example: the one pain is felt in the one place – the shared hand. It is not felt to be in the brain and any causal mechanisms in the brain are as irrelevant as the causal processes in the searchlights.[23]

Another objector asked, 'What if one of them died?' – thinking that the identity of the mental event might be somehow split this way. But if we think further about the searchlight analogy, even if one of them suddenly fuses, the one spot on the stage continues as before, cast by the remaining searchlight. Equally, death of one of the subjects of the pain changes the pain not a jot. To forestall objectors who irrelevantly point out that the luminosity of the spot would change, I hereby inform them that in my example, (1) the beams themselves are infra-red and thus invisible, (2) the visible spot is produced by a photochemical interaction with the material of the stage surface, and (3) one *or* two beams striking this material produce exactly the same intensity of visible light.

The eminent Australian philosopher David Armstrong, in his debate with Wittgenstein's student, the late Cornell Professor Norman Malcolm, briefly considers Wittgenstein's case of Siamese twins and in an unusually (for him) unperceptive remark asserts that

> . . . there are certainly two pains. Aspirin administered to twin A might take away his pain, but leave twin B unaffected.[24]

Armstrong is simply in error here about the logical mode of operation of aspirin. What the aspirin has done, surely, is interfere with twin A *having* that pain. Similarly, if one of two identically coloured post-boxes is painted a different colour then it no longer has that colour. But nothing whatever would seem to follow about the pain (or colour) of the two never having been the same in the first place!

In Wittgenstein's example, then, if the light spot analogy holds, we do seem inescapably driven to acknowledge a breach of mental privacy.

The case is certainly fascinating, but it is not immediately clear what significance it has for cases other than that of Siamese twins. It can, however, be shown to be of quite profound significance, at least for exegesis of Wittgenstein's philosophy, when we combine his treatment of this case with other of his remarks. In *Zettel*, for example, we read of how much we

> would like to change the knowledge of the place of pain into a characteristic of what is felt . . . of the private object. . . .[25]

Wittgenstein, of course, set his face against the very idea of a 'private object' and dedicated a major section of his second book, the *Philosophical Investigations*, to arguing that there weren't any private mental objects. So in this quotation from *Zettel*, he is denying explicitly that the place a pain is felt to be is a feature of the pain felt. He is saying that our strong tendency to attribute our knowledge of how we know where a pain is to something, as it were, written on the pain is wrong. (One might say something similar about colour – any place where red is, is not a feature of the colour, since the colour can exist unchanged elsewhere.)

Now this claim is not something made only once, but in many places in the Wittgenstein *corpus*. In the *Investigations*, for example, where, after dismissing an account of how we locate the direction from which a sound comes, he continues:

> It is the same with the idea that it must be some feature of our pain that advises us of the whereabouts of the pain in the body.[24]

He is saying here that pains do not come tagged with their bodily location, as they do come tagged with, say, their intensity.

Why are these quotes important? They are important for the following very important reason: If what Wittgenstein says in these passages is correct, then the Siamese twin component of the earlier example is quite superfluous. Why? Because if when two people have the same pain they really do have the same pain, then spatial separation of their bodies becomes totally irrelevant to the nature of what they feel. Pains, etc are not individuated spatially, but in their own nature; as throbbing, shooting, arching, etc. As we saw earlier, if you have toothache and I have angina then we have different pains. If you have toothache and I have toothache then we have the same pain. Toothache is not made into something different by occurring in your mouth or mine, just as red is not altered by occurring on this or that post-box.

What position is being argued towards here? Just this: when two people groan or cry out with the same pain, even when the people are separated, the immediate phenomenal cause of each groan is unitary.[27] This, in a nutshell, is the no-ownership theory: that whenever people have the same pain, then, Siamese twins or no, only one event takes place so far as consciousness is concerned. Similarly, when a meditating monk thinks, 'This consciousness is a damned elusive thing!' he is linked to whoever else anywhere in the world is thinking, 'This consciousness is a damned elusive thing.' There are not multiple events in consciousness. Most philosophers seem to think this position self-contradictory; my contention is that it is in fact Wittgenstein's account of the mind.

NINE

Merging with the Mind

By now, the no-ownership theory should be clear, as it applies to sensation and thought. What form a no-ownership account of *perception* should take, however, is not at all clear. Perhaps a personal account might help. What follows is my own 'experience for excellence'.

I had been staying on a New Zealand farm in the Coromandel peninsula, in an isolated hut surrounded by pine trees and overlooking a large sea inlet. The day was pleasantly warm and I had been reading Philip Kapleau's book *The Three Pillars of Zen*,[1] an anthology of the experiences of people practising Zen meditation. Reading along, I came across a letter written in 1953 by a Japanese executive, of how his glimpse of the nature of enlightenment had been triggered by reading a quotation originating from an early Chinese Zen work which runs:

> I came to realize clearly that Mind is no other than mountains and rivers and the great wide earth, the sun and the moon and the stars.[2]

The executive continues:

> I had read this before, but this time it impressed itself upon me so vividly that I was startled. I said to myself: 'After seven or eight years of zazen[3] I have finally perceived the essence of this statement', and couldn't suppress the tears that began to well up. Somewhat ashamed to find myself crying among the crowd, I averted my face. . . .
> . . . All the while I kept repeating that quotation to myself.
> . . . it was after eleven thirty before I went to bed.
> At midnight I abruptly awakened. At first my mind was foggy, then suddenly that quotation flashed into my consciousness: 'I came to realize clearly that Mind is no other than mountains, rivers, and the great wide earth, the sun and the moon and the stars.' And I repeated it. Then all at once I was struck as though by lightning. . . . Instantaneously, like surging waves a tremendous delight welled up in me, a veritable hurricane of delight. . . . (I) started laughing uproariously and cried out 'I've come to enlightenment! Shakyamuni and the Patriarchs haven't deceived me! They haven't deceived me!' I remember crying

out. When I calmed down I apologized to the rest of the family, who had come downstairs frightened by the commotion. . . .

Even now my skin is quivering as I write.

I read this passage feeling rather happy for the Japanese gentleman who was so tremendously moved by whatever it was that had happened to him, and then thought that if the Mind *is* no other than 'mountains and rivers and the great wide earth, the sun and the moon and the stars', then *of course* there is only one Mind, in virtue of our all being in this one world.

I got up and walked to the verandah, reflecting in a detached sort of way that Buddha had lived in the very same world in which I lived, when my attention was drawn to a tree fern about twelve feet away. I say 'my attention was drawn' to emphasis the passivity of what was happening. I felt very alert, but had no sense of agency; things were happening of themselves.

There was an air as of a charge building, a quite electric feeling of alert, intense awareness of everything in the vicinity – the colours of nature, white clouds surging across a blue sky, and gusts of wind blowing tree branches and the long grass of the fields in a single unified movement. The wind suddenly dropped and everything seemed very quiet, apart from an occasional bird call. And then in an abrupt flash that stood my hair on end, I was overwhelmingly struck by a thought that I fear the reader will find trivial, but that I found suddenly extraordinary, indeed uncanny: that when someone else sees the tree fern that I am seeing, he sees *that very tree fern*.

Laughable, is it not? Yet it came as a revelation. I stood there for how long I don't know, quite unable to move, overcome with the dawn, heart pounding and body sweating, shuddering, scarcely able to breathe. This, for me, was the rending of the temple veil, a showing of the obvious nature of the world, on which I was looking, as it were, like Adam. I was seeing the world for the very first time as it always had been, glaringly obvious before my eyes, and splashed with phenomenal properties – only *unnoticed*. The experience was showing something very, very important about the nature of *me* that I had not previously suspected. I felt part of everything; it was in me that the grass was moving. I felt I had stumbled across a great mystery; a secret 'as ancient and as lofty as the Himalayas'.[4] The sense was of coming across something long known yet forgotten; something clear as a bell in its obviousness and utterly exciting, yet not realized previously just because of its obviousness; something like Eliot's famous lines in *Little Gidding*:

> . . . the end of all our exploration
> Will be to arrive where we started
> And know the place for the first time.[5]

Of course, what I am claiming to have seen as significant, and indeed pregnant with significance, is a tautology. Of course when someone else sees what I see, he sees what I see. However, in what follows, I shall try to make clear what is significant about the experience.

What is green when I look at grass is not my experience of grass; it is the grass itself. When two people hear a Beethoven piano sonata, what they hear is a Beethoven piano sonata; it is in general nonsense to suppose that one might have different experiences from the other, but arranged in such a structurally equivalent fashion that they agree in their forms of judgement.[6] As we shall see later, what each hears is not a private, unknowable something, inside the head, but rather the one, public Beethoven piano sonata produced some distance from their bodies. As with the Siamese twins sharing a pain, the listeners intersect in the sonata! We don't stop, as subjects, anywhere short of the sonata.

Adherents of the causal (representative) theory of perception argue that we must be in error in attributing the sound we directly hear to a place exterior to our bodies. They say that what is 'really' the case is that we are caused by silent waves in the air to have private, auditory sense-data in our bodies, in our brains, or private minds, on the basis of which we infer that the location of the sound is external to our bodies.

Representationalists make the same move with vision. Since the objects we see are distant from our bodies they say we must be in error in thinking we see them directly. Because we are not 'out there' where the object is, they think that what must happen is that we are caused to have replicas of these objects in our bodies – sensations or sense-data and the like – and then unconsciously infer an external cause of the replicas. The no-ownership view, on the contrary, is that the one world is public. It is *because* there are no intermediaries to get in the way that two people can hear and appreciate the same Beethoven sonata. As in the Siamese twin example of shared pain, the no-ownership account describes the case as the minds of the listeners intersecting in the sonata. As, in the Siamese twin case, the pain that Yin feels *is* the pain that Yang feels, so the sonata that you hear *is* the sonata that I hear. There are no 'private objects' because we meet as percipients in the sonata. So far as perception is concerned, we *are* 'out there' where the object is. We all live in a common sensorium, the physical world. As subjects, we are not confined to our bodies at all.

Perceptual spaces, then, are not multiplied as the number of men perceiving. There are no such private spaces – one for you and another for me. If I may speak of an 'aural body' as the locus of the sounds a man hears (as the fleshly body happens to be the locus of physical sensations) then the aural body not only extends beyond the confines of the skin, but interfuses with the aural bodies of others, just as the sensitive flesh of Siamese twins is interfused. And the same would be true of the 'olfactory body' and the 'visual body'; they meet in the common scents of the air and in the common objects seen.

This remarkable feature of perception – that there are no intermediaries, but in some sense the subject extends to the object – has been noted before, nowhere more beautifully than by the last of the great Anglican mystical poets, Thomas Traherne, in his poem 'My Spirit'. May the reader forgive the length of the quotation.

> It acts not from a centre to
> Its object as remote,
> But present is when it doth view,
> Being with the Being it doth note
> Whatever it doth do.
> It doth not by another engine work,
> But by itself; which in the act doth lurk.
> Its essence is transformed into a true
> And perfect act.
> And so exact.
> Hath God appeared in this mysterious fact,
> That 'tis all eye, all act, all sight,
> And what it please can be,
> Not only see,
> Or do; for 'tis more voluble than light,
> Which can put on ten thousand forms,
> Being cloth'd with what itself adorns.
>
> This made me present evermore
> With whatsoe'er I saw.
> An object, if it were before
> My eye, was by Dame Nature's law,
> Within my soul. Her store
> Was all at once within me; all Her treasures
> Were my immediate and internal pleasures,
> Substantial joys, which did inform my mind.
> With all she wrought
> My soul was fraught,
> And every object in my heart a thought
> Begot, or was; I could nor tell,
> Whether the things did there
> Themselves appear,
> Which in my Spirit truly seem'd to dwell;
> Or whether my conforming mind

Were not even all that therein shin'd.
But yet of this I was most sure,
That at the utmost length,
(so worthy was it to endure)
My soul could best express its strength.
It was so quick and pure,
That all my mind was wholly everywhere
Whate'er it saw, 'twas ever wholly there;
The sun ten thousand legions off, was nigh:
The utmost star,
Though seen from afar,
Was present in the apple of my eye.
There was my sight, my life, my sense,
My substance, and my mind;
My spirit shin'd
Even there, not by a transient influence:
The act was immanent, yet there:
The thing remote, yet felt even here.[7]

This is the philosophy 'on the far side of solipsism' – solipsism without the subject, that Wittgenstein said coincided with pure realism when its consequences were correctly thought through.

Now we will approach the psychological experiment for the production of *Einfühlung* that I foreshadowed earlier. I shall construct a visual analogue of Wittgenstein's example of the Siamese twins' shared pain.

First, suppose that two people stare at a green, trapezoidal (though almost rectangular) shape long enough for a red after-image to form. Each person is then asked to project his or her after-image on to various surfaces. (The further away the surface on which one focuses one's attention, the larger the after-image appears to be.)

Suppose that each person stands a certain distance from this page and is then asked to simultaneously project the after-image on to the rectangle below:

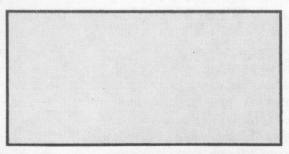

It is to be understood that each person's after-image fits exactly inside the borders of the rectangle, and that the hue, saturation and intensity of the apparent red colour is the same for each subject.

In these circumstances, the case is an exact visual analogue of Wittgenstein's Siamese twin example we considered earlier. What is occurring is that the numerically one after-image within the rectangle is simultaneously present to the two subjects.[8]

It is of course true that the after-image is not on the paper as a slide projection might be on the paper; but then the pain is not in the hand as bones are in the hand either.[9] For the point I want to make this doesn't matter. For just as the Siamese twin example is a case of two people sharing a common pain in the same place, so the preceding example is a case of two people sharing a common after-image in the same place. As subjects, they intersect in the common after-image. I take the argument in favour of this claim to have been provided already in our previous discussion of pain, though I shall now repeat and summarize it.

The issues involved are identical. We can't argue as to the existence of two distinct though identical images from their spatial location (as we might in the case of two identical though distinct billiard balls) since the images exist in precisely the same spatial location. Nor can we appeal to the multiplicity of subjects involved to split the image into two, any more than we could argue from the existence of more than one post-box that therefore the post-boxes must have more than one colour. I was once asked, 'What happens when one person's after-image appears a different shade of red from the other's?' In such a case I would say they simply don't have the same after-image, just as a magenta post-box has a different shade from a crimson one. But this doesn't affect what is the case when they do. Multiplicity of owners of a property does not of itself bring about a multiplicity of properties owned. So if the unitary after-image is to be split into two identical though distinct after-images, it must be on grounds other than spatial location or multiplicity of experiencer.

Now I shall complicate the example a little, by adding a third dimension to the image; that is, by creating a shared three-dimensional after-image.[10] The method used was a mainstay of pornography in Victorian times, creating three-dimensional images of women in various stages of undress, but will be familiar to anyone who has looked into a stereoscope. Consider the two stereoscope pictures overleaf. The reader should look 'cross-eyed' at the page and allow three images to form. By attending to the central image, its stereoscopic three-dimensional nature will become evident. The image 'juts out' of the page. Some people seem to need a dividing screen to create a stereoscopic image, but with practice, by focusing one eye on one

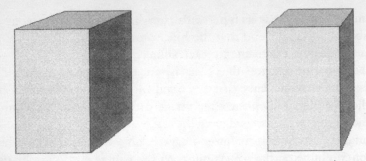

of the pictures and 'uncoupling' the other, the three-dimensional stereoscopic image can be created with no difficulty, even in the absence of a
vertical divider. Organic chemists tend to acquire this ability through regularly contemplating stereomers of complicated organic molecules. The
image produced by looking cross-eyed and attending to the resultant image
that lies between the two generating pictures produces a half-size mirror-
image version of that produced by a normal stereoscope, but it will still
serve for our purpose. If this method is used with the preceding images, the
stereoscopic image will be found to appear in three dimensions above the
plane of the page. (The reader should poke a finger into the image to verify
its location outside the plane of the paper.)

If we reflect upon the conditions of this experiment, an interesting corol-
lary emerges. This is, that the flat pictures on paper that produced the
three-dimensional cube image need not be material at all. They could
themselves be two-dimensional after-images. That is, suppose we intro-
duce a further step into our experiment and create the three-dimensional
after-image in two stages.

First, let the subject sit in a darkened room with the pictures suitably
placed, but with the right eye and right picture covered. If a flash cube is
fired, then a green, blue and yellow two-dimensional after-image will come
about through the effect on the left eye; a 'left stereomer' of the cube image
we desire to produce. By covering the left eye and left picture and quickly
repeating the flash cube procedure for the right eye and right picture, a
corresponding right stereomer will be formed. Once the after-images are
established, by moving focus, a point will be found where the images fuse
into a three-dimensional image of a cube. I suppose that technically
speaking, I should not call the image of the cube an 'after-image', since it
was not produced by a cube at all, but rather by two two-dimensional
stereomers of a cube. That is, there never was a material cube for it to be an
after-image *of*. Quibbling terminology, of course, doesn't matter very
much here. What matters is that the image of the cube occupies a position
in physical space in the sense that the person experiencing the image of the

cube might experience it as lying within, say, a real wire framework cube on a table.

If a second subject is given suitably drawn stereomers, and the procedure repeated, then the second subject can also be induced to produce a three-dimensional image of a cube that will also fit within the same wire cube on the table. Now let us suppose the experiment is done and the two subjects have each projected their image of the cube within this wire framework. (The images bear the same colours, etc.) What has been constructed here is a case of two subjects sharing a common three-dimensional visual image in a common phenomenal space. The image is outside the body of either subject, since each would describe the image as lying within the wire cube. And it is where the image is, that they meet as subjects. The image is in no sense inside the bodies of either of them. At the very best one might say that the physical conditions for the image to occur to a human perceiver (retinal effects etc), are in their bodies, but the image is clearly not; it is there in the wire cube on the table. In short, the experiment breaches our pre-reflective notion of mental privacy.

Now the non-privacy – or publicity – that I have been so carefully trying to elucidate so far as this common after-image is concerned is the same publicity that the no-ownership account attributes to ordinary physical objects. The normal line in philosophy is to take the opposite tack: to claim that publicity is impossible because of the mental privacy of perceptions. Books have been written on 'mental privacy' and how the external world is 'constructed' from private experience, saying that one person can have no idea of how another experiences the world. Perception, however, is not private at all. When two people see the same thing they really do see the same thing, just as Wittgenstein's Siamese twins are caused to cry out by a shared pain. The colours of objects are not privately owned but exist in a world of socialism – of no-ownership – of Wittgenstein's no-ownership theory of the Mind.

TEN

Wittgenstein and Mental Socialism

Proof that Wittgenstein adhered to the no–ownership theory – what I have called mental socialism – even in his later work, is easy to provide. I shall begin by quoting Moore's report of the 1930–3 lectures:

> . . . the point on which he seemed most anxious to insist was that what we call 'having toothache' is what he called a 'primary experience' (he once used the phrase 'direct experience' as equivalent to this one); and he said that 'what characterizes "primary experience" is that in its case "I" does not denote a possessor'. In order to make clear what he meant by this he compared 'I have toothache' with 'I see a red patch'; and said of what he called 'visual sensations' generally, and in particular of what he called 'the visual field', that 'the idea of a person doesn't enter into the description of it, just as a (physical) eye doesn't enter into the description of what is seen'; and he said that similarly 'the idea of a person' doesn't enter into the description of 'having tooth-ache'.[1]

Moore continues, a little further on:

> . . . he said that 'Just as no (physical) eye is involved in seeing, so no Ego is involved in thinking or in having toothache'; and he quoted, with apparent approval, Lichtenberg's saying 'Instead of "I think" we ought to say "It thinks"' ('it' being used, as he said, as 'Es' is used in 'Es blitzet'); and by saying this he meant, I think, something similar to what he said of 'the eye in the visual field' when he said that it is not anything which is in the visual field.

Having presented Moore's report, I shall now show how the no-ownership account fits perfectly with what is said in the *Investigations*. Rather than assembling endless quotes, I shall proceed by using the no-ownership theory to expound some otherwise puzzling claims made in the *Investigations* and work some of the superabundance of quotes into this exposition. What I am offering as proof that the no-ownership account is implicit in the later work of Wittgenstein is not what a logician means by 'proof', nor could it be. It is rather what is taken as proof in a court of law, evidence so compelling that no reasonable person would doubt it. I shall ask the reader to pause and reflect at the end of this chapter if any explanation other than the one I suggest could reasonably account for what Wittgenstein said.[2]

Wittgenstein had a strategy for bringing out whatever it is that leads us to our difficulties in philosophizing about first-person experience. He used exactly the same technique in many diverse places. Here is his suggestion from the *Notes for Lectures* of the 1930s:

> I do this by spreading the use of the word 'I' over all human bodies as opposed to L.W. alone.[3]

But how *could* the use of the word 'I' be spread over all human bodies? Wittgenstein writes that he wants to describe

> a situation in which we would not speak of my consciousness and his consciousness. And in which the idea would not occur to us that we could only be conscious of our own consciousness.
> The idea of the ego inhabiting a body to be abolished.
> If whatever consciousness (there is) spreads over all human bodies, then there won't be any temptation to use the word 'ego'.[4]

How would we construct a philosophy in which consciousness is spread over all human bodies? Would this not be a doctrine of Universal Mind? Wittgenstein continues (a German sentence inserted in English notes):

> Ist eine Philosophie undenkbar, die das diametrale Gegenteil des Solipsismus ist?[5]

We have already seen how such a philosophy interprets the after-image problem: when you and I have the same after-image there are not two images, yours and mine. Descriptions of the single image, in this case, are spread across two human bodies. And we have seen also how such a philosophy interprets the Will: when you and I will the same act there are not two volitions as in Cartesianism, but rather one, and the secret key to understanding Wittgenstein is that he runs the same line to explain the nature of having pain, and, indeed, all mental phenomena. Let us now examine the later work of Wittgenstein and see how this philosophy applies to it.

Consider first the claim in the *Philosophical Investigations*: that it is senseless to claim knowledge of one's own mental life. The claim is made in the *Investigations*, section 246, for the particular case of pain, and more generally on p 221, where we read:

'I know what I want, wish, believe, feel . . .' (and so on through all the psychological verbs) is either philosophers' nonsense, or at any rate not a judgment a priori.

That the claim has wide-ranging implications is clear from the parentheses in the following:

It is correct to say 'I know what you are thinking', and wrong to say 'I know what I am thinking'. (A whole cloud of philosophy condensed into a drop of grammar.)[6]

Why did Wittgenstein think one's own mental life is not a proper field for knowledge? We can glean some from idea a comparison he makes in one form or another in a variety of places. In *Investigations*, section 278, for example, Wittgenstein's imaginary interlocutor exclaims, 'I certainly know how the colour green looks to me.' Wittgenstein replied to this:

Imagine someone saying 'But I know how tall I am!' and laying his hand on top of his head to prove it.

We can imagine the man continuing, 'I'm this tall!'

A similar comparison is offered in *Zettel*, section 536, where in reply to the claim that someone has private knowledge (that another person cannot have) of the exact degree of his pain, we read:

He knows exactly how severe his pain is? (Isn't that much as if one were to say he always knows where he is? Namely here.)

Wittgenstein clearly thought the analogy worth drawing then, since he repeated it on many occasions. ('I know I'm this tall', 'I know I'm here', etc.) The subjects of these examples clearly had no idea of what particular height they had, or in what location they were. But what is its general logical point? What force does it have?

The comparison really is an instructive one, but its point has been missed. This is because commentators have taken it as saying something about pains, etc as *objects* of our mental life, whereas in fact it is a point about their *subjects*.[7] Similarly, philosophers have seized upon Wittgenstein's famous comparison of a private sensation to 'a beetle in a box' on the analogy of a pain in a private mind, and contorted themselves trying to see what argument Wittgenstein presented that allows the beetle to be done away with:

If I say of myself that it is only from my own case that I know what the word 'pain' means – must I not say the same of other people too? And how can I generalize the one case so irresponsibly?

Now someone tells me that he knows what pain is only from his own case! – Suppose everyone had a box with something in it: we call it a 'beetle'. No one can look into anyone else's box, and everyone says he knows what a beetle is only by looking at his beetle. – Here it would be quite possible for everyone to have something different in his box. One might even imagine such a thing constantly changing. – But suppose the word 'beetle' had a use in these people's language? – If so it would not be used as the name of a thing. . . .

That is to say: if we construe the grammar of the expression of sensation on the model of 'object and designation' the object drops out of consideration as irrelevant.[8]

What is really done away with in Wittgenstein's example is not the beetle, but the box! There certainly are pains – beetles; what there aren't is private minds – multiple beetle containers. The point of the comparison is to bring out that the 'beetle' must have the characteristics of a shareable universal, not of a particular thing. Thus the comment 'suppose the word "beetle" had a use in these people's language? – If so it would not be used as the name of a thing.' Indeed not. Multiple boxes would allow for numerically distinct beetles! But exactly *how* is it that the boxes vanish? I shall elaborate with a development of the comparison.

Imagine the leader of a totally lost group of hikers announcing triumphantly, 'At least we know one thing for sure – beyond any possibility of doubt – we're here!' where 'here' is wherever they happen to be. The claim is clearly a joke. The hikers know nothing at all about their location. 'Here' is not being used to identify one position among others. If we were asked what the content of the leader's 'knowledge' is, the proper reply would be that the leader doesn't have any knowledge, not about the party's position anyway.

Now the analogy in the case of pain is this: In the suffering of pain, nothing whatever is established in the experience about *who* is enduring it. In the thought 'I know I'm in pain', there is nothing to link the 'I' to one subject among others, just as in the hiker example there is nothing to link the 'here' to one place among others. Ignorance of location in the hikers' case corresponds to ignorance of who one is in the pain case. 'I' in such cases is not being used to distinguish one thing from other similar things. In a phrase that Wittgenstein uses, it 'has no neighbour'. ('I' has been spread over all human bodies.) That which has the 'knowledge' of its own state is not any one entity among others, and so 'I', in this case, does not refer. Hence Wittgenstein:

> If . . . I believe that by pointing to that which in my grammar has no neighbour I can convey something to myself (if not to others), I make a mistake similar to that of thinking that the sentence 'I am here' makes sense to me (and, by the way, is always true) under conditions different from those very special conditions under which it does make sense. E.g., when my voice and the direction from which I speak is recognized by another person.[9]

Suppose a group of zealous phenomenologists at a convention stick themselves with pins in order to acquaint themselves more intimately with the phenomena of consciousness. And let us suppose they engage in some meditative process, in order to ascertain more precisely what they can know of what is going on in consciousness. Then insofar as solely phenomenological effects are considered when the thought 'I know I'm in pain' occurs to them, there are not *many* processes occurring in the common consciousness; in truth only one event is taking place.[10]

Who is it, then, that in contemplating the pain has the knowledge? Of what entity is it knowledge about? To repeat the analogy: just as the 'here' of the lost hikers does not refer to one place among others, so the 'I' of the conscious thought 'I'm in pain' does not refer to one subject among others. No matter how many phenomenologists are at the convention, in consciousness they intersect in the numerically one pain of the pin-prick.[11]

The 'I' of consciousness – the philosopher's 'I' – does not refer to an entity at all. The 'I' of everyday life, however, achieves its reference only through this or that mouth, or by being written by this or that hand. In consciousness, what thinks is the thought, what pains is the pain, what expects is the expectation – not some entity 'I'.

That pain hurts is, of course, a commonplace. But the twenty-seventh of Shakespeare's sonnets is a fine example of an extension of the idea to other mental items. The Bard is not, of course, to blame for the italics:

> Weary with toil, I haste me to my bed,
> The dear repose for limbs with travel tir'd;
> But then begins a journey in my head
> To work my mind, when body's work's expir'd:
> For then *my thoughts*, far from where I abide,
> *Intend a zealous pilgrimage to thee*,
> And keep my drooping eyelids open wide,
> Looking on darkness which the blind do see. . . .

In the above, the thoughts themselves are the prime vehicle of the intention, not the individual person. Intentions intend, just as pains hurt. (Such attributions are more common in older Indo-European languages and

Shakespeare's use is not 'merely poetic'.) In Wittgenstein's generalization of this, as we have seen, the proposition 'p' says p. The whole nature of the thought 'Grass is green' is thinking 'Grass is green'. Consciousness belongs not to the subject but to the thought. Sometimes it forces itself through this mouth; sometimes through that mouth.

The Oxford Classicist E. R. Dodds, for example, quotes some other writers on this theme:

'The songs made me, not I them,' said Goethe. 'It is not I who think,' says Lamartine; 'it is my ideas that think for me.' 'The mind in creation,' said Shelley, 'is as a fading coal, which some invisible influence, like an inconstant wind, awakens to transitory brightness.'[12]

The picture (*Bild*) pictures, the thought (*Gedanke*) thinks, etc. The model of 'the single thinker' we considered earlier does offer a preparatory model for understanding Wittgenstein's remarks. But the more developed – and correct – model of Wittgenstein's view is that, in consciousness, the nature of a thought is just to think, so that there is not really a single thinker – only common conscious thought. The thought of consciousness, individuated by its content – not by multiple subjects – is not in any way separable from an act of thinking. As in the *Tractatus*, 'I think "p"' is really of the form ' "p" says p'. A conscious thought just *is* a thinking, the one sign becoming many symbols in its own expression.[13]

A modern equivalent would be to drop the model of brains as computers, one for each individual person, for a model of brains as essentially servo-mechanisms for a common central processor; one in which the relevant causal events have the character of universals. Thinking 'I'm in pain' would then correspond to a single process in the processor that communicates itself, more or less efficiently, to various of the remote terminals whereon the central process is expressed. (I am not saying that this is how things really are at the physiological level. I am presenting it as a 'thought-hypothesis' to show that the no-ownership theory is possible in the sense of not being logically self-contradictory. I do myself believe, however, that this *is* how things are if physiological processes are viewed as universals.)[14]

Wittgenstein, writing in the *Blue Book* of the data of immediate experience, had his interlocutor exclaim:

When anything is seen (really seen), it is always I who see it.[15]

And to this Wittgenstein replied:

What should strike us about this expression is the phrase 'always I'. Always who? For queer enough, I don't mean 'always L.W.'

This is a very interesting remark, the more so because Wittgenstein admits there is something queer in what he asserts.

He writes, 'I don't mean "always L.W.".' Now why not? Why bother to say this at all? It is surprising, because it is an *assertion*, something Wittgenstein generally avoided in his writings, preferring instead to ask questions, to lead his readers to their own conclusions. So why make the point?

He made it because the point is difficult to see but also absolutely fundamental to grasping his view of the nature of consciousness. On this particular point, he simply couldn't afford to leave the conclusion to the reader. The point is that only when I know through whose lips the word 'I' will issue do I know who is in pain, even in my own case. Until then there is nothing to distinguish one subject from another. In consciousness there is only the shared paining and in it, we poor sufferers all collapse into one. Thus Wittgenstein:

> The function 'x has toothache' has various values, Smith, Jones, etc. But not I. I is in a class by itself. The word 'I' does not refer to a possessor in sentences about having an experience, unlike its use in 'I have a cigar'.[16]

In the same discussion, over the page, he diagnoses and corrects the motive power behind solipsism; expressing correctly just what the solipsist really wants:

> What the solipsist wants is not a notation in which the ego has a monopoly, but one in which the ego vanishes.

This remark goes to the very heart of the motivation towards solipsism. On Wittgenstein's analysis, the certainty of 'I know I'm in pain' is purchased at the cost of not knowing the reference of 'I'. I can't doubt that I'm in pain when I'm in pain because there is no relation between a pain as object and a separate subject in consciousness – it is the pain itself that is paining, and announcing itself through my mouth.

Wittgenstein put this point in the *Philosophical Remarks* in what, in my opinion, is the most perspicuous and profound single philosophical remark ever made.[17] After asking where is the multiplicity in pain that justifies the 'my' in 'I feel my pain', he wrote:

> 'I have a pain' is a sign of a completely different kind when I am using the proposition from what it is to me on the lips of another; the reason being that it

is senseless, so far as I am concerned, on the lips of another until I know through which mouth it was expressed. The propositional sign in this case doesn't consist in the sound alone, but in the fact that the sound came out of this mouth. Whereas in the case in which I say or think it, the sign is the sound itself.[18]

What *is* the having of a pain by somebody – by one subject among other subjects? I have been arguing that it is not something that itself has phenomenal characteristics. The phenomenal nastiness, I have been urging, belongs to the pain, not to the having of it, just as what is coloured when we see a post-box is the post-box, not our seeing it. And in consciousness there is nothing in virtue of which a plurality of subjects of an experience can be discriminated one from another. So then how is the 'having' to be construed?

The answer, consistent with everything else that Wittgenstein wrote on this subject, is on page 68 of the *Blue Book*:

The man who cries out with pain, or says that he has pain, doesn't choose the mouth which says it.

And continuing:

The person of whom we say 'he has pain' is, by the rules of the game, the person who cries, contorts his face etc.

Yet again, we read in section 302 of the *Investigations*:

The subject of pain is the person who gives it expression.

Subjects in the plural, and thus having relations, are distinguishable not in consciousness but in behaviour, in the unitary pain's formal expression. Pain is not behaviour, but someone's *having* that pain is behaviour since in the absence of such behaviour nothing remains to link the pain to a subject.[19] The thought 'I am in pain' occurs in consciousness with the 'I' occurring as a unitary sign in Wittgenstein's sense. This is followed by many mouths opening, screaming and crying out, 'I am in pain'. In the crying out, the word 'I' is forced from many mouths and the unitary sign of the thought, of the common, unowned experience, has attained physical expression in a multitude of symbols. ('The mouth is part of the symbol' means only that knowing which mouth formed the 'I' syllable is necessary to knowing who uttered it.)[20] And so many subjects of that pain have been created.

The fundamental and profound point to grasp here is that a subject of the pain is *created* by the expression; by the use of the word 'I'. The common, unitary form is expressed multiply through diverse bodies. Prior to the word 'I' (or its equivalent in behaviour) issuing forth from this or that mouth we cannot logically discern a plurality of subjects within experience. To utter the word 'I' is to bring a subject into existence, as one such subject among others. This is a particular instance of the motivation behind Wittgenstein's philosophy of language: investigating the creative power of language; of the Word. The word 'I' creates a subject as one subject among others in its own utterance.

What, then, am I?

I am that creature whose body is involved in expressing the word 'I' whenever I express it.

Now which creature is this? The reader is reminded that the third last word of the previous sentence was written by Kimberley Cornish's hand. Which hand is my hand? Well, which hand wrote the word 'my' in the previous sentence? Suppose I move it. Of course the will to write the word 'mine' is probably moving thousands of hands throughout the world at this very instant. But the one that is mine is the one that writes the word 'mine'. (I remind the reader that Kim Cornish's hand just wrote 'mine'.) If a thousand hands write 'mine' then just by that very fact there are a thousand different subjects volitionally willing to write the word 'mine'. It is precisely this that is the secret of embodiment. My acts logically locate me as their agent. Hence Schopenhauer:

> To the subject of knowing, *who appears as an individual only through his identity with the body* [my emphasis], this body is given in two entirely different ways. It is given in intelligent perception as representation, as an object among objects, liable to the laws of these objects. But it is also given in quite a different way, namely as what is known immediately to everyone, and is denoted by the word will.[21]

It is thus that Schopenhauer thought there was only one Will! And in Wittgenstein's philosophy, this doctrine was extended to thoughts, after-images, pains etc. The generalization is obvious.

What I have been doing, then, is showing how the no–ownership doctrine fits in harmoniously with Wittgenstein's otherwise totally vatic pronouncements on the nature of mind, and indeed provides a rationale for them. The point is simply that consciousness contains no 'private' objects because it contains no individual subjects for such objects to be private *to*. And so the concept of privacy collapses.

Wittgenstein was quite explicit on this connection in the *Investigations*, section 398, and it is astounding that this has not been picked up by the commentators:

'But when I imagine something, or even actually see objects, I have got something which my neighbours has not'. – I understand you. You want to look about you and say: 'At any rate only I have got THIS'. – What are these words for? They serve no purpose. – Can one not add: 'There is no question of a "seeing" – and therefore none of a "having" – nor of a subject, nor therefore of "I" either'?

Wittgenstein continued a little further along in the same paragraph:

But what is this thing you are speaking of? It is true I said that I knew within myself what you meant. But that meant that I knew how one thinks to conceive this object, to see it, to make one's looking and pointing mean it. I know how one stares ahead and looks about one in this case – and the rest. I think we can say: you are talking (if, for example, you are sitting in a room) of the 'visual room'. *The 'visual room' is the one that has no owner* [my emphasis]. I can as little own it as I can walk about it, or look at it, or point to it. Inasmuch as it cannot be any one else's it is not mine either. In other words, it does not belong to me because I want to use the same form of expression about it as about the material room in which I sit. The description of the latter need not mention an owner, in fact it need not have any owner. But then the visual room cannot have any owner. 'For' – one might say – 'it has no master, outside or in'.

And finally, in section 399, we read:

One might also say: Surely the owner of the visual room would have to be the same kind of thing as it is; but he is not to be found in it, and there is no outside.

It is enlightening to compare this with an account Suzuki provides explicating the nature of *satori*:

This . . . is the case with all feelings, the feeling that you are an absolutely unique individuality, the feeling that the life you are enjoying now absolutely belongs to you, or the feeling that God is giving this special favour to you alone and to nobody else. But all these feelings ultimately refer to one definite subject known as 'I' which is differentiated from the rest of the world. Satori is not a feeling, nor is it an intellectual act generally designated as intuition. Satori is seeing into one's own nature; and this 'nature' is not an entity belonging to oneself as distinguished from others; and in the 'seeing' there is no seer . . .; *'Nature' is the seer as well as the object seen* [my emphasis].[22]

Suzuki's point here, expounding the Anatta doctrine, seems to be substantially the same as Wittgenstein's. And it must therefore count as support for the thesis we have been considering, which locates the source of both Wittgenstein's philosophy of mind and the Anatta doctrine in the natural mystical experience of *Einfühlung*.

There is another very puzzling claim in the *Investigations*, one as widely rejected by philosophers as the previous one about knowledge of one's own mental life. This is that statements such as 'I'm in pain' are 'expressive' rather than 'descriptive' of one's mental life. In fact this claim rests on the same foundations as the previous one about self-knowledge. Let us return to our lost hikers to see why.

The sentence 'We're here', as used by the lost hikers, says nothing whatever about their position; i.e. it is not being used to describe their location. But it can be used quite properly by the hikers when a search party is looking for them. By calling out 'We're here!' the hikers express their position to the search party who then know where (in which position among others) they are. Calling out 'Ahoy!' or even simply yelling would have accomplished the same job.

Analogously, the thought 'I'm in pain' doesn't describe the state of an entity (no more than the 'We're here' cry of the lost hikers describes a place). But when it comes out from between someone's lips in the words 'I'm in pain', we know whom to treat, just as the search party know in which place among others to seek the lost hikers. The un-owned sign becomes an individualized symbol through the locatable mouths. And just as the lost hikers' call 'We're here!' can function like shouting 'Ahoy!' or simply yelling, so saying 'I'm in pain' can (as we read in *Investigations*, section 244) 'take the place of' saying 'ouch' or of simply moaning.

This interpretation of Wittgenstein's aphorisms is supported in many places in his work. I shall quote one or two in full, from the *Investigations*, sections 404-5:

'When I say "I am in pain", I do not point to a person who is in pain, since in a certain sense I have no idea *who* is.' And this can be given justification. For the main point is: I did not say that such-and-such a person was in pain, but 'I am. . . .' Now in saying this I don't name any person. Just as I don't name anyone when I *groan* with pain. Though someone else sees who is in pain from the groaning.

What does it mean to know *who* is in pain? It means, for example, to know which man in this room is in pain: for instance, that it is the one who is sitting over there, or the one who is standing in that corner, the tall one over there with the fair hair, and so on. – What am I getting at? At the fact that there is a great variety of criteria for personal '*identity*'.

> Now which of them determines my saying that '*I*' am in pain? None.
> 'But at any rate when you say "I am in pain", you want to draw the attention
> of others to a particular person.' – The answer might be: No, I want to draw
> their attention to *myself*.–

That 'myself' is not a reference to Wittgenstein is made clear in the very
next paragraph, where he denies that in using the words 'I am in pain' he
wishes to distinguish between the person Ludwig Wittgenstein and the
person N.N., even when Ludwig Wittgenstein is the person from whose
mouth the words escape. In fact, we read further:

> It would be possible to imagine someone groaning out: 'Someone is in pain –
> I don't know who!' – and our then hurrying to help him, the one who
> groaned.[23]

How could this be? Well, let us suppose the sufferer to come awake
suffering from amnesia, after detachedly drifting in a coma. The sufferer
can easily be imagined waking up and finding it amazing that he has a male
body or fair hair, such is the extent of his memory loss. Let us further
suppose that while drifting in the coma, he feels an excruciating pain
(perhaps because his body is damaged, but the cause of the pain is irrelevant here). He involuntarily contorts and cries out. Now we would expect
him to cry out 'I'm in pain!' and of course, there is nothing logically to
prevent him. But *because* he is an amnesiac, drifting in a coma, we could
also understand him crying out, as did the person in Wittgenstein's
example, 'Someone is in pain – I don't know who!' He wouldn't know who
was in pain because he wouldn't know who he was – this is the further
contingent fact, not given just by the experience, that he has forgotten. On
the evidence of consciousness alone, he has said all that he is logically
entitled to say. Drifting in the coma, a pain is felt, prompting an urge to say
something in the hope that something can be done to alleviate it. We, the
medical staff attending the amnesiac's ward, race in to do something, and
perhaps observe screams coming from the mouths of one, two, or any
number of patients, all of which have been prompted by the one, token,
phenomenal pain. The single mental cause, like a single thunderclap shat-
tering window panes in different parts of a town, has caused effects in many
places; made now this body contort, then that one.

The oneness of the phenomenal cause is remarked on in the following
classic Zen poem:

When we clap our hands
The maid serves tea
Birds fly up
Fish draw near –
At this pond
In Sarusawa.[24]

That which is heard by the maid is the very sound heard by the birds and by the fish. There is intersection – phenomenal intersection – in the common content. There are not five or more 'private objects' involved – one for the hand-clapper, two for the maid, etc. This model also invites an obvious explanation of *Investigations*, section 409:

> Imagine several people standing in a ring, and me among them. One of us, sometimes this one, sometimes that, is connected to the poles of an electrical machine without our being able to see this. I observe the faces of the others and try to see which of us has just been electrified. – Then I say: 'Now I know who it is; for it's myself'. In this sense I could also say: 'Now I know who is getting the shocks; it is myself'. This would be a rather queer way of speaking. – But if I make the supposition *that I can feel the shocks even when someone else is electrified* [my emphasis], then the expression 'Now I know who . . .' becomes quite unsuitable. It does not belong to this game.

To see *why* it is unsuitable, imagine, as Wittgenstein supposes, that two or more people feel the shock – the same shock. Then if the numerically one shock is the cause of the one thought 'Now I know who is getting the shock; it is myself', to whom is 'myself' referring? Which one am *I*? For in the case where many people are suffering the same pain and thinking the same thought about it (i.e. Now I know who is getting the shock; it is myself) the 'I' is not referring to one among others. How can it if only one thought occurs? How can one count different occurrences of 'I' in consciousness? The apparent indubitable knowledge expressed in the claim can then be unpacked into the following translation: 'Now whoever is getting the shock knows who is getting the shock; it is whoever is getting the shock.' Hence the comment of the next paragraph:

> 'I' is not the name of a person.

Similar such statements are legion in Wittgenstein's work. Thus:

> If I give a description of my sense-datum, I don't mean to give a particular person as its possessor.[25]

What happens is that others gather who the subject of a pain or sense-datum is by seeing which body is involved in its expression; it is only thus that there *are* 'others'.

Consider also this quote from the *Notes for Lectures*, in which he is speaking of visual sense-data:

> 'How do you know it's you who sees it?', for I don't know that it's this person and not another one which sees before I point. – This is what I meant by saying that I don't choose the mouth which says 'I have toothache'.[26]

It is clear that the argument applies to action generally. A common thought thinks, 'I will raise my arm!' Which arm then raises? *That* locates its subjects!

An extension of the same argument serves to explain Wittgenstein's remarks on the means by which we know the location of our bodily sensations. This is an issue over which there has been long-standing philosophical dispute. How is it that when I feel a toothache I know it is in, say, my tooth and not elsewhere in my body? Is it a phenomenal feature of the pain that it comes located at a particular position in my body or is my knowledge of its location effected otherwise? A treatment of our knowledge of the location of a pain, on lines similar to how we have treated knowledge of subjecthood, sheds a great deal of light on Wittgenstein's remarks on the issue.

We have Malcolm's testimony in his *Memoir* that Wittgenstein thought our knowledge of the place of a pain is not a phenomenal feature of it. We read:

> . . . 'How do I know where my pain is?' I don't need to be shown where my pain is. My pointing gesture and verbal description locates the pain.[27]

And again, in the *Blue Book*, after asking in what sense a man can be said to know where a pain is before he points to it, we read:

> . . . the act of pointing *determines* a place of pain.[28]

Such behaviourist heresy is summarily dismissed in a work of the son of Wittgenstein's pupil A. C. Jackson, Frank Jackson. In his book *Perception*,[29] Jackson dismisses the claim that the place of a pain is where I would point to if asked, because of the possibility of mislocation (I could be mistaken), and tentatively attributes this doctrine to Wittgenstein in a footnote. This is more than a little unfair to Wittgenstein, in that in the very next sentence after the one that is the evidence for Jackson's attribution, we read that the act of pointing 'is not to be confused with that of finding the painful spot by probing. In fact the two may lead to different results.' A similar qualification occurs in *Philosophical Grammar*:

> Suppose I am looking for a painful place with my hand. I am searching in touch-space not in pain-space. That means: what I find, if I find it, is really a place and not the pain. That means that even if experience shows that pressing produces a pain, pressing isn't searching for a pain any more than turning the handle of a generator is searching for a spark.[30]

And in *On Certainty*:

> 'I know where I am feeling pain', 'I know that I feel it here' is as wrong as 'I know that I am in pain'. But 'I know where you touched my arm' is right.[31]

So what Jackson sees as a particularly clear difficulty for a behaviourist analysis of pain location of the sort I am about to ascribe to Wittgenstein was in fact recognized by Wittgenstein and, presumably, accommodated within his analysis. What, then, is this analysis?

It is much the same as the idea that subjects of pain (in the plural) are created as the utterances of 'I'. It is another example of the fundamental thought I alluded to earlier. The idea in this instance is that places of pain (in the plural) are created in the reference to these places. They don't exist multiply before the reference. Wittgenstein was concerned to combat the idea that we first know the location of a sensation and are only then able to point to it; that some particular psychical state or event (knowledge of the place) 'must precede every deliberate act of pointing'.[32] And since his view was that 'the act of pointing determines a place of pain' (note the absence of the definite article before 'place') it must be that prior to the act of pointing, the pain is determinately located.

It is obvious that pains do not occur in the world of physics, or at least, not straightforwardly. Amputees, for example, report pains in the place where their limbs would be if they had them – in the space external to the confines of their own bodies. And clearly, no physical examination of the place the amputee indicates as the site of his pain will reveal anything there at all – microscopes, radiation detectors, etc aren't the devices to do the job, the only pain detectors in this sense being sentient creatures. In fact it seems the only evidence we can have in such a case – that a pain is where a sufferer indicates it to be – is his indication; it seems impossible to get to it any other way. But then this is still a long way short of Wittgenstein's claim. It is undeniably true that our evidence for the location of a pain is what a sufferer of it says and does, but how are we to get from this truism to the claim that the pain is not in itself determinately located prior to the expression?

We need to remind ourselves once again that the pain, as a property of sentient creatures (not a 'thing'), can be suffered by others. So let us return to the ward full of sufferers that we visited earlier. We describe the suffering consciousness, whose thoughts, in a stoically expressionless silent soliloquy, run something like this:

> I wish I could get an anaesthetic quickly! It even hurts to breathe. The pain's coming again – under my ribs on the right! Aargh!

The pain is not yet located in physical space, in one location among others. As doctors we might observe inflammation, or characteristic muscle spasms. But we have no awareness of the pain as such (unless we suffer it too!). And I have set up the case so that the location of the pain is not being expressed by its sufferers. All that is definite is that the thought 'There's the pain, under my ribs on the right' is occurring – i.e. one token thought.

Now we can understand Wittgenstein's view if we take seriously the metaphor of pain-space, with the rider that people with the same pain occupy the same, one, pain-space. In this pain-space, intense concentration is being directed upon the pain – 'There it is, on the right – how it hurts!' But the concentration hasn't yet fixed on any point of the physical world; it isn't directed to any point in space; only on to the pain. In our capacity as doctors, we might then utter the words, 'Point to the pain now!' – to observe twenty hands rise to point at twenty different appendices. Hey presto, suddenly the one appendix pain is located in twenty different places. Prior to the pointing, the pain is not determinately here or there. What is determinately the case is only that the pain is being felt on the right in pain-space; not that it is being felt at co-ordinates (x_1, y_2, z_3), (x_1, y_2, z_3), ... (x_1, y_2, z_3) in the physical world.

How, then, should we conceive 'pain-space'? Pain-space is just the body image of the 'incorporeal being' of Aquinas's contemporaries, the common consciousness – the body of Buddha.[33]

The no-ownership theory, then, accounts for the three characteristic Wittgensteinian theses about the mind:

1 It is senseless to claim knowledge of one's own mental life.
2 Statements such as 'I am in pain' are expressive, rather than descriptive.
3 Pointing gestures *determine*, rather than report, the location of pain.

I ask the reader, how else could the many quotes from Wittgenstein I have adduced be interpreted? And yet the consequences of my case being correct are not inconsiderable. It follows that the philosophy of mind in the *Investigations* is the same no-ownership theory that commentators are unanimously agreed was abandoned in the thirties. And more importantly, it follows that for the half-century since his death, not a single commentator has correctly understood Wittgenstein's philosophy of mind. I shall quote again the passage from Anscombe and Geach's *Three Philosophers*:

> . . . some of Aquinas's contemporaries, who shared his view of thought, held that what really thinks is not a man but a single . . . intelligence that somehow manifests itself through all the many human organisms.

These philosophers, it is now clear, were early no-ownership theorists. And, if my interpretation of the Anatta doctrine is correct, they were also crypto-Buddhists. The single intelligence would be the Buddha nature, which every aspirant is supposed to realize on enlightenment is undivided and shared by all sentient creatures; knowingly by the enlightened and unknowingly by the unenlightened.

Something like this comes out in the following Zen story from Suzuki's third volume.[34] A monk had asked the formalized question, 'Who is the Buddha?' thereby indicating that he craved instruction. The dialogue is as follows:

> The monk called Hui-chao asked Fa-yen, 'Who is the Buddha?'
> Yen replied, 'You are Hui-chao.'

The dialogue is puzzling if we understand Yen to be speaking to Hui-chao, since he has offered no instruction at all, merely repeated his name. But the point is the reference of 'you'. If we take him instead to be speaking to the 'single intelligence manifesting itself through all the many human organisms' of Aquinas's contemporaries, the point is clear. Fa-yen is addressing this intelligence – the Buddha-nature – and reminding it that in this instance, it happens to be Hui-chao, the one through whose mouth it is so ignorantly asking the question of its own nature.

The connection between atheistic Buddhism and Communism has been pointed out before, not least by Professor Zaehner. Communism, of course, viewed petit bourgeois mysticism askance, but there is one way in which mysticism can be highly relevant to Communism, at least insofar as one can use the term mysticism for the no-ownership theory of mind. It lies in solving the ultimate dilemma of the revolution. This dilemma was expressed with great clarity by Professor Carew-Hunt in a *Spectator* article, later expanded into a handbook for the SIS.[35] (By a pleasant touch of irony, it was Philby who sponsored this handbook.) Carew-Hunt pointed out that it was a central part of Marxist belief that from the revolution

> there would eventually develop a genuine communist society in which men would agree to abandon their individuality, of which property is an expression, and live solely in and for the collective whole. Yet to believe that they will ever voluntarily do this is the very extreme of utopianism. The tension between the individual and society is a natural one, and it is not resolved by getting rid of one of its elements, any more than is the equilibrium of a pair of scales restored by removing one of its balances. There is nothing in Marx's teaching to show how this transformation of human nature will be brought about; while in *The State and Revolution* Lenin dismisses the question as one to which there can be no answer and which no one has the right to ask.

Wittgenstein's mental socialism – the no-ownership theory of Mind – was the means by which this goal could be accomplished. Men could be induced, by Wittgenstein's philosophical method, 'to abandon their individuality, of which property is an expression, and live solely in and for the collective whole'. Indeed, far from thinking it 'the very extreme of utopianism' to believe that men 'will ever voluntarily do this', Wittgenstein had done precisely this in turning his back on his own fabulous inheritance and working, at great risk to himself, to defeat Hitler. It might turn out, I think, not merely that Philby knew his Marxist theory backwards, but that he supported Professor Carew-Hunt publishing these thoughts in the belief that he himself – from his Cambridge instruction – knew the solution to the great unsolved problem of Communism. He knew it from understanding the philosophical method of his guru. Wittgenstein's subtle philosophical method, I suspect, led to his students at Cambridge adopting Communism as a religious revelation. Cornford and Bell were to die for it; Blunt and the others were to live their lives in its light. It was the original Aryan doctrine of consciousness, propounded by a Jew – or near-Jew. And through the work of Wittgenstein's disciples, it helped defeat Hitler.

ELEVEN

Avicenna and Averroes

It certainly assists in comprehension of the no–ownership theory to study its history, its suppression and its later re-emergence with Schopenhauer. The history of the doctrine covers so much territory that it is unrealistic to do more than touch upon some salient points within the space of a work such as this.[1] Nonetheless, it is worthwhile to demonstrate that it does *have* a history and to demarcate its position in the intellectual controversies of the past two millennia. It is also remarkable that it appears to have been espoused by Moses Maimonides, the great Rabbi.

Because the doctrine was twice suppressed in Europe, first in 1277 AD, and again in 1513 AD, there is considerable ignorance about the extent of the philosophical literature dealing with it. I shall focus upon Ibn Sina and its transfer to the University of Paris, where the doctrine was subject to the single greatest condemnation of the Middle Ages. Understanding the arguments Aquinas forged against it will help us to understand more of the doctrine itself.

Ibn Sina was an eleventh-century Persian philosopher who is better known in the West by the Latinized version of his name, Avicenna. (I shall use this version from here on.) Besides being perhaps the greatest philosopher between Aristotle and Aquinas, he was also a physician of the very highest calibre. His *Canon of Medicine* is the most famous single work in the history of medicine, not excluding those of Hippocrates and Galen, and it was taken as authoritative until the eighteenth century. (It was also the second book ever printed in Arabic.)

Avicenna adhered to a limited version of the no–ownership theory under which the intellect had an aspect that was not individual. He used this doctrine to account for the phenomena both of ordinary human intellection and of mystical union with the divine. His philosophy was enormously influential in the Muslim world and penetrated through Spain to the University of Paris, where it had a profound effect upon the thought of St Thomas Aquinas, amongst others. The question of the sources of Avicenna's doctrine is still not settled and I take this opportunity to point out a possible source that appears to have been over-looked in the literature.

One of the many interesting aspects of Avicenna's thought is a contro-versy extending over nearly a thousand years concerning a mysterious 'oriental philosophy' to which he referred in his writings. Precisely what he was referring to, and the role it played in his system of thought, is still very much a mystery. Puzzlement about it has produced a stream of books and scholarly articles in the last three or four decades, the general upshot of which is that the 'Oriental Philosophy', if it is anything at all, is not some-thing whose origins were *geographically* oriental. The Avicennan scholar Dmitri Gutas has described it as a 'scholarly hoax, or non-issue, of immense proportions that has consistently hampered research, especially Western Arabic studies'.[2] But belief that Avicenna had a distinctive and somewhat mysterious oriental philosophy goes back many, many centuries, indeed to his own time. Even Roger Bacon, for example, referred to Avicenna's *Philosophia Orientalis*.[3]

What was it supposed to be? So far as can be determined at this remove, the original work was destroyed, in 1151 AD. Gutas quotes the medieval historian Bayhaqi in support of this:

As for the complete Eastern Philosophy and the Throne Philosophy, the Imam Ismail al-Barhazi said they were in the libraries of Sultan Masud ibn-Mahmud at Ghazna. [They remained there] until the libraries were put to fire by the Gurid and Oguz troops of the king of Jibal, al-Husayn [Jehan-suz] in the year 546[/1151].[4]

As to its contents, therefore, we are largely ignorant, and given the historical vicissitudes, it seems unlikely that a complete copy might have reached Roger Bacon. But stranger things have happened, and in fact the *Philosophia Orientalis* was not lost in its entirety. Fragments of what appear to be part of it, to do with logic, were printed in 1910 in Cairo. And these fragments have been the subject of vitriolic scholarly dispute.

Most scholarly opinion seems to side with Gutas, who derides all attempts to locate a genuinely oriental source for Avicenna's ideas as ranging from the ridiculous to the fantastic.[5] On the other hand Avicenna does mention that he divides scholars into 'Occidentals' and 'Orientals'[6] and we also need to take account of a passage in Afnan's study of Avicenna in which he presents a translation of his words in the *Mantiq*:

And it is not improbable that certain sciences may have reached us from else-where than the side of the Greeks. . . . we then compared all these with that variety of science which the Greeks call logic – and it is not improbable that it may have a different name among the orientals. . . .[7]

Commentators rightly see this passage as very important, and they have contorted themselves trying to account for what Avicenna might have meant by saying 'from elsewhere than the side of the Greeks'. Corbin, in his commentary on Avicenna's visionary recitals, makes much play on the meaning of 'oriental', interpreting it in a novel, non-geographical sense, as a sort of pun. For Corbin, 'oriental' has the sense of the direction of the dawn light, as a metaphor for orienting oneself correctly in philosophy for the receipt of mystical illumination.[8] Gutas opposes this violently and believes that Avicenna's statement that he acquired knowledge 'from a direction other than that of the Greeks' must be treated in terms of his theory of intuition; that 'This "direction" is, of course, Intuition.'[9]

To say 'of course', however, seems a little swift, for the fact of the matter is that no one knows for certain, and we can only assign probabilities on the basis of the fragmentary evidence that has come down to us. But let us, in opposition to both Corbin and Gutas, follow the natural way of taking the passage and allow that 'direction' might really have a straightforward and literal geographical sense. Where else, in the tenth century, were there 'sciences' that a brilliantly intelligent and widely read man could rank with the sciences of the Greeks?

Let us remember that Avicenna was, above all else, a physician and that Ayurvedic medicine – which is undeniably one of the sciences that reached him from 'elsewhere than the side of the Greeks' – did come from India. And there was work done in India – so far as we know, independently of the Greeks – on logic.[10] Balkh, where Avicenna's father lived, had been a centre of Yogacarin Buddhism, and contained the ancient and wealthy Nawbahar monastery, mentioned in reports of Chinese monks travelling to India. The monastery was attacked by Muslims in AD 663 and apparently destroyed; but a Persian geography book dated around AD 982 (two years after Avicenna's birth) speaks of Balkh as 'a resort of merchants . . . very pleasant and prosperous' and as 'the emporium of Hindustan'. It also describes the remains of Nawbahar as containing 'paintings and wonderful works'.[11]

During the time of the Abassid Caliphate (AD 750-1258), individuals of enormous influence in Baghdad had family links to Nawbahar. A book on Hindu religious beliefs had been translated for the vizier Yahyia al-Barmaki. On the background of the Barmak family, Sachau, in the preface to his translation of Al-Biruni's work on India, notes that

Another influx of Hindu learning took place under Harun, AD 786-808. The ministerial family Barmak, then at the zenith of their power, had come with the ruling dynasty from Balkh, where an ancestor of theirs had been an official in the Buddhistic temple Naubehar. . . . Of course, the Barmak family had been converted, but their contemporaries never thought much of their profession of Islam, nor regarded it as genuine. Induced probably by family traditions, they sent scholars to India, there to study medicine and pharmacology. Besides, they engaged Hindu scholars to come to Baghdad, made them the chief physicians of their hospitals, and ordered them to translate from Sanscrit into Arabic books on medicine, pharmacology, toxicology, philosophy, astrology, and other subjects.[12]

The milieu, therefore, is one in which Hindu/Buddhist thought is not only far from dead but is demonstrably having an influence. This influence was particularly marked in philosophy and medicine/pharmacology/toxicology and these were overwhelmingly the fields that Avicenna made his own. On the Arab medical translations, we have the following on the authority of Dr Cyril Elgood:

I have . . . mentioned the names of one or two Indians who were in residence in the court at Baghdad. That these were not rare and occasional adventurers is clear from the remarks which the author of the Firdaus-ul-Hikmat makes when describing some Indian remedies. For he adds that he had collected such treatment of diseases by Indians as were easy and well known to the people of his part of the world. He was writing in AD 850, probably at Merv. Not only their practice but also their theory must have been well known in those times. Manka had translated an Indian book on poisons into Persian: Sanjahl, another Indian, had translated Charaka into Persian which had been retranslated into Arabic.[13]

Indian medicine, then, was influential in the Arab world and Avicenna was a physician. Furthermore, the mention of Charaka is particularly significant. Charaka was the redactor of a very curious Hindu work attributed to one Agnivesa, concerned primarily, but not solely, with medicine, and known ever since Charaka's redaction as the *Charaka Samhita*. It was composed in the first few centuries of our era, and it was translated into Persian and thence into Arabic about AD 800. What makes it important is that Avicenna refers to Charaka by name in the *Canon of Medicine*, showing, thereby, a direct connection to an Indian writer.[14]

There are also other references in Avicenna's medical work to Indian sources. For example, Book 1 of his *Canon of Medicine* (section 1037) informs us that 'The Indians have specified which leeches are venomous.[15] Now there is not very much on leeches in the *Charaka Samhita*, but there is a chapter on the topic in the *Sushruta Samhita*, the other classic work of

Ayurvedic medicine, which there are other reasons for believing that Avicenna knew.[16]

If we make the not uncharitable assumption that Avicenna actually read the texts he referred to and that the texts have not been corrupted since Avicenna's time, then, if Charaka states anything about the self being common to all, Avicenna was aware of that doctrine also. If we now turn our attention to Book IV of the *Charaka Samhita* we come across our theme. Here are some representative verses:

> After Lord Atreya concluded his talk, Agnivesa asked – Whatever your lordship said about commonness between the universe and the Person is quite correct. (Kindly tell us) What is the purpose of describing this commonness?
>
> Lord Atreya said – O Agnivesa! listen to me. Seeing the entire universe in the Self and vice versa gives rise to true knowledge. On seeing the entire universe in his Self one realises (the truth) that self alone is the agent of happiness and misery and none else. Though associated with cause etc under the influence of previous actions, after realizing the identity of the Self with the universe, he rises for salvation.[17]

And later:

> When one thinks himself spread in the universe and vice versa, and has the vision of the great and the small . . ., his serenity based on knowledge is not affected.[18]

Lord Atreya, then, identified this unification with the universe (that I have presented as the fruit of transcendence of the subject/object link) as 'nirvana'. Whether this is correctly translated as 'extinction' is a point very much at issue and, if our own investigation is correct, somewhat misleading. One might accept 'individual extinction' perhaps, but if the no–ownership account is correct, there have never been any individual consciousnesses anyway. Clearly, if Avicenna read this chapter in the *Charaka Samhita*, a work to which he refers, there can be no question but that he was aware of the doctrine we have been discussing and of its role in Indian religion. Now what was Avicenna's philosophy of the self?

We know that his own philosophy of mind allowed that an aspect of the intellect was not individual, but rather common to all. Commentators have found a similar doctrine in Aristotle, and therein located Avicenna's source; but it is only *arguably* in Aristotle whereas, as we have seen, it is explicitly present in Indian writings. In view of a centuries-old puzzle about an 'Oriental Philosophy' that Avicenna refers to as reaching him from a source 'other than the Greeks', these references, totally unnoticed in the literature, are of capital importance. It is not to be wondered at that they have escaped the philosophical historians, for they are not philosophical references, but medical references containing a philosophical theme.

Avicenna flourished in reasonable geographical proximity to India, in Khorasan, at the (then) remote east of the Islamic world. But the next act in the drama we are viewing was staged in the far West, in Spain, apparently far from any Indian influence. Its main actor was the vehicle through whom the no-ownership account passed through to Christendom and the Scholastics: the Islamic philosopher Ibn Rochd, better known to the latinized West as Averroes. Because of his writings on Aristotle, and his labours in commentary, Averroes was universally referred to in medieval times as 'the Commentator', his veneration for Aristotle being a byword.

The interesting feature of Averroes' philosophy of mind is that he explicitly adhered to a full no-ownership account of the intellect. He was certainly familiar with the earlier work of Avicenna towards a partial no-ownership position.[19] Had Averroes extended his idea to all mental faculties, he would have anticipated Wittgenstein's account of the mind by some eight hundred years.

India was wide open to trade with the Islamic world, and we have a particularly noteworthy record of a trade link to India involving the family of another prominent Iberian from the very same city as Averroes. This was the great Jewish Rabbi, Moses Maimonides, who became a doctor at the court of Saladin. He was a contemporary of Averroes, and was born in the same city, Cordova, in AD 1135, nine years after Averroes. Colette Sirat notes that

> The family of Maimonides was engaged in maritime commerce with India; the shipwreck and death of his brother David brought about their ruin.[20]

David Maimonides drowned in the Indian Ocean, which is a long, long way from Spain, but in fact the Jewish Indian trade was extensive and represented a clear link between India and Spain.[21] Maimonides is also interesting in that we find our theme in his work also. It is worth diverting a moment to examine what he wrote.

He begins by speaking of God as an intellect, and argues that He himself, the thing that He apprehends and the act of apprehension are equally the Divine Essence – in other words that subject, act and object are one. He then extends this from the creator to the creature and writes that

> numerical unity of the intellect, the intellectually cognizing subject, and the intellectually cognized object, does not hold good with reference to the Creator

only, but also with reference to every intellect.[22]

What, one is impelled to ask, must follow when the same object is grasped intellectually by *two* intellects? Would not identity of intellect with cognized object mean, on this account, identity of cognizing subjects also, so far as cognizing does not involve separate bodies? Our theme is clearly at hand and, despite its apparent Aristotelian garb, the researcher again comes across the ubiquitous smell of India, this time via Maimonides's family trading connections.

We know that Maimonides did read Averroes, if not before his exile from Spain, certainly later, when domiciled in Egypt,[23] and in Averroes, as in Maimonides, our theme is presented explicitly:

> Zaid and Amr are numerically different but identical in form. If, for example, the soul of Zaid were numerically different from the soul of Amr in the way Zaid is numerically different from Amr, the soul of Zaid and the soul of Amr would be numerically two, but one in their form, and the soul would possess another soul. The necessary conclusion is therefore that the soul of Zaid and the soul of Amr are identical in their form. An identical form inheres in a numerical i.e. a divisible multiplicity, only through the multiplicity of matter. If then the soul does not die when the body dies, or if it possesses an immortal element, it must, when it has left the bodies, form a numerical unity.[24]

All souls, therefore, are one and thus there is no *individual* immortality.

Now this doctrine, presented by Averroes, whether Hindu/Buddhist resurrection or new creation, caused an immediate problem for Christianity. This is because for Christianity (as, indeed, for Judaism and Islam) the gap between creature and Creator is absolute. Without there being a component of the individual intellect multiplied as the number of bodies, what could one make, for example, of the doctrine of individual rewards and punishments in the after life?[25] That is, what could remain that would be subject after death either to reward for virtue or punishment for vice, if the intellect is not intrinsically individual? Indeed, what could be made of the doctrine of personal immortality at all? And most troubling of all, what was there to distinguish the mental life of the creature from that of the Creator?

The effect of this doctrine was to place Aristotle and Greek philosophy under a cloud, for Aristotle (rather than fabulous India) was presented as the doctrine's source. Aristotle had been introduced to the West via Arab translations which included Averroes's commentaries. The clear non-Christian origins of these translations, and the theologically suspect account of the soul they carried, subjected Aristotelians and Averroists at the University of Paris to increasingly unfavourable scrutiny from the ecclesiastical authorities.

Averroes's no-ownership position on the soul, however, appealed to a growing number of Masters. Of these, the most prominent was Siger of Brabant, who, on the matter of the unicity of the intellect, followed Averroes explicitly. In 1266, the papal legate (and future Pope) Simon of Brion cited Siger as the leader of a rebellious faction at the arts faculty. The *Encyclopaedia Britannica* article 'Siger', commenting on his last book, *Treatise on the Intellectual Soul*, says that it

> discusses his basic belief that there is only one 'intellectual' soul for mankind and thus one will. Although the soul is eternal, individual human beings are not immortal.

If the *Britannica* article is correct about Siger's view on the unity of the will, then we see in Siger a further movement towards the full no-ownership position, for we would be dealing with a thirteenth-century anticipation of Schopenhauer. There are not multiple 'wills', diverse as the number of men, but a single will expressing itself through all willing creatures. I am not *inventing* parallels here: they are real. This is the identical doctrine that we see in Schopenhauer and Wittgenstein.

One does not need to be a genius to see the logic of how it works in Schopenhauer. We can also see how it works in Averroes. And one can reason out how a logically identical doctrine about the intellect might have worked in Siger, though the destruction and loss of many of his works makes it unlikely that we will ever know precisely to what extent his evident anticipation of Schopenhauer penetrated and informed his thinking.[26]

This is not a small loss. Even so acute a philosopher as Frege, Wittgenstein's predecessor and mentor in applying mathematical logic to philosophy, in evident ignorance of the enormous upheavals in mediaeval times over just this question of privacy, managed to founder even while glimpsing a way out:

> . . . it is impossible to compare my sense-impression with that of someone else. For that it would be necessary to bring together in one consciousness a sense-impression, belonging to one consciousness, with a sense-impression belonging to another consciousness. Now even if it were possible to make an idea disappear from one consciousness and, at the same time, to make an idea appear in another consciousness, the question whether it were the same idea in both would still remain unanswerable. It is so much of the essence of each of my ideas to be the content of my consciousness, that every idea of another person is, just as such, distinct from mine. But might it not be possible that my ideas, the

entire content of my consciousness might be at the same time the content of a more embracing, perhaps divine, consciousness? Only if I were myself part of the divine consciousness. But then, would they really be my ideas, would I be their bearer? This oversteps the limits of human understanding to such an extent that one must leave its possibility out of account.[27]

For Frege to simply dismiss from consideration the possibility that consciousness might be public on the grounds he adduces is surely just shortsightedness. Does such a possibility really overstep 'the limits of human understanding'? Why *does* 'a sense-impression belonging to one consciousness' *by that very fact alone* have to differ from a 'sense-impression belonging to another consciousness'? Why did Frege think that in this area no serious philosophical investigation could be mounted? The reason, probably, is that he had never come across the idea as a serious philosophical possibility. He had no idea that it had already been considered, six hundred years previously, but that its Islamic and Christian investigators had been killed or frightened into silence. Frege therefore was blind to any need to probe here at all. The idea that consciousness is one and undivided in all, an idea that recurs East and West and that was current among the Aryans of the East virtually from the invention of writing, had been pushed underground.

The connection I am drawing through Indian thought, Averroes and Siger on the one side, through to Schopenhauer and Wittgenstein on the other, should be obvious. For it is surely clear by now to what end in Wittgenstein all these developing fragments of doctrine are tending. To Wittgenstein's credit, he not only grasped the prime importance of what Frege dismissed; he probed it to its limits, indeed, formed his philosophy of mind upon it, and fully recognized its religious implications. Wittgenstein, though, was far from the first, and Von Wright's claim that he had no philosophical predecessors is hopelessly incorrect.[28]

In modern times proponents of the views we have been examining have tended to be outside the serious philosophical mainstream. In olden times they were certainly in the serious mainstream, but were dealt with rather differently. In Baghdad, Hallaj had been crucified for arguing in their favour. Paris, as ever, was a shade more civilized.

TWELVE

The Arguments: Aquinas and Strawson

We shall now turn to consider some of the arguments with which Thomas Aquinas destroyed the first European incarnation of the no-ownership theory of the mind. As a translator says, 'His refutation of the leaders of the Averroist movement at the University, particularly of Siger of Brabant, formed the chief controversy of his life.'[1]

The controversy against the no-ownership theory established Christian doctrine on the nature of the soul, and so has an intrinsic interest of its own. Aquinas stated his purpose in Chapter 1 of *De unitate* in the following words:

> Of late there has sprung up an erroneous doctrine about the intellect on the part of many men who take their starting point from certain works of Averroes. They assert that the intellect, which Aristotle called the possible intellect (he also inaptly named it 'immaterial'), is evidently a kind of substance separate, by its very nature, from the body, yet in some way united to the body as its form; and further that this possible intellect is one for all men. . . .
>
> At this time it will not be our method to show that the aforesaid position is erroneous as being repugnant to the truth of Christian faith: this is through death nothing of the souls of men survives except the one common intellect. Thus would be destroyed any possibility of retribution, of rewards and punishments, or any diversity in recompenses.
>
> However, we intend to show that their position is not less in conflict with the principles of philosophy than it is with the testimony of faith.

Those of Aquinas' arguments I consider occur in various of his works,[2] and for our purposes, some of them need to be met and some do not. The Wittgensteinian no-ownership account, of course, is more comprehensive than the position of the Latin Averroists, who thought only the intellect (and perhaps also the will) to be one for all men.

The critical *theological* consequence of the no-ownership theory was clearly foreseen by Aquinas, for, criticizing the Averroists, he wrote:

. . . according to their reasoning, we can conclude absolutely that there is only one intellect – and not merely one for all men.

For if there is only one intellect, then, according to their argument, it follows that there is only one in the whole world, and not simply one for all men. Therefore our intellect is not only a separate substance, but also it is God himself, and any plurality of separate substances is rendered impossible.[3]

It is worth pointing out that Aquinas viewed the doctrine he condemns here far more favourably at an earlier stage in his thinking. It was also viewed more favourably by earlier Catholic doctors. We have, for example, the early Aquinas on the agent intellect, saying that 'some Catholic doctors with much probability have made God Himself the "intellectus agens" '.[4]

What Aquinas says here (where his 'with much probability' rider indicates tentative agreement) clearly contradicts his later position in the *Summa Theologica*. He came to see individuation as a problem, as is clear from his critical statement of the full no-ownership account of intellection:

. . . the intellection of one thing – for example, of a stone – is but one, not only in all men, but even in all intellects.[5]

Now the reply of the no-ownership account is that the content of the intellection of one thing is indeed one for all men (for God too): indeed, as a point of logic, it must be one if it is to be intellection of that thing. As in Frege and Maimonides, the content is, and must be, common. The intellecting, however – the act – is multiple via behavioural expression of the content through its multiple human vehicles. Aquinas would seem to be right, however, that the no-ownership theory can provide no account of how multiplicity might come into the thinking of disembodied intelligences. Indeed, Nicholson, expounding the nature of the unitive state of Islamic mystics, quotes Hallaj:

In that glory is no 'I' or 'We' or 'Thou'. 'I', 'We', 'Thou' and 'He' are all one thing.[6]

This doctrine, which is implicit in much of Sufism, was, in this explicit statement, as objectionable to Muslims as it was to Aquinas. Hallaj seemed to be claiming that he was God. Accordingly, he had his hands and feet cut off and was crucified in Baghdad for blasphemy. Sufis, from that time on, have been understandably more circumspect in advertising the nature of mystical union.

Another of Aquinas's concerns, apparently connected with the previous consideration, was that the doctrine had catastrophic *moral* consequences.

This comes out in the following passage:

> If, therefore, there should be but one intellect for all men, it would follow neces-
> sarily that there would be but one intelligent being and consequently one will
> and one agent using, according to the dictates of his own will, all those attrib-
> utes by which men are differentiated from one another. Furthermore, from this
> fact it would likewise follow that there would be no difference among men as
> regards free election of the will; but the same things would be done by all if the
> intellect (in which alone resides the sovereignty and command over all the other
> powers) is one and the same in different men – a supposition evidently false and
> impossible. For such a doctrine is in opposition to facts that are clearly
> apparent. And it likewise would destroy the whole science of morality and all
> that pertains to the conservation of organized society which, as Aristotle says, is
> natural to all men.[7]

But does this view really 'destroy the whole science of morality'? Might
it not rather lead to virtue in that, to the extent that the doctrine is grasped,
individual egotism is no longer the source of action? On this doctrine, to the
extent that one acts egotistically, one simply misunderstands the nature of
what one is doing – the very nature of action itself. The left-wing publisher,
Victor Gollancz, with whom Wittgenstein corresponded, collected several
stories from the world's religious literature illustrating this theme and
presented them in his anthology *A Year of Grace*. Here is one that Gollancz
attributes to the nineteenth-century Indian renunciate, Ramakrishna:

> There was a monastery in a certain place. The monks residing there went out
> daily to beg their food. One day a monk, while out for his alms, saw a landlord
> beating a man mercilessly. The compassionate monk stepped in and asked the
> landlord to stop. But the landlord was filled with anger and turned his wrath
> against the innocent monk. He beat the monk till he fell unconscious on the
> ground. Someone reported the matter to the monastery. The monks ran to the
> spot and found their brother lying there. Four or five of them carried him back
> and laid him on a bed. He was still unconscious. The other monks sat around
> him saw at heart; some were fanning him. Finally someone suggested that he
> should be given a little milk to drink. When it was poured into his mouth he
> regained consciousness. He opened his eyes and looked around. One of the
> monks said, 'Let us see whether he is fully conscious and can recognise us.'
> Shouting into his ear, he said, 'Revered sir, who is giving you milk?' 'Brother,'
> replied the holy man in a low voice, 'he who beat me is now giving me milk.'[8]

The no-ownership account, then, does indeed force a change in how we
conceive of action and Aquinas was quite correct to complain that it
permits ultimately of only one agent. Perhaps he is even correct to

complain that it 'would destroy the whole science of morality'. The holy man of Gollancz's story saw only one agent – God – for everything. However, even if Aquinas's complaint is justified, it does not follow that the doctrine is therefore false.

Did the Saint have a knock-down argument against the no-ownership theory that does demonstrate it to be false on logical grounds? Though he appears to claim that he does, what he has is something rather different. He argues first that the no-ownership account is not in accord with our ordinary pre-reflective beliefs about the nature of human beings and then that our ordinary pre-reflective beliefs have not been demonstrated to be self-contradictory by the no-ownership account.

Thus, he discusses Plato's opinion concerning the union of the intellectual soul with the body, writing:

> Plato and his school held that the intellectual soul is not united to the body as form to matter, but only as mover to moveable, for he said that the soul is in the body as a sailor in a boat.[9]

Aquinas's objection is that on this view, the unity of a man is done away with; that 'a man is not one simply, and neither consequently a being simply, but accidentally'.[10] He thought this was sufficient to show the no-ownership account to be false, for he writes in his reply to objections in the *Summa Theologica*:

> I answer that, It is absolutely impossible for one intellect to belong to all men. This is clear if, as Plato maintained, man is the intellect itself. For it would follow that Socrates and Plato are one man; and that they are not distinct from each other except by something outside the essence of each. The distinction between Socrates and Plato would be no other than that of one man with a tunic and another with a cloak; which is altogether absurd.[11]

Absurd or not, in this very form, the clothes analogy is given in the *Bhagavad Gita* from the mouth of the god Krishna:

> Who thinks that he can be a slayer,
> Who thinks that he is slain,
> Both these have no (right) knowledge:
> He slays not, is not slain.[12]

> Never is he born nor dies;
> Never did he come to be, nor will he
> ever come to be again:

Unborn, eternal, everlasting he – primeval:
He is not slain when the body is slain.

If a man knows him as indestructible,
Eternal, unborn, never to pass away,
How and whom can he cause to be slain
Or slay?

As a man casts off his worn-out clothes
And takes on other new ones (in their place),
So does the embodied soul cast off his worn-out bodies
And enters others new.[13]

The clothes analogy is clearly not original with Aquinas. In the East its antiquity is even venerable. It might indeed be false, but it is not, on the face of it, absurd. Why can't it be that 'man is not one simply, and neither consequently a being simply, but accidentally'? Couldn't something like this be *discovered*? And if it is discoverable, then it is not absurd, but an hypothesis to be investigated; something that might fall within the domain of legitimate scientific inquiry and perhaps turn out to be true. What then were Aquinas's reasons for thinking it to be impossible?

They appear to me to be neither insignificant nor fully convincing. He argued that a man cannot just *be* an act of understanding (an intellectual soul whose essence is just to understand) – as he says Plato maintained – for this reason:

that it is one and the same man who is conscious both that he understands and that he senses. But one cannot sense without a body.[14]

Aquinas then, given that a man is not just the intellect, is led to investigate the principle of his composition. How is the intellect related to the whole of which it is a part: what is the principle of its union? On the union of soul and body, Aquinas writes:

But some philosophers, indeed, seeing that the conclusions reached by Averroes' road could not show how this individual man thinks, have turned aside into another road. They say the intellect is united to man as a mover; and so, inasmuch as unity is produced by the conjunction of body and intellect, as by the union of a mover and the thing moved, so the intellect is a part of this man. Hence the operation of the intellect is attributed to this man, just as the operation of the eye, which is to see, is attributed to him. . . .

It must be asked of one holding this theory, first of all, what kind of individual this is whom we call Socrates. Is Socrates the intellect alone – that is, the mover (motor)? Or is he moved by that which is the body, and yet animated by a vegetative and sensitive soul? Or is he a composite of both?

It seems from their position that the third opinion should be held: namely, that Socrates is a being composed of both.[15]

Aquinas then argues that this is to throw away the *unity* of man. He quotes Aristotle,[16] that Socrates 'is a substance of a unique nature, not after the manner of Ilias, a city composed of parts, but a being of one existence'.[17] But whether supported by Aristotle or not, this is just the point at issue, and needs support independent of the mere opinion of a philosophical authority. This is what the Saint now attempts to provide:

> But if you say that Socrates is not an absolutely unified being, but a unity of a sort resulting from the aggregation of mover and moved many difficulties would result.

What are these difficulties? The first of them is that

> only in that totality which is a unity is the action of a part the action of the whole. . . .

Aquinas illustrates what he is getting at by the example of a sailor in a ship, the sailor corresponding to the intellect and the ship to the body:

> . . . we do not say that the sailor's ability to understand is attributable to the totality comprised by the sailor and his ship, but that understanding belongs to the sailor alone; and in like manner . . . to understand will not be the act of Socrates, but of the intellect alone which makes use of the body of Socrates.

He continues that

> even if it is granted that an intellect is united to Socrates as moving him, this does not prove that understanding is in Socrates, or that he understands; because understanding is an act which is in the intellect alone.

What does it mean to say that 'understanding is an act which is in the intellect alone'? On the no-ownership account, to the extent that an act of understanding is individualized as this or that person's, it is expressed via this or that body. And this is essential to it; this is what 'your act of understanding' as opposed to 'my act of understanding' is. So an 'act of understanding' really is, for a no-ownership theorist, essentially this person's or that person's. What is in 'the intellect alone' is just the common content, in which no distinction can be drawn between thinking and thought. And it is this that is uniquely neither mine nor yours. The nettle in this account for Aquinas, will be the nature, not of the individualized acts of understanding, but of the common, unowned content. And there is a passage in which Aquinas expresses what he feels is the difficulty. In some anthologies of quotations from Aquinas's work it is taken as *the* passage that definitively refutes the Averroist doctrine of the unicity of the intellect:

> Again, this is clearly impossible whatever one may hold as to the manner of the union of the intellect to this or that man. For it is manifest that, supposing that there is one principal agent and two instruments, we can say that there is one agent absolutely, but several actions; as when one man touches several things with his two hands, there will be one who touches, but two contacts. If, on the contrary, we suppose one instrument and several principal agents, we might say that there are several agents, but one act; for example, if there be many drawing a ship by means of a rope, there will be many drawing and one pull. If, however, there is one principal agent, and one instrument, we say that there is one agent and one action, as when the smith strikes with one hammer, there is one striker and one stroke. Now it is clear that no matter how the intellect is united or coupled to this or that man, the intellect has the precedence of all the other things which appertain to man; for the sensitive powers obey the intellect, and are at its service. Therefore, if we suppose two men to have several intellects and one sense, – for instance, if two men had one eye, – there would be several seers, but one sight. But if there is one intellect, no matter how diverse may be all those things of which the intellect makes use as instruments, in no way is it possible to say that Socrates and Plato are otherwise than one understanding man. And if to this we add that to understand, which is the act of the intellect, is not effected by any organ other than the intellect itself, it will further follow that there is but one agent and one action; that is to say that all men are but one 'understander', and have but one act of understanding, in regard, that is, of one intelligible object.[18]

Indeed it will. But to take this as a *reductio* seems to me a bit too quick. The no-ownership theorist produces a theory of the mind that he thinks takes due account of the conceptual separability of the mind from the body (as Cartesianism, with its reliance on mysterious, unarticulated individuating principles for minds, does not). He claims that when two men understand the same intelligible object, behavioural differences aside, there is but one act of understanding and thus, so far as consciousness alone is concerned, one 'understander'. But he does not have to say, it seems to me, that there is one understanding man, period.

The account needed here is of what it is to understand. For the no-ownership theorist, Socrates and Plato are not 'one understanding man', just as Yin and Yang, the Siamese twins are not one suffering man, despite their unitary phenomenal hurting. The no-ownership position is that so far as consciousness alone is concerned, there are not multiple understanders or multiple sufferers (when the object of understanding or suffering is the same). But there certainly are multiple understanders and sufferers when human behaviour is taken into account.[19]

The no-ownership theorist asks how Aquinas thought intellects were multiplied among men, if not via the diversity of human behaviour. Interestingly the saint does grant that it is not in the nature of intellects to be plural:

. . . those others who try to prove that God could not create many intellects of the same species, present a clumsy argument, believing that this would involve a contradiction.

Now, though we should grant that it is not of the nature of an intellect to be multiplied, we cannot presume that for such an intellect to be multiplied would imply a contradiction. For even though the cause of some quantity would not be in the nature of a being, still nothing would prevent its possessing this perfection from some other cause; just as a heavy body has the tendency by its own nature not to be above lighter bodies; nevertheless, for such a heavy body to be thus above does not involve a contradiction; though to be thus above would be, according to its own nature, contradictory. Thus, even if the intellect, by nature, were one for all men because of not having any natural cause for multiplication, still this multiplication could be allotted to it by a supernatural cause: nor would this imply any contradiction.

This fact we emphasize, not only in view of the immediate problem, but more in order that the same argument may not be extended in other discussions. For, in the same way, one might be able to conclude that God could not cause the dead to rise, and that sight might not be restored to the blind.[20]

Reading this passage, we ask ourselves how Aquinas thought it possible for immaterial intellects (which on the face of it, lack any feature in virtue of which one can be picked out from another) to be distinguished. And the Saint piously informs us that while it is not in the nature of intellects to be distinguished, God can do it – supernaturally. This is singularly unhelpful to those of us who are curious as to the logical means by which He can so supernaturally intervene. It is an answer which in any case even the pious are less inclined to accept immediately nowadays. The point the Saint is making is that the non-Averroist position is not self-contradictory and that whatever the power of the Averroist critique of individuating principles for disembodied intelligences, it fails to establish that there couldn't be such an individuating principle.

Aquinas asks how the intellect is united to Yin or to Yang. The no-ownership answer (not, incidentally, that of Averroes or Siger) is that it is linked in the same way as is their shared pain, and is made multiple by making use of their bodies and in no other way. In itself the intellect is not the property of any subject, but when its pronouncements issue forth through Socrates's mouth or through Plato's mouth we thereby listen to Socrates's intellect or Plato's intellect. Likewise, Socrates's height could have been identical with Plato's height. Yet when we measure Socrates's body and Plato's body, we are measuring the height of Socrates and the height of Plato. The intellect is Socrates's or Plato's to the extent that it is expressed through Socrates or Plato. Such a theory might indeed be false, even absurd, but it is not made false or absurd in the mere assertion that it is.

Aquinas's chief worry is that he sees a no-ownership theorist as committed to holding that 'in no way is it possible to say that Socrates and Plato are otherwise than one understanding man', and that the unity of an individual is thereby done away with. Socrates and Plato, however, are distinguished by their bodies, time of birth, personalities, relations to others and so on; but not by their understanding of something in those cases when their understanding is the same. For how could they be if their understanding is the same? In these cases there is no multiplicity in the understanding, but it certainly would not seem to follow that no distinction of person is possible on *other* grounds. The distinct entities Socrates and Plato simply happen to intersect where their mental life is common. Is this really a doctrine so absurd to be dismissed out of hand? I think the reader will agree that the foregoing arguments seem a little thin to damn people on.

I shall conclude this chapter by examining a modern argument against the no-ownership theory. It was developed by Peter Strawson and published in his book *Individuals*.[21] The version of the no-ownership theory that Strawson expounds and then demolishes, however, is not Wittgenstein's, but subtly different from it.

I said earlier that my pains are those that involve my body in their expression, whichever body is 'mine' being determined in part by the body involved in actively expressing the sign 'mine', thus making it into an individuating symbol. Strawson's no-ownership theory offers a very different criterion for what my pains are. On the Strawsonian account of the no-ownership theory, my pains are those pains causally dependent on the state of a certain body – Kimberley Cornish's. Now this is to break my active involvement in my own mental life and turn it into something purely passive, with catastrophic consequences for the no-ownership theory, as we shall see.

Strawson presents his point in the following passage in somewhat technical philosophical prose, that we shall unpack in a moment:

When [the no-ownership theorist] tries to state the contingent fact, which he thinks gives rise to the illusion of the 'ego', he has to state it in some such form as 'All my experiences are had by (i.e. uniquely dependent on the state of) body B'. For any attempt to eliminate the my, or any expression with a similar possessive force, would yield something that was not a contingent fact at all. The proposition that all experiences are causally dependent on the state of a single body B, for example, is just false. The theorist means to speak of all the experiences had by a single person being contingently so dependent. And the theorist cannot consistently argue that 'all the experiences of person P' means the same thing as 'all experiences contingently dependent on a certain body B'; for then his proposition would not be contingent, as his theory requires, but analytic. He must mean to be speaking of some class of experiences of the members of which it is contingently true that they are all dependent on body B. The defining characteristic of this class is in fact that they are 'my experiences' or 'the experiences of some person', where the idea of possession expressed by 'my' and 'of' is the one he calls into question.[22]

In a nutshell, Strawson's argument is this: 'My experiences' can't *mean* 'experiences dependent on the state of Kim Cornish's body' because it is conceivable that I might have a pain dependent upon the state of someone *else*'s body (sympathetic labour pains might be an example) so the claimed identity would be merely contingent. It would presumably even be possible to have a pain dependent upon the state of another's body that the other person didn't have at all. (I might feel a pain, for example, when the thumb of some totally anaesthetized person is struck with a hammer.)

Now the reason why Strawson's argument doesn't work against Wittgenstein's version of the no-ownership theory is simple, and can be presented in a sentence: If I have a pain that another man expresses, then he has that same pain too. There is no contingent link involved. To the extent that what the other person is expressing is a pain, then he must have it too. If he is merely simulating expressing a pain, then on that very ground, he is not expressing a pain. One cannot express a pain without having it – one can at most only pretend to. In Strawson's version, however, where the criterion is not active expression, but passive bodily damage, a person need not feel a pain when his body is damaged and the way is open to drive in the contingent/necessary wedge.

It then would be possible for me to have another pain (that the other person didn't feel) when another person's body is damaged. But on Wittgenstein's version, whichever body expresses the word 'my' in 'my pain' when I use the words is, because of this, *my* body. The very utterance of 'my' locates its subject logically.

I have said that my pains are those that involve my body in their expression. Strawson asks, 'But might you not feel that pain when the bodies of others express that pain?' The reply is simply, 'Of course; when they have it too!' I never said that *only* my body expresses a particular pain – the point is only that multiple having relations do not exist prior to the expression. The whole question depends upon how I pick out *my body*. It is picked out by the words 'My body' issuing forth from this body, from that body etc. Each occurrence creates an individual owner or subject of experience out of the unowned universal mind. Strawson asserts that when the no-ownership theorist

> tries to state the contingent fact, which he thinks gives rise to the illusion of the 'ego', he has to state it in some such form as 'All my experiences are had . . . by body B' . . . where the idea of possession expressed by 'my' . . . is the one he calls into question.

This presenter of the no-ownership theory states the contingency in the following form: All *my* experiences are expressed through Kimberley Cornish's body, just as is the word 'my' when I happen to use it. The Strawsonian question in this case is 'But might you not have an experience that another person expresses?' And the reply is that to the extent that he expresses it then we both have that experience. But if I express the word 'my' through the lips of Joe Bloggs, then I *am* Joe Bloggs – those are *my* lips. There is just no criterion of personal identity for consciousnesses independent of expression of the first person pronoun and its correlates.

Conclusion

Readers who have come so far will be conscious of having covered rather a lot of territory. Our investigation has embraced many topics in the history and geography of ideas, touching on issues in metaphysics, epistemology, history, comparative religion and psychology. It has been concerned with the nature of man, mortality, magic and even mystical union, and has dealt with such contrasting personalities as Schopenhauer, Wagner, Wittgenstein and Hitler. Each path on this journey has been to help us find our way around uncharted territory and to make plausible a hypothesis concerning the source of the doctrines that led to the Holocaust – and indeed influenced the whole twentieth century – that otherwise would seem fantastic.

It has long been a discredited and hateful argument of the anti-Semitic fringe of politics that Jews somehow brought the Holocaust upon themselves. It was because Jews did XYZ that the Holocaust happened and therefore they – the victims – are to blame for it. The XYZ factors that are appealed to are various; all of them are objectionable beyond words and in any case not intrinsically different from the allegations the Nazis themselves presented to justify their persecutions. But even were some of the allegations true, it is of no relevance at all. Whatever 'the Jews' might have done, nothing humanly justifies what was visited upon them.

On the other hand, from the Jewish side of the divide, the Holocaust must be – is – profoundly disturbing religiously. It is *the* defining event of post-Biblical Jewish history, yet the Holocaust had no prophets. To a religious Jew, it is clear that Yahweh beyond any possibility of argument turned his back upon His people and delivered them into the hands of a great persecutor who inflicted upon them all the curses of Deuteronomy. Only a remnant of European Jewry passed through the consuming fires to sanctuary. Why did it happen? From a religious point of view, why did Yahweh bring it about? And how can we explain the Divine Silence?

To a man of no religious belief, there is nothing to explain. Horrible things just do happen, because human nature is horrible – and with

232

Diaspora Jews relatively powerless and at the mercy of the nations amongst which they dwelt, it is not at all surprising they should have been subject to particularly horrible things. It is a waste of time to draw a specifically religious lesson from what happened. The Holocaust is just the climax of 'The Longest Hatred'; that is, of an anti-Semitism going back millennia.[1] It was different in degree, but no different in kind, from the horrors visited upon other minorities such as the Armenians, the Gypsies, the Rwandans and many others.

This writer, however, as the reader is aware, thinks that the Holocaust had very little to do with traditional anti-Semitism and that those of no religious belief who assimilate its causes to traditional anti-Semitism condemn themselves to historical ignorance. About this extermination, there was something different. To bring out what happened, however, requires that the metaphysics of Nazism be examined rather more closely than it has been hitherto. I have attempted to locate the source of the Holocaust in a perversion of early Aryan religious doctrines about the ultimate nature of man.

Adolf Hitler, from his schoolboy encounter with Wittgenstein, came to understand 'the meaning of history' in terms of the unowned mind taking multiple individuals as its vehicle. He viewed history as a struggle of forms, of unitary racial wills. He saw the Aryan will taking bodies within the Aryan race as its vehicles. Because of this Wittgenstein-inspired doctrine, Hitler came to study Schopenhauer's crucial summary and explanation of the Hermetica in terms of this very doctrine. That is, Hitler was thereby able to develop the powers of fascination – which I have described as magical powers – that ultimately propelled him to the German leadership and let him set in train the Holocaust. Note that the causal sequence traced out here that led to the Holocaust crucially depends upon Wittgenstein's philosophy of mind. I very briefly touch here, as lightly as I can, upon a thought that might occur to a Hasidic Jew, and that is more fittingly a matter for Jewish, as opposed to gentile, reflection: the very engine that drove Hitler's acquisition of the magical powers that made his ascent and the Holocaust possible was the Wittgenstein Covenant violation, for had the family been practising Jews, Ludwig could not have held the no-ownership theory to be true.

Our investigation, of course, has not focused solely upon the Holocaust. Inevitably, in a book dealing with a great philosopher, we have been drawn into philosophy. We have considered such impenetrable philosophical chestnuts as the nature of subjecthood, of consciousness, of eternity and death. We have seen a novel method of attack on these chestnuts; Wittgenstein's method, whose promise is, not merely that they might be soluble, but that they contain their answer within themselves if we only know how to look. Remarkably, the method of looking – so long and difficult in the finding – is simply to allow ourselves to be struck by commonplaces.

What are these commonplaces? The ones we considered are these: when I say 'I', I thereby distinguish myself from others; when I say 'now' I distinguish the time of utterance of the word from other times of its utterance. These really are commonplaces, 'grammatical rules' that no one would dispute. But they are also, when considered from another standpoint, statements of the new science that Wittgenstein invented and bequeathed to his philosophical posterity – 'philosophical grammar'.

Just as Wittgenstein claimed, 'a method has been found'. Wittgenstein's life – when he wasn't fighting Hitler – was devoted to sketching a map of this intellectual region that it is the task of his successor cartographers to fill in. The sketch is of something new; a sort of Euclideanization of concepts – a study of the 'logic of our language'. The point is that to engage in this intellectual enterprise, we must look at commonplaces differently. We must delve into what they 'show' rather than into what they 'say'. The distinction is Wittgenstein's and I hope to have made a small contribution by showing how it works in his philosophy. It is utterances of 'I' that create multiple subjects, and utterances of 'now' that create a temporal location for mental events. The result of this elucidation is that we are enabled to grasp by what means the *Logos* – the Divine Word – creates us all as individuals at a particular point in time. So another view of our endeavour is to see it as a study of the logical mechanism of Divine Creation. It is entirely apt that such a study should come to us, as has so much of our knowledge of the Divine, out of Judah. It is a tragedy that it came entangled, as I have tried to demonstrate, with the Holocaust.

The theme of Divine Creation, whether described as philosophy or as theology or as *a priori* grammar, is not a small study. And neither has it been a contrived study. We have pursued an idea, a 'single thought' – endlessly recurrent – across continents and thousands of years, expressing itself again and again through the most various of human vehicles; at and in sundry times and diverse places. As with Schopenhauer, the book has been written to convey a 'single idea', but the conveyance of it has required a book.

What has been established? At the least I think we have established that there really is a philosophy 'on the far side of solipsism' that had not been articulated clearly and that yet affected us all profoundly. Our investigation has been, as Wittgenstein remarked, returning again and again to the same place from different directions; the effect each time being to 'produce that knowledge that consists in the fact that we see the connections'.[2] We now know our way around.

Appendix
A Note on Clausewitz, Hitler and Prince Ludwig Adolf Wittgenstein

Hitler, according to Werner Maser, had made a deep study of the work of Carl von Clausewitz, the German military theorist. Maser quotes Josef Popp, who relates

> that in 1913 and 1914 his twenty-four-year-old lodger was constantly sending him out to the Munich University library and other libraries and bookshops to fetch him the books he needed. These dealt primarily with political economy, art history, foreign policy and warfare, this last category including Clausewitz's *Three Confessions* and *On War*. . . .[1]

Hanfstaengl recalls seeing *On War* (*Vom Kriege*) amongst Hitler's books in the early twenties, and says that Hitler could quote from Clausewitz 'by the yard'.[2] He also recalls Hitler addressing an audience in Munich's Bürgerbräukellar, and complaining:

> Not one of you has read Clausewitz, or if you have read him, you haven't known how to relate him to the present.[3]

Hitler obviously thought that *he* knew how to relate Clausewitz to the present. This sounds a little like the 'discovery of the meaning of history' made at the *Realschule* and adverted to in *Mein Kampf*. We shall return to this later.

Hitler also had a deep admiration for Napoleon, making a special point of visiting his tomb following the German conquest of Paris. Commentators, for obvious reasons, have seen nothing in these facts needing any special explanation. They have taken them as obvious aspects of Hitler's personality: that is, he would have read Clausewitz because Clausewitz is the classic theorist of war and the attraction of Napoleon as the self-made emperor of France is also obvious.

Besides his classic *Vom Kriege*, however, which appeared in 1832, Clausewitz also wrote a work on Napoleon's Russian campaign. In fact although Clausewitz is thought of as pre-eminently a German military theorist, he saw action against Napoleon while serving not in the Prussian but in the *Russian* army. Clausewitz had entered the Russian service in 1812 and served under the command of Ludwig Adolf Wittgenstein, Prince of Sayn-Wittgenstein-Ludwigsburg and Field Marshal of Russia, the man whose son's wife was to elope with Franz Liszt. Clausewitz had borne a letter from the Chief of Staff of Prince Ludwig Adolf Wittgenstein's army to General Yorck, which successfully persuaded Yorck to defect from the French cause – the 'convention of Tauroggen' as it became known to history. That is, the actions of Clausewitz, serving under the directions of Prince Ludwig Adolf Wittgenstein, had played a significant role in ensuring the Napoleonic defeat in Russia. (Ludwig Adolf! – what striking first names this man had and how might they have struck intelligent Linz schoolboys in History class in 1904!)[4]

Clausewitz's descriptions of Wittgenstein's valour are damning in their faint praise: he is always 'resting his troops' or 'losing a day's march' or 'one day's march further back'. When Wittgenstein acted with great generalship in the Russian cause, Clausewitz attributed his deeds to the intervention of others, thus weakening the praise he gave. We read, for example, that 'Even if Wittgenstein did not act without express orders from Kutuzov and the emperor, he nevertheless provided the first impetus for extending the campaign as far as the Elbe. . . .'[5] It is just possible, then, that the work of Clausewitz might have exerted its fascination for Hitler, not only for its theory of war, but for its connection to the Wittgensteins. If this train of thought is worth following up then we might examine Clausewitz's account of the Russian campaign with a view to the Wittgenstein connection and perhaps even with a view to gaining an insight into the execution of Plan Barbarossa; that is, of Hitler's invasion of the Soviet Union.

If we turn to Clausewitz's account of the Russian campaign, we notice the following highly significant passage:

According to the author's recollection of Wittgenstein's headquarters at this time, it was Wittgenstein who fought for the successive advances toward Königsberg to cut off Macdonald, and then the pursuit of the marshal to the Vistula. But Wittgenstein himself was only drawn from one step to the next by Macdonald's late arrival [at Tilsit], by the isolation of General Yorck, by the negotiations with him, and finally by the conclusion of the convention and the danger in which this placed Macdonald. It would have been a different matter if 30,000 men had been waiting for the Russians behind the Niemen or even the

Pregel. It is nearly certain that the Russian campaign would then have reached its conclusion at the Prussian frontier.

Although we are not inclined to see the events of this world as resulting from individual causes but always take them as the complex product of many forces, so that the loss of a single component can never produce a complete reversal (but only a partial transformation relative to the significance of the component), we must nevertheless recognize that great results have often arisen from seemingly small events, and that an isolated cause, strongly exposed to the workings of chance, often brings forth universal effects.

This is true of Yorck's convention. It would be unreasonable to believe that, had it not been for the decision General Yorck reached at Tauroggen on the evening of December 29, Bonaparte would still occupy the French throne and the French would still rule Europe. Such great results are the effects of an infinite number of causes, or rather forces, most of which would have retained their strength even without General Yorck; but it cannot be denied that the decision of this general had enormous consequences and in all likelihood very considerably speeded up the final outcome.[6]

Clausewitz then goes on to recommend a lightning attack on Moscow as the means by which Russia might be conquered. The important feature of the above extract, however, is that Clausewitz, despite his always grudging remarks about Ludwig Adolf Wittgenstein, allows that an action initiated under Wittgenstein's command – that is, the subverting of General Yorck – was, in the enormity of its consequences, responsible for speeding up the French defeat. Were it not for the infinity of causes affecting historical events making him reluctant to say so, Clausewitz seems to incline to the view that this was the decisive event in the overthrow of Napoleon. A Wittgenstein, then – generally ungallant in the field – had, by devious means, brought about the French defeat, or at least vastly accelerated it.

To military historians reading Clausewitz, the above passage is interesting, but of no great import in their view of history. It is only one of many *aperçus* to be found in his work. But if our own hypothesis about the crucial importance of the Wittgenstein family in modern history is correct, then the passage is of very great significance. First it would have confirmed Hitler in his prejudice against the Wittgensteins. Secondly, it would explain his confidence that he alone – rather than his ignorant generals – could understand the significance of what Clausewitz was saying. Napoleon had been overthrown by Ludwig Adolf Wittgenstein, the saviour of St Petersburg. No wonder the German generals, and all later historians, had no idea what Hitler was talking about! And perhaps this is the explanation of his policy towards Leningrad – the former St Petersburg. Unlike other Russian cities, Leningrad was to have been reduced to rubble by artillery fire and left, like Babylon, as a witness for future ages. Historians have taken Hitler's attitude towards Leningrad to have been determined by his hatred of it as the birthplace of the Bolshevik revolution. My own suggestion is that he hated it because it had been saved by Ludwig Wittgenstein. It was a *different* Ludwig Wittgenstein, of course, but it is possible, in the depths of this fascinating psychopathic mind, that the very *name* – as a sort of conditioned reflex – was the trigger for the urge to leave the entire city in ruins.

History might even have displayed a sense of humour of sorts. What a delicious irony, that 130 years later, streaming in through the ether from Soviet spies in England, came the saving manna from heaven – the Bletchley Park decryptions of German army plans. Throughout the entire nine-hundred-day siege of Leningrad the starving defenders knew exactly how to combat the Germans. Leningrad – the once and future St Petersburg – saved once by Ludwig Adolf Wittgenstein in the nineteenth century, was also saved by Ludwig Wittgenstein in the twentieth, as, just possibly, was the entire Soviet Union.

Hitler, of course, sensed that something was wrong. He became increasingly convinced of betrayal, that his military plans were being leaked to his enemies. Some commentators have taken this as evidence of paranoia, but he was absolutely correct. Not only did the enemy know what his plans were, they knew exactly what they were even before the German commanders in the field. Bletchley Park decrypted orders from German headquarters – sometimes three thousand a day – quicker than did the innumerable German code clerks in the bloody vastness of Russia. Whatever the hopeless appearance of the Allied position at the time, Wittgenstein's long and lonely labours at Trinity helped to ensure that Hitler was beaten strategically by 1941.[7] Perhaps memories of *Realschule* beatings at Hitler's hands were Wittgenstein's consolation as he patiently discussed logic with Alan Turing, listened to the ever more convincing news reports that the Wehrmacht was being slowly cut to pieces and saw film of the endless lines of German soldiers being led off to captivity after Stalingrad. Sadly, the great strategic defeat of Hitler that he made possible could not put out the fires of the crematoria for four more long years.[8]

Pictures

Joseph Joachim

Princess Wittgenstein

Franz Liszt

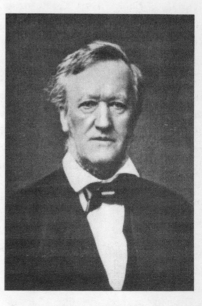

Richard Wagner

Notes

Introduction

1 Hitler refers to him in his *Tabletalk* as the 'one good Jew' for this very reason. He is mentioned also in Hitler's joint effort with Dietrich Eckart, *Bolshevism from Moses to Lenin*.

2 28:15.

3 *Victorian Parliamentary Papers*, 1950/51, Report 12, vol 2, p 156-. The report is available on microfiche in the library of Latrobe University, Victoria, Australia.

4 A summary of Chapter 1 was published in the New York Zionist periodical *Midstream* in 1994. A slight variant of the *Midstream* paper was the cover feature of the Australian literary periodical *Quadrant* in April of the same year.

Chapter 1

1 Janik and Toulmin's book *Wittgenstein's Vienna* (Simon & Schuster, 1973) is a good introductory source which, despite its title, is not specifically on Wittgenstein. Another good source is Robert S. Wistrich's work *The Jews of Vienna in the Age of Franz Joseph* (Oxford University Press, for the Littman Library, 1990). There are numerous others.

2 Monk's book, *Ludwig Wittgenstein: The Duty of Genius* (Jonathan Cape, 1990), is now the standard received account of Wittgenstein's life and is the source for much of what follows. Brian McGuinness's book, *Wittgenstein: A Life* (Duckworth, 1988), is also indispensable.

3 Monk, p 7. W. W. Bartley writes of Wittgenstein's father (*Wittgenstein*, Open Court, second edition 1994, p 76): 'In creating the iron and steel industry of the Danube Monarchy (most of it situated in Bohemia and thus after 1918 in the new state of Czechoslovakia), Karl Wittgenstein had won a position in his country comparable to that of Andrew Carnegie in America and rather like that of the Krupp family in Germany; in fact, Carnegies, Krupps, Schwabs, and Wittgensteins were guests in one

another's homes prior to the war.'

4 See, for example, the references to Karl Wittgenstein and his Prager Eisenindustrie-Gesellschaft in Richard Rudolph, *Banking and Industrialization in Austria-Hungary*, Cambridge University Press, 1976.

5 Monk, p 14.

6 Monk, p 12.

7 Bartley, p 35.

8 Monk, p 376. Bartley's claim that Wittgenstein was homosexual was slammed by every commentator of note when he first raised it, but he has been completely vindicated by the above passage and other passages in Monk's book. It is, I believe, of crucial historical importance.

9 McGuinness writes on this (p. 52): 'The stammer had disappeared by the twenties, when he spoke with the clear high voice not uncommon among those who have overcome an impediment.'

10 McGuinness, p 32.

11 McGuinness, p 32.

12 McGuinness, p 19, and Monk, p 50.

13 'Ludwig versaumte damals in Linz, wo er die Realschule besuchte, viele Unterrichtsstunden; im zweiten Semester 1903/04 waren es, im Jahre darauf sogar.' Kurt Wuchterl and Adolf Hubner, *Wittgenstein*, Rowohlt Taschenbuch Verlag GmbH, Reinbek bei Hamburg, May 1979, p 28.

14 Monk, pp 15-16.

15 McGuinness, p 51. *Saujud* = filthy Jew, *Saupreuss* = filthy Prussian.

16 Franz Jetzinger, *Hitlers Jugend*, Vienna 1956 (translated as *Hitler's Youth*, by Lawrence Wilson, Foreword by Alan Bullock, Greenwood Press, Connecticut, p 71).

17 Monk, p 15.

18 Alan Bullock, *Hitler: A Study in Tyranny*, Penguin, 1980, p 26.

19 The complete original photograph is available from the German Archives at Koblenz. It has appeared in a number of publications, none of which have noted Wittgenstein's presence. I mention here the unnumbered pages following p 95 in Walter C. Langer's book *The Mind of Adolf Hitler*, a wartime O.S.S. publication, republished in England in 1973 by Book Club Associates by arrangement with Secker & Warburg. A more accessible source for this photograph is the illustrated and abridged version of William L. Shirer's *The Rise and Fall of the Third Reich*, Bison Books, 1987, p 17. The photo on p. 11 and on the dust-jacket is cut from the upper right section of the group photograph. It appears to be the photograph of an age group, not a class.

20 I take this opportunity to express my profound appreciation of the efforts of Adrian Paterson and Glyn Taylor and of the cooperation of

Graeme Sinclair, Assistant Commissioner of the Victoria Police Department. The examination was very thorough and included ear and facial ratio comparisons.

21 *Mein Kampf*, Hutchinson, 1974, p 4.

22 *Mein Kampf*, p 113.

23 Bradley Smith, *Adolf Hitler* (Hoover Institute Publications, Stanford, 1967), p 85.

24 *Mein Kampf*, p 47.

25 *Mein Kampf*, p 48.

26 *Mein Kampf*, p 48.

27 McGuinness, p 19.

28 McGuinness, p 55.

29 Robert S. Wistrich, *Weekend in Munich*, Pavilion Books, 1995, p 31.

30 John Toland, *Adolf Hitler*, Ballantine Books, New York, 1976, p 183.

31 Ernst Hanfstaengl, *Missing Years*, Eyre & Spottiswoode, 1957, p 50.

32 Monk, p 443. Monk's report here is one of many testifying to Wittgenstein's habit of correcting people.

33 Theodore Redpath, *Ludwig Wittgenstein: A Student's Memoir*, Duckworth, London, 1990, pp 56-57.

34 Robert G. L. Waite, *The Psychopathic God*, Basic Books, New York, 1977, p. 43.

35 See Monk, pp 314-15.

36 McGuinness, p 2.

37 Monk, pp 314-15.

38 Readers are referred to the relevant section in Monk, or to Wittgenstein's book *Culture and Value*, (Blackwell, 1980), pp 16, 18, 19, 20, 21 and 22 for details. P 18 has the line 'Even the greatest of Jewish thinkers is no more than talented. (Myself for instance.)' That is, after Hitler's accession to power, on a programme of hatred of Jewish influence and Jewish thought, Wittgenstein was prepared to describe himself not merely as a Jew, but as the greatest of Jewish thinkers.

39 Monk, p 5.

40 An undated English translation by a 'Mrs Malcolm' was published as *Debit and Credit* by Lock & Co in London, late last century. The novel concerns the thwarting of the designs of the wicked Jew, Veitel Itzig, by the hero, the ethnically pure Anthony Wohlfart.

41 Monk, p 279.

42 Monk, p 114.

43 *Encyclopedia Judaica*, Vol 11, article 'Linz', p 262. I owe this valuable reference to Rabbi John Levi of Temple Beth Israel, Melbourne, Australia. The 1910 *Britannica* (11th edition) gives the population of right-bank Linz

in 1900 as 58,778 and of Ursahr, on the opposite bank of the Danube, as 12,827. Hitler's family doctor, Eduard Bloch, in his article 'My Patient, Hitler' in *Collier's* (15 March 1941, p 34), stated that when Hitler was a boy of thirteen 'Linz was a city of 80,000 people'.

44 Werner Maser, *Hitler* (translated by Peter and Betty Ross, Allen Lane, 1973, p 165). Wittgenstein, incidentally, was enrolled as a Catholic, not as a Jew. (See McGuinness, p 52.) This is relevant when taken in tandem with Jetzinger's report that Hitler's 'filthy Jew' comment was made not to a Jew, but to a boy of Jewish descent *who presented himself as German*. Bradley Smith's *Adolf Hitler*, p 88, breaks down the school ethnically as 1 Italian, 1 Serb, 4 Czechs and 323 Germans, and religiously as 299 Catholics, 14 Protestants, 1 Greek Orthodox and 15 Jews. To readers curious about the detailed school records, Professor Raul Hilberg informed me that they were removed by the Nazis. Present whereabouts are unknown. The fact of removal would seem to indicate that there was something to conceal.

45 See Monk's chapter 'Confessions', pp 361-84, or the report of Wittgenstein discussing his sins with Bertrand Russell, pp 64-5. On p 68, Monk writes that contrary to Lytton Strachey's opinion that Russell wanted to 'keep Wittgenstein all to himself', the truth was that Russell 'would have been only too glad to be spared the evening-long examinations of Wittgenstein's "sins", to which he had been subjected all term'.

46 Monk, p 368.

47 I am not, of course, trying to defend Hitler here, but making a point. I should also mention that one of the items Wittgenstein confessed to, at least at Cambridge, was that he was Jewish.

48 McGuinness, p 52.

49 The reference to 'A shower' is interesting. One hypothesizes (and I stress that this is *all* one can do) that if there were a shower room and Wittgenstein was circumcised, this latter fact would thereby have become common knowledge. And since Wittgenstein showed all the signs at Cambridge of robust good health (going on regular long country walks, for example) one must wonder if his being forbidden to do gymnastics at school had more to do with this fear than with ill-health, particularly since he and brother Paul had already tried to join a gymnastics club, but had been rejected *on grounds that they were Jewish*. It is curious that the very first sentence after the 'shower' reference concerns his relationship 'to the Jews', which seems rather an odd juxtaposition from a nominal Catholic, but is readily explicable if he had been forced to think about what circumcision might mean. During the Great War, faced with the prospect that he might have to share sleeping quarters with the other men (which would have involved public undressing), Monk writes (p 120) that his prayer was:

'from which God release me'. A lot here hangs on whether or not Wittgenstein was circumcised.

50 The Lyons restaurant incident, of course, occurred not in France, but in one of the well-known chain of English restaurants, akin, for this explanatory purpose, to McDonald's.

51 The absence of general anti-Semitic persecution at the school is supported by Maser, who writes of Hitler (p 165): 'had he encountered any definite anti-Semitic manifestations at school he would surely have stressed in *Mein Kampf* that six of his classmates had been Jews'.

52 Monk, p 114.

53 To readers curious about what the confession might have been I note here my belief that Wittgenstein was analysed by psychiatrist Alfred Adler, the case being reported by him in *The Neurotic Constitution*.

54 *Mein Kampf*, pp 378-9.

55 Maser, p 165.

56 Waite, p 173.

57 On Mahler, see W. W. Bartley's *Wittgenstein* p 76.

58 McGuinness, p 18.

59 William A. Jenks, *Vienna and the Young Hitler*, Columbia University Press 1960, p. 53.

60 Oxford University Press edition, 1988, p 206.

61 Joachim Fest, *Hitler*, translated by Richard and Clara Winston, Penguin, 1982, p 19.

62 Jetzinger, pp 71-2.

63 Hermine Wittgenstein, 'My Brother Ludwig', in *Recollections of Wittgenstein*, p 2. Hermine's supposition is in fact wrong and Ludwig was a year *younger* than the boys in his class. Hitler was a year *older* than the other boys in *his* class. Thus Hitler, who had been born within six days of Wittgenstein, was forced to endure having this young, homosexual, billionaire heir two years in front of him.

64 Albert Speer, *Inside the Third Reich*, Phoenix, 1995, p 156.

65 *Mein Kampf*, p 283.

66 *Mein Kampf*, p 282. Note that it is not the *Austrian* princes!

67 *Mein Kampf*, p 286.

68 The boundaries of the county endured virtually unchanged from the time of Charlemagne to 1975, when it was enlarged and became Siegen-Wittgenstein.

69 Monk, p 278.

70 Who, incidentally, around this time had his mother purchase an expensive grand piano.

71 Princess Carolyne Wittgenstein (d. 1887) was originally Russian and

married a Sayn-Wittgenstein, and so was not descended from old Moses Meier, but fifteen-year-old schoolboys at provincial schools might not appreciate the distinction, given that the Meier Wittgensteins were culturally sophisticated multi-millionaires. Cosima Wagner (1837-1930) was educated in Paris by two very strict governesses selected by Princess Wittgenstein, and is commended by Nietzzzsche in *Ecce Homo* ('Why I am so Clever') for her exquisite taste. The significance of Princess Wittgenstein's relationship to Cosima Wagner will be brought out in the next chapter.

72 Dietrich Fischer-Dieskau, *Wagner and Nietzsche*, Sidgwick and Jackson, 1978, p 52.

73 Fischer-Dieskau, p 207.

74 Toland, p 180.

75 *Wittgenstein*, p 198.

76 *Mein Kampf*, p 282.

77 *Karl Wittgenstein: Politico-economic writings*, John Benjamins Publishing Company, Amsterdam/Philadelphia, 1984. This valuable volume has an introduction by J. C. Nyiri and Brian McGuinness and an English summary by J. Barry Smith.

78 Nyiri, p. 191.

79 *Die Fackel* 56 (October 1900), p 7.

80 McGuinness, p 16. Hitler believed that Jews had caused the Great War. That the Austrian Archduke whose assassination *precipitated* the war was an enemy of Haus Wittgenstein, is therefore worthy of note.

81 See, for example, Frank Field's study of Karl Kraus, *The Last Days of Mankind*, Macmillan, 1967, p 237.

82 *Mein Kampf*, p 54.

83 McGuinness, p 15. Whether Karl Wittgenstein was a Jew is a moot point. Certainly, as a baptised Christian, he was not a Jew so far as the Jewish community was concerned. On the other hand, there is no doubt that the yet-to-come Nazis would have had a different opinion. I suppose one of the truly dreadful ironies of what I am suggesting is that Hitler's anti-Semitism arose from contact with an individual whom no orthodox Jew would consider was a Jew at all.

84 Nyiri, p 56. In fact, despite this, Karl Wittgenstein appears to have accepted the need for some protection of agriculture and for protection of cartels.

85 Hitler, *Secret Conversations with Hitler*, edited by Edouard Calic, John Day, New York 1971, p 66.

86 *Die Fackel* 31 (February 1900), p 3.

87 McGuinness, p 15. Compare Hitler describing the work of the Jew

(p 288 of *Mein Kampf*) on 'masses of people, numbering millions, moved from peasant villages to the larger cities to earn their bread as factory workers'.

88 Rudolph, p 108.
89 *The Jews of Vienna in the Age of Franz-Joseph*, p 511.
90 No 32, February 1900, pp 22-3.
91 McGuinness, p 14.
92 Wistrich, p 510.
93 Rudolph, p 96.
94 Hitler, *My New Order*, Angus and Robertson, 1942, pp 27-8.
95 McGuinness, p 17.
96 The best source is Peter Vergo, *Art in Vienna 1899-1918*, Phaidon, 1975. A colour picture of Klimt's 1905 portrait of Wittgenstein's sister is on p 182 of Vergo's book and the location of the original is given as the Bayerische Staatsgemaldesammlungen in Munich. Another good source on the Secession is James Schedel, *Art and Society: The New Art Movement in Vienna*, 1897-1914, Sposs, Palo Alto, California, 1981. I also mention Gottfried Fliedl's biography *Gustav Klimt*, Benedikt Taschen Verlag, (English transl. Hugh Beyer), Cologne, 1994.
97 Cf Jones, p 19. Otto Weininger, of whom Hitler quoted Dietrich Eckart as saying that he was the 'one good Jew' because he killed himself for being Jewish (*Table Talk*, p 141), Schwarzspanierstrasse suicided on 4 October 1903 in the same house in Vienna's where Beethoven died. Admiration for Beethoven must have been at almost cultish dimensions about this time. Alan Janik quotes a report that Ludwig Wittgenstein attended the funeral, though this might not be significant, because the funeral was a very public event. (See Alan Janik's paper 'Wittgenstein and Weininger' in *Wittgenstein and His Impact on Contemporary Thought*, Hölder-Pichler-Tempsky, Vienna, 1978, pp 25, 29.)
98 McGuinness, pp 17-18.
99 There is a photo of it taken at the fourteenth Secession exhibition of 1902, in Vergo's book, p 67. On the dates, one would imagine it was already in Karl Wittgenstein's possession when Ludwig started at the school. Did Ludwig say anything in art class, one wonders? Talking of Karl Wittgenstein, Bruno Walter refers to the Klinger 'half-nude' Beethoven, which 'had found its way to his home from the Sezession Exhibition'. (Bruno Walter, *Theme and Variations*, Hamish Hamilton, 1948, pp 168, 179.)
100 Jones, pp 40-1.
101 Monk, p 8.
102 Toland, p 45.

103 'One should gaze long and hard upon something like Kokoschka's Self Portrait, in order to gain a halfway understanding of the monstrous inner-nature of this idiot-art' – *Alfred Rosenberg Selected Writings*, edited by Robert Pois, Cape, 1970, p 150.

104 Vergo, p 156.

105 This is supported by Toland (p 39), who writes that 'a neighbour per-suaded Professor Alfred Roller, director of scenery at the Royal Opera, to take a look at Hitler's paintings and advise him on his career'. Toland dates the Roller offer to early February 1908.

106 Wulf Schwarzwaller, *The Unknown Hitler*, translated from the German by Aurelius von Kappau, edited by Alan Bisbort, Stoddart, Ontario, 1989, p 28.

107 Vergo, p 40.

108 Fliedl, p 156.

109 Vergo, p 84.

110 The design of the St Louis exhibition room by Hoffmann (among whose sins was a penchant for abstract paintings) contrasts with Roller's design of the exhibition room of the fourteenth Secession exhibition in 1902. The reader is referred to the photographs in Vergo's book.

111 Werner Maser, *Adolf Hitler: Legende, Mythos, Wirklichkeit*, Bechtle Verlag, Munich and Esslingen, 1971, translated as *Hitler*, by Peter and Betty Ross, Allen Lane, 1973. Futura edition 1974, p 65. I would make somewhat more of Maser's comment, were it not that in 1898 Hitler was only nine or ten years old.

112 Vergo, p 78.

113 Bartley, p 90.

114 Bartley, pp 90-1.

115 Bruce F. Pauley, *From Prejudice to Persecution: A History of Austrian Anti-Semitism*, University of North Carolina Press, 1992, pp. 207-8.

116 We noted earlier both that the Jewish population of Linz in 1880 was 533 and that the city's population in 1903 was 80,000. Even allowing for fourteen years of growth to 1903, the Jewish population would not have been more than about 1%. In Vienna, the proportion of Jews was at least 6%. In 1910, 8.63% of Vienna was Jewish. (William A. Jenks, *Vienna and the Young Hitler*, Columbia University Press, 1960, p 119.)

117 Hitler, *My New Order*, p 371.

Chapter 2

1 See Monk, p 351.

2 Bartley, pp 34-5.

3 Bartley, p 35.

4 One of Hitler's themes in the early Munich years of the Nazis was Jewish war profiteering.

5 Sandra Darroch, *Ottoline*, Coward, McCann and Geoghan, New York, 1975, p 212.

6 *Encounter* 41 No 2 (August 1973), pp 23-9, reprinted with revisions as 'Wittgenstein: A Personal Memoir' in *Recollections of Wittgenstein*, edited by Rush Rhees, Oxford University Press, 1984, pp 12-49. All references to Mrs Pascal's 'Memoir' will be to this revised edition, which, for this passage, is p 17.

7 Paul Engelmann, *Letters from Ludwig Wittgenstein*, Blackwell, 1967, p 53.

8 Bartley, p 116.

9 Norman Malcolm, *Ludwig Wittgenstein: A Memoir*, Oxford University Press, revised 1966, p 30.

10 G. E. R. Gedye, *Fallen Bastions*, Victor Gollancz, 1939, p 35.

11 Wittgenstein's criticism of Frank Ramsey, with whom he corresponded about this time, was that he was 'a bourgeois thinker'. Let us note that this is a left-wing epithet. Wittgenstein, therefore, did not see *himself* as a bourgeois thinker. One wonders what adjective he would have applied.

12 Paul Feyerabend, *Killing Time*, University of Chicago Press, Chicago, 1995, p 20.

13 Page, Leitch and Knightley, *Philby*, revised edition, Andre Deutsch, 1969, p 64. Penrose and Freeman, on the other hand, give Maclean's starting date at Trinity Hall as Autumn 1929 (p 77).

14 In one of those odd coincidences that sometimes fall upon researchers, when chasing up references to Joseph Joachim and his time with Felix Mendelssohn, I came across Wilfred Blunt's biography of Felix Mendelssohn, *On Wings of Song* (Hamish Hamilton, 1974), in which he acknowledges the advice of his brother Anthony in its production.

15 There is some doubt about Philby, but the verdict of most historians is that (like Maclean) he bestowed his sexual blessings in an unbiased fashion upon both sexes. At any rate, Burgess claimed to have had an affair with him. (John Costello, *Mask of Treachery*, William Morrow and Company, New York, 1988, p 201.) And Burgess and Philby were seen in bed together in America as late as 1951. (Costello, p 545.) Philby is reported to have said that at school 'I buggered and was buggered'.

16 Julian Bell, 'An Epistle', reprinted in I. Copi and R. Beard, *Essays on Wittgenstein's Tractatus*, Routledge & Kegan Paul, 1966, p 68. Like Hitler on the Jewish boy at the *Realschule*, Bell also thought Wittgenstein's indiscretion worth commenting on: 'Moments when lovers part, or when they meet, Omniscient Wittgenstein grows indiscreet' (p 69).

17 Peter Wright, *Spycatcher*, Heinemann Australia, Melbourne, 1988,

pp 255-6.

18 Bell died in Spain fighting for the Republic and wrote a letter to the *New Statesman*, saying 'we are all Marxists now' (Page et al, p 72). Like Blunt, Burgess, Watson and Wittgenstein, Bell was an Apostle.

19 Monk, pp 256-7. Burgess was elected an Apostle in November 1932 (Page et al, pp 65 and 68). The nuclear spy Alan Nunn May, incidentally, was at Trinity Hall with Maclean (Page et al, p 67).

20 Costello, pp 151-2.

21 Andrew Boyle, *The Climate of Treason*, Hutchinson, 1979, pp 107-8. Boyle's source is attributed to several eye-witnesses, one of whom was Lady Llewelyn-Davies.

22 'An Epistle', quoted from above.

23 Costello, p 154. This might seem to contradict what I argue later. I take comfort from the recorded precedent of Blunt instructing Michael Straight to prepare for his spying assignment in the United States 'by breaking all his ties with the left. He was to use his grief at Cornford's death as a pretext for cutting himself off from the Cambridge Communists' (Costello, p 268.) If this was Blunt's strategy for Straight, the 'black beast' business with Wittgenstein might have been equally feigned. Both Guy Burgess and Kim Philby also adopted strategies of concealing their Communist beliefs and appearing to move to the right. (See, for example, Goronwy Rees, *A Chapter of Accidents*, The Library Press, New York, 1972, pp 116-17.) Making one's friends appear to be one's enemies was a standard practice of *Konspiratsiya*.

24 The *Cambridge Review* listings of students and addresses locates Wittgenstein in D3 of Bishop's Hostel and Blunt in A2.

25 'An Epistle'.

26 Brother of Michael Ramsey, future Archbishop of Canterbury. Frank Ramsey died aged twenty-six on 19 January 1930 at Guy's Hospital, where Wittgenstein was to work as a porter during the war.

27 Wittgenstein had also stayed with the Ramseys following his return to Cambridge. Lettice Ramsey, after her husband's death, set herself up in a photography business, Ramsey and Muspratt. (See Owen Chadwick, *Michael Ramsey: A Life*, Oxford University Press, 1991, p 392, and Richard Deacon, *The Cambridge Apostles*, Robert Royce, 1985, p 117.)

28 The sanitised ASIO surveillance reports on the late A. C. Jackson, released under the thirty-year rule and reporting the period 1952–1966 alone, cover 28 pages. (Australian Archives, item A6119/89;2288 – JACK-SON, Allan Cameron.) Gasking was under suspicion because of his public stance urging (during the Korean War and despite the presence of his own country's combat troops there) that an Australian delegation be sent to the

'peace conference' in Peking.

A certain Miss Ruth Loewe, who was 'under consideration for employment of a Top Secret nature', gave Gasking's name as a referee. The Victorian Regional Director of ASIO, on 3 February 1952, asked for an 'urgent check' on her and a minute back to the Regional Director, dated 15 March 1954, mentions an 'adverse trace held against Professor Gasking'. (Miss Loewe and her relatives were judged to be loyal and respected citizens and she departed for the USA on the *Orsova*, embarking 28 January 1955. What work she did in the United States I do not know.) (Australian Archives, item A6119/89;2311 and 2312 – GASKING, Douglas.)

29 'An Epistle', p 68.

30 Quentin Bell, *Elders and Betters*, Pimlico, 1995, p 203.

31 The house, which Wittgenstein built for his sister, became the Bulgarian embassy in Vienna after the war. This, in itself, must strike the reader as suspicious. Certainly the embassy had to go somewhere, but there must have been very many great houses in Vienna. What, one thinks, are the probabilities here? The style of the house was modernist – therefore at odds with the canons of Stalinist architectural excellence – and Communist Bulgaria was hardly likely to flout the received standards of Communist aesthetics.

32 Costello, p 137.

33 Goronwy Rees, p 123.

34 B. Penrose and S. Freeman, *Conspiracy of Silence*, Vintage Books, New York, 1988. Klugmann, despite his Party background, also wormed his way into the Strategic Operations Executive in Cairo during the war. Klugmann's address in Trinity College, at K2 Whewell's Court, was very close to Wittgenstein's at K10.

35 Page et al, p 64.

36 Peter Stansky and William Abrahams, *Journey to the frontier. Julian Bell and John Cornford: their lives and the 1930s*, Constable, 1966, p 90.

37 Monk, p 343. George Thomson, the classicist of King's, was elected to the Apostles in 1923 and converted to Communism by Wittgenstein's friend Roy Pascal in 1934. (Costello, pp 191, 197.)

38 I am, of course, presenting this process as Hitler saw it. Karl Wittgenstein did *not* 'degrade art'.

39 Readers should remember that there had been a failed revolution in Russia at the very time when Hitler and Wittgenstein were at school together, in which Trotsky – later a Viennese resident – played a role. Trotsky, as president of the St Petersburg Soviet in 1905, was the leader – insofar as there was one – of the first Russian Revolution.

40 The mathematician (and Bletchley Park cryptologist) Alan Turing

accused Wittgenstein of introducing 'Bolshevism' into mathematics (Monk, p 419), a sentiment also shared by the Oxford philosopher/ historian R. G. Collingwood with respect to his philosophy.

41 Wittgenstein, *Philosophical Investigations*, Blackwell, 2nd edition, 1958, p viii.

42 Monk, p 260.

43 Costello, p 250.

44 Monk, p 260.

45 John Moran, 'Wittgenstein and Russia', *New Left Review*, LIII, May–June 1972.

46 *Recollections of Wittgenstein*, p 205.

47 Monk, pp 353-4.

48 Theodore Redpath, p 99.

49 Norman Malcolm, *A Memoir*, p 30.

50 Selwyn Grave, *A History of Philosophy in Australia*, University of Queensland Press, 1984, pp 76-83, and Jan T. J. Srzednicki and David Wood, *Essays on Philosophy in Australia*, Kluwer Academic Publishers, Dordrecht, 1992, p 29. I have benefited from a conversation with Graeme Marshall of the University of Melbourne on this topic, though Marshall, of course, is not responsible for the way in which I have represented the information he gave me. Gasking, in the grand tradition of Cambridge Communists, worked with encrypted government communications in Brisbane on his return to Australia, before taking up his position at Melbourne University.

51 Selwyn Grave, p 83. Professor David Armstrong of Sydney, who was on the Melbourne philosophy faculty as a young man and who knew both Gasking and Jackson, remarked to me that in his opinion, Jackson's politics were even more leftist than Gasking's.

52 Interested readers are referred to Richard Hall's book *The Rhodes Scholar Spy*, Random House Australia, 1991. Milner (who read philosophy at Oxford) spent a week in Vienna in August 1935, though Wittgenstein appears to have been *en route* to Moscow at this time. Sanitized ASIO surveillance records on the Melbourne Wittgensteinians and on Milner and former Cambridge economics student Eric Russell (father of the Australian ambassador to the United States under the Keating government) are available from the Australian Archives. ASIO records show that it was not aware that Paul's wife – Frank Ramsey's sister and Wittgenstein student – was the sister of the Archbishop of Canterbury, though the expression 'sister of the Archbishop' features in a transcript of a telephone conversation between the Communist Bernie Taft and Jackson, arranging a meeting between Jackson and Judah Waten.

53 Every single American who attended pre-war Cambridge – some 600 individuals – was investigated by the FBI after Michael Straight named some Americans as Trinity cell members/Communist sympathizers. (Costello, p 597.) This includes Wittgenstein's student the late Cornell professor Norman Malcolm and many others. In Britain, the vetting procedure expanded from the 2,000 names originally contemplated to some 58,000 individuals. (Nigel West, *Molehunt*, Weidenfeld and Nicolson, 1987, p 87.) If these did not include *all* Trinity College staff, the investigating authorities were simply incompetent.

54 Monk, p 354.

55 Theodore Redpath, *Ludwig Wittgenstein: A Student's Memoir*, Duckworth, 1990, pp 36-7.

56 Page et al, pp 28-9.

57 Deacon, pp 200-5, and Costello, pp 189-90. Once a common list has been constructed from these two sources, it is a routine, though tedious, matter to compare them with a list of Trinity members in the *Cambridge Review*, Extra Numbers.

58 Costello, p 639, claims that his list is 'accurate and complete'.

59 Nigel West, *Seven Spies Who Changed the World*, Secker and Warburg, 1991, p 117.

60 Seale and McConville, p 93.

61 David Cannadine's biography of Trevelyan (*G. M. Trevelyan: A Life in History*, HarperCollins, 1992, p 21), however, does reveal that: 'During the late 1930s, Trevelyan went out of his way to help Burgess find a job, and according to Andrew Boyle it was Trevelyan's personal intervention with Cecil Graves, the Deputy Director-General and a personal friend, that eventually secured for Burgess a position with the BBC.'

62 Deacon writes of Hardy, however: 'Quarrels with various prominent figures in Cambridge led to his leaving for New College, Oxford, where his left-wing influence was very marked. In his rooms at Oxford he flaunted a photograph of Lenin on his mantelpiece' (p 73).

63 Fania Pascal, 'A Personal Memoir', in Rhees, p 22.

64 Later (p 26) Mrs Pascal states that Skinner moved to Pye's and that 'During the war he was on war priority work.'

65 'A Personal Memoir', p 23.

66 Norman Malcolm, *A Memoir*, p 28.

67 Seale and McConville, p 55.

68 J. N. Findlay, 'My Encounters With Wittgenstein', *Philosophical Review*, Vol 4, 1972-3, pp 171-4. Quoted in Bartley, pp 192-3. Some writers have claimed the recruitment agent was the classics tutor Andrew Gow, a belief encouraged by Blunt's embellishment to Gow's obituary in the

London *Times* (4 January 1978, referred to in Costello, p 147). I think, however, it is a good hypothesis that anything Blunt encouraged the reader to believe is false. Gow was *not* the recruiter.

69 The guru-worship reported here continues to the present day, as any reader familiar with products of the academic Wittgenstein industry will attest.

70 'A Personal Memoir', p 18.

71 Deacon, p 101.

72 *Recollections of Wittgenstein*, pp 207-8.

73 *Philosophical Investigations*, p 226.

74 Drury, in Rhees, p 122.

75 Monk, p 347.

76 Page et al, p 76.

77 Page et al, p 75. Maclean said he wanted to get the Russians 'out of the muck'. The choice of career here was also Wittgenstein's choice after the Great War, in order to 'get the peasantry out of the muck', to cite the phrase he used again and again when explaining his goals and educational views to friends and colleagues' (Bartley, p 85). One also recalls Wittgenstein's first impression of the *Realschule* students as 'muck'. Was Maclean's use of words here an echo of his guru's?

78 Monk's spelling is incorrect. His name was David Haden-Guest.

79 Monk pp 347-8.

80 Monk, p 348.

81 Robert Skidelsky, *John Maynard Keynes*, Vol 2, Macmillan, 1992, p 292.

82 Costello, p 164. Kamenev, a high Comintern official and, like Bukharin and Zinoviev, to fall under Stalin's scythe, was married to Trotsky's sister.

83 Cf Costello, p 165.

84 Costello, p 644.

85 'A Personal memoir', p 14.

86 *Economist*, 30 September-6 October 1995, p 125.

87 Peierls, unfortunately, was responsible for recruiting Klaus Fuchs to the Manhatten Project, evidently in ignorance that Fuchs was a Soviet spy. At any rate, he won a libel action against Richard Deacon, who claimed that Peierls supplied atomic secrets to the Russians and also, rather imprudently, that he was dead. (West, p 107.)

88 'A Personal memoir', p 14.

89 McGuinness, p 62.

90 McGuinness, p 62.

91 Costello, p 191.

92 C. Haden-Guest, *David Guest. A Scientist Fights for Freedom*

(1911–1938). A Memoir, Lawrence & Wishart, 1939.

93 Haden-Guest, p 59.

94 'The great Wittgenstein' seems a highly unusual description from the lips of an Englishman. One thinks perhaps of 'the great Caruso' – but hardly of 'the great Russell' or 'the great Moore'. This unusual expression crops up again in the biographies, however, with the Professor of Mathematical Logic at Moscow University, Sophia Janovskaya, saying to Wittgenstein's face in Moscow, 'What, not the great Wittgenstein?' (Monk, p 351.) Haden-Guest had been teaching mathematics and physics in Moscow at the Anglo-American school prior to Wittgenstein's visit, but whether this explains what one smells as a linguistic curiosity is unclear.

95 Haden-Guest, p 59.

96 Haden-Guest, pp 95-6.

97 Haden-Guest, pp 97-8.

98 Costello, p 203.

99 Page et al, pp 65, 68.

100 Wright, p 252.

101 George Paul, the Wittgenstein student who taught at Melbourne University and married Frank Ramsey's sister Margaret (also a member of the Communist Party), was a specialist in the philosophy of perception. He is best known for his paper 'Is there a Problem about Sense-Data?' (*Proceedings of the Aristotelian Society*, Supplementary volume 15, 1936), but also produced 'Lenin's Theory of Perception' (*Analysis*, 5 August 1938).

102 Redpath (pp 18-19) lists some of those attending Wittgenstein's lectures as Alice Ambrose, Abraham Gans, Francis Skinner, George Paul, Rush Rhees, R. L. Goodstein, Charles Hardie, A. G. M. Landau, Alister Watson, John Wisdom and Peter Dupré. Of these, at least Paul, Landau and Watson were Party members.

103 Haden-Guest, p 69.

104 Cornforth does not say so, but these, presumably, were Maurice Dobb, Roy Pascal, J. D. Bernal or J. B. S. Haldane. (Costello, pp 198 and 531. Haldane was passing secrets to the Communist Party during the war, while working on secret projects for the Admiralty.) It would be nice to know the names of the 'four or five' other students mentioned. Were any of them the Cambridge spies?

105 Haden-Guest, p 98.

106 Cornforth married Klugmann's sister, Kitty, another Party member, and their flat above a pawnbroker's shop in King Street was a meeting place for selected Communist students and academics. Unaccountably, James Klugmann, like Blunt and the others, was engaged to work for the

Intelligence agencies, Klugmann for Special Operations Executive in Cairo.

107 Francis Skinner, Wittgenstein's lover, also volunteered for the International Brigade. ('A Personal Memoir', p 24.)

108 'A Personal Memoir', p 40.

109 Cornford was killed in Spain on 28 December 1936, the day after his 21st birthday. (Deacon, p 114.)

110 Wright, Chapter 17.

111 Wright, p 251.

112 Admiralty Research Laboratory.

113 Wright, p 253.

114 Wright, pp 255-6.

115 Wright, p 256.

116 Costello, p 193.

117 Redpath, p 47. My emphasis.

118 *Encounter*, 41 No 2, August 1973, pp 23-9. A revised version of this article appears in the anthology edited by Rush Rhees, *Recollections of Wittgenstein*, pp 12-49.

119 Costello, p 197.

120 Monk, p 272.

121 Costello, p 198.

122 Costello, p 199.

123 'A Personal Memoir', p 22.

124 'A Personal Memoir', p 22.

125 'A Personal Memoir', p 31.

126 My speculation about Duranty here is not being used to support the thesis of this chapter; that Wittgenstein was the Cambridge recruiter. Rather, the point is that if he *were* the recruiter, Duranty fits the bill as his crippled friend. But of course, should British Home Office and French passport records support this hypothesis about Duranty being in Brittany, then the Wittgenstein/recruiter hypothesis would be correspondingly strengthened.

127 Duranty was also a black magician and had sodomized, among others, the former Trinity College student Aleister Crowley, in the practice of ritual magic. (Duranty married Crowley's first 'Scarlet Woman', the opium addict Jane Cheron.) It is of interest that around this time Wittgenstein produced his 'Remarks on Frazer's Golden Bough', in which he treated magic very seriously indeed. Wittgenstein was no sceptic about magic, but sought to understand its nature; how it could *represent*. The relationship between Wittgenstein's philosophy of mind and his views on magic and the occult will be brought out later in this book. (My source for the above

THE JEW OF LINZ

details of Duranty's life is S. J. Taylor, *Stalin's Apologist*, Oxford University Press, 1990, pp 11, 18, 22, 23, 130.)

128 Seale and McConville, 130.

129 Monk, p 349. The fact that Keynes, one of the twentieth century's most prominent homosexuals, refers to Wittgenstein, another homosexual, as an 'intimate friend of mine' perhaps indicates a closer form of relationship than one might otherwise take to be the case. I have no independent evidence of this, beyond the above passage, their joint Apostle membership, the fact that they lived together for a short period in 1929, and modern sociological studies of homosexual promiscuity.

130 Monk, p 350.

131 Monk, p 352.

132 Taylor's book on Duranty begins: 'When he wasn't in Berlin having his wooden leg readjusted, or in St Tropez basking in the sun, or in Paris at the races in the Bois de Boulogne, the *New York Times* man in Moscow could usually be found among the throngs at the bar of the Metropol Hotel.' I note that Rees records Burgess returning from the south of France immediately the German-Soviet non-aggression pact was signed. (Rees, p 149.) That Duranty had a house in the south of France therefore might turn out to be significant.

133 Penrose and Freeman, p 524. The authors unfortunately omit a reference to the edition of *The Times* from which the quote is taken.

134 Costello, pp 251-52.

135 Seale and McConville, p 20.

136 Redpath, p 53. See also 'A Personal Memoir'.

137 McGuinness, p 32.

138 Seale and McConville, p 76.

139 Soviet composers had absolutely no prerogative to write for Western concert pianists on their own initiative. Prokoviev therefore must have had Party endorsement and instruction to write for Paul Wittgenstein. Why should Paul Wittgenstein have been so favoured?

140 This information comes from a recently published book honoring Prinz Heinrich Sayn-Wittgenstein, the top-scoring German night fighter ace of the Second World War, and outlining his family background – Werner P. Roell, *Laurels for Prinz Wittgenstein*, Independent Books, 1994, pp 27-9.

141 These passages, incidentally, enable us to focus a little more closely upon the family background of Princess Carolyne Wittgenstein. Her husband, Prince Nicholas, was the youngest son of this Field Marshal Ludwig Wittgenstein, who was mentioned by Tolstoy. See Alan Walker, *Franz Liszt*, vol 2, *The Weimar Years 1848-1861*, p 28.

142 Redpath, p 53.

143 West, *The Illegals*, pp 135-6.

144 Costello, pp 278-9.

145 West, *The Illegals*, p 31. 'His younger brother was a pianist with an international reputation.'

146 Christopher Andrew and Oleg Gordievsky, *KGB The Inside Story*, Hodder & Stoughton, 1990, pp 159-60.

147 Deutsch is variously said to have been torpedoed in the North Atlantic (Nigel West) or captured by the Gestapo in Vienna and executed (Oleg Gordievsky). In my opinion, the simplest hypothesis is that Stalin had him murdered.

148 Cf Seale and McConville, p 255.

149 Paige, Leitch and Knightley, p 223.

150 Author.

151 Monk, p 353.

152 My particular enquiry to Lady Rothschild concerned details of the transfer of the Wittkowitz steel plant, a transaction whose details she wrote to me that her son would provide, but his tragic suicide has meant that I have had to rely upon Morton's account in his book on the Rothschild family. Roland Perry (p 83) claims that Guy Burgess, as a Rothschild employee, was flown to Vienna and reported back the exact Nazi demands on Wittkowitz. Wright's book incorrectly gives her maiden name as 'Mayer', not 'Mayor'.

153 Wright, p 215.

154 Rupert Butler, *Legions of Death*, Sheridan, 1994, p 31.

155 W. J. West, *The Truth About Hollis*, Duckworth, 1989, p 46.

156 John Wheeldon, 'A Conversation with Albert Glotzer on Trotsky', *Quadrant*, November 1995, pp 38-43.

157 Wright, pp 316-17.

158 Wright, p 320.

159 West, *Seven Spies*, pp 98, 221.

160 West, p 99.

161 Anthony Cave Brown, *The Secret Servant: The Life of Sir Stewart Menzies, Churchill's Spymaster*, Penguin, 1987, p 198.

162 West, *Molehunt*, pp 114-15.

163 Costello, p 599.

164 West, *Molehunt*, Weidenfeld and Nicolson, 1987, p 115.

165 Roland Perry (p 35) notes that Lord Rothschild's mother, Rozsika, 'was descended from a Habsburg court Jew'. Austria seems very close in so very many of the threads of this tapestry we are weaving.

166 West, p 115.

167 Costello, p 632.
168 Costello, p 242

Chapter 3

1 An accessible version of the 1850 paper (originally in the *Neue Zeitschrift fur Musik* of 3 and 6 September 1850) is given in Albert Goldman and Evert Sprinchorn's *Wagner on Music and Drama*, Gollancz, 1970, pp 51-9. A version of the 1867 reissued paper is given in the Bison Books edition *Judaism in Music and Other Essays* of the 1894 translation by W. Ashton Ellis, commissioned by the London Wagner Society.
2 *Wagner and Nietzsche*, p 52.
3 *Wagner and Nietzzsche*, p 207.
4 William Wallace, *Liszt, Wagner and the Princess*, Kegan Paul, Trench, Trubner & Co, 1927, p 19.
5 Richard Wagner, *My Life*, translated by Andrew Gray, Cambridge University Press, 1983, p 538.
6 Andreas Moser, *Joseph Joachim. A Biography*, translated by Lilla Durham, Philip Wellby, 1901, pp 74-5. There is a copy of this now rare volume in South Australia and I take this opportunity to express my appreciation to the staff of the State Library of Victoria for their efforts in locating it.
7 Ernest Newman, *The Life of Richard Wagner*, vol 3 (1859-66), Cassell, 1945, pp 269-71.
8 Sacheverell Sitwell, *Liszt*, Cassell, 1934, revised edition 1955.
9 Du Moulin, Eckart, *Cosima Wagner*, Alfred A. Knopf, New York, 1930, vol 1, p 61.
10 Bartley, p 198.
11 Moser, pp 8-9. 'Pepi', of course, is an affectionate diminutive of 'Joseph'.
12 Moser, pp 34-5.
13 Monk, writing of Fanny Figdor, in his biography of Wittgenstein (p 5), confirms this: 'One of her cousins was the famous violin virtuoso, Joseph Joachim, in whose development she and Hermann played a decisive role. He was adopted by them at the age of twelve and sent to study with Felix Mendelssohn.
14 Kurt Wuchterl and Adolf Hubner, *Wittgenstein*, Rowohlt Taschenbuch Verlag, Reinbek bei Hamburg, May 1979, p 19.
15 Moser, p 39.
16 Moser, p 50.
17 Moser, pp 56-8.
18 McGuinness, p 19. I note also this passage in Wagner's 1867 paper on

Judaism in Music concerning Robert Schumann (p 118): Into this passivity sank Robert Schumann's genius too, when it became a burden to him to make stand against the restless, busy spirit of the Jews; it fatigued him to have to keep watch on all the thousand single features which were the first to come under his notice, and thus to find out what was really going on. So he lost unconsciously his noble freedom, and his old friends – even disowned by him in the long run – have lived to see him borne in triumph by the music-Jews, as one of their own people!' Clearly the Wittgenstein family was associated with Mendelssohn and with the Schumanns through the Wittgenstein daughters. Might the Wittgensteins, therefore, have counted as 'music-Jews'? Whatever the case here, there is no doubt at all that they would have counted as 'music-Jews' through Joachim, who had a life-long friendship with Clara Schumann. I shall demonstrate that Wagner's 'music-Jews' were in fact the Wittgensteins.

19 See the city entries in the *Encyclopedia Judaica*.

20 Moser, pp 133-4. The square brackets in 'W[ittgenstein]' are in Moser's original; they have not been added by me.

21 Moser, p 134.

22 *My Live*, pp 501-2.

23 Jacob, Katz, *The Darker Side of Genius: Richard Wagner's Anti-Semitism*, University Press of New England (Tauber Institute for the Study of European Jewry), 1986, p 94.

24 Edited by Stanley Sadie, Macmillan, 1980, vol 9, p 653.

25 Joachim visited England annually from 1862 and received an honorary Cambridge doctorate from Trinity College. One wonders if this might not explain Wittgenstein's choice of college at Cambridge.

26 Paul Holmes, *Brahms: his life and times*, Baton Press, 1984, p 49.

27 See Walter Niemann, *Brahms*, Cooper Square Publishers, New York, 1969, pp 77-8, and Malcolm MacDonald, *Brahms*, Dent, 1990, pp 57-9.

28 Bartley, p 76. Bruno Walter had to flee the Nazis, as did Joachim's children, though their Jewish ancestry was not such as to condemn them under the Nuremberg Laws.

29 *The Darker Side of Genius*, p 94.

30 *Letters From and To Joseph Joachim*, selected and translated by Nora Bickley, Vienna House, New York, 1972, p 319.

31 Newman, vol 3 (1859-66), p 276.

32 Katz, p 65.

33 Katz, p 67.

34 *Judaism in Music*, pp 106-7.

35 Du Moulin-Eckart, vol 2, pp 466-7.

36 *Theme and Variations*, p 27.

37 *Theme and Variations*, p 168. The 'Ludwig Wittgenstein' mentioned by Walter was not the philosopher, but his uncle.

38 'For myself, I have the most intimate familiarity with Wagner's mental processes. At every stage in my life I come back to him.' Quoted in *Hitler Speaks*, p 227.

39 *Judaism in Music*, p 121.

Chapter 4

1 Blackwell, 1982, vol 1, p 8e.

2 Drury, p 161.

3 *Mein Kampf*, p 10.

4 Quoted in Waite, p 46.

5 Drury, p 158.

6 *Tractatus* 5.631 (Ogden's translation).

7 Arthur Schopenhauer, *The World as Will and Idea*, translated by E. F. J. Payne, Dover Books, New York, 1966, p xii. Following Schopenhauer, Payne renders Pliny's remark in Latin.

8 *Table Talk*, p 720. There are quotations from Schopenhauer scattered in other of Hitler's speeches and written works, including *Mein Kampf* and the neglected joint effort with Dietrich Eckart, *Bolshevism from Moses to Lenin*, Hoheneiehen-Verlag, Munich, 1924.

9 Maser, p 124.

10 *On the Will in Nature*, translated by E. F. J. Payne, Berg, New York/Oxford, 1992, pp 102-28.

11 Quoted by Toland, p 87.

12 D. W. Hamlyn's otherwise excellent study, *Schopenhauer* (Routledge & Kegan Paul, 1980), does not even have an entry on magic or the occult in the index.

13 'Animal Magnetism and Magic', in *On the Will in Nature*, p 107.

14 Ludwig Wittgenstein, *Wittgenstein's Lectures*, edited by Desmond Lee, Blackwell, 1980, p 21, and G. E. Moore, 'Wittgenstein's Lectures in 1930-33', *Mind*, vol LXIV, no 253, January 1955, p 26.

15 P. F. Strawson, *Individuals*, Methuen, 1959, p 97.

16 'History', in Emerson's *Works*, 1888, p 1, cited by McGuinness, *Wittgenstein: A Life*, p 224. This passage was brought to my attention by Professor Peter Woolcock of the University of South Australia. The 'favourite thought' is in fact a Christian heresy.

17 Maser, p 125.

18 *Notebooks*, p 49, but the entire section around p 85 is also worth considering.

19 Ralph Waldo Emerson, *Essays and Other Writings*, E. W. Cole,

Melbourne, undated, p 21.

20 Quoted in P. J. Davis and Reuben Hersh, *The Mathematical Experience*, Penguin, 1984, p 52. Davis and Hersh's reference (p 431) to Shafarevitch's original lecture is 'Uebereinige Tendenzen in der Entwicklung der Mathematik', *Jahrbuch der Akademie der Wissenschaften in Goettingen*, 1973, German 31-6, Russian original 37-42. Shafarevitch was a corresponding member of the Soviet Academy of Sciences and former laureate of the Lenin Prize. He is intellectually suspect outside Russia for his anti-Semitism and ought to be suspect inside it.

21 S. T. Coleridge, *The Eolian Harp*, II 44ff. It is not the place here to trace Coleridge's antecedents, who have in any case been the object of countless PhD theses. Suffice it to mention here the virtually unanimous agreement of scholars that his major sources were German.

22 This fundamental idea – Schopenhauer's 'single thought' – has been grasped, with varying degrees of firmness, at sundry times and in diverse places. In Europe, an anticipation of Schopenhauer's doctrine raged among the scholastics from the early thirteenth century until 1531. Outbreaks of the doctrine at the University of Paris led to action by the Archbishops of Paris and Canterbury, rightly fearful of its theological consequences for the unity of a person. St Thomas Aquinas, in the major philosophical controversy of his life, was sufficiently incensed to unleash a polemical treatise against the doctrine, insisting upon its catastrophic moral consequences. The Archbishop of Canterbury issued an edict, never revoked, forbidding that it should ever be taught at Oxford. (Anthony Kenny, *Aquinas*, Oxford University Press, 1980, p 27.) It flared here and there in the schools for the next three centuries until the fifth Lateran Council, on 19 December 1513, laid a formal anathema on any who should espouse it. The 1513 condemnation nowadays makes delicious reading, so I shall quote parts of it to convey the flavour and the feelings that had been aroused. (General Council Bull *Apostolici Regiminis*, in H. Denzinger, *Enchiridion Symbolorum Definitionum Declarationum*, edition 32, no 738, Herder, Freiburg im Breisgau, 1963. Denzinger editions after 1965 have it marked as 1440.) Van Steenberghen considers of this condemnation in 1277 by the Archbishop of Paris that 'This resounding condemnation can be considered the most important of the Middle Ages. . . .' (F. Van Steenberghen, *The Philosophical Movement in the Thirteenth Century*, Nelson, 1955, p 94.) The condemnation attributes the source of the doctrine to Satan. The reader has been warned.

'The sower of cockle, the ancient enemy of the human race . . . has declared to sow and make grow in the Lord's field some pernicious errors which at all times were rejected by that faithful concerning in particular the nature of the rational soul; viz that . . . it is one and the same in all men. . . . . We therefore wish to use the appropriate remedy against this error, and with the approval of the Council we condemn and reprove all those who assert that the intellectual soul . . . is one and the same in all men, or who raise doubts in this matter. The intellectual soul is not only truly, of itself and essentially the form of the human body, as it is stated in the canon of Clement V, our predecessor of blessed memory, issued by the Council of Vienna, but . . . according to the number of bodies into which it is infused, it can be, has been and will be multiplied in individuals. And since truth in no way contradicts truth, we define as altogether false every assertion contrary to the truth of illumined faith; and, that it might not be lawful to dogmatize otherwise, we more strictly forbid [it]: and we deem all who hold to the assertions of this error as sowers of the most damnable heresies, to be thoroughly detestable heretics and infidels, destroyers of the catholic faith who ought to be shunned and punished.'

Chapter 5

1 Paul Lawrence Rose, *Wagner, Race and Revolution*, Faber and Faber, 1992, p 95.

2 Rose, p 98.

3 Michael Tanner, *Wagner*, HarperCollins, 1996, pp 142-3.

4 Tanner (p 109) writes of the Rhinemaidens in Wagner's *Ring*: 'It is then that they inform Alberich about what could be done by someone who stole the Gold and made the Ring out of it, and the first shadow falls over the music, to chilling effect, as Woglinde says "Nur wer der Minne Macht versagt . . ." (Only he who forswears love . . .).' I suggest that a dream of Wittgenstein's (recorded in Monk's biography, pp 279-80) that features a Jewish Hitlerian character in a motorcade – i.e. one who has successfully forged the Ring of world-conquest – named variously 'Vertsagt', 'Vertsag', 'Verzagt' or 'Pfersagt' derives from this very scene, which, to the musically literate Wittgenstein, must have been pregnant with meaning.

5 Ogden's translation, Routledge & Kegan Paul, 1922, republished with corrections, 1933.

6 Monk, p 243.

7 Monk, pp 243, 408.

8 This has not always been the case. A very interesting study with a plethora of references to positive descriptions in the original Pali texts is provided in Rune Johansson's book, *The Psychology of Nirvana* (Allen and Unwin, 1969). Johansson demonstrates that the popular view that nothing positive can be said about nirvana, that Buddhism is an apophatic mysticism – an eastern *via negativa* – is simply wrong.

9 Wittgenstein knew descriptions of both states from William James's book, *The Varieties of Religious Experience* (Random House, New York, 1929) pp 391-3.

10 E. Conze, *Buddhism: its essence and development*, Harper & Row, 1975, p 201.

11 D. T. Suzuki, *Living by Zen*, Rider, 1986, p 50. See also p 72.

12 Graham Reed, *The Psychology of Anomalous Experience*, Hutchinson, 1972, p 114.

13 R. E. L. Masters and Jean Houston, *The Varieties of Psychedelic Experience*, Holt Rinehart and Winston, 1966, p 15.

14 Masters and Houston, p 166.

15 T. S. Eliot, *Four Quartets*, Faber and Faber, 1972 edition, p 44. (*The Dry Salvages* II. 206-12.) Eliot's approach to these matters was catholic in a very broad sense and certainly not limited to Christianity. Section III of *The Waste Land*, for example, is the *Fire Sermon* of Buddha.

16 M. H. Abrams, *The Mirror and the Lamp*, Oxford University Press, 1953, p 347.

17 The connection of these states with anti-Semitism, as in Eliot, Wagner, Shafarevitch, Pound, etc, not to mention Hitler, is one of the substantial points to be demonstrated in this book. *Why* it is associated with anti-Semitism is intensely interesting and takes us into matters essentially religious. Eliot's anti-Semitism is too well known to require documentation:

> And the Jew squats on the window sill, the owner
> Spawned in some estaminet of Antwerp,
> Blistered in Brussels, patched and peeled in London.

18 Abrams, p 347.

19 *Don Juan*, III, civ, 6-8.

20 *Childe Harolde's Pilgrimage*, Canto III, lii.

21 Canto III, lv.

22 Canto IV, clviii

23 I point out that reports of these experiences occur also in James's *Varieties of Religious Experience*, in the chapter 'Mysticism', pp 370-420. The following is quoted from James by Brian McGuinness ('The Mysticism of the Tractatus', *Philosophical Review*, vol 75, 1966. McGuinness's reference is to p 324, but in my edition it is on p 386): '*To return from the solitude of individuation into the consciousness of unity with all that is* [my emphasis]; to kneel down as one that passes away and to rise up as one imperishable.'

The late Douglas Gasking, a former pupil of Wittgenstein's, assured me in conversation that Wittgenstein knew James's book backwards. In fact, from Gasking's testimony to me, on one occasion Wittgenstein loaned a

copy of it to a student suffering from depression – I presume Gasking himself. There are also Wittgenstein's words in the letter to Russell of 22 June
1912 (*Letters to Russell, Keynes and Moore*, Cornell University Press, Ithaca,
1974): 'Whenever I have time I now read James' *Varieties of religious
experience*. It does me a lot of good.'

24 The relevant sections occur in the *Notebooks 1914-16*, pp 72 ff, recording his thoughts from June to the end of the year 1916, and in the *Tractatus*,
in the remarks beginning with a '6'.

25 *Notebooks 1914-16*, p 82e. A very similar remark is made in *Tractatus*
5.641.

26 *The World as Will and Idea*, pp 178-9.

27 Let me bolster this with the following quote from Plotinus on contemplation (*Enneads* IV.2, from the translation of Stephen MacKenna, William
Benton, Chicago, 1982, p 159): '. . . it should be borne in mind that, in contemplative vision, especially when it is vivid, we are not at the time aware
of our own personality; we are in possession of ourselves, but the activity is
towards the object of vision with which the thinker becomes identified.'
There is something of especial interest about the mind being reported here,
which matters, I think, for more than just psychology.

28 Quoted in P. M. S. Hacker, *Insight and Illusion*, Clarendon Press,
Oxford, 1972, p 100 (footnote).

29 G. Pitcher, *The Philosophy of Wittgenstein*, Prentice Hall, New Jersey,
1964, p 8.

30 Gudmundsen, in his *Wittgenstein and Buddhism* (Macmillan, 1977,
p 111), writes that a demonstration that some of Wittgenstein's ideas were
derived from the Mahayana would be a 'philosophical bombshell', and
argues against it. He attributes the similarities to 'similar stimuli' – these
being philosophical problems, not experiences. But it is worth pointing out
that the similarities are very close, even to examples. The 'eye in the visual
field' metaphor of *Tractatus* 5.6331, that sees but is not an object of sight,
occurs also in the canonical Buddhist texts (and, I should remark, in
Augustine – *The Trinity*, Book IX, 3, iii). This, incidentally, is followed in
Tractatus 5.64 with the claim that 'Here it can be seen that solipsism, when
its implications are followed out strictly, coincides with pure realism.' *The
Brown Book* (p 108), gives as an example of a meaningless question: 'Where
does the flame of a candle go to when it goes out?' This is the very form of
words Buddha used to dismiss as meaningless questions about what happens to the enlightened person after death. For the moment, however, let
the reader accept that *dhyana* and *Einfühlung* seem very similar, and attend
to what develops.

31 Drury, *The Danger of Words*, p ix.

32 McGuinness, 'The Mysticism of the Tractatus', p 305. McGuinness (p 327) acknowledges Erich Heller's article 'Ludwig Wittgenstein, Unphilosophical Notes' (*Encounter* 72, 1959, p 42) as his source.

33 McGuinness also acknowledges the help of Miss P. von Morstein in locating the passage in Act III, scene 1 of *Die Kreuzelschreiber*. McGuinness describes Ludwig Anzengreuber (1839-89) as 'a considerably lesser Austrian dramatist', which is somewhat unfair. He was, in fact, a luminary of nineteenth-century Austrian drama and a number of biographies have been written of his life. *Die Kreuzelschreiber* (1872) is perhaps best described as a comedy along the lines of *Lysistrata*.

34 Wittgenstein, Blackwell, 1967, p 123.

35 *Philosophical Review*, vol 74, 1965, p 3. Wittgenstein's English was at this time evidently rather poor. Miss Anscombe suggested what Wittgenstein meant in her *Introduction to Wittgenstein's Tractatus*, p 173. In the *Lecture on Ethics*, he actually spoke of his 'experience for excellence'. I have followed Miss Anscombe in the above, though I am not at all convinced she is correct. McGuinness's footnote (p 326) makes one suspect that he meant to talk of his experience *par excellence*, i.e. the one that mattered above all others. Interested readers might like to pursue the references to 'the miracle *par excellence*' in section 51 (p 251) and elsewhere of *The World as Will and Idea*.

36 From a slightly different tradition, consider also the canonical Hindu *Isa-Upanishad* (1,7 – a similar verse is attributed to Vagasaneyi in the *Samhita-Upanishad*, vol I of *Sacred Books of the East*, edited by F. Max Mueller, Oxford, 1879-85, p 312, quoted in R. M. Bucke's *Cosmic Consciousness*, Dutton, New York, 1973, p 240): 'When to a man who understands, the self has become all things, what sorrow, what trouble can there be to him who once beheld that unity?'

37 Drury, in Rhees, p 132.

38 Here is Emerson again, in the *Essays* ('The Oversoul', p 170): '. . . within man is the soul of the whole; the wise silence; the universal beauty, to which every part and particle is equally related. . . . And this deep power in which we exist, and whose beatitude is all accessible to us, is not only self-sufficing and perfect in every hour, but the act of seeing and the thing seen, the seer and the spectacle, the subject and the object, is one. We see the world piece by piece, as the sun, the moon, the animal, the tree; but the whole, of which these are the shining parts, is the soul.'

39 The following quote from Frege's article 'Thoughts' (reprinted in *Logical Investigations*, edited by Peter Geach, Blackwell, 1977, p 21) might be of interest to an historian of ideas, since it is clear from Geach's preface that Wittgenstein had read the article: 'If everything is idea then there is no

owner of ideas.' This is solipsism without the subject.

40 'Notes For Lectures', p 297. Compare also *Tractatus* 5.62: 'What the solipsist *means* is quite correct; only it cannot be said, but makes itself manifest.'

41 Here is Russell's impression of Wittgenstein in December 1919, from *Letters to Russell, Keynes and Moore* (p 82): 'I had felt in his book a flavour of mysticism, but was astonished when I found that he has become a complete mystic. He reads people like Kierkegaard and Angelus Silesius, and he seriously contemplates becoming a monk. It all started from William James's *Varieties of Religious Experience*, and grew (not unnaturally) during the winter he spent alone in Norway before the war, when he was nearly mad. Then during the war a curious thing happened. He went on duty to the town of Tarnov in Galicia, and happened to come across a bookshop, which, however, seemed to contain nothing but picture postcards. However, he went inside and found that it contained just one book: Tolstoy on The Gospels. He bought it merely because there was no other. He read it and re-read it, and thenceforth had it always with him, under fire and at all times.'

42 Richard Wagner, *The Artwork of the Future*, reprinted in A. Goldnan and E. Sprinchorn, *Wagner on Music and Drama: A selection from Richard Wagner's prose works*, Victor Gollancz, 1970, p 184.

43 Hermann Rauschning, in *Hitler Speaks*, writes (p 232): 'His own esoteric doctrine implies an almost metaphysical antagonism to the Jew. Israel, the historic people of the spiritual God, cannot but be the irreconcilable enemy of the new, the German Chosen People. One god excludes the other. At the back of Hitler's anti-Semitism there is revealed an actual war of the gods.' In a speech in the Reichstag, in March 1938, Hitler remarked: 'Nations are the creations of gods of will. . . .' (*My New Order*, p 374.)

Chapter 6

1 'The later Wittgenstein, in my view, has no ancestors in the history of thought.' G.H. Von Wright, *A Biographical Sketch*, p 27. A version that is an update of the one in Norman Malcolm's *Ludwig Wittgenstein: A Memoir* (Oxford University Press, 1958) is given in Von Wright's *Wittgenstein*, Blackwell, 1982, pp 13-34, and this is the version referred to here and hereafter.

2 On Majer, Halbfass refers to a paper of R. F. Merkel, 'Schopenhauer's Indien-Lehrer', *Jahrbuch der Schopenhauer-Gesellschaft*, 32 (1945/48), 158-81.

3 Wilhelm Halbfass, *India and Europe*, State University of New York Press, Albany, New York, 1988, p 106.

4 Halbfass, p 107. Halbfass refers again to Schopenhauer's *Handschriftlicher Nachlass*, Deussen XI, 459.

5 Halbfass, p 110.

6 *The World as Will and Representation*, vol I, pp 356-7.

7 Halbfass, p 111.

8 'Das Ich, das Ich ist das tief Geheimnisvolle!' Wittgenstein, in the *Notebooks 1914-16*.

9 Kabir, *The Bijak of Kabir*, translated by Linda Hess and Shukdev Singh, North Point Press, San Francisco, 1983, p 24.

10 *Varna* is an old Sanskrit word which means colour. It implies the division of a group of people according to colour, i.e. the means of distinguishing between the Aryan invaders of India (who coined the term) and the original Dravidian inhabitants.

11 Alfred Rosenberg, *Selected Writings* (ed Robert Pois), Jonathan Cape, 1970, pp 42-4.

12 Rosenberg, pp 42-4.

13 Francis King, *Satan and Swastika: The Occult and the Nazi Party*, Mayflower, 1976, p 241. There are a number of similarly interesting quotes in Paddy Padfield's biography of Himmler.

14 Rauschning, *Hitler Speaks*, p 92.

15 *Mein Kampf*, p 283.

16 King, p 172.

Chapter 7

1 The black magician Aleister Crowley, a Trinity College student, claimed to have been Iamblichus in a former birth.

2 Joan Miller claimed in *One Girl's War* (Brandon Book Publishers, Dingle, Eire, 1986, p 45) – which was banned in the UK – that Crowley was involved in the death of Maxwell Knight's wife in the Overseas Club 'after some sort of occult misadventure'. (Knight was the head of MI5's B5(b), the counter-subversion department.) Knight sent his agents along to Crowley's Satanic ceremonies, ostensibly to keep an eye on what was going on at them. The hapless agents, of course, in order not to blow their cover, would have had to participate in the rituals. That Knight's role here might have been a matter not of national security, but of recruitment for a coven, is suggested by other details in Miller's book. Grant's and Symond's biographies of Crowley have further details, as does Anthony Masters, biography of Maxwell Knight (*The Man Who Was M*, Blackwell, 1984, p 68), which states: 'Knight told his nephew, Harry Smith, that he and Dennis Wheatley went to Crowley's occult ceremonies to research black magic for Wheatley's books. "They jointly applied to Crowley as novices

and he accepted them as pupils," Smith told me.' This last sentence ought to provoke a good deal of reflection. Crowley sodomizzzed Walter Duranty and Tom Driberg (later secretary of the British Labour Party) – both probable Soviet agents – in their pursuit of magical powers. Masters outlines Crowley's involvement with Knight and Ian Fleming (the James Bond author) in the Hess defection on pp 126-9 of his book, as does John Pearson on p 110 of his biography, *The Life of Ian Fleming* (Cape, 1966), which includes a copy of a letter from Crowley concerning Hess.

3 *Parerga and Paralipomena*, translated by E. F. J. Payne, Oxford, 1974, vol 2, pp 227-309.

4 'The Artwork of the Future', in *Wagner on Music and Drama*, p 181.

5 R. G. Collingwood, *The Principles of Art*, Oxford University Press, 1938, pp 59-61.

6 Collingwood, p 64.

7 Collingwood, pp 65-7.

8 Rauschning, pp 208-12.

9 I particularly recommend Wagner's essay 'The Artwork of the Future', describing both the nature of 'knowing through feeling' and 'the awakening of the individual will as the universal will'. How Wagner's vision was brought to political rather than artistic fruition is plainly evident to anyone who has read the essay and then watched Leni Riefenstahl's film of the 1934 Nuremberg rally, *Triumph of the Will*.

10 I add the rider 'as characterized by Collingwood' to emphasize that I am not asserting that magic involves any violation of the laws of physics.

11 Collingwood, pp 68-9.

12 Why *do* cheer teams chant this? Why *is* it effective? What was the overwhelming power of chants such as 'Ein Reich, Ein Volk, Ein Führer' that so paralysed the political intellect that they made eminently sensible Germans of their own free will give up the right to change their own government?

13 The Bürgerbräukeller assassination attempt appears to have been the same event over which Wittgenstein was to cut Malcolm dead for years for doubting that 'the British national character' would allow the security agencies to deal in murder. As it happens, the British agencies turned out to have had nothing to do with it.

14 Heinrich Hoffmann, *Hitler was my Friend*, Burke, 1955, pp 135-7.

15 Quoted in John Lukacs, *The Duel*, Oxford University Press, 1992, footnote, p 39.

16 *Hitler: A Study in Tyranny*, p 35.

17 *Parerga and Paralipomena*, vol I, 'Essay on Spirit Seeing', p 229.

18 'Animal Magnetism and Magic', in *On the Will in Nature*, pp 106-7.

19 Readers who can accept what modern physicists say about the notion of 'quantum entanglement' – a non-causal action at a distance – ought to be less inclined to dismiss Schopenhauer's idea than were the nineteenth-century mechanists, though I do not think Schopenhauer's theory is by any means committed to such a revision of causality.

20 It is not *quite* as difficult as all that. Just because some subjects are unhypnotizable, we do not thereby reject hypnosis as a phenomenon.

21 *Parerga and Paralipomena*, vol I, p 229.

22 Deuteronomy 18: 10-12. There is certainly a Jewish mystical tradition and the Kabbala is quite clearly magical, but the nature of Jewish magic does not – cannot, because the very idea is unthinkable – involve a magician compelling Yahweh.

23 Byron refers somewhere to affectionately riding the waves and stretching out his hand to stroke the white caps as though the surf were a horse's mane. Perhaps what Byron expressed, together with the unstable medium of water and the shaking caused by galloping hooves, is the explanation of Poseidon's disparate spheres of activity.

24 All the quotations are from Schopenhauer's brief essay referred to earlier. I have replaced the Latin in the originals by the English translations of E. F. J. Payne in the footnotes of his English translation of *On the Will in Nature*.

25 Giulio Cesare Vanini, *De admirandis arcanis*.

26 Rauschning, pp 240-3.

27 Maser, pp 167-8.

28 Rauschning, p 233.

29 Quoted in Charles Bracelen Flood, *Hitler: The Path to Power*, Houghton Mifflin, Boston, 1989, p 244.

30 Rauschning, p 238.

31 There is a booming, but largely fringe literature on Hitler and the occult. With few exceptions, it is, in my opinion, of very little value.

32 Secker & Warburg, London, 1993, p 31.

33 Marion Meade, *Madame Blavatsky*, Putnams, New York, 1980, p 449.

34 Josephine Ransom, *A Short History of the Theosophical Society*, Theosophical Publishing House, Adyar, 1938, reprinted 1989, p 21.

35 Ransom, p 17.

36 Ransom, p 17.

37 Meade notes in her natal horoscope of Madame Blavatsky that she was born at Ekaterinoslav, 35:01 E. Longitude; 48:27 N. Latitude, on 31 July 1831.

38 It is remarkable that Stalin was a Theological student in Tiflis, where Madam Blavatsky lived, and where her grandfather was a high state official.

If the well-known Blavatsky interests inspired the young Stalin to a bit of occult dabbling also, then the grounds for his otherwise mysterious expulsion from the Tiflis Seminary would be mysterious no longer. Certainly, his daughter's unforgettable description of his death scene and Milovan Djilas' descriptions of a sense of strain suddenly descending during his conversations with him are only too familiar to anyone with a knowledge of how the occult is said to work.

39 Helena Petrovna Blavatsky, *The Secret Doctrine*, Theosophical Publishing House, 1893, p 210. For readers interested in following up what might turn out to have been a fundamental source passage for the twentieth century, there is a section devoted to the mystical meaning of the Swastika, pp 103-6.

40 Ludwig Wittgenstein, 'Remarks on Frazer's Golden Bough', reprinted in *Philosophical Occasions 1912-1951*, edited by Klagge, James and Nordmann, Alfred Hackett Publishing Company, Indianapolis & Cambridge, 1993, pp 116-17.

41 In a remark in the *Notebooks* of 8 July 1916. He actually says, 'There are two godheads: the world and my independent I.'

Chapter 8

1 Emerson, R. W., *Emerson's Essays*, Essay 9 (the over-soul), Collins, London, undated, p 159.)

2 Moore, p 14. This judgement must be treated with respect, since it was Moore who used just this distinction to flail Idealist philosophers in a famous philosophical paper, *The Refutation of Idealism*. One would expect Moore to be awake to any philosopher foolish enough to overlook it. But Moore was nonetheless wrong in accusing Wittgenstein of this error, for Wittgenstein did distinguish between the act and the object; the only difference between Moore and Wittgenstein in this respect being simply that Wittgenstein, as we shall see, drew the distinction correctly.

3 It is even possible that the 'superficial' theory Wittgenstein dismisses might have been his *own* invention, lately discarded. Russell, for example, acknowledged his debt to Wittgenstein in *Logic and Knowledge* (edited by R. C. Marsh, p 226.)

4 *Tractatus*, 5.541.

5 *Tractatus*, 5.5421.

6 In Weitz, p 31.

7 Richard Wagner, 'Erkenne dich selbst', *Bayreuther Blätter*, February-March 1881, translated as 'Know Thyself' by W. Ashton Ellis, reprinted in *Religion and Art*, Bison Books, 1994, p 264.

8 David S. Shwayder, 'On the Picture Theory of Language', in *Essays on*

Wittgenstein's Tractatus, eds. Irving M. Copi, and Robert W. Beard, Routledge and Kegan Paul, 1966, p 307.

9 For a comparison with Buddhist thought consider a passage by Dr Walpola Rahula, an internationally reputable Buddhist monk, and D Phil supervisor at Oxford, who writes of the doctrine of the five aggregates (*Zen and the Taming of the Bull*, Gordon Fraser, 1978, p 41): 'These five aggregates together, which we popularly call a being, are dukkha itself (samkharadukkha). There is no other being or "I" standing behind these five aggregates who experience dukkha. There is no unmoving mover behind the movement. It is only movement. In other words, there is no thinker behind the thought. Thought itself is the thinker. If you remove the thought there is no thinker. Here one cannot fail to notice how this Buddhist view is diametrically opposed to the conception of Cartesian cogito.' Readers familiar with the names of some eminent modern Buddhist scholars might be aware that K. N. Jayatilleke, author of *Early Buddhist Theory of Knowledge* (Allen and Unwin, 1963, see p 10), was admitted to Wittgenstein's classes in his rooms at Whewell's Court, in the years 1945-7. One trusts they conversed.

10 The great German philosopher/logician, Frege, clearly espoused the alternative, relational view; he separated the *act of thinking* from the *content of thinking*. For Frege, the act of thinking is something private to a subject while the content of the thought is something public. In Frege's writings, the subject/act/object trichotomy is patent. Thus Frege on the thinker and publicity of the mental (G. Frege, *Logical Investigations*, edited by Peter Geach, Blackwell, pp 25-6): 'He is the owner of the thinking, not of the thought.'

11 Jaakko Hintikka, 'On Wittgenstein's "Solipsism"', Copi and Beard, p 160.

12 'Token' is a philosophical term invented by the American philosopher C. S. Peirce, whose use is illustrated by the word 'Mississippi' in which there are said to be four *type* letters and eleven *token* letters. The standard position in the philosophy of mind is that two people can share the same mental act only in the sense of their having two distinct token acts of the same type. The no-ownership position, on the contrary, is that they intersect in the same token mental act.

13 For documentation of this claim, I refer readers to any library with a Philosophy of Mind section and ask that a book be chosen at random. Those wanting a more specific reference will be comforted in a moment by a discussion of the views of the young Peter Strawson.

14 *Philosophical Investigations*, [s]253.

15 *Individuals*, p 97. I do not know if Sir Peter still adheres to this position. Peter Geach presents a similar view in *Truth, Love and Immortality*

(Hutchinson, 1979, p 111) though it is unclear if this is his own view or that of the philosopher McTaggart.

16 *Individuals*, p 97.

17 'Instantiations' is another ugly jargon word very much used here in place of 'instances', to, as it were, cook the vocabulary within which the issue is to be decided.

18 I have been unable to locate these exact words in Wittgenstein's writings, but Moore presents virtually identical formulations in his report of Wittgenstein's lectures in *Mind*, vol LXIV, pp 13-14. The claim 'das gegebene ist subjektlos' does occur in Carnap's *Aufbau*, however (quoted, without a page reference, in Bernard Williams's article 'Wittgenstein and Idealism', *Royal Institute of Philosophy Lectures*, vol 7, p 81), and it is a fair bet (without deprecating Carnap) for historical reasons that its source was Wittgenstein. To anticipate a little, the claim is stronger than that the objects of our mental states are public – it applies to the acts of experiencing those objects when such acts are conceived as Cartesian events in consciousness; as further items over and above the object that we are conscious of. It is just this that is radical in what I am about to present.

19 Frege, pp 25-26. There is also Augustine's comment in *On Free Choice of the Will*, (translated by A. S. Benjamin and L. H. Hackstaff, Bobbs-Merrill, Indianapolis, 1980, chapter XIV, book 2): 'No part of truth is ever made the private property of anyone; rather it is entirely common to all at the same time.'

20 The Preface to the *Tractatus*.

21 *Philosophical Remarks*, p 91.

22 *Blue Book*, p 55. The example is used again in later work, so it is not simply an idiosyncrasy of the thirties. See, for example, the *Philosophical Investigations* section 253.

23 Adherents of the 'identity' theory of mind hold that *the having of a pain* is a brain-process, not that *the pain* is a brain-process.

24 D. M. Armstrong and Norman Malcolm, *Consciousness and Causality*, Blackwell, 1984, p 116.

25 *Zettel*, section 498.

26 *Investigations*, II, viii, p 185. See also *Last Writings on the Philosophy of Psychology*, edited by G. H. von Wright and Heikki Nyman, Blackwell, 388, p 53e. This last demonstrates that he adhered to this view at the end of his life.

27 To those philosophers busily making mental distinctions and caveats here, I must ask them to cease and desist: the position being presented is that when two people have the same pain, they have the same *token* pain, *not* two tokens of the same type.

Chapter 9

1 Beacon Press, Boston, 1967. Also Anchor Press, New York, 1980.

2 Kapleau's footnote, p 205, attributes the executive's immediate source to Dogen's *Shobogenzo*. Stryk and Ikemoto (*Zen*, Doubleday, New York, 1965, p 63) give Dogen's dates as AD 1200-53. Kapleau states that it is originally found in *Zenrui No 10*, an early Chinese Zen work. Compare the following famous text from the *Svetasvatara Upanishad*:

> Thou art the fire
> Thou art the sun
> Thou art the moon
> Thou art the starry firmament
> Thou art Brahman supreme:
> Thou art the waters – thou
> The creator of all.
> Thou art woman, thou art man;
> Thou art the youth, thou art the maiden.
> Thou art the old man tottering with his staff.
> Thou facest everywhere.
> Thou art the dark butterfly.
> Thou art the green parrot with red eyes.
> Thou art the thunder-cloud, the seasons, the seas.
> Without beginning art thou,
> Beyond time, beyond space.

Though this sounds superficially like a hymn to some other being, however unlikely it seems, it is in fact addressed to the reader, though not to the reader as 'one amongst others'.

3 Zazen is the practice of Zen meditation.

4 R. C. Zaehner, *Our Savage God*, pp 210-11.

5 *Four Quartets*, V, vii-ix. Hugo von Hofmannsthal produced the following – lovely – aphorism: 'Depth is hidden. Where? On the surface?' quoted in H. Finch, *Wittgenstein – The Later Philosophy*, Humanities Press, New Jersey, 1977 (opposite p 1). On p 238, Finch quotes the following from Aristotle's *Metaphysics*: '. . . for, as the eyes of bats are dazzled by sunlight, so it is with human intelligence when face to face with what is by nature most obvious.'

I add here that this is Plotinus's interpretation of what is meant by the Platonic anamnesis. I have found a footnote of Merlan's, expounding Plotinus on Plato, helpful (Merlan, p 76): 'When Plotinus speaks of the timelessness of anamnesis he seems to mean that the condition of this kind of remembering should not be expressed by the formula "I remember the ideas I once saw", but by another, viz. "I now am conscious of seeing the ideas which I have always seen, though unconsciously". In other words, we do not really remember ideas, we see them and precisely in virtue of the same faculty by which I saw them before incarnation. And this faculty should not, of course, be called memory. Thus, anamnesis is actually the raising of unconscious knowledge to conscious one.' R. T. Wallis, in *Neo-Platonism* (Scribner's, New York, 1972, p 80), writes, more clearly than Merlan, of '. . . Plotinus' interpretation of Plato's description of knowledge as Recollection as denoting not a temporal recovery of what the soul knew in the past, but an awakening to what her true self knows eternally.'

6 I am denying here the validity of the 'colour reversal argument' – that you might undetectably experience as red (or anything else) what I experience as green.

7 Included in *The Oxford Book of English Mystical Verse*, pp 71-3.

8 I shall present the claim for unbelieving philosophers in this form: the same 'token' after-image is simultaneously present to the two subjects. We shall pierce the murk surrounding the type/token distinction a little later.

9 How this is so will become clearer when we examine our knowledge of the location of our pains.

10 I note that the psychological literature on imagery includes reports that establish not merely the logical possibility of after-images being three-dimensional, but the actuality. Consider Alan Richardson, *Mental Imagery*, Routledge, 1969, pp 24-5: 'Most subjects do experience a memory after-image if the object is illuminated by a brief and brilliant flash under background conditions of total darkness. With such a brief exposure no appreciable movement of the eye in relation to the object is possible and an after-image of great clarity and detail can result. In a study by Gregory, Wallace and Campbell (1959) using a 110 joule 1 milli-second flash tube, positive after-images of several seconds duration were produced. In one instance it was found that the flash illumination of a corridor produced an after-image *which changed in perspective as the subject moved* [my emphasis]. This latter phenomenon is easy to replicate for oneself using an ordinary photographer's flash gun. If one is in a dark room, facing a chair at a distance of about 10 feet when the flash occurs, it is possible, for example, to walk towards a point 2 or 3 feet to the left of the chair and to observe the imaged chair *from a constantly changing angle as one approaches it* [my emphasis].'

Chapter 10

1 *Mind*, vol LXIV, No 253, January 1955, p 13. It was Moore's notes of these lectures that were the source of Strawson's attribution (*Individuals*, p 97) of the no-ownership theory to Wittgenstein.

2 The passage from William James, quoted in the *Investigations*, section 342, where the deaf mute Ballard reports that he had wondered 'How came the world into being?', is followed a page or two later by James quoting Professor Herzen on the experience of awakening from anaesthesia: 'During the syncope there is absolute psychic annihilation, the absence of all consciousness; then at the beginning of coming to, one has at a certain moment a vague, limitless, infinite feeling – a sense of existence in general without the least trace of distinction between the me and the not-me.' (*The Principles of Psychology*, University of Chicago, 1988, p 177.) If the reader tabulates the occasions traceable in Wittgenstein's life, or in the books he read where reference is made to transcendence of the subject/object link, he will fill a sizeable notebook. In any event, it is evident that the idea we are tracing has links to Wittgenstein from many sources.

3 *Notes for Lectures* p 281.

4 *Notes for Lectures*, p 282.

5 Is it impossible to imagine a philosophy that would be the diametrical opposite of solipsism?

6 *Philosophical Investigations*, p 222.

7 The same misunderstanding has occurred in interpreting 'the private language argument' – than which no more sterile verbiage has been produced since the Scholastics.

8 *Investigations*, section 293.

9 *Blue Book*, p 71.

10 For the benefit of those who think the terminology meaningful, I am saying that only one *token* event is taking place. The thought is a shared, token mental act.

11 Merlan, p 132, writes that '. . . publication of the literary remains of Husserl brings some surprises'. Merlan continues: 'Time and again Husserl felt that phenomenology seems to amount to transcendental solipsism, time and again he tried to prove that it did not have to be so. One of his attempted proofs reads somewhat like this. "When we continue with the transcendental reduction (i.e. ascend to the constitution of the world of objects in subjectivity or consciousness), we ultimately are lead (sic) to a point where we transcend the realm of personal transcendental consciousness and find ourselves in the realm of a completely impersonal transcendental consciousness. In other words (which are not Husserl's own), we find that personal transcendental consciousness is constituted by an impersonal transcendental consciousness (the affinity to Fichte's ideas is obvious). But this being so, suddenly any plurality of personal 'consciousnesses' disappears."' I do not care myself for either Husserl or phenomenology, but feel honour bound not to hide scripture from devotees.

12 *The Greeks and the Irrational*, University of California Press, Berkeley, 1951, pp 100-1.

13 I like to think of the move from 'common single thinker' to 'common thinking thought' as paralleling the move in Oriental thought from the Hindu identity 'Atman = the one Brahman' to the Buddhist denial of even the unitary Atman. As Asvagosa presented the Buddhist view of the *Visuddhimagga*

> The deed there is, but no doer thereof;
> Suffering there is, but none who suffer.

14 The analogy is an important one. Reflective readers will realize that it shows the no-ownership account to be consistent if Cartesianism is consistent, and that objections to it must be directed not at logical inconsistencies but rather towards the empirical question of whether this model in fact corresponds to the reality. If Cartesianism is a possible account of the mind, then the no-ownership account is likewise not a theory that can be dismissed on logical grounds; it is a waste of time looking for *internal* inconsistencies in the position, as, we shall see later, for example, Aquinas did. This is because both Cartesianism and the no-ownership account are *mental cause* theories, differing only as to the nature and number of the mental causes invoked. In fact one is not far wrong to consider the no-ownership account to *be* Cartesianism, but with the proviso that the mental cause is considered to be a universal, not a particular. And Cartesianism about the mind might be false, but it does not seem incoherent (except, perhaps, on the very nettle of the individuation of multiple mental subjects to which the no-ownership theory is impervious). Other things being equal, the no-ownership account would seem preferable on Ockhamist grounds. In fact if the causality involved is formal rather than efficient, it is just barely possible that the theory can squeeze past the 1513 condemnation to orthodoxy. Christian orthodoxy has been, since Aquinas, the Aristotelian doctrine that the soul is the form of the body. On the no-ownership account, while the content of an individual's mind is public, the individual's experiencing that content as an individual, as something separate from the content, consists in the content informing the bodily expression, which expression by the body is then the 'having' of its informing cause by an individual.

15 *Blue Book*, p 61.

16 *Wittgenstein's Lectures 1932-1935*, edited by Alice Ambrose, University of Chicago Press, Phoenix edition, 1982, p 21.

17 I am well aware that this is rather a strong claim to make. I am classing it with remarks such as Kant's, that Cartesians confuse the unity of experience with the experience of a unity. That Wittgenstein's remark is

profound, of course, does not entail that it is *true*, but I rather incline to think it might be.

18 Wittgenstein found the point important enough to repeat on several occasions. On p 11 of Moore's reports of the 1930s lectures, for example, we read that Wittgenstein distinguished 'between what he called "the sign" and "the symbol"', saying that whatever was necessary to give a sign meaning was part of the "symbol" so that where, for instance, the sign is a sentence, the "symbol" is something which contains both the sign and everything which is necessary to give that sentence sense.' Moore continued that Wittgenstein 'illustrated this by saying that if a man says "I am tired" his mouth is part of the symbol. . . .'

19 Stoical behaviour, where the suffering is born as expressionlessly as possible, is, of course, just another species of behaviour; not something different from behaviour.

20 There is the interesting comment on p 24 of *Wittgenstein's Lectures 1932-1935*: 'If when people spoke, the sounds always came from a loudspeaker and the voices were alike, the word "I" would have no use at all: it would be absurd to say "I have toothache". The speakers could not be recognized by it.' The point here concerns not just how the speakers might or might not be recognized – the point is that I would not be able to distinguish myself from others whenever someone else said the same thing. ie the self-other distinction for such speakers collapses.

21 *On the Will in Nature* vol I, 18, p 100.

22 *Living by Zen*, pp 73-4.

23 *Philosophical Investigations*, section 407.

24 Blyth, *Zen and Zen Classics*, vol 1, Hokuseido, Tokyo, 1960, p 73.

25 *Notes for Lectures*, p 309. Similarly, we could ask who owns the cube after-image. There isn't one for you and a different one for me, since it is shared in common by each of us.

26 *Notes for Lectures*, pp 310-11.

27 Malcolm, p 49.

28 *Blue Book*, p 50.

29 *Perception*, p 83.

30 *Philosophical Grammar*, p 393.

31 *On Certainty*, section 41, p 7. Readers should also look at *Remarks on Colour*, p 51, section 261.

32 *Blue Book*, p 50.

33 In favour of the view is the way it renders clear why non-philosophers automatically reject the question 'How do you know your pain is where you sincerely point to?' But it might seem that there remain other difficulties. One objection that has been raised (by Dr Bruce Langtry of the University

of Melbourne, in conversation) is that this view precludes one from saying that the pain *caused* me to point to my appendix. The reasoning, of course, is that if my pain's being in Cornish's appendix at co-ordinates (x,y,z) *consists in* my sincerely pointing there then the pain that is there cannot also *cause* me to point there.

But the reasoning fails. It is not that the pain *that is there* causes me to point, but that the pain *simpliciter* causes me to point. As in our example, the unitary appendix pain, as cause, induced twenty hands to point, as effects, to twenty different spatial locations. The causal efficacy attaches to the pain, not to pain-in-a-location. It is as with thunderclaps. That which possesses the causal efficacy when a thunderclap causes the windows to shake in many locations is derived from the unitary source. That which shakes the many windows *here* is the thunderclap *there*. And that which moves the many hands in the world is the one pain in pain-space.

34 *Living by Zen*, p 103.

35 Robert Carew-Hunt, 'The Theory and Practice of Communism', reprinted in *The Faber Book of Espionage*, edited by Nigel West, Faber, 1994, pp 268-70.

Chapter 11

1 The best presentation of how our theme has emerged in Western thought is Philip Merlan's study *Monopsychism, Mysticism, Meta-consciousness*, Martinus Nijhoff, The Hague, 1969.

2 Dmitri Gutas, *Avicenna and the Aristotelian Tradition*, E. J. Brill, Leiden, 1988, p 3.

3 In the 11th edition of the *Britannica* (Cambridge, 1910, vol III, p 63) we read that among Avicenna's works 'There is also a *Philosophia Orientalis*, mentioned by Roger Bacon, and now lost, which according to Averroes was pantheistic in tone.'

4 Gutas, p 117, quoting Bayhaqi, Tatimma, 56/68.

5 Gutas, p 130, footnote.

6 See F. E. Peters, *Aristotle and the Arabs*, New York University Press, New York, 1968, p 167.

7 From *Mantiq*, pp 2-4, quoted in Soheil M. Afnan, *Avicenna, His Life and Works*, Greenwood Publishing Group, 1980, pp 89-90.

8 Henri Corbin, *Avicenne et le recit visionnaire*, Departement d'Iranologie de l'Institut Franco-Iranien, Teheran. An abridged English translation of this has been published by Pantheon Books, New York, 1960.

9 Gutas, p 175.

10 With Greek kingdoms having flourished in the Punjab, there is no doubt that Vidyabhusana was correct in seeing some Greek input in the

development of Indian logic. But he also established evidence of a very early home-grown Indian logical tradition.

11 *Hudud al-Alam* (The Regions of the World – A Persian Geography, AD 982) translated by V. Minorsky, edited by C. E. Bosworth, E. J. W. Gibb, Memorial Volume, second edition, Luzac, 1970, 21a 67 (p 108).

12 *Al Beruni's India*, edited by E. C. Sachau, S. Chand, Delhi, 1964, p 000.

13 Cyril Elgood, *A Medical History of Persia and the Eastern Caliphate from the Earliest Times Until the year AD 1932*, Cambridge University Press, 1951, p 372. The author of the Firdaus-ul-Hikmat referred to here by Elgood was Abu-I-Hasan Ali ibn Sahl (ibn) Rabban al-Tabari. Of Tabari's Firdaus-ul-Hikmat, Elgood writes (p 372): 'It obtained an immediate success and was widely quoted. The text, but not unfortunately a translation, has been made available lately by its publication by the Sonnar Druckerei of Berlin. Of this work, the seventh and final part concludes with 36 chapters devoted to Indian medicine.'

14 See G. N. Bannerjee, *Hellenism in Ancient India*, Munshi Ram Manohar Lal, first revised edition, Delhi, 1961, pp 153-4: 'In the earliest Arab author Serapion, the greatest of the Hindu physicians, Charaka, is mentioned by name; in the Latin translation, he is named as "Xarch Indus, or Xarcha Indus". Avicenna calls him "Apud, Sirak Indum", "Rhazes in quit Scarac Indianus", and again says "dixit Sarac".' Bannerjee's source is not Avicenna directly, but T. F. Royle's *Essay on the Antiquity of Hindu Medicine*, for which he regrettably provides no date or publisher. Despite careful perusal, I was unable to locate his original in Gruner's translation of the *Canon of Medicine*, but then Gruner's translation is incomplete.

15 Gruner's translation, p 512.

16 I am confident, on the basis of the leech reference, that Avicenna knew the *Sushruta Samhita* also, but will rest the case, for the moment, on the *Charaka Samhita* alone. I point out, however, that diabetes mellitus is described in the *Sushruta Samhita* as a distinct disease (Benjamin Lee Gordon, *Medieval and Renaissance Medicine*, Philosophical Library, New York, 1959, p 543.) and was not so described by a European physician (Thomas Willis) till the seventeenth century. Avicenna, however, as Gordon notes (p 542), has 'a full and accurate account on the subject of diabetes'. One *must* suspect Indian influence here, as the Greek medical accounts of diabetes are incomplete, subsuming all cases to diabetes insipidus. Elgood (*Medicine in Persia*, Paul B. Hoeber, New York, 1934, p 15) writes of Sushruta and Charaka that 'Recently it has been shown that the works of these two Indian sages were available in Arabic in the seventh century under the title of "Kitab-i-Shaushura-al-Hindi".'

17 Book IV (*Sarirasthanam*), chapter 5, verses 6-7 (p 441).

18 Verse 20.

19 Richard Walzer, *Greek into Arabic*, Cassirer, 1962, p 26.

20 Colette Sirat, *A History of Jewish Philosophy in the Middle Ages*, Cambridge University Press, 1985, p 157.

21 We can note from *A History of the Jewish People*, edited by H. H. Ben-Sasson (Harvard University Press, Cambridge, Massachussetts, English translation 1976, p 468) that 'In the Muslim Orient the Jews remained an integral part of the economic life of the city. Documents found in the Fostat Genizah reveal that large-scale Jewish trade in the Indian Ocean continued in the twelfth century, as is implied in the Responsa of Maimonides, which date from that period.'

22 Moses Maimonides, *Guide for the Perplexed*, transl. Shlomo Pines, Dover, New York, 1950, 1, 68.

23 Dominique Urvoy, *Ibn Rochd* (Averroes), translated by Olivia Stewart, Routledge, 1991, p 123. Leo Africanus states that while still in Spain, Maimonides was a pupil of Avenzoar in medicine and of Averroes in philosophy. (Cf Gordon, p 220.) But since Maimonides was only ten when the family fled Spain, this is overwhelmingly unlikely.

24 Averroes, *The Incoherence of the Incoherence*, in two volumes, translated and introduced by S. Van den Bergh, Luzac, Leiden, 1954, reprinted 1978, pp 28-9.

25 On the account I have been presenting, what is multiplied as the number of bodies is not the intellect, but the *having of* the intellect. There are as many having relations as there are humans expressing intellectual things. Intellectual matters involve people's bodies in their expression, but *that which* is expressed; the intellect, is common to all men. Critics, of course, must argue that the unexceptionable commonplace that 'the intellect is common to all men' (and not, say, to animals or insects) is true in some other sense, and means something different from how I am interpreting it.

26 The *Oxford Dictionary of the Christian Church* informs us (p 1274) that in a lost work, *De intellectu* (whose existence is attested to by quotations from it by an early sixteenth-century Italian writer), Siger did apparently reply to St Thomas. Van Steenberghen's *Aristotle in the West* (Louvain, 1955, pp 215-18) reports that 'up to the present' fourteen authentic works of Siger have been recovered, and offers a few words about the writings known to be lost.

27 Gottlob Frege, 'The Thought: A Logical Enquiry', reprinted in *Essays on Frege*, edited by E. D. Klemke, University of Illinois Press, 1968, p 521.

28 The American psychologist William James was an undeniable influence upon Wittgenstein. Here is a passage linking him directly to the contro-

versies we are investigating (*The Principles of Psychology*, p 346): 'I confess that the moment I become metaphysical . . . I find the notion of some sort of an *anima mundi* thinking in all of us to be a more promising hypothesis, in spite of all its difficulties, than that of a lot of absolutely individual souls.'

Chapter 12

1 Sister Rose Emmanuella Brennan SHN, in her introduction to Aquinas's *On the Unicity of the Intellect*, Herder, 1946, p 201.
2 They are definitively stated in the *Summa Contra Gentiles*, chapter LIII (circa AD 1261-4), in the *Summa Theologica*, Q 76 (circa AD 1266–72), and in *De unitate intellectus contra Averroistas*, chapters V, VI and VII (circa AD 1269). The dates are from David Knowles's guide *The Evolution of Medieval Thought*, Vintage Books, New York, 1962, pp 260, 271, 272.
3 *De unitate* – Aquinas stated his purpose in the opening words of Chapter 1 of this work.
4 The agent intellect was understood to be that which in the perception of 'intelligibilia' plays the same role as light in the perception of colour. The quote is from *Lib. ii. Sentent. dist.* 17, quaest 2, art. 1.
5 *De unitatate*, p 268. This, as we saw, was the doctrine of the great Rabbi, Moses Maimonides, though for all that it must be still wrong as Jewish theology.
6 Reynold A. Nicholson, *The Mystics of Islam*, George Bell, 1914 (reissued in Penguin Arkana, 1989, p 152).
7 Aquinas, *On the Unicity of the Intellect*, p 258.
8 First published 1950. Penguin edition, 1955, p 470.
9 *Summa Contra Gentiles*, translated by the English Dominican Fathers from the Leonine Edition, Burns Oates, London, 1923, chapter LVI, p 134.
10 *Summa Contra Gentiles*, p 138.
11 *Summa Theologica*, Q76, Art. 2.
12 Emerson's poem 'Brahma', evidently based on this, runs:

> If the red slayer think he slays,
> Or if the slain think he is slain,
> They know not well the subtle ways
> I keep, and pass, and turn again. . . .
> They reckon ill who leave me out;
> When me they fly, I am the wings;
> I am the doubter and the doubt,
> And I the hymn the Brahmin sings.

13 Translated by R. C. Zaehner, *Hindu Scriptures*, Everyman, II, 19-22. In an unconscious echo of Aquinas, Zaehner's worry in *Our Savage God* was

that the idea of this verse was the justification of the American mass-murderer Charles Manson; that he had arrived at the same position as the writer of the *Gita* through mystical experiences induced by the drug LSD.

14 Aquinas argued this point, that one cannot sense without a body, in *Summa Theologica*, Q 75, Art. 4. That Wittgenstein thought the opposite is apparent in Moore's 'Notes of Wittgenstein's Lectures 1930–33' (*Mind*, January 1955, p 13). The following passage (from *Wittgenstein's Lectures*, edited by Alice Ambrose, University of Chicago Press, 1982, pp 22–3) is as clear a support of this (and of my interpretation of Wittgenstein) as can be imagined. It is worth quoting in full: 'How . . . does a person enter into the description of a visual sensation? If we describe the visual field, no person necessarily comes into it. We can say the visual field has certain internal properties, but its being mine is not essential to its description. That is, it is not an intrinsic property of a visual sensation, or a pain, to belong to someone. There will be no such thing as my image or someone else's. The locality of a pain has nothing to do with the person who has it: it is not given by naming a possessor. Nor is a body or an organ of sight necessary to the description of the visual field. The same applies to the description of an auditory sensation. The truth of the proposition 'The noise is approaching my right ear', does not require the existence of a physical ear it is a description of an auditory experience, the experience being logically independent of the existence of my ears. The audible phenomenon is in auditory space, and the subject who hears has nothing to do with the human body. Similarly, we can talk of a toothache without there being any teeth, or of thinking without there being a head involved. Pains have a space to move in, as do auditory experiences and visual data. The idea that a visual field belongs essentially to an organ of sight is not based on what is seen.'

15 *De unitate*, p 245.

16 Aristotle, *Metaphysics* Book VIII.

17 *De unitate*, p 246.

18 *Summa Theologica*, 1a, lvi, 2.

19 It is via bodily behaviour that the Wittgenstein no-ownership theory accounts for the link between the unowned intellect and the body. The Averroist no-ownership theory attempted to account for the link in terms of 'phantasms' which were *both* incorporeal and in the bodily organs.

20 *De unitate*, VII, p 267.

21 Methuen, 1957.

22 *Individuals*, pp 96–7.

Conclusion

1 *The Longest Hatred* is the title of a book by Robert S. Wistrich. In using

this term, I most certainly do not want to label Dr Wistrich – for whose work I have the very greatest respect – as 'a man of no religious belief'.
2 'Remarks on Frzer's Golden Bough', p 35.

Appendix

1 Maser, p 133.
2 Hanfstaengl, p 162.
3 Hanfstaengl, p 163.
4 Hitler's favourite teacher at school was the History teacher Dr Pötsch, to whom he devotes a nostalgic passage in his *Mein Kampf* description of the *Realschule*. The passage runs: 'Professor Dr Ludwig Pötsch, my secondary school teacher in Linz, was the ideal embodiment of this principle. An old gentleman, of kindly yet incisive manner, he had the gift of dazzling eloquence which not only enthralled, but literally carried away his pupils. Even today I cannot recall that grey-haired old man without emotion.' In due course, Dr Pötsch was sent a luxury leatherbound version of *Mein Kampf* with a dedication written in the hand of the Führer himself. Pötsch replied with a curt expression of thanks, which pointed out that his name was not *Ludwig*, but *Leopold*. (Cf. Jetzinger, op cit, pp 69-70.) Students of Hitler aware of this gaffe might have thought it a natural, but silly mistake. But *Ludwig*? I wonder if from our perspective, it might not reveal something about Hitler's psychology, that the man he praises for teaching him the meaning of history was called 'Ludwig'. It would be a fascinating exercise for a trained statistician to compile a list of first names of people Hitler appointed to government positions and compare the frequency of 'Ludwigs' here with those in the general population. It ought to be possible to estimate the probability that some factor other than chance was responsible for the observed distribution, if, indeed, it turns out to be significantly skewed. (I publicly place my bet now that it would be.)
5 Clausewitz, 'The Campaign of 1812 in Russia', in *Historical and Political Writings*, edited and translated by Peter Paret and Daniel Moran, Princeton University Press, 1992, p 198. I note that Wittgenstein is mentioned in two places in *Vom Kriege* also, though in very much less detail than in this work.
6 'The Campaign of 1812 in Russia', p 200.
7 Besides Wittgenstein's likely recruitment of the Cambridge spies, Alan Turing – who was introduced to Wittgenstein by the spy Alister Watson in 1937 – used the logical ideas of Wittgenstein, whose lectures he attended, in designing the bombes, the machines that did the deciphering. He certainly took classified Government Code and Cypher School materials back to Cambridge and discussed logical issues with Wittgenstein during this period. (Andrew Hodges, *Alan Turing: The Enigma*, Simon and Schuster,

New York, 1983, pp 151-2.) Costello (p 689) quotes a letter of Turing's from as early as 1933: 'Am thinking of going to Russia some time in the vac, but have not quite made up my mind. I have joined an organization called the "Anti-War Council". Politically communist. Its program is principally to organize strikes amongst munitions and chemical workers when the government intends to go to war.' If I am correct about Wittgenstein, it is a certain bet that the Russians would have had their own bombes and a duplicate of Bletchley. And just as Bletchley won the Battle of the Atlantic for Britain, so the Russian reconstruction of the Bletchley machines must be expected to have been decisive in the East.

8 There is a very poignant and moving recollection of Walter Eytan, a Jew working at Bletchley Park, in *Codebreakers* (ed. F. H. Hinsley and Alan Stripp, Oxford University Press, 1994, p 60). '. . . in late 1943 or early 1944 we intercepted a signal from a small German-commissioned vessel in the Aegean, reporting that it was transporting Jews, I think from Rhodes or Kos, *en route* for Piraeus *zur endlösung* ('for the final solution'). I had never seen or heard this expression before, but instinctively I knew what it must mean and I have never forgotten that moment.'

Index